EDWARD
and
ALEXANDRA

EDWARD
and
ALEXANDRA

Their Private and Public Lives

Richard Hough

CORONET BOOKS
Hodder and Stoughton

Copyright © Richard Hough 1992

First published in Great Britain in 1992
by Hodder & Stoughton, a division of Hodder Headline PLC.
Trade paperback edition, 1993.
This edition 1994.
A Coronet paperback.

A John Curtis Book

The right of Richard Hough to be identified as the author of
this work has been asserted by him in accordance with the
Copyright, Designs and Patents Act 1988.

10 9 8 7 6 5 4 3 2 1

British Library Cataloguing in Publication Data

Hough, Richard
Edward and Alexandra : Their Private and
Public Lives. – New ed
I. Title
941.08230922

ISBN 0-340-61724-1

Printed and bound in Great Britain by
Cox and Wyman Ltd, Reading, Berks.

Photoset by Rowland Phototypesetting Ltd,
Bury St Edmunds, Suffolk.

Hodder and Stoughton Ltd
A Division of Hodder Headline PLC
338 Euston Road
London, NW1 3BH

For Jackie

Contents

Illustrations

Bertie as a young rider at Balmoral (*author's collection*).

With his wistful sister Alice (*Christopher Hibbert's collection*).

As a young soldier after returning from Canada and the United States (*Christopher Hibbert's collection*).

As a twenty-one-year-old student at Cambridge (*Weidenfeld & Nicolson Archives*).

Sandringham House in 1862 (*author's collection*).

Sandringham House from the gardens (*The Hulton-Deutsch Collection; Weidenfeld & Nicolson Archives*).

Bertie embarking on HMS *Hero* at Plymouth for his extensive tour of Canada and the United States (*author's collection*).

Less than two years later Bertie was engaged to Alix. This is Frith's painting of the marriage ceremony on 10 March 1863 in St George's Chapel, Windsor (*reproduced by gracious permission of Her Majesty The Queen; Weidenfeld & Nicolson Archives*).

Bertie and Alix and Prince Eddy, their first child, in 1864 (*author's collection*).

The Prince and Princess of Wales in 1868 (*Bassano & Vandyk; Weidenfeld & Nicolson Archives*).

Marlborough House, Bertie's and Alix's London home (*Victoria and Albert Museum; Weidenfeld & Nicolson Archives*).

The Prince and Princess of Wales in 1870 (*author's collection*).

Bertie soon after he recovered from typhoid fever, probably at Cowes in July 1872 (*Christopher Hibbert's collection*).

A thanksgiving procession and service in St Paul's Cathedral took place on 27 February 1872 to celebrate Bertie's recovery (*author's collection*).

During the winter of 1875–6 Bertie, without Alix to her chagrin, made an extensive tour of India and Ceylon. Between formal occasions the slaughter was formidable. This is Bertie's first elephant (*author's collection*).

*

The children in 1876 (*Windsor Castle. Royal Archives © 1992, Her Majesty The Queen; Weidenfeld & Nicolson Archives*).

Part of the dining-room at Marlborough House (*Windsor Castle. Royal Archives © 1992, Her Majesty The Queen; Weidenfeld & Nicolson Archives*).

Bertie and some of his cronies, 1889 (*Windsor Castle. Royal Archives © 1992, Her Majesty The Queen; Weidenfeld & Nicolson Archives*).

The Tranby Croft house party before the cheating scandal (*Weidenfeld & Nicolson Archives*).

Bertie at Baden while taking the waters (*Christopher Hibbert's collection*).

Bertie at forty-one, Alix at thirty-eight with Queen Victoria in 1883 (*Bassano & Vandyk; Weidenfeld & Nicolson Archives*).

Minnie, the Dowager Tsaritsa of Russia, with her sister Alix and Bertie, Copenhagen, 1900 (*author's collection*).

Lillie Langtry (*Mrs Jenny Tricker's collection*).

Sarah Bernhardt (*author's collection*).

The Countess of Warwick, previously Lady Brooke – 'the Babbling Brooke' (*The Hulton-Deutsch Collection*).

Alice Keppel, Mrs George Keppel, the favourite and longest lasting (*The Hulton-Deutsch Collection*).

The new King and Queen (*Mrs Jenny Tricker's collection*).

The procession, passing Guildhall, at their delayed Coronation, 9 August 1902 (*author's collection*).

Sir John (Jackie) Fisher, a favourite of both Bertie and Alix (*author's collection*).

Lord Charles (Charlie B.) Beresford, who fell out with both Bertie and Fisher (*National Portrait Gallery; Weidenfeld & Nicolson Archives*).

Sir Frederick (Fritz) Ponsonby, Bertie's loyal secretary (*Windsor Castle. Royal Archives © 1992, Her Majesty The Queen; Weidenfeld & Nicolson Archives*).

Lord Esher, wise adviser and *éminence grise* (*author's collection*).

The King (*Windsor Castle. Royal Archives © 1992, Her Majesty The Queen; Weidenfeld & Nicolson Archives*).

Sir Ernest Cassel (*Weidenfeld & Nicolson Archives*).

*

The faithful-unto-death Charlotte Knollys, Woman of the Bedchamber to Alix for fifty-five years (*Windsor Castle. Royal Archives © 1992, Her Majesty The Queen*).

Author's Note

I am especially grateful to Christopher Hibbert, an earlier biographer of Edward VII, who guided me to many sources he had previously explored and lent me useful material. Peregrine Churchill kindly, and to my great benefit, opened up for me the Lord Randolph Churchill letters, which brought new light to bear on his grandfather's relationship with the Prince of Wales. The voluminous Carrington Papers in the Bodleian Library revealed especially the many-sided nature of the Marquess of Lincolnshire's long and unique friendship with the Prince of Wales, and later when he became King. Mrs Jenny Tricker applied her remarkable knowledge of this period to my manuscript, correcting factual mistakes and solecisms. Tom Pocock as always bore in mind my needs as he went about his own research and was materially helpful.

Too many other people to list here with whom I have discussed this remarkable couple have contributed in large and small measure to my understanding of them. As a biographer for many years of subjects whose lives, in one way or another, overlap in time or association this dual biography, I must acknowledge posthumously the considerable contribution, from my old files, of conversations with Queen Victoria's last surviving grand-daughter, Princess Alice of Athlone, and Earl Mountbatten of Burma when I was working on my dual biography of his parents and official history of the family. Similarly, my access to archives at that time, including the Royal Archives, has proved again of value. Many of the references to the Royal Archives have stemmed from published works, especially from Georgina Battiscombe's wonderful biography of Queen Alexandra (1969), the nearest we have to an official biography, and the late Sir Philip Magnus's *King Edward VII* (1964). To both of these biographies I owe a great deal.

The staff of the London Library, the Bodleian Library, the RUSI Library and the New York Public Library were, as always, marvellously helpful. Candida Brazil was a tower of strength during the early stages of research; and Jackie Gumpert (as the dedication suggests) dealt speedily and with her usual efficiency with early drafts of the text.

February 1992   RICHARD HOUGH

Some Nicknames

AFFIE: Prince Alfred, fourth child of Queen Victoria and Prince Albert, later Duke of Edinburgh and Duke of Saxe-Coburg and Gotha

ALIX: Princess Alexandra of Denmark, later Princess of Wales and Queen Alexandra

BERTIE: Prince Albert Edward, first-born son of Queen Victoria and Prince Albert, Prince of Wales and later King Edward VII

EDDY: Prince Albert Victor, Alix and Bertie's first born

GEORGIE: Prince George Frederick Ernest Albert, later King George V, Eddy's younger brother

LENCHEN: Princess Helena, fifth child of Queen Victoria and Prince Albert, later Princess Christian of Schleswig-Holstein-Sonderburg-Augustenburg

MINNIE: Princess Dagmar of Denmark, sister to Alix, later Empress of Russia

OLD MAC: Lady Macclesfield, Alix's long-time Lady of the Bedchamber

TORIA: Princess Victoria, second daughter of Alix and Bertie

VICKY: or 'Pussy' when a baby, Princess Victoria, first-born child of Queen Victoria and Prince Albert, later Princess Frederick of Prussia and Empress of Germany

WILLI: William, Prince of Denmark, later King George I of Greece

Chronology

II, dies and is succeeded by his son William (Kaiser William II)

1890   10 September, Bertie becomes involved in the Gordon-Cumming baccarat cheating, and the subsequent trial, 1–9 June 1891, as witness

1891   17 May, Alix becomes a grandmother for the first time – Louise's child

1891   9 November, Bertie's fiftieth birthday, and Alix fails to return home for it

1891   24 December, the long dispute with Lord Charles Beresford settled by Lord Salisbury

1892   14 January, Eddy dies while engaged to Princess May of Teck

1893   6 July, Georgie marries Princess May of Teck

1898   27 February, Bertie meets Alice (the Hon. Mrs George) Keppel

1898   Bertie is introduced to Sir Ernest Cassel at Newmarket and a close friendship, to their mutual advantage, rapidly develops

1898   Bertie meets Miss Agnes Keyser

1900   4 April, Bertie and Alix closely escape assassination at Brussels

1901   22 January, Queen Victoria dies and Bertie and Alix become King Edward VII and Queen Alexandra

1901   9 November (Bertie's birthday), Georgie and May become Prince and Princess of Wales

1902   11 April, Alix to Copenhagen to celebrate the eighty-fifth birthday of her father, King Christian IX

1902   31 May, Boer War ends

1902   24 June, Bertie, 'suffering from perityphlitis',

is operated on by Sir Francis Treves, leading to the postponement of his Coronation

1902   9 August, Bertie and Alix crowned

1902   9 November, Kaiser at Sandringham for Bertie's sixty-first birthday celebration

1903   April–May, Bertie visits Portugal, Italy and, most importantly, France

1903   5 October, Alix leaves for Darmstadt and wedding of Princess Alice of Battenberg and Prince Andrew of Greece

1904   12 April, *Entente Cordiale* with France signed

1904   23 June, Bertie embarks for Germany for naval conversations with the Kaiser

1905   31 March, Kaiser lands at Tangier instigating the Morocco crisis

1905   April, Alix visits Portugal on her own

1907   May, Bertie takes Alix to Paris privately

1907   23 September, Bertie signs Anglo-Russian Convention

1907   20 June, Bertie invites the Kaiser and Kaiserin to visit England on 11 November

1908   8 April, Herbert Asquith, as new Prime Minister, kisses hands with Bertie in Biarritz, attracting some criticism

1908   20 April, Bertie and Alix embark on an extensive Baltic tour

1908   6 June, Bertie and Alix embark happily on a visit to the Tsar and Tsarina of Russia at Reval

1909   8 February, Bertie and Alix embark with heavy hearts for Berlin

1909   26 May, Bertie's horse wins the Derby again to his – and national – delight

1909   4 November, 'People's Budget' passed by the House of Commons and immediately rejected by the Lords

1910   22 February, Bertie opens Parliament for the last time

1910   27 April, Bertie returns to London from Biarritz in low spirits and poor health

1910   6 May, Bertie dies

1918   16 July, the deposed Tsar of Russia and his family assassinated

1925   20 November, Alix dies

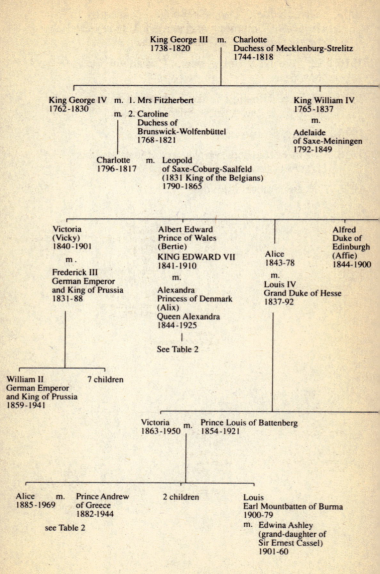

King George III
1738-1820
m. Charlotte
Duchess of Mecklenburg-Strelitz
1744-1818

King George IV
1762-1830
m. 1. Mrs Fitzherbert
m. 2. Caroline
Duchess of
Brunswick-Wolfenbüttel
1768-1821

King William IV
1765-1837
m.
Adelaide
of Saxe-Meiningen
1792-1849

Charlotte
1796-1817
m. Leopold
of Saxe-Coburg-Saalfeld
(1831 King of the Belgians)
1790-1865

Victoria
(Vicky)
1840-1901
m.
Frederick III
German Emperor
and King of Prussia
1831-88

Albert Edward
Prince of Wales
(Bertie)
KING EDWARD VII
1841-1910
m.
Alexandra
Princess of Denmark
(Alix)
Queen Alexandra
1844-1925

See Table 2

Alice
1843-78
m.
Louis IV
Grand Duke of Hesse
1837-92

Alfred
Duke of
Edinburgh
(Affie)
1844-1900

William II
German Emperor
and King of Prussia
1859-1941

7 children

Victoria
1863-1950
m. Prince Louis of Battenberg
1854-1921

Alice
1885-1969
m. Prince Andrew
of Greece
1882-1944

see Table 2

2 children

Louis
Earl Mountbatten of Burma
1900-79
m. Edwina Ashley
(grand-daughter of
Sir Ernest Cassel)
1901-60

TABLE 1

King Edward VII

simplified family tree

Edward
Duke of Kent
1767-1820

m.

Victoria
of Saxe-Coburg-Saalfeld
1786-1861

12 children

Queen Victoria
1819-1901

m.

Albert
Prince of
Saxe-Coburg-Gotha
1819-61

Helena
Princess Christian
of Schleswig-Holstein
(Lenchen)
1846-1923

Louise
Duchess of Argyll
1848-1939

Leopold
Duke of Albany
1853-84

m.

Helen of Waldeck
1861-1922

Alice of Athlone
1883-1981

Beatrice
Princess Henry of
Battenberg
1857-1944

Arthur
Duke of Connaught
1851-1942

Alexandra
1872-1918

m.

Nicholas II
Emperor of Russia
1868-1918

Irene
1866-1953

m.

Prince Henry
of Prussia
1862-1929

3 children

4 children

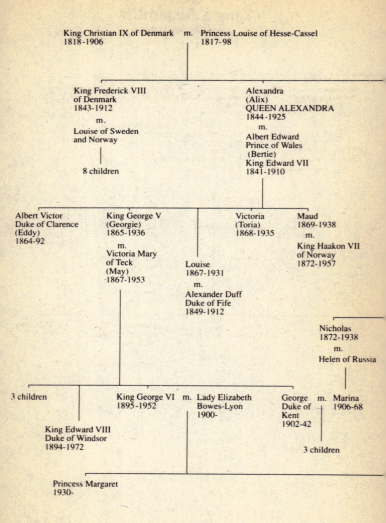

King Christian IX of Denmark m. Princess Louise of Hesse-Cassel
1818-1906   1817-98

King Frederick VIII
of Denmark
1843-1912
m.
Louise of Sweden
and Norway

8 children

Alexandra
(Alix)
QUEEN ALEXANDRA
1844-1925
m.
Albert Edward
Prince of Wales
(Bertie)
King Edward VII
1841-1910

Albert Victor
Duke of Clarence
(Eddy)
1864-92

King George V
(Georgie)
1865-1936
m.
Victoria Mary
of Teck
(May)
1867-1953

Louise
1867-1931
m.
Alexander Duff
Duke of Fife
1849-1912

Victoria
(Toria)
1868-1935

Maud
1869-1938
m.
King Haakon VII
of Norway
1872-1957

Nicholas
1872-1938
m.
Helen of Russia

3 children

King George VI
1895-1952

m. Lady Elizabeth
Bowes-Lyon
1900-

George
Duke of
Kent
1902-42

m. Marina
1906-68

King Edward VIII
Duke of Windsor
1894-1972

3 children

Princess Margaret
1930-

TABLE 2

Queen Alexandra
simplified family tree

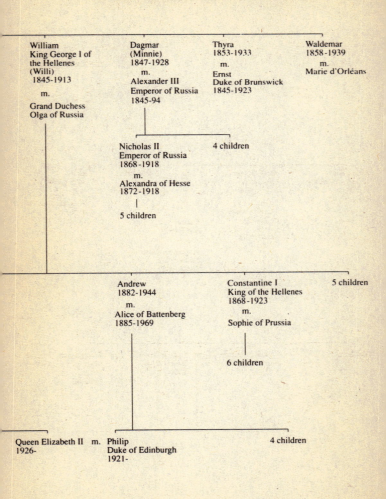

William
King George I of
the Hellenes
(Willi)
1845-1913

m.

Grand Duchess
Olga of Russia

Dagmar
(Minnie)
1847-1928

m.

Alexander III
Emperor of Russia
1845-94

Thyra
1853-1933

m.

Ernst
Duke of Brunswick
1845-1923

Waldemar
1858-1939

m.

Marie d'Orléans

Nicholas II
Emperor of Russia
1868-1918

m.

Alexandra of Hesse
1872-1918

5 children

4 children

Andrew
1882-1944

m.

Alice of Battenberg
1885-1969

Constantine I
King of the Hellenes
1868-1923

m.

Sophie of Prussia

6 children

5 children

Queen Elizabeth II   m.   Philip
1926-   Duke of Edinburgh
                             1921-

4 children

1

The Arrival

'She comes! the Maid of Denmark . . .
To be our Queen of Love'
                    Martin Tupper

No one could remember having seen the Prince of Wales *running* before, neither General Knollys, the Comptroller, nor the Groom of the Stole, Lord Spencer, nor the rest of His Royal Highness's Household* assembled on the quayside. The crowds, the boom of the welcoming cannon still in their ears, adored it.

There had been both grace and a swagger to the manner of the royal yacht's entry into Gravesend harbour and her coming alongside the pier. The Danish flag flew from the foremast, the union flag at the jack, both confirming an easterly wind, and a foully cold one at that.

The Prince of Wales and his party were late, their carriages having been delayed *en route* from Windsor, which was the cause of the Prince's haste to greet his bride. She was Princess Alexandra of Denmark, at eighteen 'the most beautiful Princess in all Europe', according to the Prince's elder sister.

Not one of the thousands present – in the street, crowded

* See page 415 for definitions of Household functions.

at windows like screaming chicks in their nests, perched precariously on rooftops – had seen before this lovely young woman who would one day become their Queen. When she stepped out on to the deck from the yacht's stateroom, there was renewed cheering, which increased deafeningly yet again when the Prince of Wales opened wide his arms and embraced his bride warmly, holding her to him for some time.

'Huzza! huzza! huzza!' Hats were in the air, many of those thrown from the wherries and launches and other small boats clustered about the yacht, landing in the water. 'Ain't she lovely!' 'Lucky Prince!', sighs from the women, lewd expletives from the men, rose from the crowd who could now see on the yacht's deck the nabobs in glittering uniform, the ladies in long sequin-edged coats, bonnets and furs against the cold, gathered about the couple with much bowing and curtseying.

The Prince, scarcely taller than his bride-to-be and preceded by sixty of Kent's prettiest girls who strewed flowers in their path, then led her down the gangway into the open landau that was to take them to the railway station. Before this day, 7 March 1863, Prince and Princess had been together for only a few hours, but gave the impression that they had known one another all their lives. The Princess, in a grey dress, violet mantle and white bonnet she had made herself, sat beside her father, heir to the throne of Denmark, while her mother and the Prince sat opposite.

There was to be no opportunity to exchange more than a few words between the four of them, and the unremitting cheers made these almost inaudible. Besides, their duty on this of all days was to give their attention to the welcoming thousands, to smile and wave a hand. Up the High Street they went, through the town's market-place, festooned with evergreens and orange blossom, the people particularly dense here, many standing on the stalls, past the Town Hall with its massive Doric portico and the figures of Wisdom, Truth and Justice. They then turned into the London Main Road, past St George's Church and its tomb of Pocohantas – though that was out of sight – then up the steep narrow Windmill Hill, where people at the windows dropped early daffodils into the landau, and into the short street leading to Gravesend railway station.

Here a special reception room had been prepared for them. They stepped on to the red carpet and made their way inside, failing to note the pictures tastefully hung on the walls for this day, including *Mine Own* by Maclise and *The Measure of the Wedding Ring* by Halliday, appropriate if a little premature. The chairman of the South-Eastern Railway Company, Lord Caithness, greeted the party with a deep bow. Then he led them to their carriage and, to everyone's further delight, mounted the footplate of the locomotive, *Maid of the South*, and took the controls.

There was no respite for the young couple on the short railway journey to the terminus at the Bricklayers' Arms on the south side of London Bridge. His Lordship maintained the speed at no more than 15 mph so that the citizens on both sides of the track, who sometimes threatened to spill on to it, would have the opportunity to glimpse the figures, the Prince on one side and the Princess on the other side, through the open windows. There were decorations even out here in the country, flags and bunting on cottages and barns and cowsheds, flags fluttering from haystacks, offsetting the darkness of this chilly, cloudy day.

The journey across London to Paddington by way of the Mansion House and St Paul's Cathedral, Temple Bar and Pall Mall, Piccadilly and Park Lane, was beset by obstacles and frustrations, moments of wonder and several near catastrophes. The decoration of the streets was as impressive as the organisation was awful. There were triumphal arches along the city's streets, there were flags and heraldic devices, banners and streamers by the mile. 'Never in the long history of our great city', ran one account the following day, 'have so many citizens been on our streets, nor given our newest citizen such a welcome.'

Less extravagant language was used to describe the control of these crowds, who spilt on to the path of the procession. At one point, a mounted charge with drawn sabres was resorted to, and it was later reported that some people had died in the press of numbers. Outside the Mansion House a mounted officer of the Blues charged to clear the way, one of his horse's forelegs somehow becoming enmeshed in the rear wheel of the landau, halting it. In a moment the carriage would be upset, the officer thrown. Princess Alexandra, showing her initiative and quick-thinking, merely reached out a hand much experienced in dealing with horses, soothed the beast with a word and calmly extracted the leg as if this were an everyday occurrence. Then she returned to the smiling and waving.

Alix 'had a charming way of treating a crowd as if they were intimate friends', wrote one friend of hers later, 'and she was so nervous that people would get hurt that she appealed to those nearest to her to look after the children.'

From time to time – and the journey took four hours – someone attempted to kiss the Princess's hand, and she was not in the least put out. At other moments in this bewildering, deafening experience, she spotted faces at the windows of grand houses that were comfortingly familiar: her cousin, Princess Mary Adelaide, her aunt, the Duchess of Cambridge, and the Duchess's lady-in-waiting, Lady Geraldine Somerset. And in Piccadilly the Prince recognised the Prime Minister, Lord Palmerston, Miss Angela Burdett-Coutts of the banking family and reputedly the richest woman in the land, Lord John Russell and others.

Again like the marriage before her, the road for Alix was sometimes rough, adding to the demands and exhaustion of the journey. But the children running alongside, without shoes but with smiles on their faces, and the equally boisterous happy dogs, caught her eye, too, reflecting her deep love for both and presaging the happy part of her life to come.

Hyde Park marked the climax of the welcome. One observer reported:

The Royal procession, which had wound its way so far beneath the forest of steeples, of public buildings, of clubs and merchant palaces, with their undergrowth of private dwellings and galleries erected for the occasion, entered at Hyde Park Corner on a novel phase.

The Princess had been welcomed with naval, military and civic greetings, with the voice of ships at sea, the joyous clamour of multitudes on shore, the deep reverence of England's capital, with every emblem of loyalty and love which taste could suggest; and now, amid a running and ever-renewed roll and current of hearty English cheering, she passed into Hyde Park to enjoy an imposing spectacle which there awaited her – an army of volunteers, citizen soldiers numbering 17,000 men, representing all arms of the services, congregated to prove their fidelity and zeal to the Royal house of England.

The royal train from Paddington Station arrived two hours late at Slough, the nearest station to Windsor. It was almost dark in this awful weather and the rain borne on the east wind was pouring down. It had been planned that the carriage would halt briefly at Eton College so that the boys could greet the royal couple and present an address of welcome. It was too late and too wet and the first stop was therefore their final destination, Windsor Castle.

In spite of the conditions there were still many people lining Thames Street and the High Street of the town, though they were scarcely visible in the flickering light of the gas-lamps and the pelting rain. The guards, wearing capes, stepped forward smartly at Henry VIII's Gateway and saluted. The horses, hating every yard of this journey, now had only to drag the coaches up the steep hill to St George's Gateway, where at last, beneath the towering ramparts, there was bright light and shelter.

Bertie's younger brothers and sisters raced towards the coach before it had stopped, Prince Alfred (Affie) leading the pack, then Helena (Lenchen), Louise (Loosy) and the others, down to little five-year-old Beatrice, the most excited of them all. Bertie watched indulgently as Alix embraced and kissed them in turn, even Affie the eldest who responded rather bashfully.

The Queen herself, looking so small and pinched and old in her grief, held back in the doorway, but managed to conjure up a smile as Bertie led forward his bride, who curtseyed deeply before the Queen embraced her. 'Dear Alix', she wrote later, 'was looking like a rose.'

Lady Mary Meynell was to write later of the reason for the extraordinary enthusiastic devotion Princess Alexandra inspired: 'Perhaps it was the romantic idea of the Sea King's daughter coming to our shores after the series of worthy but uninteresting German Princesses who had been dumped down upon us for centuries.'

Queen Victoria, so sensitive to emotion, dined privately that evening, and was struggling with tears in her room later when there was a gentle knock on the door and Alix, looking radiant, entered. 'She came and knelt before me with the sweet loving expression that spoke volumes,' the Queen wrote later in her journal. 'I was much moved and kissed her again and again.'

So many were the rooms and tortuous the passages in this great castle that Alix had to be led to her father and mother's bedchamber. Here she embraced them in turn, but did not remain long for they were all tired almost beyond bearing. When the door of her own room was at last shut by the chambermaid, Alix noticed that a long scroll of white satin lay on her dressing-table. Upon it was an elegantly printed poem, 'A Greeting to the Princess Alexandra' by Martin Tupper:

> She comes . . . [Alix read]
>   To be our Queen of Love;
> She comes! His young and beauteous Bride,
>   Behold her at the Prince's side,
> His truest crown, his joy and pride –
>   She comes! All blessings on her!
> Our ALBERT-EDWARD's happy choice,
>   Making the world's great soul rejoice
> That such a Prince has won her.

and on and on, verse after verse.

Then Alix collapsed into her bed. After this night in the silent castle, there would be only two more alone before she shared her bed with the young man she had met only briefly and scarcely knew.

2

A Serene Childhood

> *'Only three people have ever really understood the Schleswig-Holstein business – the Prince Consort, who is dead – a German professor, who has gone mad – and I, who have forgotten all about it.'*
>
> Lord Palmerston

Denmark is a kingdom of 16,000 square miles, one-third the area of New York State; a peninsula shaped like a fist which divides the North Sea from the Baltic Sea. The capital, Copenhagen, is on one of the largest of the islands in the Baltic which appear to have splintered from the mainland and drifted east towards Sweden. Schleswig and Holstein were two duchies which together formed the wrist separating Denmark from the great land mass of Germany.

This buffer area was of great value and significance to the independently minded Danish people, who were perpetually fearful of the avarice and aggrandisement of the kingdom of neighbouring Prussia. Unfortunately, the Danish people had made some recent diplomatic decisions which had led to the destruction of their fleet by Admiral Nelson in 1801 and, by allying themselves with Napoleon Bonaparte, to the loss of the whole of Norway, a Danish dependency, in 1814.

Although militarily debilitated, impoverishment had improved their national character and by the middle of the nineteenth century they were known as a liberal and cultured people. 'The Danes as a race are kind-hearted, honest and simple-minded,' observed a contemporary. 'In the intellectual world they have always maintained an honourable position; in science, literature, and in art they can boast of names worthy of being ranked with the best of other countries.'

These descendants of the ferocious Vikings who had also more recently mastered the Swedes had become a peace-loving and romantic people, living almost entirely off their rich land. 'The cult of the idyll', perhaps thanks to Rousseau and the eighteenth century, held a great attraction for them, and those who had the opportunity spent the summer 'in the country', renting houses or rooms, depending on what they could afford, in the most beautiful spots available.

'The pleasures of nature were, however, reserved for the summer. In the winter the people of Copenhagen were left to their own devices, to entertainment in the home, song and dance, and occasionally, for the more well-to-do, a private chamber concert. Interest in music was widespread. . . .'

Rulers of Denmark could be traced back to the euphonious Gorm the Old, who died in about 940. Since 1448 the House of Oldenburg, with deep German roots, had provided the monarchs, almost all of them called Frederick or Christian. Another Christian of a different dynasty – Prince Christian of Schleswig-Holstein-Sonderburg-Glücksburg – was destined to become King Christian IX and to rule the little nation for forty-three years. This decent, honest, not particularly brainy fellow nearly did not rule at all. As a young man in 1837 he was deputed as Denmark's representative to congratulate Queen Victoria on her accession to the throne. He liked what he saw of the country, and liked the Queen. Encouraged by a kinswoman, Augusta, Duchess of Cambridge, who had married one of Victoria's uncles, he let it be known that he would like to marry and be Consort to the Queen. She seemed to like him, too. They had lunch *à deux* and 'it is not at all certain that he has not made some impression on the Queen,' reported the Danish Ambassador.

The following year, Prince Christian contrived to return

for the Coronation, which seemed an appropriate time to 'pop the question'. It appears that he never succeeded in doing so, or was rebuffed, and Victoria married Prince Albert of Saxe-Coburg-Gotha instead.

Prince Christian found a less difficult and a more handsome bride in the Duchess of Cambridge's niece, Princess Louise of Hesse-Cassel. Louise, with her hour-glass figure, beautifully formed face, and grace of movement and comportment, made a stunning impression wherever she ventured, especially on the streets of Copenhagen where she walked, without escort, smiling at those who greeted her.

Louise shared Christian's firm beliefs in religion and solidarity of the family, was cheerful and gay and a great deal brighter than her husband. She conformed to the Danish love of music and played the piano beautifully. Her one flaw was a hereditary form of deafness caused by the development of spongy bone forms in the ear – osteosclerosis – which tends to worsen with age. Together they made a handsome and popular pair. 'Prince and Princess Christian are such charming people,' Queen Victoria's eldest child once told her, 'so full of tact and quiet that they soon put one at one's ease.'

For the present the Danish throne remained occupied by the dissipated and gross Frederick VII, a distant relative of the Christians, whose only merit was infertility, and who was married morganatically (and for the third time) to his one-time mistress. Meanwhile, Christian served as a full-time Horse Guards' officer, and very fine he looked mounted on a seventeen-hand charger. But the £800 a year he earned in the 1850s was all the family had, so they lived austerely in what was pretentiously called the Yellow Palace (*Det Gule Pala*).

This palace was no more than a substantial grace-and-favour town-house, set among others of like size, close to the King's palace and with a fine garden. Here on 1 December 1844 was born their first daughter, Princess Alexandra Caroline Marie Charlotte Louise Julia, known to friends and family all her life as Alix. The first four Christian children, Prince Frederick, Princess Alix, Prince William (Willi) and Princess Dagmar (Minnie) were all born within five years of each other and formed a close and loving group, and also made a particularly handsome quartet. Although well disciplined by their parents, their education was sketchy. What there was of it was undertaken at home, not to protect them from the outside world but because an army officer's pay did not run to private education. Their mother taught them music, art, German and French, while they became fluent in English from their British nursemaids. Their father introduced them to outdoor sports, from acrobatics to horse-riding, and they all grew up fit and active, known among their relations and friends as cheerful extroverts given to practical jokes. Only Minnie among them showed any curiosity about the intellectual world, although they were all musically talented.

Alix and Minnie were especially close, sharing a sparsely furnished bedroom, helping one another with their dressmaking and the few lessons they were taught. No photographs were taken of these children until adolescence, the cost in the late 1840s being prohibitive, and their mother was such a poor artist that she limited herself to unhelpful back views only. But the first photographs, taken when they were around fourteen, confirmed that Alix was the prettier of the two sisters. This is supported by several accounts, including that of Bessie Carew, recounted in a book of memoirs by her host from a visiting yacht:

We saw a go-cart drawn by a goat, which was led by a very smart-looking footman in a green and gold livery, with another one behind. Someone who looked like a ladies' maid or nurse was walking beside the cart. Seated in the cart was a most beautiful little girl about eight years old wearing a little fur bonnet. 'That', said Sir Henry Wynne, 'is the little Princess Alexandra of Denmark.' She waved to us gaily as she went by.

The presence of two liveried footmen appears to contradict the impression of an austere domestic life, for the Court did at least provide for the maintenance of a proper dignity for the future royal family.

The Christians were also given the use of a much larger house than the Yellow Palace, a fine dwelling in the French château-style called Bernstorff, after the family that built it in the eighteenth century. Here Alix and the other children

were determined that his wife should not come. Countess Donner was outraged when she heard this and announced publicly that she would be present anyway. The Christian family, and Alix herself, could do nothing and were fearful of some public scene. In the event, the Countess changed her mind, or perhaps she never had any intention of attending.

'Such was Princess Alexandra at the age of sixteen,' an earlier biographer has written. 'A young and lovely girl, probably not ignorant but certainly unsophisticated and, because of the circumstances of her upbringing, of necessity inexperienced in the ways of the great world.'

The Christian family was unsullied by morganatic marriages and indisputably royal. All the children were good-looking and had been brought up in a healthy and highly moral household. The economy of brains and wealth among these six children were not reckoned to be a handicap. Their Protestant religion was a bonus almost beyond reckoning by the non-Catholic dynasties of Europe.

For those who felt responsible for ensuring the continuity of royal lineages, Princess Alix of Denmark had been a serious candidate well before her confirmation. Her parents were aware of this, and prints of the photograph taken when she was fourteen were sent to many members of the Hesse-Cassel network. This pre-mating signal, they could be sure, would be recognised in all the qualifying royal palaces of Europe, and in Russia.

3

A Difficult Upbringing

'I had no boyhood . . .'
The Prince of Wales to Lord Esher

With the birth of a boy at Buckingham Palace at forty minutes past ten on the morning of 9 November 1841, the mother both set a precedent and 'suffered far the most severely' of all her nine confinements. Not for seventy-nine years had a reigning sovereign given birth to an heir.

The ancestry of this heir to the English throne was pure German on both sides. After Queen Victoria had decided in favour of Prince Albert of Saxe-Coburg-Gotha rather than Prince Christian of Denmark, the British monarchy retained the pure Germanic strain it had acquired with the first of the Hanoverians. It also established a strong prejudice in the Queen in favour of all that was Prussian, a fact that was later to trouble still further the relationship between her and her eldest son.

Queen Victoria had acceded to the throne on the death by asthma of her uncle, King William IV, on 20 June 1837. She was eighteen and could be very earnest. 'I am very young,' she conceded, 'and perhaps in many, though not in all things, inexperienced, but I am sure, that very few have more real good will and more real desire to do what is right than I have.'

Like Alix's mother, Princess Christian, Victoria was highly principled, possessed strong family feelings and loyalty, had no pretensions to intellectuality (but unlike the Dane felt ashamed of her inferiority), was deeply religious in a simple anti-evangelical belief, and was a romantic at heart. Unlike the future Queen of Denmark, Victoria had a scarcely concealed fear of death, was hot-tempered, superstitious, inflexible in resolve, highly nervous and could be extremely peremptory. In appearance, the contrast was as wide as the North Sea which geographically separated Dane from Briton. At four feet eleven inches, Victoria was seven inches shorter than Princess Christian, and her Hanoverian chin, plump fingers and dumpy figure ('a distingué figure tho' not very good,' wrote Lady Wharncliffe kindly) was in sharp contrast with the appearance of the Danish Princess. But even as a teenage girl, Victoria's friends and contemporaries recognised her unsurpassed *regality*: 'Her regal nature cannot be ignored. It is present in all that she does.'

The most important and surprising feature of the early years of Victoria's reign was her relish in her role as Queen. She had her beloved Prime Minister, Lord Melbourne, who had nursed her through the difficult apprenticeship, smoothed the bumps and filled in the potholes along the royal highway. He was kind, tactful, concerned, firm yet respectful on all occasions. How could she manage without Lord Melbourne? she asked herself every day.

By 1839 she was being pressed to consider marriage. She knew subconsciously that it must happen, but for the present she determined to give herself up to her duties, and the satisfaction they gave her.

Victoria had known her cousin Albert, Prince of Saxe-Coburg-Gotha, since early childhood and very much liked him. When pressed by her uncle, King Leopold of the Belgians, to consider this young man as a husband, she retorted sharply, 'All the reports of Albert are most favourable. I might like him as a friend, and as a *cousin*, and as a *brother*, but not *more*. . . .'

It had been arranged that in the early autumn of 1839 Prince Albert, accompanied by his elder brother, Ernest, should make a visit to England. Victoria dreaded it. She did not wish to be provoked by Lord Melbourne, Uncle Leopold or anyone else into a vulnerable position with this German cousin.

Albert arrived, and a metamorphosis overwhelmed her at this new meeting. The Queen was tempestuously in love; a passion had been aroused that was to burn for twenty-two years, and then endure as a warm, glowing and irreconcilable grief that only death nearly forty years later could douse. She found Albert 'quite charming, and so excessively handsome'. He possessed 'such beautiful blue eyes, an exquisite nose, and such a pretty mouth with delicate moustachios and slight but very slight whiskers: a beautiful figure, broad in the shoulders and fine waist; my heart is quite *going. . . .*'

The courtship proceeded at a pace that had everyone breathless. On that first evening they danced a quadrille, and later as a spectator she observed that 'it is quite a pleasure to look at Albert when he gallops and valses, he does it so beautifully, holds himself so well with that beautiful figure of his'.

That night Queen Victoria went to bed with her head spinning with love for this handsome German Prince and, being a decisive young woman (of twenty), let it be known the very next day to Lord Melbourne that she had changed her mind about marriage. Court and political circles rang with the excited murmurs that the match was as good as made. They inevitably reached the ears of Albert himself, who noted that 'V. had almost decided to choose me as her future husband and would probably make her declaration personally to me.'

Later he exclaimed, 'the climax has come upon us with surprise, before we could have expected it'. In a moment the Prince found himself having lunch, 'several times', with his future mother-in-law, the Duchess of Kent, and his betrothed. He brought along with him, almost as if he were a bodyguard, his great greyhound Eos ('Dawn'). One advantage about marrying a Queen was that you were saved 'the arrangements'. Still breathless and bewildered, Albert learned that the wedding would be on 10 February 1840, a mere three months ahead. 'While I shall be untiring in my efforts and labours for the country to which in future I shall belong, I shall never cease to be a true German, a true Coburg and Gotha man,' he declared. Never were truer words written.

Prince Albert had many things in common with Queen Victoria, the most significant being the unsatisfactory nature of their immediate forebears and their own determination to correct this record of debauchery, improvidence and heaven knows what other failures of character. Even as a young girl, Victoria was well aware of the dreadful nature of the Georges, and she was already eleven years old when the deplorable George IV died on 26 June 1830 and she became heir to the throne. While Victoria's childhood was miserable and lonely, and her mother's improvidence was notorious, she grew up with otherwise good examples before her, as if the nation was determined to help her lead a monarchical renaissance.

Albert had been born on 26 August 1819, three months and a week after the birth of his future wife. His father, Ernest I, Duke of Saxe-Coburg-Saalfeld, was quite as profligate and debauched as any King George of England. His mother, Princess Louise of Saxe-Coburg-Altenburg, was only sixteen when she married this awful man; and Albert was only five when the marriage broke down and Louise left. Albert never saw her again, but for all his life he retained affectionate memories of her.

The Coburg family took over responsibility for the education and upbringing of Ernest and Albert, and a good job they made of it, appointing an understanding yet firm, scholarly, patient and humane tutor, Herr Florschütz. 'Thus', as the boys called him, became for Albert almost a double surrogate parent on whom he depended for advice and comfort throughout his childhood.

Two other figures featured in Albert's upbringing, a tall, kind, strong Swiss named Cart, who, appropriately, carried him up and down stairs when he was too young to tackle them himself. The other was a remarkable and somewhat sinister man, Baron Christian Friedrich Stockmar. Stockmar was a German diplomat and physician of Swedish descent, who became part of the Court of Coburg where he earned his baronetcy in 1831. As mentor to Prince Albert, and trusted friend of Queen Victoria, Stockmar supervised Albert's education while acting the part of *éminence grise* at Coburg and Windsor.

With only one year between them, the Coburg Princes were as devoted as twins. Ernest was much less handsome than his brother but also more robust. Albert suffered congenital weaknesses from birth and like many of his kind became a hypochondriac. He had small resistance to germs and a need for frequent rest, even as a young man. By nine o'clock he was ready for bed, but as Victoria's Consort he would be called upon to endure long, formal dinners and late-night balls. In the event he nodded off over the entrée, sat out most of the dances and slipped away to bed as soon as this could be decently engineered.

Any sort of stress led to insomnia and neuralgia, and he suffered with his teeth through his boyhood and after. At the end of 1838, before he made that fateful journey to England and while on a cultural tour of Italy with Stockmar, he was struck down with 'the most violent toothache I have ever had to bear'. It was an abscess. On the night of New Year's Eve, 'when in Coburg the postilions ride trumpeting through the town', the abscess burst. Years later, Albert remembered the pain and then the relief. All the while his mind played on his homeland and the Rosenau, the summer residence set in a fairyland of forest, hills and rivers four miles from Coburg, which remained his spiritual home during all those years ahead in England and Scotland.

Albert did not at the time know it, but Stockmar's presence on this tour of Italy was to assess his suitability as a husband for Victoria. His findings, imparted first to King Leopold, were mixed. Considering Albert's all-male upbringing, it is not surprising that 'he will always have more success with men than with women, in whose society he shows too little empressement, and is too indifferent and retiring'. Stockmar also noted his weak health on the one hand, and his intelligence, kindness and amiability on the other. Stockmar's report, to all interested parties, which included the Duchess of Kent and Lord Melbourne, was a qualified 'Yes'.

In the brief period between engagement and marriage, Albert sought solace, searched his conscience, and fought his doubts in the land of his birth and in the company of the brother whose future absence in his life filled him with melancholy. 'Sobered and sad, he sought relief in his brother Ernest's company; the two young men would shut themselves up together, and, sitting down at the pianoforte, would escape from the present and the future in the sweet familiar gaiety of a Haydn duet.'

There was no escaping the irony of the words 'love, honour and obey' in the tremendous, triumphant wedding ceremony on 10 February 1840 at the Chapel Royal, St James, and there was greater irony in the Queen's insistence that they should not be omitted. Albert's role was without precedent. No one had given a hint of his duties for the excellent reason that no one knew. There would be plenty of advice available to the Queen, but Albert knew full well that she would accept or reject this entirely at her own judgment. She would, Albert felt confident, 'love and honour' him, if her evident passion and trust were a guide. But 'obey'? He could not even envisage giving orders, at least for the foreseeable future.

There had been a proposal during their engagement that Albert might be offered a peerage after the wedding. Victoria, already sensitive to any possible interference in her power – however slight – had the foresight to see the potential danger of this move and warn off her future husband. 'The English', she had written to justify her decision, 'are very jealous of any foreigner interfering in the government of this country, and have already in some of the papers expressed a hope that you would not interfere. Now,' she continued on a placatory note, 'though I know you never would, still, if you were a peer, they would all say, the Prince meant to play a political part.'

A 'foreigner'? Of course he was a foreigner, but Albert had entertained some sort of hope that he might become an adopted Englishman while retaining his love for the country of his birth. After all, since 1689 the British monarchy had been in the hands of foreigners, Germans since 1714. The British had succeeded in absorbing them, had they not, in spite of the guttural accents which had echoed in the royal palaces down the years?

But for the present, on their wedding day and their Windsor honeymoon, these two young people, the groom so tall and handsome, the bride so small and plain, could surrender to the joys of new love. 'I NEVER NEVER spent such an evening!!!' Queen Victoria recorded in her journal. 'My DEAREST DEAREST DEAR Albert sat on a footstool by my side, & his excessive love and affection gave me feelings of heavenly love & happiness, I never could have *hoped* to have felt before! – really how can I ever be thankful enough to have such a *Husband*!'

More than three years of Victoria's high-minded reign had not rid the Court of all its Hanoverian detritus and malicious gossip. There was still plenty of suspicion polluting the air, from the Cambridges for example. The Duke of Cambridge was the sixth son of George III and, therefore, uncle to Victoria. He had married Princess Augusta of Hesse-Cassel,* who became one of the Queen's greatest bugbears. 'An infamous woman', Victoria once described her. The tiresome children of George III scrapped like turkey-cocks among themselves and formed into pro- and anti-Victoria groups. Further angst and vituperation set in with the arrival of Albert – a Coburg outsider among the Hanoverians. There seemed to be no end to this internecine warfare, which stretched Albert's patience and nerves to their limit.

There was also the constant and irritating intrusion in their domestic life by Baroness Lehzen, Victoria's Lady Attendant, who saw her influence and importance reduced by Albert's presence and was a source of much mischief-making. More fundamental was the imbalance of power and influence between husband and wife. Albert had had perforce to consider deeply the inevitable unmasculine role of playing second

* She lived to ninety-two and saw Victoria's Golden Jubilee.

fiddle to his wife while retaining his dignity (which he guarded carefully) and finding himself something useful to do. 'My future life', he wrote to his friend, Prince Löwenstein, 'is high and brilliant, but plentifully strewn with thorns.'

There were many more political and domestic conflicts to overcome in those early months of marriage, and it is to the immense credit of this young, inexperienced, highly charged, temperamental and passionate couple that their relationship and love prevailed.

In the midst of this tumult of adjustment and efforts towards stabilisation, Victoria knew, by the third week in March 1840, that she was pregnant. She dreaded childbirth and had confessed to this fear many times. Had not her cousin Princess Charlotte, the only child of George IV, died in childbirth, thus bringing about her own accession? What would happen to the monarchy if she suffered the same fate? And Victoria was so small. She was therefore greatly relieved to hear that her own *accoucheurs* predicted an easy birth.

Then three months later, riding with Albert in an open carriage up Constitution Hill, a man in the crowd advanced and fired one pistol, and, with Albert's arms flung protectively about his wife, he fired again with a second. The father of John Millais, his painter son at his side, seized the miscreant. The Queen's calm comportment was much admired and attracted a cheering crowd.

The Queen gave birth, six weeks prematurely and without difficulty, to her baby on 21 November 1840. Albert sat behind a screen with his mother-in-law in the bedroom at Buckingham Palace. Here they were informed by Dr Charles Locock that the baby was 'a fine healthy princess'. Albert experienced a fleeting moment of disappointment before the midwife presented the child to him, wrapped in a flannel. From that moment, he thereafter claimed, he felt that he was truly an Englishman. To his brother he wrote: 'Albert, father of a daughter, you will laugh at me.'

The Queen was not in the least put out by the child's sex. 'Never mind, it will be a boy next time,' she confidently predicted. The baby was christened Victoria Adelaide Mary Louise, and for the present was called Pussy, later Vicky.

The Queen had no inclination to nurse the baby and obtained a wet-nurse from – where else? – Cowes, a stone's throw from the house where she would die a few months before this child's own death, sixty years later.

Everyone remarked on Albert's love for Pussy, which was never matched by his love for his later children, and certainly not by the next one. The year between the birth of the first and second child was fraught with troubles in the royal household. The causes were numerous. Of equal awfulness for the Queen were the loss of Lord Melbourne on 30 August when he resigned as Prime Minister and the increasingly appalling relationship between Albert and Baroness Lehzen. For four years Victoria had seen Lord Melbourne almost every day. He was her surrogate father, adviser, guide and protector, and to her his role of Prime Minister was merely incidental. She did not know how she would manage without him and unwisely quarrelled with his successor, the Tory Sir Robert Peel.

As for the Queen's Lady Attendant, it was as inevitable as the cycle of the moon that there would be continuing conflict with Albert. Since she was five years old, Victoria had owed Lehzen a great deal, but Lehzen had become jealous, a gossipy virago and a mischief-maker of the first order. Worst of all, her presence led to blazing rows between Victoria and Albert. It was months before Lehzen was at last prevailed upon to leave.

Wise old Melbourne knew that the Queen, with her abiding dislike of the new Tory Prime Minister and Government, would perforce have to rely even more heavily on her husband. In a final parting homily Melbourne wrote to his Queen:

Lord Melbourne has formed the highest opinion of HRH's [Albert's] judgement, temper and discretion, and he cannot but feel a great consolation and security in the reflection that he leaves Your Majesty in a situation in which Your Majesty has the inestimable advantage of such advice and assistance. Lord Melbourne feels certain that Your Majesty cannot do better than have recourse to it, whenever it is needed, and rely upon it with confidence.

If only she had followed this advice more closely. Melbourne's departure coincided with a sudden loss of health in little Pussy. The nursery quarters were the responsibility of Mrs Southey, sister-in-law of the poet, and about as ill-organised as Southey's verse. She would later be sacked in a clean-up by Albert, but for the present the baby was clearly being wrongly fed. '*Only* asses' milk,' instructed the Queen in early November while in the throes of fretfulness, anxiety and fear of the confinement that lay ahead. She also felt seedy and depressed. Her mother wished that she had not conceived again quite so quickly, and she did not disagree.

A few days after the new diet had been decreed for her first born, Victoria felt the final rumblings of the arrival of the second. Early on the morning of 9 November she called for Mrs Lilly, who in turn called for Dr Locock. She had premonitions that she was in for a bad time, and she was quite right. The pains were barely supportable even though 'dearest Albert' was at her bedside holding her hand throughout. Later in the morning she knew that the climax was fast approaching and that the agony would soon end.

THE ACCOUCHEMENT OF HER MAJESTY
BIRTH OF A PRINCE OF WALES

The *Times* Office
Quarter-Past Eleven o'clock AM

We have the utmost pleasure in announcing that at 10 minutes to eleven o'clock this morning her Majesty was safely delivered of a Prince.

The official bulletin which appeared a little later was as follows:

The Queen was safely delivered of a Prince this morning at 48 minutes past 10 o'clock.
    Her Majesty and the Infant Prince are going on well.

James Clark MD
Charles Locock MD
Robert Ferguson MD
Richard Blagden MD

'It was taken to the Ministers for them to see,' pronounced the Queen baldly. They were waiting in attendance and examined the infant closely, deciding unanimously that 'it' looked robust and well.

Bertie's arrival could not have been more timely, a precursor to a lifetime of promptitude. The whole of London, and in the provinces when the news was learned, went into a tumult of celebration, formalised by the Lord Mayor's Show, which happily coincided to the hour with the birth.

At a Privy Council meeting the Archbishop of Canterbury was enjoined to prepare a form of Prayer and Thanksgiving to Almighty God for Her Majesty's safe delivery of a Prince, to be said in all churches and chapels in England and Wales. This was complied with at amazing speed; and with equal pace two verses were added to the national anthem for a spontaneous invasion of the stage at the Adelphi Theatre, where *The Maid of Honour* was playing.

> Oh, Lord, in bounty shed
> Joys round the Infant's Head,
> Shield him from harm:
> Hear now a nation's prayer,
> Guard England's youthful heir;
> Make him thy special care;
> God save the Queen

'Nothing could exceed the enthusiastic acclamation with which the last verse was received,' ran one report, 'and the manifestations of loyalty and joy displayed by the audience in all parts of the house exceeded anything which we have witnessed.'

What pleased the baby's mother most was that he so closely resembled his father; equally pleasing was to hear 'the Boy' (as she insisted on calling him) so described by others. She had resolved that he must be brought up to resemble his father in every respect, and that no impediment towards this aim must on any account be countenanced. He could not, of course, quite match the qualities of character and behaviour of Albert, but with God's help and her guidance this goal must be striven for. 'You will understand', the Queen wrote to her Uncle Leopold in Belgium, 'how fervent are my prayers, and I am sure everybody must be, to see him resemble his father in *every, every* respect, both in body and mind.'

As to the choice of name, for the Queen it was a pity that there had to be more than one. She would have preferred simply Albert, but Lord Melbourne intervened and suggested that this name had 'not been so common nor so much in use since the Conquest' and that it might be preceded by 'a good English appellation', like Edward. The Queen reluctantly compromised on Albert Edward. To avoid confusion, he came to be known in the family as Bertie, and that was that.

The baptism took place in St George's Chapel, Windsor, on 25 January 1842, a crisp, sunny day, with the Archbishop of Canterbury officiating. Considering Bertie's appetite and later girth, it was appropriate that the baby's cake was eight feet wide. 'You will have heard', the Queen wrote to Uncle Leopold, 'how perfectly and splendidly everything went off on the 25th. Nothing could have done better and *little* Albert (what a pleasure that he has that *dearest* name!) behaved so well.'

Bertie's early childhood was not unhappy, but it was beset by misfortunes which were to multiply as the years passed. The first misfortune was simply to be the second child. Like an entertainer who follows the star turn, Bertie was unfortunate to have an older sister blessed with so many qualities. Vicky, as Pussy soon became, was the prettiest baby imaginable, with fair hair and enormous blue eyes; she was precociously bright and eager for attention, which was never lacking. Albert took her out daily in a carriage with open windows through which the little Princess cheered and waved back at the crowds, thrilled at the excitement she created. She did have a sharp temper when she was reproved or frustrated, but she was soon all sweetness again. She was indeed dreadfully spoilt, but charm and liveliness melted any resentment at this.

While Vicky was forgiven rare misdemeanours, and basked in the limitless love of father, mother, governess and the rest of the nursery staff, Bertie was made to feel the less loved, the second to catch the eye of all who entered the nursery, especially by his father who sometimes seemed to ignore him altogether.

One-year-old Vicky did not at first take kindly to this intrusion in the nursery, but after a few days curiosity got the better of her and she soon became reconciled to her brother's presence. She was a contented child and, with the reformation of the nurseries by Albert himself and the appointment of Lady Lyttelton as governess, she was in good hands. Lady Lyttelton, who figured equally in Bertie's young childhood, was the widowed daughter of Lord Spencer, who was responsible for the Reform Bill of 1832, a wholly admirable and sensible woman who also sported a keen sense of humour.

Baron Stockmar, who had become Albert's confidant, took a keen interest in the upbringing of the two children, and was the only person whose reforming zeal would have been welcome. His beliefs were far ahead of the times, with emphasis on fresh air and sun and sensible, fresh food. He had the complete trust of Victoria and Albert, who co-operated with him in drawing up a joint resolution covering their own conduct as parents: 'That they should be brought up as simply as possible and that they should be as often as possible with their parents (without interfering with their lessons) and place their greatest confidence in them in all things.'

Giving time to all his children was something Albert welcomed daily. He loved noting every advance in their behaviour and development and played with them until sometimes they were exhausted. The Queen could not spare the same amount of time, and anyway while they were still infants she felt more distaste than love for them.

As the months passed it became increasingly evident that Vicky was much quicker and brighter than her brother. Comparisons were made, to Bertie's disadvantage, often within his hearing. It says much for him that these in no way lessened his love and admiration for her, and she, for her part, did not take unfair advantage of her superior skills.

Bertie was just one year old when he was taken for his first ride in a train, marking his association with the age of invention and advancement in all types of industry and transport which his life was to encompass. The Great Western Railway had been operating out of Paddington and all the way to Bristol since 1837. The Queen had made her first journey a few weeks earlier from Slough into London in a special coach and with the chairman of the railway, Dan Gooch, on the footplate to acknowledge the honour and to ensure that Her Majesty was safe.

Victoria and Albert were for ever on the move between their residences and on social and duty visits. Their children did not always travel with them, but they did so often enough to plant the seed of restlessness in their son, who, in adult life, was content to remain at two places only – Sandringham and Marlborough House – for more than a few days.

For about three years Bertie was admired without qualification and lived a life of nursery contentment. After a visit from the Gladstones, William reported, 'The Prince of Wales has a very good countenance . . . his manners very dear and not shy,' while his wife Catherine described him as 'a fine fair satisfactory baby'. The historian Macaulay qualified his praise, finding him 'pretty but delicate looking'. 'A fair little lad, rather of slender make,' wrote Archbishop Benson, while Lady Lyttelton wrote of him at the age of one: 'He is very intelligent and looks through his large clear blue eyes, full at one, with a frequent very sweet smile.'

Queen Victoria was, in the 1840s, at the height of her child-conceiving period. A daughter, Alice, was born on 25 April 1843, another son, Alfred, on 6 August 1844, Helena (Lenchen) on 25 May 1846, Louise (Loosy) on 18 March 1848 and Arthur on 1 May 1850. The last son, Leopold, was born on 7 April 1853, and the afterthought, Beatrice, on 14 April 1857. This fecundity had an unfortunate effect on the behaviour and performance of Bertie. The others did not appear to be affected by the sharing of attention among so many, but Bertie seems to have been born with unusual sensitivity and need for love.

Lady Lyttelton, who knew him better than anyone else through his early childhood, provided him with much of this love. She was often deeply touched by his sensitivity, and especially by his love for his sister Alice, nearly eighteen months younger than himself. He was six when Lady Lyttelton reported that he was 'much improved in size and manliness'. He was also

continuing most promising for kindness and nobleness of mind. His sister had been lately often in disgrace and . . . his little attentions and feeling on the sad occasions have been very nice – never losing sight of her, through a longish imprisonment in her own room, and stealing to the door to give a kind message, or tell a morsel of pleasant news – his own toys quite neglected, and his lovely face quite pale, till the disgrace was over.

Lady Lyttelton also noted early signs of 'passions and stampings', and a little later this excellent woman observed that he was 'uncommonly averse to learning'. He was brought up bilingually in German and English, but his French teacher had a difficult time interesting him in her language. Lady Lyttelton, too, had trouble holding his attention for any length of time, and worse, he practised 'getting under the table, upsetting the books and sundry other *anti-studious* practices'. However, she qualified this by writing that he was 'passionate and determined enough for an aristocrat, but he still has his lovely mildness of expression, and calm temper in the intervals'.

The situation was not in the least helped by the fact that his younger sister nearest to him in age was as bright as Vicky, thus sandwiching him between them. Alice soon caught him up and remained ahead at lessons, while Vicky took to teasing him about his stutter, which had now developed. By eight years of age, Bertie had become a real handful and was far behind in most lessons except handwriting, drawing and music, all of which he enjoyed.

The more Bertie fell behind, the more his parents determined that he should work harder for longer hours to make up for his deficiencies. Visitors noted how good and natural his manners were, as he offered his hand, bowed and saluted. It was the one department where there appeared some hope that he might eventually emulate his father. As for his lessons, the Queen determined that he 'ought to be given *entirely* over to the Tutors and taken *entirely away* from the women'.

In the event, at the age of eight Bertie was put into the hands of one exclusive male tutor, Mr Henry Birch, whose name belied a fine, and certainly non-violent, teacher from Eton College. Birch soon regretted his decision to agree to devote his life, for the present anyway, to a boy who might be 'the once and future King' but at this stage was wilful, recalcitrant, 'extremely disobedient, impertinent . . . and unwilling to submit to discipline'.

'Poor Bertie!' people would say. 'Poor, poor Bertie!' If he had not been heir to the throne, his parents would have worried less, but although Victoria was strong and fit, a bad attack of typhoid or diphtheria, which were rife in the land, could make Bertie into King Edward VII overnight. Sensible Birch was not the only one to press for a more normal life for his charge. 'I have always found that boys' characters at Eton were formed as much by contact with others as by the precepts of their tutors.' With no other boys of his own age about, 'he has no standard by which to measure his own powers'.

Neither his mother nor his father could agree. Victoria, who had herself been brought up lacking almost all contact with other children, 'had a great fear of young and carefully brought up boys mixing with older boys and indeed with any boys in general, for the mischief done by bad boys and the things they may hear and learn from them cannot be overrated'.

Lord Esher once wisely wrote:

Without the stimulus of competition, surrounded by the disturbing influences of regal state, deprived of the freer companionship of boys of his own age, it is not surprising that the Prince of Wales, although he never rebelled, passively resisted the high pressure of his father's system of education. . . . Referring to those days, he regretted the decision which isolated him during the crucial years of his later boyhood from contact with his equals in age and intellectual attainments.

With no experience of how to behave with boys of his own age, when the total ban was faintly relaxed and several carefully vetted boys from Eton were summoned to Windsor Castle to play with Bertie and his younger brother, Affie, Bertie was inclined to assault them to establish his superiority, leading to complaints from the headmaster. That experiment was soon stopped. Later, Bertie's governor, Colonel the Hon. Robert Bruce, attributed his charge's odd behaviour with others of his age to his lack of experience with 'those checks and restraints, and those practical lessons in what is due to others, and ourselves, which belong to the ordinary social intercourse of equals'.

One boy who always escaped Bertie's bullying was Charles Carrington (later third Baron and Marquess of Lincolnshire), who wrote of this period:

[Both boys] were strictly treated and brought up – Prince Alfred was the favourite, but I always liked the Prince of Wales far the best. He had such an open generous disposition and the kindest heart imaginable. He was a very plucky boy and always ready for fun, which often got him into scrapes. He was afraid of his father, who seemed a proud shy stand-offish sort of a man not calculated to make friends with children – individually I was frightened to death of him!

Victoria and Albert remained adamant that Bertie's life should remain unnaturally circumscribed. Birch found that he was expected to be the boy's companion day and night. It was to his credit that Bertie developed a deep affection and respect for him, which proved the death-knell of the relationship. Albert, who had himself depended upon and dearly loved his tutor, Herr Florschütz, could not tolerate seeing the happiness Birch gave Bertie. Contentment hinted at inactivity in his twisted judgment. Also, Victoria suspected that Birch's religion was too High Church and might brush off on her son. The man was also talking about being ordained. What next?

Birch was promptly replaced, and Bertie was heartbroken. In an upbringing that was mishandled throughout, this was the worst thing to happen to the young Prince of Wales. His new tutor was Frederick Waymouth Gibbs, a stiff, unimaginative pedant with none of Birch's warmth. Almost the first words Bertie uttered to him were, 'You cannot wonder if we are somewhat dull today,' speaking for himself and his brother Alfred. 'We are sorry Mr Birch has gone. It is very natural, is it not?'

Bertie detested Gibbs from the start, and it did not help that at the same time his father ordered a more demanding regimen than ever – seven hours a day at his books, six days a week. Stockmar supported this pressure of work, believing it to be the only way to recover lost ground in the boy's education. No one, least of all the Queen to whom they were addressed, had listened to the wise words of Lord Melbourne: 'Be not over solicitous about education. It may be able to do much, but it does not do as much as is expected from it. It may mould and direct the character, but it rarely alters it.' Expecting to do just that, no wonder Victoria brushed this aside. *They* were going to alter Bertie's character – they were going to alter it so that it precisely conformed to *dear* Albert's.

For the present, however, at around the age of ten, Bertie's character was as far distant as Windsor from Coburg from conforming to Albert's. The unremitting pressure of work led him into frightful and destructive rages, when he was likely to throw anything he could lay his hands on at anything or anybody in sight – usually Gibbs himself. Or he might 'stand in the corner stamping with his legs and screaming in the most dreadful manner'. 'A very bad day,' this tutor recorded. 'The P. of W. has been like a person half silly. I could not gain his attention. He was very rude, particularly in the afternoon, throwing stones in my face. . . .'

His German and French teachers believed that the cause of these tempers was too intense a programme of work. 'You will wear him out early,' Dr Voisin wisely warned Gibbs. 'Make him climb trees! Run! Leap! Row! Ride! . . . He has the moral sentiments in a high degree. For instance, such a love of truth that he is ready to be a witness against himself.' Dr Becker sounded the same warning note to Prince Albert himself, defending Bertie's 'profound religious feeling, a great straightforwardness, and a sense of truth to such an extent as I scarcely ever witnessed in a child of his age'.

Bertie's parents' ears remained closed, and the killing regime continued as before. When he was included in a royal visit to Ireland, his tutors followed like shadows, maintaining the same pressure as if at home. Even at sea, Latin, history, French and science lessons continued. Tantrums were met with chastisement, boxed ears and raps across the knuckles with a stick.

Bertie remained longing for love – the love he had once received first from Lady Lyttelton and then from Birch – and someone to love. He wanted more than anyone to love his father. This was virtually impossible when he received from him only the admonition and dark scowls of disapproval insisted upon by the Queen.

A narrow but sharp beam of light settled briefly on Bertie's life when he was thirteen in 1855. Victoria and Albert made a state visit to Paris and the French royal family, and they took Bertie and Vicky with them. For Bertie it was the beginning of a love affair with Paris that was to last for all his life. As soon as he was able, and when he felt a need for the beauty and freshness, the unique charm and friendliness of the people, the appreciation of fine wines and food, he would cross the Channel and race along the *chemin de fer* in his special carriage to the Strasburg terminus.

Writing in 1906 with the *Entente Cordiale* safely signed, an early biographer of Bertie recorded that 'This first visit to France unquestionably marked an epoch in the boyhood of the Prince of Wales. . . .' His mother, too, was enchanted with the people and the city. 'Imagine this beautiful city, with its broad streets and lofty houses, decorated in the most tasteful manner possible [she wrote in her journal], with banners, flags, arches, flowers, inscriptions, and, finally, illuminations; full of people, lined with troops. . . .'

Bertie and his beautiful older sister were especially admired. Bertie went to his first ball, staring about him in wonder at the illuminated decorations and the dresses of the French royal family. He himself created a sensation in his kilt and sporran, and no one regarded it as anachronistic that a future Hanoverian King of England should be dancing – and with what *bravura*! – in Scottish national costume. He was simply *ravissant*.

Besides the Empress Eugénie, sparkling with diamonds, and the Emperor Napoleon III, there was present in the throng of whirling figures Prince Jerome Bonaparte, who was said to have been earmarked for the English throne if Nelson had not won at Trafalgar and Wellington at Waterloo.

Then there was Bertie's *tête-à-tête* carriage drive with the Emperor through the packed Paris streets, Bertie 'chatting and joking, while his host smoked a large cigar'. 'I should like to be your son,' Bertie remarked poignantly. He equally fell for the charms of Empress Eugénie, who later sent him a lock of her hair entwined with a hair from the Emperor's head and the head of her baby son.

Besides the firing of cannon and displays of fireworks, Bertie – again in his fetching kilt and sporran – knelt in prayer beside his mother at the tomb of Napoleon I, once the most feared and hated man in England.

'May my sister and I stay for a little longer?' Bertie ventured just before they were due to leave. 'I am afraid that the Queen and Prince Albert could not do without you,' the Empress replied.

Bertie promptly retorted, rolling his 'r's gutturally, as he did for all his life, 'Don't fancy that, for there are six more of us at home, and they don't want *us*.'*

The departure was almost as tumultuous as the arrival. At 10 a.m. on 27 August the imperial carriage left St Cloud, where they had been staying, 'the inhabitants and the municipal body cheered her as she passed under the same triumphal arch which was erected for her arrival,' wrote *The Times* correspondent, conditioning his enthusiasm only by pointing to one mistake: 'With all this it is right to observe that some disappointment was felt at the Queen passing in state through

---

* He was not so far wrong at that. Later in the same year, the Queen wrote to the Queen of Prussia: 'I find no special pleasure in the company of the elder children . . . and only very occasionally do I find the rather intimate intercourse with them either easy or agreeable.' The only years she could 'do' with children were between about three and ten.

Paris in a close carriage – no one could see her features.'

At the Strasburg terminus 'the Queen, leaning on the Emperor's arm, entered the station. She saluted those about her and proceeded to the Royal Train, while the band of the 9th Regiment of the Voltigeurs of the Guard played "God Save the Queen".'

On their return to England, Bertie was at once despatched to Osborne, the house the Queen had purchased on the Isle of Wight to get away from it all. Its function for Bertie was quite the reverse, more a crammer than a place to relax, for he was in for a period of especially intense study to make up for the lost six days in Paris. (He always loathed Osborne and sold it the moment he became King.)

Now the fact that Bertie was 'pale and trembling' at the prospect was typically misinterpreted by his mother as his distress at separation from her and Albert – 'his first long separation'.

Nevertheless, a corner of the blanket that had half-suffocated him for years had been lifted momentarily, and he recorded that there was a real world outside which one day, in the not too far distant future, he might venture into on his own. Soon he would be fourteen, and was already keenly conscious of his destiny.

4

A Little Learning

'A good set'
Prince Albert on Bertie's tutors

The Prince of Wales's life was much changed by the marriage of his diminutive, pretty and intelligent elder sister in January 1858, when he was sixteen and she seventeen. Her groom was an amiable German Prince, Frederick of Prussia (Fritz), and heir apparent to the throne. This match gave Queen Victoria immense satisfaction, tightening the ties ever closer with Germany – once the homeland of her beloved Albert.

As early as the evening of the wedding day, 25 January, the Queen began a correspondence with her eldest daughter which was to run into hundreds of thousands of words and continue until her death. The subjects of this correspondence were equally numerous, and until Bertie married he was one of the most frequently mentioned preoccupations of mother and daughter. By March of the same year, Victoria is opening her heart, and its agony, to her newly married daughter, and nothing shows more clearly her regret that Bertie is her first-born son:

Affie [Prince Alfred] is going on admirably; he comes to luncheon today and oh! when I see him and Arthur and look at . . . ! (You know what I mean!) I am in utter despair! The systematic idleness, laziness – disregard of everything is enough to break one's heart, and fills me with indignation.

The loss of Vicky in the household was felt keenly by everyone, and Bertie was among those who shed tears on the quayside at Gravesend when she and her husband embarked on the journey to her new home. In spite of childhood tiffs, the two first born were very close. Soon after this, Bertie was separated from Affie, his nearest brother in age, in companionship and interests. Prince Alfred was a good-looking and bright boy, set for the Royal Navy, but meanwhile his parents feared that his character, and his education, might be adversely affected by Bertie's baleful proximity.

While Vicky was settling down to married life in Berlin, Bertie was effectively exiled from his family. In a further outrageous misjudgment, Queen Victoria and Baron Stockmar had between them decided that he should be banished to a house called White Lodge in Richmond Park. Prince Albert dutifully agreed.

Here, in the spring of 1858 after his confirmation, Bertie was incarcerated with the loathed Gibbs and the more sympathetic Revd Charles Feral Tarver, who was to concentrate on teaching Latin and religion. The other gaolers were two army majors and a 'thoroughly good, moral and accomplished' youngish man, Lord Valletort, who had never been to school, having been too busy looking after his invalid father.*

These five men were 'what is commonly called a good set', Albert wrote hopefully to Stockmar. 'I anticipate no small benefit to Bertie.' White Lodge was to be, in effect, a one-man finishing school prior to university. In a lengthy memorandum, Albert instructed his team in a 'rigorous code of disciplinary rules', in lessons on 'appearance, deportment and dress' on the one hand and 'manners and conduct towards others' on the other. His son was to learn how 'to acquit himself creditably in conversation' and avoid, at rest, 'lounging ways, such as lolling in armchairs and sofas' and, in

---

* He succeeded to the title as fourth Earl of Mount Edgcumbe and remained in royal service for most of his long life, ending up as ADC to Queen Victoria.

motion, to eschew 'a slouching gait with hands in the pockets'. 'He must borrow nothing from the groom or the game-keeper', at all times exercise 'the most scrupulous civility', and above all 'avoid anything approaching a *practical joke*'. In order one day to become 'the first gentleman in the country', he must for the present enjoy personal relations with only 'those in official attendance upon him' – namely these five guardians, and perhaps a close relative or two, but not if they were young.

No games were there for him [wrote his friend and near-contemporary, the future Lord Redesdale], no free association with playmates of his own age. . . . He was sent to Oxford, but strict care was taken that he should have no part in the life of the university. He might hear lectures – he might see nothing. It was as if you were to send a lad to the theatre and set him down in the stall with his back to the stage. The first time that I saw the Prince of Wales was when his father brought him to Eton, as a little boy of twelve, to hear the 'speeches' on the Fourth of June. What a diversion for a child of his age, to listen to us sixth-form boys spouting Demosthenes, Aeschylus, Cicero! I can see his poor bored little face now. It was pitiful.

It took just three months for this desperate White Lodge scheme to prove a fiasco. The first crack occurred when one of the military 'gentlemen-in-waiting' wrote on 27 July 1858 to Albert's Private Secretary:

A continuance of the present system will not be beneficial to the Prince. Mr Gibbs has *no* influence. He and the Prince are so much out of sympathy with one another that a wish expressed by Mr Gibbs is sure to meet with opposition on the part of the Prince. . . . I quite understand the Prince's feelings towards Mr Gibbs, for tho' I respect his uprightness and devotion, I could not give him sympathy, confidence or friendship.

The Queen, who had been such an admirer of Gibbs and of his firm resolution, suddenly did a *volte-face*. The White Lodge incarceration ended and Gibbs rapidly retired in October 1858. 'Bertie was much affected at parting from him,' she wrote hopefully, but, as she admitted to Vicky in Berlin, '[Gibbs] has failed completely the last year and a half with Bertie – and Bertie did what he liked! No-one can understand the cause and it makes it more difficult for us now. However,' she consoled herself, 'I have great confidence in Colonel Bruce.'

The Hon. Robert Bruce, the younger brother of the eighth Earl of Elgin, was forty-five years old and a colonel in the Grenadier Guards. Prince Albert wrote of him, with incredible inaccuracy, that 'he has all the amiability of his sister [Lady Augusta], with the great mildness of expression'. 'Mildness', however, was probably the very last characteristic Queen Victoria was seeking.

Bruce was to hold the new rank of 'Governor to HRH The Prince of Wales' and was to take up his duties on 9 November 1858, Bertie's seventeenth birthday. Like the previous quintet of guards, Bruce did not lack for instructions in the execution of his 'monstrous trust'. Even after all these years of failure, the purpose of this 'trust' was still to make Bertie a facsimile of his father. The trouble was that no one was in a position to point out to the Queen and her Consort that this was an unachievable goal. Albert, unlike the light-hearted, cheerful Fritz – Vicky's husband – was of a different strain of Prussian blood and in almost every respect was a reverse image of his anglicised Hanoverian son.

Bertie learned from observation, conversation and example, and absorbed hardly anything from books and scarcely listened to anything theoretical or hypothetical. He learned early to appreciate the joys of smoking and drinking. Prince Albert, like his wife, abhorred cigars and cigarettes, and a touch of claret in his seltzer water was his idea of going the whole hog. Bertie, even in boyhood, loved women* as they loved him, and he could not have too much of the social life. His father was fearful of the first and disliked mixing with a lot of people. He was completely comfortable and secure only with his wife, who arranged and instructed and guided him in all matters. Everyone remarked on Bertie's charm and natural good manners, and while Albert was extremely

---

* At sixteen, in the course of a 'cultural tour' of the continent, he once contrived to get mildly drunk and kiss a pretty German girl. Gladstone, whose son was one of the party, on being informed described the incident as a 'squalid debauch'.

courteous people were not actually captivated by him: he was too unbending for that.

Robert Bruce, strengthened even further by promotion to major-general, led his cohorts into the final campaign to convert his charge into a mini-Albert. They should have saved themselves the trouble, as the first communiqués indicated – although these were in the form of 'gloomy' reports from the Queen to Vicky in Germany. 'Oh! dear, what would happen if I were to die next winter! One shudders to think of it: it is too awful a contemplation. [Bertie's] journal is worse a great deal than Affie's letters. And all from laziness!'

More cultural tours were planned when all Bertie desired was to follow in the footsteps of his governor rather than his father and become a soldier. He had always loved the pomp and ceremony of soldiering, of what he regarded as the romance of war. Since infancy he had had plenty of opportunity to watch troops performing their marching evolutions, or to wave them off to the Crimean War and hear the tales of battle on their return. He treasured his own toy gun and when he lost it, and Louis Philippe happened to be staying, he later received as a present a *fusil de munitions* as replacement.

Besides the ceremonials, what Bertie enjoyed most about the military life was the colour and variety of uniforms, decorations, sashes, buttons, headgear, belts, swords and side-arms. He had first been drawn to the attraction of clothes on his sixth birthday, when, with Vicky, Affie and little Alice, he had been present at an inspection of troops and a *feu de joie*. His own uniform for the occasion had been ordered by royal command from a Bond Street tailors, who were to 'make several suits of clothes of new fashion and materials . . . made from a Turkish design. One of the jackets was bright blue, lined with crimson silk and trimmed with braid. Another was of dark lake with white, and a third of maroon with blue.' In addition, 'a variety of waistcoats were provided of different colours varying from plain black to white sateen, while a fancy tartan was employed for the trousers'.

As if this were not enough to sow the seeds of royal clothes-consciousness at an early age, at about this time

Bertie had been togged out in his first Scottish kilt and its ornaments, 'the jewels that set off the bonnet and sporran and plaid', and the *sgian-dubh* worn in the stockings.*

Eleven years later, the most memorable of his seventeenth birthday presents was an allowance for buying his own clothes. It was a liberation all the more exciting for being unexpected, although naturally conditioned by warnings like 'We do *expect* that you will never wear anything *extravagant* or *slang.*'

The complaints soon followed. Prince Albert warned Vicky, prior to Bertie's first visit to her in Berlin, that she would find 'unfortunately that he took no interest in anything but clothes, and again clothes. Even when out shooting he is more occupied with his trousers than with the game.'

In the event, the visit was a tremendous success. Everyone liked Bertie, and he made a lifelong friend of his brother-in-law. Vicky found him much improved, but the Queen complained that his excitedly favourable report on return was about theatres, parties and people and not about 'the finer works of art'.

Undeterred, Albert decided to press ahead with Bertie's further ventures into the world of art and culture. This time Rome was to be his destination. The plans were drawn up within days of Bertie's return from Berlin. And what comprehensive plans they were, as his father spent hours drawing up lists and detailed instructions late at night by the light of his special reading lamp. Even Victoria was satisfied with their demanding complexity. There was to be not only an Italian tutor in the party, but also an archaeological guide, Joseph Barclay Pentland, and John Gibson, the distinguished émigré British sculptor, to take Bertie round the marble busts.

This new expedition began with the departure from London on 10 January 1859, and the journey ended circuitously, with many cultural halts *en route*, at the Hotel d'Angleterre in

* It was typical of his father, however, to commit every sort of wardrobe solecism with his Scottish dress.

Rome on 4 February.* Almost before his valet had unpacked his bags, Bertie was hard at it. Three days later, Bruce was able to report back to his master:

He learns by heart in the morning before breakfast, and prepares for his Italian master who comes from 10 to 11 a.m. He reads with Mr Tarver from 11 to 12, and translates French from 5 to 6 p.m. and has the next hour in the evening for private reading or music. He has a piano in his room. The afternoon is devoted to the inspection, under expert guidance, of ancient monuments and ancient and modern works of art. . . .

Dinner parties with all the best cultured people in Rome, or attendance at the opera or theatre, occupied the evenings. Although there were rebellions in private, without exception the eminent guests were impressed, even enchanted, by the young man. One of them, the American historian John Lothrop Motley, compared his profile with that of the Queen (not a very good example), but 'the complexion is pure, fresh, and healthy, like that of most English boys, his hair light brown, cut short, and curly. His eyes are bluish-grey, rather large and very frank in his expression; his smile is very ready and genuine; his manners are extremely good.' Others spoke of his 'engaging disposition', and Robert Browning described him as 'a gentle refined boy', while Edward Lear commented, 'Nobody could have nicer or better manners.'

Back home Victoria and Albert knew nothing of this. All they received were gloomy reports from General Bruce: 'His thoughts are centred on matters of ceremony, on physical qualities, manners, social standing, and dress.' As for Bertie's own journal, which he was obliged to send home regularly, his parents thought the entries dull and uninspiring. 'I am sorry you were not pleased as I took pains with it,' he wrote, 'but I see the justice of your remarks and will try to profit by them.'

Internal political friction, and then war involving Austro-Hungary, northern Italy and France, cut short Bertie's

* Bertie's sister Vicky gave birth to the future Kaiser William II while he was travelling across Europe, a figure who would be troublesome to Bertie, and a disaster to the world at large.

cultural tour. Escape in a British man o'war enlivened things, as HMS *Scourge* headed for the security of Gibraltar. With the programme and routine broken, he had an unexpected release. There were trips into Spain and, on the way home, a visit to his cousin, the amiable King Pedro V of Portugal. There was, according to Bertie's journal, 'plenty of larking'. This ceased abruptly on his return home.

Stockmar and the Queen had already laid down a programme for him devised at an 'educational conference' on 30 August 1859, which included a three-month cramming session at Edinburgh, followed by the completion of his education at both Oxford and Cambridge universities. In Scotland he lived at the Palace of Holyroodhouse, with shooting parties strictly forbidden, and to his fury at Oxford he was not allowed to live in college and was consigned to gloomy Frewin Hall, an independent establishment off Cornmarket Street.

General Bruce remained as supervisor, and Albert reminded him that 'the only use of Oxford is that it is a place for *study*, a refuge from the world and its claims. You are aware of the principles which we have laid down after anxious reflection.' The General was by now very much aware of these 'principles', and so, increasingly, was the outside world, which was showing alarm at the relentlessness of Bertie's instruction. The Vice-Chancellor of Oxford, no less, contributed some verses called 'A Prince at High Pressure', which *Punch* published on 24 September, one of which ran:

> When next the boy may go to swell the farrago,
> We haven't yet heard, but the Palace they're plotting in;
> To Berlin, Jena, Bonn, he'll no doubt be passed on,
> And a drop in for a finishing touch, p'haps at Gottingen.

Victoria and Albert's anxieties about their son continued unabated, and Vicky in Berlin, busy enough with her own family, was subjected to a series of complaints and appeals to use her influence to bring about improvements in her brother's behaviour and record. 'Bertie's propensity is indescribable laziness,' Albert wrote yet again. 'I never met in my life such a thorough and cunning lazybones. It does grieve me when it is my own son, and when one considers that he might be called upon at any moment to take over the reins of government in a country where the sun never sets.'

While conceding that Bertie might be working harder at Edinburgh, the Queen complained to her daughter that he had 'not improved in looks; the mouth is becoming so very large and he will cut his hair away behind and divide it nearly in the middle in front, so that it makes him appear to have no head and all face. It is a frightful coiffure.'

Then there was the matter of Bertie's weight. Even before he was seventeen, it was clear that he had inherited his mother's tendency to plumpness and her healthy appetite which caused it. Earlier, he had been given strict diet sheets, laying down in detail the quantity and nature of his food and drink: claret to be mixed with seltzer water in hot weather, sherry with tap water in cold weather, a light breakfast only – bread and butter, tea and an egg. At Oxford he had his own chef to deal with the dinner parties he was expected to give, and, as he loved rich food and could choose his own menu in conjunction with his chef, many were the dishes 'which an experienced and prudent liver will carefully avoid', as his father complained.

His parents also hated Bertie's smoking, and would have been alarmed if they had had any idea how heavy it was – already half-a-dozen cigars a day, supplemented by around twenty cigarettes. The Queen especially abhorred – as well as his haircut – Bertie's tendency to wear '*loose* long jackets – so slang', and *slippers*.

It was Bertie's sunny disposition and resilience that led him to survive this storm of unremitting criticism. Everyone who met him at university attested to his cheerful nature, easy manners and general agreeableness. Among the many nabobs attracted to the Prince by his charm and enthusiasm were members of the notorious Bullingdon Club, who were mainly rich, raffish and unprincipled young men who represented between them everything which Victoria and Albert deplored.

Increasingly, Bertie succeeded in escaping from the

General and went hunting with his cronies, including Harry Hastings, 'the wicked marquess'.

These bloods had good hands, they were regular in nothing except their attendance at the meets, they read no book except the half-yearly *Racing Calendar* and they indulged in the noxious habit of smoking [a biographer of Edward VII has written]. In this circle Sir Frederick Johnstone, who attained notoriety ten years later in the Mordant divorce case, was a close friend; another was Henry Chaplin, over whom the Prince had a strong influence.

Later, on transferring to Cambridge, Bertie found a friend who was to be of great significance in his life, Nathaniel (Natty) Rothschild, and became reacquainted with Charles Carrington, one of the boys who had earlier been invited up from Eton to Windsor Castle as an occasional outside companion. 'The Prince of Wales lived at Madingley Hall, just outside Cambridge,' Carrington wrote in his diary. 'He entered into all our sports and fun – and rode hard and well with the "drag" which Natty Rothschild and I kept; and he was immensely popular with all classes.'

Bertie also found for the first time a tutor who was sympathetic, attracted his interest and from whom he actually learned something useful – though he would not have admitted it at the time. He was Charles Kingsley, Regius Professor of Modern History, the only teacher to make a serious mark on the entire course of Bertie's education. Kingsley's unpatronising, unacademic manner struck a chord in his student's mind. Bertie actually looked forward to his lectures: not exactly with the fire of excitement of a good day's hunting with his cronies, but not with the dread which lectures usually aroused in him.

In keeping with this unusual episode in Bertie's academic upbringing, the reports and results from both Oxford and Cambridge were better than his parents had expected. The Dean of Christchurch, Henry Liddell, expressed himself 'quite satisfied' with Bertie's performance, and added that he found him 'the nicest fellow possible, so simple, naïf, ingenuous and modest'.

When Bertie visited Germany again in the Easter vacation

of 1860, Stockmar was greatly impressed by his improvement in comportment, manner, speech and in other departments. Prince Albert, delighted at this communication, wrote back thankfully and with uncharacteristic common sense:

That you see so many signs of improvement in the young gentleman is a great joy to us. For parents who watch their son with anxiety, and set their hopes for him high, are in some measure incapable of forming a clear estimate, and are apt at the same time to be impatient if their wishes are not fulfilled.

Two stories about Bertie were widely spread about this time, both of which reflected well on his character. The first occurred while he was at Edinburgh, when the chemistry lecturer was explaining the immunity from pain of certain conjurers who applied hot irons, which had been heated to a very high temperature, to their naked flesh.

'Now, sir,' the professor continued, addressing Bertie, 'if you have faith in science you will plunge your right hand into that cauldron of boiling lead and ladle it out into the cold water which is standing by.'

'Are you serious?'

'Perfectly.'

'If you tell me to do it, I will,' said Bertie – and did so without further hesitation, or pain.

The second act, which showed his kindness, had a wider audience. He was just alighting from his carriage in a crowded street when he noticed a blind man and his dog experiencing great difficulty in trying to cross the road. Bertie at once made his way to the man and steered him decisively through the traffic to the other side. Some time later he received a massive inkstand inscribed: 'To the Prince of Wales. From one who saw him conduct a blind beggar across the street. In memory of a kind and Christian action.' Bertie never discovered who it was, and the gift became one of his most highly prized possessions.

Bertie was still bent on finally getting into the army. How could his parents refuse any longer? He had followed their bidding, he would soon be nineteen, and they surely *must* see that the discipline and companionship of a fine regiment would do him no end of good. But it was not yet to be. His mother and father, supported as always by Stockmar and General Bruce, had other plans for him: a royal tour, no less.

The Canadians had contributed generously to the Crimean War, levying a regiment which fought under Lord Raglan. It was clearly desirable that some royal acknowledgment should be made to this sacrifice. The Queen was asked if she would like to make an official visit, and at the same time open the new railway bridge spanning the St Lawrence river and lay the foundation-stone of the Federal Parliament building in Ottawa.

The Queen was now forty-one years old but already dreaded the demands of a long journey, less for the physical strain than the wear and tear on her nerves. She declined, but in an inspired moment, she told Albert, after discussions with the Prime Minister, Lord Palmerston, she had decided to send Bertie instead. The Prince of Wales on his first official visit to a foreign land: would he be up to it? How would he behave? Bertie was so weak and might commit the most terrible blunders, offending their friends across the Atlantic. The doubts rang through the private conversations between Victoria and Albert like seeds on the wind, before and after the decision had been made. But now it *was* made, and they were left with only the prayers for its success.

5

Bertie Breaks Out

'A Very Great Jam and Very Little Dancing'
Bertie in New York

HMS *Hero* might have been a survivor from the Battle of Trafalgar fifty-five years earlier, a fine ship-of-the-line with marked tumblehome, black ports pierced in her hull for her ninety-one guns, fore, main and mizzen masts reaching high into the sky, each sprouting three yards. Nothing, it at first seemed, spoilt the symmetry and sturdy grace of this battleship until the eye was caught by the anachronistic black tube emerging from amidships, spouting a whisp of smoke.

The *Hero* was, technically, a Screw 2nd Rate, and in adverse weather conditions, or coming in or out of harbour, the auxiliary steam-power could be employed, although it was considered poor seamanship and every pound of coal had to be accounted for. In fact, the *Hero* was only a year old and was among the last of a line of wooden sailing ships going back to a time before Queen Elizabeth I's fleet which drubbed the Spanish Armada in 1588. Already under construction were the first ironclads, which, to the dismay of old-time admirals, would rely chiefly on their engines, 4,000 hp or more, giving them a speed of fourteen knots.

Bertie, viewing for the first time the man o'war which was

to transport him to the New World, had never seen a more romantic sight in his life. Anchored nearby were the fine new frigates *Ariadne* (two funnels), the *Emerald* and the much smaller *St George*, all three to act as escort to the mighty *Hero*. The backdrop of Plymouth Hoe with its enduring maritime associations, and the hills of Devonshire half lost in the misty sunshine, completed the scene.

In honour of the occasion and Bertie's presence beside his father, the yards were manned on all the ships; a royal salute of twenty-one guns crashed out, to be followed by the Royal Marines' band on the quarterdeck of the *Hero* opening the first bars of 'God Save the Queen' as the sound of the salute faded. Perfect!

The first farewells of this send-off had taken place the previous day, 9 July 1860, at Osborne. Here Bertie had embarked in the royal yacht *Victoria and Albert* with his father, while the Queen and his sister Alice and brother Arthur followed in the second yacht, *Fairy*. It had been a pleasant and easy passage down the Channel, in sight during daylight of the beautiful Hampshire, Dorset and Devonshire coasts.

The arrival of so many of the royal family made this a great day for Plymouth. Sailing-boats and steam launches bustled to and fro across the bay, a larger launch bearing the Worshipful Mayor of Plymouth and his party. The Mayor in his full robes was piped on-board the *Hero*, and Bertie greeted him formally and received an address from the city.

Watched critically by his father – and even he could find no fault – Bertie replied with grace and *savoir-faire*, referring to 'some of the great works of nature and human skill of a great land' that he would soon be seeing, and thanking the city for its good wishes. Then it was time for the last farewells – the bow and embrace for the Queen, who gave him a handsome ring; the bow and shaking of hands with Prince Albert; the embrace for Alice, and finally for little Arthur, just ten years old, standing shyly beside his big sister.

Anchors were raised shortly before 4 p.m., and on the hour the four vessels under a full spread of sail made their stately way out of the harbour and into the open sea, HMS *Hero* in the vanguard. Awaiting them as escort for the first part of the voyage was Vice-Admiral Sir Charles Fremantle's Channel Squadron. It was the most impressive sight at sea Bertie had ever witnessed, and he remained on the bridge in the late afternoon sunshine watching the great men o'war taking up station on either side of the *Hero* and her frigates. They had a fair wind down the Channel and were soon working up speed to eight knots.

Bertie's personal escort was a formidable one, too. Besides the ubiquitous General Bruce, with his mass of maps and guide-books to the places in Canada they were to visit, there was the Secretary of State for the Colonies in the dour form of the Duke of Newcastle. (As Secretary for War at the time of the Crimean War, it was widely believed that he was responsible for the early scandals of that campaign. For Palmerston to sack him would have been tantamount to admission of the charges, so His Grace had been moved sideways to look after the colonies.) Apart from lending importance and gravitas to the royal suite, the Duke was to prepare Bertie for 'the pertinent political issues', which really meant the never-ending French–Catholic hostility towards their Anglo-Saxon 'oppressors' in Canada.

Then there was the Earl of St Germans representing the Queen in the numerous formalities lying ahead; Bertie's two equerries, Major Christopher Teesdale and Captain Charles Grey; and his physician, Dr Henry Acland. There was no one near Bertie's age, and they formed a party of grave, bearded worthies as company for the four months of the tour. Almost the only laughter that was heard would emanate from Bertie himself, who was in tremendously spirited form because of his relative freedom and in anticipation of what lay ahead.

The coast of Newfoundland was sighted two days early on 23 July. The four ships entered Conception Bay, first noted and named by the Portuguese early in the sixteenth century, while Captain James Cook later charted all this coast after helping to drive out the French in 1762. Bertie first trod the soil of the New World at St John's, the capital of

Newfoundland, and became quite lyrical about the scenery, which he compared to Scotland's. 'It is a very picturesque seaport town,' he wrote to his mother. 'The harbour is remarkably pretty.'

There now began the seemingly endless formal occasions and addresses. Bruce wrote all the speeches, which kept him busy, and Bertie did not in the least mind delivering them, with increasing ease and authority. He even quite liked it. But the trouble was that he also had to listen to the addresses of welcome (fourteen of them in the first few days), and almost every worthy measured the length of his address by the import and distinction of the occasion, which were considered to be very high.

The Duke of Newcastle was especially impressed by Bertie's comportment. 'His manners with the people were frank and friendly without any mixture of assumed study to gain popularity by over-civility,' he reported to the Queen. Bruce, more waspishly, wrote that Bertie 'acquitted himself admirably, and seems pleased with everything, himself included'.

For four weeks the Prince of Wales's party toured the outer periphery of Canada – Newfoundland,* Nova Scotia, Prince Edward Island, New Brunswick – staying in government houses, inspecting the local volunteers and important buildings, receiving and giving addresses, attending formal lunches and dinners, all the time the centre of attention of the hospitable people who did not normally enjoy much excitement in their lives. The burden of it all on Bertie was relieved by the balls, at which he danced 'with notable skill and grace' to the very end – twenty-four dances out of twenty-four on one occasion, his short figure whirling about with great panache, to the delight of the local ladies.

Never before had Bertie experienced so much freedom to enjoy himself, demonstrate his natural good manners and mix with the general public. He would never, for all his life, be seen as anything but a unique and awesome figure, heir to

* On leaving the province, Bertie was presented with an enormous Newfoundland dog, which he called Cabot after the explorer. A better present could not have been found. He loved dogs for all his life and usually had one beside him.

the throne of the greatest power on earth and later King-Emperor, but he became as near as he ever would to being regarded as 'one of us' among these cheerful, straightforward and egalitarian settlers of north America.

By the second week in August HMS *Hero* was making her way up the St Lawrence river, and on the 18th the battleship anchored off Quebec. The chief functions of the tour now began, and for the following weeks Bertie was engaged in meeting Canada's hierarchy, conferring knighthoods on behalf of the Queen and visiting the Heights of Abraham at Quebec, where General Wolfe fell in action. At Montreal he drove in the last rivet of the mighty two-mile-long Victoria Bridge, and at Ottawa he laid the corner-stone of Parliament House for the two provinces of the now united colony, the most significant political occasion of the tour. But the most pleasing personal occasion was the arrival from England of two young men of his own age, Edward Montagu, the future eighth Earl of Sandwich, and another of the old Etonians who had been an occasional companion at Windsor Castle, Charles George Eliot, son of the Earl of St Germans. It was an enormous relief to have confidants and fellow gossips in the midst of all the tiresome pomp and glory.

The youngsters of the party enjoyed a break in the daily routine at Niagara Falls, one of the last sights they were taken to. The falls had been illuminated for the occasion, and Blondin, the French acrobat, had been called in to perform one of his heart-stopping acts: clear across the falls on a tightrope, wheeling a man in a barrow. When he arrived at the royal enclosure to receive a bag of gold as a reward, the Frenchman asked Bertie if he would like to make the return journey. Bertie was quite prepared to be sporting and agree, to the delight of his young friends, but when the Duke and Bruce learned what was going on they hastened over and prohibited the act. So Blondin ascended a pair of stilts instead and strode back across his tightrope.

Shortly before leaving England, the American President, James Buchanan, on learning from his Ambassador in London of the Prince's tour of Canada, had suggested that he might like to include an informal visit to his country in his itinerary.

Victoria and Albert would have been very doubtful about this diversion, which might diminish in Canadian eyes the honour of the state visit to their country, but they had both known and come to admire Buchanan when he had earlier been Ambassador in London. So, with certain restrictions – he was to travel incognito and stay in hotels and never in private houses, except the White House – Bertie was allowed to accept the invitation. It was a momentous decision.

Therefore, after Niagara, the party travelled by train to Hamilton, on the border with the United States. Here, on 19 September, Bertie enjoyed his last ball on Canadian soil, once again unselfconsciously revealing both his skill and pleasure at dancing. 'Never has the Prince seemed more manly or in better spirits,' wrote one reporter. 'He talked away to his partner . . . he whispered soft nothings to the ladies as he passed them in the dance, directed them how to go right, & shook his finger at those who missed the figures . . . in short was the life of the party.' The same reporter informed his readers that the Prince was more pleased with a pretty girl than 'all the state ceremonies and reception addresses of which he has been the honoured object'.

On the following day there assembled in the town the Governor-General of Canada, the Prime Minister, members of the Government and others of the hierarchy who had welcomed and looked after him for the past weeks. There was also a great and mixed crowd to give him a final cheer 'and expression of loyalty': Protestant Orangemen (who had not all behaved well), Catholic French and even a party of Indians, who had so intrigued Bertie and shown their loyalty so vehemently.

On 20 September 1860 Bertie and his party crossed the Detroit river and set foot for the first time on United States' soil. The most extraordinary part of Bertie's tour lay ahead.

In Canada it had been almost a century since the French had suffered defeat at the hands of the British; in the United States it was only forty-six years since Britain had burnt down Washington, and there had been a good deal of mutual suspicion since then, to say nothing of the mass

Irish immigration following the terrible potato famine.

The British Ambassador in Washington, Lord Lyons, had organised the itinerary himself and was to accompany Bertie and his party to every destination. And what an itinerary it was! Chicago, St Louis, Cincinnati, Pittsburgh, Richmond, Baltimore, Philadelphia, New York, Albany, Boston and Portland Maine, besides Washington itself, were some of the towns and cities on the list. When it was all over, Bertie's memories were of the immense distances – 1,000 miles between St Louis and New York alone – and the weariness of the never-changing landscape of the Midwest; the enthusiasm and informality of the people he met – a bit too informal for Lord Lyons and the Duke sometimes; the frontier-newness of the towns; and the combined eagerness and disorganisation of the arrangements.

In Philadelphia, in order to avoid the press of the crowds, Bertie was hustled to a private door of his hotel. But there he was refused entry because he had no credentials. Was this the consequence of travelling incognito? At length he persuaded the doorman that he was indeed the Prince of Wales, and 'these are my equerries'. He then ran up the stairs and was guided to his rooms. Here he surprised the hotel's proprietor, 'who, with a picture of the royal family under his arm, was directing the servants to arrange the disordered furniture. . . . Surprise soon gave way to amusement, and it was considered a good joke all round.'

In Washington President Buchanan held a levee in honour of Bertie at the White House. 'Anyone came who liked,' Edward Montagu recalled. 'There was no order of any kind, no presentations; the people scrambled by in the greatest confusion, many of them not recognising the Prince or President. For a time the Prince was immensely amused.'

At a tremendous levee in New York City, 'which may well rank with the most magnificent "jams" in history', there was chaos and near mayhem. In a mocking report on the events covering the whole front page, the *New York Times* wrote:

It may be said that the finest thing which 'four hundred select committee men' of New York could do to entertain the Prince of Wales was to invite to the Academy of Music exactly five hundred more than the house would hold, amuse them by opening a pitfall in the floor, and crush their toilettes into an undistinguishable mass of splendour.

Bertie was received by the stately Mrs Morgan, wife of the financier, 'in a cloud of crape alive with diamonds'. Neither she nor Bertie could find the dais for the speech-giving, and Bertie at five feet seven inches *needed* a dais. But someone had forgotten to erect it, and everyone wanted to see the pair of them, especially to examine the Prince of Wales. 'The whole mass of the people on the floor surged and swayed to and fro in a kind of well-bred impatience in their eagerness to see him.'

Suddenly there was a great crash and a large portion of the floor just in front of Bertie gave way. Guests who did not fall in were encouraged to disperse elsewhere for sandwiches, and doctors and carpenters were summoned. No one was badly hurt, but the carpenters were still hammering away at midnight,* and, as the *New York Times* headlined its report, there was 'A Very Great Jam and Very Little Dancing'.

New York had been *en fête* from the moment of Bertie's arrival:

After 11 o'clock in the morning [Friday, 12 October] there was but little business done. Buyers and sellers alike were anxious to see the Prince. Stores closed, American and English flags were in the windows. The Prince arrived in a revenue cutter at Harriet Lane and was taken to Castle Gardens where he was welcomed by the Mayor. Later he left to review the 1st Division and when the review was over, the Prince and party entered carriages, and accompanied by the military, proceeded to the City Hall in front of which he received a marching salute. The line was then reformed, and the Prince was escorted to his rooms in the Fifth Avenue Hotel. The demonstration was among the very best which has ever been made by the City. During the day there were not less than 200,000† people either looking on or taking active part in the welcome.

---

* In the haste of the operation, one of them was nailed down under the repaired floor and spent the rest of the night hammering to be released.
† The population of New York in 1860 was something over 300,000.

If there was not much room for dancing at the New York levee, elsewhere in the United States Bertie enjoyed as many balls as in Canada. He followed the same policy at all of them, doing his duty with the local elderly matrons as quickly as possible before swinging into action with the young beauties. One girl at the Cincinnati ball was 'the belle of the evening', wrote the man from the *New York Times*. 'She laughed and chatted and flirted with the Prince in the most bewitching manner, and completely bound him hand and foot for the brief hour of her triumph.'

At Washington he stayed at the White House with the President* and his niece, Miss Lane. 'I thought Miss Lane a particularly nice person, and very pretty,' Bertie noted. During the three days in Washington, Bertie visited the Capitol ('very striking') and George Washington's old house ('in very bad repair'), planting a chestnut tree near the first President's grave.

By the time the party reached their embarkation point at Portland, Maine, even Bertie had had enough and was thankful to see the familiar silhouette of the *Hero* again. It was a tiresome, long, uncomfortable and occasionally hazardous voyage home in terrible weather, but the battleship brought back to England a young man who had experienced much more than his nineteenth birthday during his absence. His life had been changed, no less, by this long visit. The self-assurance of which he had been almost deprived while growing up had been as firmly planted as his chestnut tree at Mount Vernon. As well, he had been on centre stage for four months and played his part marvellously. Everywhere he had met affection and admiration. President Buchanan wrote to the Queen:

He has passed through a trying ordeal for a person of his years, and his conduct throughout has been such as becomes his age and station. Dignified, frank and affable, he has conciliated, wherever he has been, the kindness and respect of a sensitive and discriminating people.

* It was less than a month to Abraham Lincoln's election in Buchanan's place, leading to the outbreak of the Civil War.

Lady Augusta Stanley was one of the many people who noted the change on his return: 'He is grown and has become much more manly, while he retains that sort of youthful simplicity and freshness which give his manners such charm.'

Even General Bruce gave him high marks and wrote of Bertie's 'development of mind and habit of thought', but warned, somewhat self-evidently, that the trip might stimulate a 'longing for independence'. On a less personal note, the Duke of Newcastle wrote of the time in Canada: 'The attachment to the Crown of England has been greatly cemented, and other Nations will have learnt how useless it will be in case of war either to tamper with the allegiance of the North American Provinces or to invade their shores.'

Within a few days of arriving home Bertie returned, philosophically enough, to the tedium of university life. In his new-found wisdom he knew it would not last for long, and that the enlargement of his mind and the world that was awaiting him had brought him close to maturity.

6

Prince Albert's Agony

'The things . . . that are laid on our shoulders . . . are not to be told.'

Prince Albert

The storms of the Atlantic which had so badly delayed Bertie's return from the United States had been a great source of anxiety to his mother. To his father, as always in a high state of nervous tension, the days without news of HMS *Hero* were frustrating and vexing, for it meant that his son's education was being delayed and the strict timetable worked out so painstakingly with the Queen disrupted.

Assuming that they must be untrue, Albert had been greatly put out by the favourable reports from Canada and the United States. For Bertie to be a success in anything had long since been written off in Albert's mind. In passing on Bruce's early communication to Stockmar, Albert resorted to sarcasm: 'From Canada we have the best possible accounts. Bertie is generally pronounced "the most perfect production of nature".'

Later, when still receiving nothing but good news, Albert jumped upon Bruce's reference to Bertie being pleased with himself. He at once took up his pen and expressed to Bertie his own feelings of distaste: 'You appear to be under the delusion that the tumultuous welcome was for *him* [you]. It was nothing of the kind. It was simply an expression of loyalty to the Queen.'

On the day Bertie returned to Windsor Castle, his renewed pleas to join the army were brushed aside by his father. The most that he could hope for was reconsideration when his education was complete. He was going back to university, and in three days' time at that. General Bruce, who had warmly supported Albert's decision, would accompany him, of course.

How was it possible that this German Prince, intelligent and capable of normal affection and understanding, could commit so many hideous errors in dealing with his eldest son? The fact that the Queen supported him at every stage, and showed no more affection for the boy than he did; that his tutor and then his guardian were quite unfit for their tasks; and that Baron Stockmar, guide and mentor to both Victoria and Albert, was a misguided, self-satisfied, devious old ass: it has to be said in the end that Prince Albert, the Prince Consort (as was his title after 1857), was quite unfit to bring up the heir to the throne of his adopted nation.

The decline in Albert's health and the increase in his misfortunes and miscalculations stretched back over the 1850s to the Great Exhibition of 1851, for which he was always to be remembered even if it did nearly kill him. He suffered chronic catarrh and a digestion that could tolerate only the plainest food, and not even that if he was agitated by anxiety or anger.

Observing Albert's method of working, wise old Palmerston begged the Queen to make him work specified hours and then to relax and think no more about it instead of 'endlessly harassing himself'. A perennial strain on his nervous system stemmed partly from his unpopularity in the country. He had a reputation even among the lower classes for stiffness, a lack of humour and 'foreign ways'. His determination to remain a German – '*Ein treuer fester Coburger zu sein*' – was almost a part of his marriage vows and he made no attempt to conceal it. It was astonishingly insensitive to talk in German to his children in the presence of others, to go hunting in soft leather thigh boots and an open-necked shirt, and to show his displeasure at any hint of jolly familiarity.

Anti-German and therefore anti-Albert feeling was whipped

up by the onset of the Crimean War in 1854, and all the raging jingoism that it occasioned. It was so strongly rumoured that Prince Albert would be consigned to the Tower of London that thousands gathered at the gates to watch him go in, while newspaper attacks on him became so virulent that he had to be defended in the House of Commons and the Upper House. 'I have been quite miserable,' Albert admitted to Stockmar, and he could hardly eat because of the digestive reaction. Later, the attacks on him died out when the fighting began and attracted the full attention of the nation.

Labouring over numbers of self-imposed tasks above his regular duties, his health deteriorated further. 'The things of all sorts that are laid on our shoulders, i.e. on *mine*, are not to be told,' he complained to Stockmar; and then for a while he could not even write to him owing to acute rheumatism. When he could, his letters were full of woe about his 'frightful torture', 'terrible suffering' and 'the long nights of sleeplessness and pain'. (He was thirty-six years old.)

A year or two later, in August 1859, after taking upon himself the task of opening the meeting of the British Association (for the advancement of science), he agonised over the writing of his speech. 'I read thick volumes, write, perspire, and tear what I have written to shreds in sheer vexation,' he wrote to Vicky in Berlin. No wonder he had 'one of his stomach attacks, which makes him look fearfully ill', as the Queen reported.

After visiting Bertie at Oxford in October of the same year, he was struck down by a gastric attack that lasted two weeks, and he was confined to bed 'with cramp at the pit of my stomach'. 'I am tired to death with work, vexation and worry,' he told Stockmar early in the new year (1860). By now advanced hypochondria had set in and every day the Queen was told, without asking, the state of his health and the onset, or threatened onset, of some new malady.

'We have been a good deal plagued lately with tiresome and annoying business, which unfortunately dear Papa will take too much to heart,' the Queen told Vicky, 'and then it makes him unwell always – and affects his sleep. He really ought not to do so, because it makes one's life so difficult if one minds things so much.'

It was in this same year that Albert became almost obsessionally preoccupied with the threat of invasion from France, and the way the French navy was challenging British command of the seas. He blamed the Admiralty and directed it to lay down more warships – urgently. This, and the 'general affairs of Europe', brought on 'mental fatigue, emotional disturbance and overstrain'.

The thought of going to see his beloved Vicky later in the year cheered him up, and he also arranged to visit the Rosenau and scenes associated with his happy childhood. Unluckily, this break from the demanding round of work and worry was interrupted by a road accident which could well have ended his life. He was returning to Coburg from shooting when the four horses of the carriage in which he sat alone suddenly bolted. They were travelling at a great speed when they came upon a level crossing with the bar down for an imminent train and a stationary wagon already waiting to cross. A collision was inevitable, and Albert opened the carriage door and hurled himself into the ditch.

In the crash that followed, one of the horses was killed and the others bolted towards the castle. Albert's injuries were not serious, but there was a lot of blood about the face. When rescue came he turned away the doctor, instructing him to look after the seriously injured coachman. The Queen did not see him until he had been bandaged and was lying on his valet's bed. She was reassured that his features would not suffer. 'Oh! God! What did I not feel!' she exclaimed in her journal. 'I could only, and do only, allow the feelings of gratitude, not those of horror at what might have happened, to fill my mind.'

A further setback to what was to have been a happy holiday was the sudden death of Albert's stepmother, the Dowager Duchess of Coburg, which filled his mind with foreboding and deep gloom. The day before he and Victoria were due to begin their journey home, he went for a walk with his brother through countryside they had known so well as boys. Albert halted at a spot with a familiar view and the emotions it aroused were too much for him. Ernest glanced towards him and saw that he had a handkerchief to his face. Thinking that the cuts on his face had reopened to cause bleeding, he was about to offer help when he saw that his brother was crying.

'I'm sure that this is the last time I'll gaze on this scene I love,' Albert remarked tearfully. When Ernest pooh-poohed his prediction, Albert sobbed more violently than ever. It was a poignant fraternal moment between the two men.

It was two years before Bismarck was to deliver his 'blood and iron' speech, but already aggressive expansionism was becoming evident in Prussian policy. *The Times* was publishing articles hostile to Prussia in the autumn of 1860 and continued to do so throughout 1861. Matters were exacerbated by the arrest of a British officer on a Prussian train following a dispute over a seat. Captain Macdonald was tried and gaoled, the public prosecutor remarking on the boorish, arrogant behaviour of English tourists generally.

The response to this in England was a renewal of attacks against Prussia, each one like a stab wound to Albert. 'What abominable articles *The Times* has against Prussia!' he wrote to Vicky. 'A total estrangement between the two countries may ensue, if a newspaper war be kept up for some time.'

The end of a miserable year for Albert was marked by a message of cheer from the Prime Minister for Victoria and himself. Quoting Pope, Palmerston wrote:

> May day improve on day, and year on year,
> Without a pain, a trouble, or a fear.

The very next day, Albert's cousin, the King of Prussia, Frederick William IV, died, making Vicky and her husband now Crown Prince and Crown Princess, next in line for the throne. This was rapidly followed by the death of Albert's doctor, who was the only fatality in a railway accident. 'An incalculable loss!' lamented Albert, his most persistent patient. Six weeks after this, Victoria's mother, the Duchess of Kent, expired at Frogmore House, Windsor, throwing the Queen into paroxysms of grief. Albert, too, was heard sobbing loudly by himself in the library at Windsor, and then – as sole executor – he had to tackle the task of sorting out the Duchess's chaotic estate. At the same time, Victoria's beloved physician, Sir James Clark, became seriously ill at the age of seventy-five. Was there no end to the woe?

The affairs of state, and estate, and these deaths all proved too much for Albert, who went about looking like death himself, with terrible toothache among numerous other ailments. 'Dear Papa never allows he is any better or will try to get over it, but makes such a miserable face that people always think he is very ill. . . . His nervous system is easily excited and irritated, and he's so completely overpowered by everything,' Victoria wrote to her eldest daughter.

As this terrible year of 1861 wore on, it became more and more evident that Albert was in danger of losing his reason, as he had long since lost his health. Victoria revealed her anxiety about him in almost every letter to Vicky at Coburg. 'You say no one is perfect but Papa,' the Queen wrote on 1 October. 'But he has his faults too. He is very often very trying – in his hastiness and over-love of business – and I think you would find it very trying if Fritz was as hasty and harsh (momentarily and unintentionally as it is) as he is!' And a week or two later, she said ominously: 'I feel now to be so acquainted with death, and to be much nearer the unseen world.'

Happily ignorant of all the recurrent and debilitating crises his father was going through, Bertie was having the time of his life in Ireland. The Queen had suddenly changed her mind about the army, something she had previously declared to be impossible. Perhaps the discipline might help make a man of him? Perhaps those who had for so long been advocating greater freedom for the Prince of Wales might be right?

On 13 March 1861 Albert had been sent to Cambridge to meet General Bruce. Bruce had been as firmly opposed to military training for Bertie as his master, but when Albert seemed to have changed his opinion, he instantly did likewise. Bertie was summoned to hear the news, facing the solemn faces of the two men who had controlled almost every waking minute of his life for so long.

His heart lifted when his father told him that he was to proceed to Ireland, where he was to be attached to a battalion of the Grenadier Guards 'to learn the duties of every grade from Ensign upwards'. It is probable that he scarcely heard the further details and conditions nor recognised their absurdity. In ten weeks he was expected to rise to the rank of brigadier-general, be capable of commanding a battalion and 'manoeuvre a Brigade in the field', a process which normally took twenty years. He was also to master the social life of a soldier in all its intricacies, customs, language and shibboleths, while at the same time living outside the Guards' mess, for it would be quite improper for a prince of royal blood and heir to the throne to mix with his young brother officers.

Instead, Bertie would live in his own quarters, which had been requisitioned from General Sir George Brown (C-in-C Ireland) himself. Senior officers of his regiment were to be invited twice a week, while once a week he would be guest of honour of other regiments. On Sundays and one other evening he was to read and dine privately in his own quarters in the company of General Bruce only. And that was that.

Nevertheless, Bertie loved the life at the Curragh Camp, the military ceremonies, the day-long sound of marching feet, the bark of commands, the constant to-ing and fro-ing. Above all, he was fascinated by the colourful guards' uniform and the flash of swords. However constrained in his movements, he still managed to enjoy some measure of comradeship, and was able to see something of an old friend from his childhood, Lord Derby's son Frederick Stanley.

The absurdity of the programme was evident from the start. He had scarcely learned the simpler points of marching on parade when his parents, with the Duke of Cambridge, the army C-in-C, arrived to check on his progress. Victoria expected to see him marching at the head of his battalion. Instead, he was in the ranks and General Bruce confessed that Bertie could only perform the duties of a subaltern.

Colonel Percy, Bertie's commanding officer, warned him that he was 'too imperfect in your drill, Sir. Your word of command is indistinct. I will *not* try to make the Duke of Cambridge think you are more advanced than you are.' The Duke did not receive that impression, but at least his expectations were not high considering that Bertie had been in uniform for only a few weeks. Albert, predictably, was deeply disappointed and expressed doubts as to whether Bertie would ever make a soldier, but what could you expect considering 'the idle tendencies of English youth'?

Bertie took all this with his usual equanimity and continued to enjoy camp life. He soon became practised at the art of evading the authority of his governor and increasingly enjoyed the company of his fellow officers. As his official biographer put it, 'Under the influence of his comrades in camp near his own age his outlook on life widened and he was introduced to dissipations which were new to him. He learned for the first time something of the meaning of unimpeded liberty.'

At that time it was considered quite usual for some of the more raffish Grenadiers to keep a woman in the camp just as they might stable half-a-dozen hunters. Bertie's sexual innocence became the subject of amusement among his fellow officers and, after one hectic night, several officers persuaded (without much difficulty) 'a vivacious young actress', Nellie Clifton, to slip into Bertie's quarters and his bed. Bertie found the experience enthralling and enlightening. In the gossipy conditions of a mess of rich officers with time on their hands, news of this practical joke spread rapidly, and later to London. But for the time being it was kept from his father and mother.

Queen Victoria and the Prince Consort had an abundance of worries already. Relations between Britain and Prussia were going from bad to worse just at the time of King William I's Coronation, to which Victoria sent Lord Clarendon, her Foreign Secretary, to represent her. Letters between Victoria and Vicky expressed their mutual regret, but they were powerless to intervene and improve the situation.

Victoria was always depressed by the return to Windsor from Balmoral. From the isolation of her Scottish castle with its beautiful mountain scenery and fast-running burns, the journey brought her back to the reality of her problems and old griefs. 'Pain is chiefly felt by dwelling on it, and can thereby be heightened to *an unbearable extent*,' wrote Albert sympathetically.

If only he had heeded his own axiom and not dwelt so self-indulgently on *his* health. His visit to Stockmar at the end of October 1861 also led him to dwell on how much he missed him

– the one man to whom he could open his heart and discuss his troubles with complete frankness and confidentiality. Two weeks later grave news arrived from Portugal. Albert's cousin, King Pedro V, of whom the whole family was fond, had a younger brother, an equally admirable man, who contracted typhoid and died swiftly on 6 November. Five days later Pedro himself succumbed to the same disease. 'It is an almost incredible event!' the Queen wrote to King Leopold, 'and a real European loss! He was so attached to my beloved Albert.' Before the year was out a third brother was dead.

'You know my love for Pedro,' Albert wrote in agony to Stockmar; while to Clarendon, back home from the Coronation, he mused, 'Do you not, like me, wonder at the cause of good men being cut off in the midst of their usefulness [Pedro was just twenty-five], while bad ones are left to do harm with apparent impunity?'

Viewed in retrospect it seems that the nature, and increasing acceleration, of events over the following days had a dreadful inevitability. Two days before King Pedro's death, Victoria wrote in her diary: 'Our dear Bertie's 20th birthday. May God bless and protect him and may he turn out well.' Three days later a letter arrived for Albert from Stockmar, a man who had always shown little faith in Bertie's character and was quick to pass on bad news of him, exposing the scandal of Bertie's affair which had continued at the Curragh.

Prince Albert was stunned and so shocked by this news that when he took the letter to show to Victoria she knew that something dreadful had happened before she read it. No decision was made by Bertie's parents for four days. At first they thought it might stem from malicious gossip, but it seemed to be finally confirmed by one of Albert's gentlemen-in-waiting, Lord Torrington, who had been in Albert's service for many years. He was one of the two gentlemen who had been despatched to Coburg in January 1840 to invest him with the Garter and escort him to England for his marriage. He could be relied upon 'to know everything' and was sometimes laughingly known as *The Times*'s correspondent at Windsor Castle'. When asked by Albert if the news about

Bertie's actress was true, Torrington answered in the positive without hesitation.

In Albert's eyes, the implications were too terrible to contemplate. Had he been infected with syphilis? Had he conceived a child? Would any suitable bride now contemplate marriage? How open to blackmail was he? The answer to the last question was an emphatic 'Yes'. Feeling ill and weary almost beyond bearing, Albert sat down to write what he regarded as the most important letter he had ever written. It took no account of the fact that most young men of Bertie's age and of the class with whom he was mixing had an affair or two before marriage and that their parents were thankful that they would not enter the matrimonial bed completely inexperienced.

But Prince Albert, at the best of times inhibited about sex, wishing that the Good Lord had ordered things differently, and already and for months in a state of nervous tension amounting to irrationality, was no longer master of his judgment or action. The typhoid germ that was to kill him had already entered its incubation period. The letter was from a man enraged and doomed, grief-stricken and fatally afflicted.

Prince Albert was writing to his son 'with a heavy heart upon a subject which has given me the greatest pain I have yet felt in my life'. His son had 'become the talk and ridicule of the idle and profligate'. The actress to whom he had succumbed was already known in low circles as 'The Princess of Wales'. She would probably have a child, with him as the reputed father.

If you were to try and deny it, she can drag you into a Court of Law to force you to own it & there with you (the Prince of Wales) in the witness box, she will be able to give before a greedy Multitude disgusting details of your profligacy for the sake of convincing the Jury, yourself cross-examined by a railing indecent attorney and hooted and yelled at by a Lawless Mob!

And so it continued for page after page.

In answer to Bertie's shocked and contrite answer, Albert had to admit that he had shown repentance, 'but no forgiveness can restore you to the state of innocence and purity which you have lost, and you must hide yourself from the sight of God'.

Prince Albert told the Queen that she was not to know 'the disgusting details'. 'Oh! that boy – ' she responded, 'much as I pity him I never can or shall look at him without a shudder as you can imagine.'

Albert was already suffering several symptoms of the typhoid which was rapidly developing, including insomnia and muscular pains in all parts of the body. Victoria, who had seen her beloved Albert through so many illnesses, real and imagined, was not greatly alarmed at first. In a brief discussion with her, he told her, 'I do not cling to life. You do, but I set no store by it. I am sure if I had a severe illness I should give up at once, I should not struggle for life. I have no tenacity of life.'

Worse than this, over the next days Albert appeared to be courting death, although this was not apparent at the time because not even the Queen knew how ill he was. Suffering from a severe cold, he fulfilled an engagement to inspect new buildings for the Army Staff College at Sandhurst. It poured with rain and he returned soaked through and shaking with cold.

Two days later, perhaps because he suspected that he would never see him again and that he must make a final attempt to reform his son, he took the train to Cambridge. It was a cold and stormy day. They went for a long walk and were seen to be in earnest conversation, the small undergraduate in gown and mortarboard pacing beside the taller Prince, who bent ever earnestly towards his son. Somehow, preoccupied with the lecture he was receiving, Bertie missed a turning in the town and they were out for longer than they had planned.

The next day back at Windsor, Albert expressed himself as reassured by the meeting but in great pain in his back and legs. It was his last outing. The fever was seizing him, sometimes relaxing and then strengthening its hold, each time leaving the Queen despairing of hope for him and then restoring it. Albert would dress some days and move about his rooms, then pronounce himself exhausted and take to his bed. The restlessness and uncertainty were creating an equally exhausting effect upon those concerned for him, especially the Queen herself.

Somehow, to everyone's astonishment, Albert succeeded

in dealing with another crisis, this one of international dimensions, between Britain and the northern states of America, now at war with the Confederacy of the south. A Unionist warship had intercepted a British ship on the high seas, forced her to stop and took off several men, envoys of the southern government *en route* to London. 'The *Trent* affair' threatened relations between London and Washington so seriously that war appeared imminent. Albert was shown the strong ultimatum to be sent to the North American Government, considered it needlessly belligerent and suggested a change of wording which was accepted. It was said, in the emotional aftermath of Albert's death, that his last act had been to save another Anglo-American war. Be that as it may, it required a great effort in his weakened condition to apply his concentrated attention to this document.

He could not have done so on 7 December, one of his worst days. The doctors conceded that he was less well. 'I went to my room,' wrote the Queen, '& cried dreadfully and felt oh! as if my heart must break – oh! such agony as exceeded *all* my grief this year. Oh, God! help and protect him!'

The doctors knew now that it was typhoid, but named it only as a fever. It would have to run its course, eased only by some stimulus and opiates, and by persuading the Prince to keep down a little food. His mind began to wander increasingly but recovered, and he became quite rational for a while, calling his wife *Fräuchen* (little woman) and *Weibchen* (little wife) from time to time.

Bertie was called to Windsor from Cambridge by his sister Alice, who was a tower of strength and common sense amidst grief and near hysteria. A bulletin told the public that the Prince Consort's illness was rather more serious than had been expected:

For some days His Royal Highness has been suffering severely from an attack of gastric fever, and is at present much weakened by the disorder. It need not be said that the best medical skill has been called to his aid, and we hope it will be in our power shortly to announce an improvement in the state of the royal patient.

The first edition of *The Times* on 14 December 1861 carried a brief, mournful bulletin: 'HRH the Prince Consort passed a restless night, and the symptoms have assumed an unfavourable character during the day.' The third edition of this newspaper reported 'a slight improvement', but it was short-lived. Princess Alice played some of her father's favourite music on the piano and then joined others of the family, including brother Ernest summoned from Coburg, on their knees. The Queen knelt close to Albert's head, Alice on the other side, Bertie and Lenchen at the foot, the others about the room.

'I bent over him [the Queen later wrote] & said to him *"Es ist Kleines Fräuchen"* & he bowed his head; I asked him if he would give me *"ein Kuss"* & he did so. He seemed half dozing, quite quiet.'

The Queen raised herself to her feet and walked out of the room to sit down alone for a moment. Alice soon recalled her, taking her arm, and she knelt again as before. 'Two or three long but perfectly gentle breaths were drawn,' the Queen wrote later, 'the hand clasping mine and . . . *all, all,* was over.'

It was shortly before eleven o'clock at night on 14 December 1861, a date that was scored into the Queen's memory as surely as the lettering upon the great monument that was later erected to Albert's memory in Hyde Park. The Queen stumbled away to her own room, weeping inconsolably. A little later her children entered one by one; she told them in turn that she promised to live for them. Bertie embraced her warmly.

'Indeed, Mama, I will be all I can to you.' She kissed him several times.

'I am sure, my dear boy, you will.'

The Queen, at forty-two, had lost the one prop which had supported her through the past twenty years. How could she reign without him? people everywhere asked, and a flood of royalist affection spread across the country. 'The day which announced throughout the land the death of the Prince Consort was a day of universal gloom,' Gladstone recalled later.

The nation has just sustained the greatest loss that could possibly have fallen upon it [began *The Times* leader]. Prince Albert who a week ago gave every promise that his valuable life would be lengthened to a period long enough to enable him to enjoy, even in this world, the fruit of a virtuous youth and a well-spent manhood, the affection of a devoted wife and of a family of which any father might be proud – this man, the very centre of our social system, the pillar of our State, is suddenly snatched from us.

True to his word, Bertie relieved his mother of a number of duties which were urgent and essential but which, in her prostrate condition, she was incapable of handling. Letters of condolence were pouring in and Bertie answered, in his own hand, the most urgent. To the Prime Minister, Lord Palmerston, he wrote:

I cannot tell you how touched my mother was by your kind and sympathising letter.

You know the loss which we have sustained, and how irreparable it is to her, to us, and to the country for whom he lived.

My mother wished me to tell you that her life would now be but a life of duty, which she would perform to the best of her abilities, but that her worldly career was closed for ever.

She bears this fearful calamity with a courage which is touching to witness, and you can I feel sure feel for us, who have lost one of the best of fathers who can never be replaced.

The Queen was advised to leave Windsor and all its tragic and too-recent memories and retreat to the peace of Osborne, and Bertie accompanied her to Gosport before returning to take part in the arrangements for his father's funeral. This took place in St George's Chapel on 23 December and, because his mother felt unable to attend, Bertie stood in for her, acting with great dignity while reflecting the grief that he was feeling.

Bertie's grief was genuine and deep, inflamed by remorse. In his humility he believed that it was his own fault that he had never succeeded in becoming close to his father, that he had let him down by failing to give satisfaction over his education. 'He was always kindness itself to me,' he wrote to Charles Carrington. 'Though I fear I have often given him pain by my conduct.' He did not for one moment blame his father for his chilly reception when he returned from North America, the one occasion when he thought he had done well. Bertie's expectations about himself had always been low and were governed largely by the rating of his parents, which never seemed to rise significantly.

Clarendon believed 'the poor boy knows of his mother's dislike of him, but seems to have the good taste not to speak of it'. All the same, he took it for granted that, with the death of his father, however unsatisfactory a son he may have been, he would be given certain duties to perform, beyond writing a few letters. He was, after all, at the age of twenty, Prince of Wales and heir to the throne, in a much more important position than he had been when his father was still alive. He reckoned without the effect of Albert's death upon his mother. And why should he? It came as a shock to all those who knew her intimately – family, senior politicians and courtiers alike. Who could have reckoned on a metamorphosis on this scale? But, then, who knew the extent of the Queen's dependence on Albert? Not Lord Palmerston, nor his fellow Liberal statesman Lord Granville, nor even Princess Alice, the eighteen-year-old daughter close to both parents.

Granville accurately diagnosed the shock effect of Albert's death on the Queen without foreseeing the consequences:

The loss to the country is great: to the Queen is irretrievable. . . . The Prince of Wales has behaved with great affection and feeling. The Princess Alice has shown singular tact and feeling. I own I was afraid that the Queen's nervous system would have given way . . . her future is fearful. Having given up [for] 20, every year more, the habit of ever deciding anything, either great or small, on her own judgement, the situation is immense for her to conduct the affairs of her family, her Court and of the Country. And who has she upon whom she can lean?

The answer was, on the ghost of her beloved. She made this clear on the day after Albert's funeral when she wrote to her uncle, King Leopold, of her *'firm* resolve, my *irrevocable decision*, viz. that *his* wishes – *his* plans – about *every*thing, are to be *my law*! And *no human power* will make me swerve from *what he* decided and wished. . . .'

The shock of grief led either to total breakdown and surrender, or to decisions, firm resolutions and uncompromising judgments. She would rule as if he were still there beside her. As for the cause of this catastrophe, her finger pointed unerringly at one figure – that of the Prince of Wales.

After the first hours of mourning when she was too stunned to think, she began considering again the reason for her husband's fatal illness. It was the affair of the Curragh Camp, there was no doubt of that, 'the *one* great sorrow which cast him so utterly down', she wrote as early as a month before he died. After his death, his doctors diagnosed the cause as overwork and worry – and that could only mean worry over Bertie. He had killed his father.

The Queen wrote to Vicky to confirm to her that it was indeed Bertie's lapse which had so weakened Albert and left him without hope for the future and deprived him of any defence against the fever. Vicky, as nearly rebuking her as she felt she could go, begged her to 'be kind, pitying, forgiving and loving to the poor boy for Papa's sake'.

The Queen was having none of that. 'All you say about poor Bertie is right and affectionate in you; but if you had seen what I saw, if you had seen Fritz struck down, day by day get worse and finally die, I doubt if you could bear the sight of the one who was the cause. . . .'

Discussing Albert's death with Lord Hertford, who found her 'the most desolate and unhappy of God's creatures', the Queen claimed again that the cause was 'that dreadful business at the Curragh'. Lord Hertford had the courage to disagree. 'Oh, no, Madam,' he told her.

One of the doctors summoned to Albert's sick-bed was William Jenner, Holme Professor of Clinical Medicine at University College, who had established the difference between typhus and typhoid fever back in 1851. He had established to his own satisfaction that it was 'the drains of Windsor' which had caused the typhoid fever. They were in a terrible condition, but so they were throughout the land at that time. Sanitation scarcely existed. Following a dry summer, Victoria and Albert had decided one evening on a cruise up the River Thames. It was a very brief one. The banks were thick in human excreta and the stench overpowering.

One in three male deaths at that time was traceable to fever. Yet plenty of people survived typhoid fever. One of them was Albert's second son, Affie, the following year. It was the will to survive as much as the strength that mattered. In a revealing and indiscreet moment in conversation with Lord Derby, 'The Queen [Derby reported later] talked freely of the Prince [Albert]: "he *would* die – he seemed not to care to live." Then she used the words "He died from want of what they call pluck."'

But Bertie remained the prime culprit for the foreseeable future in the Queen's eyes. Unable to tolerate the thought of him 'living in the house, doing nothing', the Queen and Lord Palmerston decided that a long journey was the solution. Prince Albert had made preliminary plans for Bertie to visit Palestine and the Near East in 1862. Now the date of departure was to be advanced to 6 February, and the length of the journey extended to five months.

Bertie's eastern caravan consisted of General Bruce, three equerries and a doctor, and Canon Arthur Stanley, who was summoned at very short notice from his duties as Regius Professor of Ecclesiastical History at Oxford. He hated the idea, but in the event got on very well with the Prince and on his return was made Dean of Westminster as a reward, fell in love with Bruce's sister, Lady Augusta, a close friend of the Queen, married and became deeply involved in Court life. So he was glad he went.

After stopping at several courts *en route*, the party embarked in the royal yacht *Osborne* at Trieste, disembarking at Alexandria on 1 March 1862. It soon became clear to Stanley that his pupil had little interest in history or archaeology, although he did his duty cheerfully enough, glancing at temples and tombs and other ruins, though sometimes treating himself to a rest. Stanley noted, for example, that on 6 March while the remainder of the party was off to see some tombs, Bertie 'was sitting in front of the tent smoking and reading [the latest bestseller] *East Lynne*'.* He also went on strike at Thebes five days later: 'Why should we go and see the tumbledown old Temple – when we get there, nothing

---

* The only novel he ever completed, which he read a number of times.

to be seen – like going to Rome to see the theatre of some-body and only two stones left.'

As always when abroad, what Bertie really wanted was sport. He was never far from his guns but, apart from Nile crocodiles, it was not until they reached Palestine and some gazelle appeared that there was good shooting. 'Immediately all the energy of the poor boy revived,' it was observed. Hares and vultures, larks, owls and quail – even lizards – all fell to his guns, and many of his victims were stuffed to take home.

The party became a minor crusade at one point, fifty ser-vants and one hundred Turkish cavalry escorting them across the desert to Jerusalem, enjoying enormous picnic lunches on spread rugs and dinners with local notables. For a number of days there was not a ruin to be seen, and Bertie loved every minute of it.

General Bruce was less enthusiastic. He also picked up a fever, which was to prove fatal after he returned to England. Bruce had been in attendance on Bertie for so long that Bertie had become used to him and was quite grieved at his death. 'I lost in him a most useful and valuable friend,' he wrote, thinking rather of the good times they had had together and forgetting the innumerable disputes.

The Queen set her eyes on her now-bearded son on 14 June 1862. 'Bertie arrived at ½ past 5,' she wrote in her journal, 'looking extremely well. I was much upset at seeing him and feeling his beloved father was not there to welcome him back. He would have been so pleased to see him so improved, and looking so bright and healthy. Dear Bertie was most affection-ate and the tears came into his eyes when he saw me.'

She added later in some relief that he was 'most anxious for his marriage'. Even before Prince Albert died, the decision had been reached that the only way to keep Bertie out of further mischief was for him to marry as soon as possible. The Queen was inflexibly determined about this, and did not wish to compromise relations with her son until a wedding had taken place. She stuck to this resolve and there were no repetitions of the scenes and accusations of those terrible December days. All was sweetness and light between them for the present.

7

The Search

'Oh! if you would find us one!'
Queen Victoria to her eldest daughter
referring to a bride for Bertie

Long before Bertie's fall from grace, the Queen, Prince Albert, Baron Stockmar and King Leopold were all giving serious thought to a bride for him. In July 1858 *The Times* had the cheek to list possible candidates. There were only seven in all, which was hardly surprising considering that she had to be Protestant by law, a princess by inheritance, and not older and not too much younger than Bertie himself. 'We must look out for princesses for Bertie – as his wife ought not to be above a year or 2 younger than him, therefore 14 or 15 now, pretty, quiet and clever and sensible,' the Queen wrote to Vicky. 'Oh! if you would find us one!' She added one more important condition: she must not 'knock under' from the strain of being married to Bertie.

While Bertie was in North America it was hoped that a possible bride would greet him on his return – not in person, but in the new and rather daring practice of presenting a photograph as the first step. Those on the short list included Princess Marie of the Netherlands, 'clever and lady-like' but neither very pretty nor strong; Princess Hilda of Dessau was a possibility but 'rather old', whereas the Princess of Sweden was 'rather young'; that left Princess Anna of Hesse, probably the favourite, or having 'the fewest disadvantages' as Vicky put it, but she did have poor teeth, an incipient twitch in her eyes, a gruff voice and she frowned too much. Also she was 'a poor dresser'.

There were others, but the photograph that Vicky sent first was of Princess Elizabeth of Wied. She was pretty all right but, with portrait photography still rather primitive, perhaps the picture did not do her justice. Anyway, Bertie took one look and turned away. What he kept telling them was that he was interested only in love and that he would just as soon choose a commoner if he loved her. Vicky, like her parents, wanted to cement the German link with an appropriate bride from Germany – best of all from Coburg.

But, becoming frantic by the end of 1860, Vicky felt duty bound to send the photograph of 'Prince Christian of Denmark's lovely daughter':

I have seen several people who have seen her of late – and who give such accounts of her beauty, her charms, her amiability, her frank natural manner and many excellent qualities. I thought it right to tell you all this in Bertie's interest, though I as a Prussian cannot wish Bertie should ever marry her. I know her nurse who tells me that she is strong in health and has never ailed anything. . . . I must say on the photograph I think her lovely and just the style Bertie admires, but I repeat again that an alliance with Denmark would be a misfortune for us here.

The Queen agreed (8 December 1860) that Alexandra was 'indeed lovely', but 'What a pity she is who she is!' And a few days later, on the Princess's prospects she wrote: 'That must not be.' Though quite ignorant of all this, Alix's chances of becoming the Princess of Wales and later Queen Consort of England were remote indeed.

There were three reasons for ruling out the Danish Court. First Victoria and Albert wanted a German princess. Second, the present King was a drunken roué with a mistress, even if Princess Alix was only distantly related to him. But also she was related through her mother to the Hesse-Cassels, a notoriously high-spirited and frivolous family in the Queen's eyes.

Then quite suddenly in February 1861 Victoria began enquiring further about Princess Alix: 'Do you hear anything about her?' 'I hear almost every week about her,' the gossip of Berlin replied, 'but never mentioned it as I thought you did not wish to hear anything more about her and were determined not to give her another thought.' Vicky then wrote of her 'gentle and ladylike manner and sweet voice and expression' besides many other qualities which were reiterated in later letters.

The reason for this surprising turn was not that the Queen had changed her mind. It was because the most interested party had seen Alix's photograph and expressed a great deal of interest in it. It was difficult, even for the super-authoritarian Prince Albert, to brush aside these paeans of praise from his beloved Vicky *and* his son's admiration for the Princess's photograph. The urgent need for Bertie to marry was a further consideration, and when the English Court learned that the Russian imperial family was becoming interested in this Danish Princess for the Tsarevitch, Albert took his son into his confidence and went so far as to write to Bertie that 'it would be a thousand pities if you were to lose her'. Vicky put it more pithily: 'It would be dreadful if this pearl were to go to the horrid Russians.'

Vicky's next task was to meet and make the acquaintance of this Danish 'pearl'. This was engineered through the Mecklenburg-Strelitz family. The Grand Duchess Augusta was a cousin of Queen Victoria and when Vicky learned that Alix and her mother were to visit Strelitz in late May, Vicky innocently enquired if she and Fritz could come too.

Strelitz is a pretty town north of Berlin and set among the lakes of Brandenburg, and they arrived by train from Berlin on 2 June 1861, eager to set their eyes on the Princess. 'The meeting', Vicky reassuringly wrote to her mother, 'seems to be as natural as possible and neither the mother nor Augusta or anyone else here seemed to think it's anything else than the merest accident.' As to Alix, well, she exceeded all

Vicky's high expectations, and a few days later she wrote in lyrical detail to the Queen at Windsor:

It is very difficult to be impartial when one is captivated [she began], and I own I never was more so – I never set eyes on a sweeter creature than Princess Alix. She is lovely! . . . She is a good deal taller than I am, has a lovely figure but very thin, a complexion as beautiful as possible. Very fine white regular teeth and very fine large eyes – with extremely prettily marked eyebrows. A very fine well-shaped nose, very narrow but a little long – her whole face is very narrow, her forehead too but well shaped and not at all flat. Her voice, her walk, carriage and manner are perfect, she is one of the most ladylike and aristocratic looking people I ever saw! She is as simple and natural and unaffected as possible – and seems exceedingly well brought up.

No mother could have asked for a more comprehensive account of a potential daughter-in-law than Vicky provided in a letter running to many pages. The Queen was told that Alix had a mark on her neck* 'from an accident of neglected cold' and, more ominously, that her mother was very deaf. She reassured the Queen that she spoke English and German without the slightest accent† as well as her natural Danish and Swedish and French. 'You may go far before you find another princess like Princess Alix – I know you and Papa would be charmed with her.'

Victoria and Albert decided that a meeting between the young couple was Vicky's next task and they conspired to bring this about at Baden-Baden late in September. At this time Alix would be at Rumpenheim with the rest of her family, and many more Hesse-Cassels, while German army manoeuvres would be taking place conveniently close by. As Bertie was with the Grenadier Guards it seemed reasonable that he should be sent to observe them, although he was well aware that the true purpose of this mission was to meet and learn for himself whether or not this Danish Princess would make a suitable bride.

---

* This later led to her adoption of a jewelled 'dog collar', which remained fashionable for some fifty years.
† Not strictly true. For all her life Alix spoke English with a Danish accent.

Alix, however, had been told nothing and was extremely surprised when on the morning of 24 September she was told that she was going on an excursion to the town of Speyer to study the beauties of the cathedral there. She was further astonished when her mother instructed her to put on her very best dress, especially as they were to travel by train, with all its attendant smut and dust.

The whole exercise then took on a melodramatic flavour. Both parties travelled incognito, as if that would throw the newspapermen off the scent. But even the bishop, who 'happened' to be in his cathedral when Bertie arrived with his party, including General Bruce, immediately recognised him and insisted on taking him on a detailed tour, which badly threw out their rendezvous timetable.

The Danish party on the other hand were well on time, but eventually in late morning there was a meeting 'by chance' and appropriately in front of the altar of the cathedral's chapel. There was some rather intense bowing and clicking of heels while introductions were conducted. 'I felt very nervous,' Vicky noted later, and no one could blame her. Alix was far more poised and pulled together at sixteen than Vicky felt herself to be and chatted naturally to Bertie for some fifteen minutes. 'I don't think it would be possible to find a fault in her behaviour,' Vicky told the Queen.

The crisis to this melodrama occurred when, as was inevitable, the news became widely known that the Prince of Wales had been seen in the company of the beautiful Danish Princess. The idea of a marriage link between the English monarchy and little Denmark caused outrage and consternation in Berlin. Had not the Queen herself expressed a wish to tighten further the links between Prussia and the British Empire? That most ardent Prussian nationalist, Albert's brother Ernest, Duke of Coburg, passed on to the now aged Baron Stockmar this grave news. The Prussians had for long been bent on acquiring from Denmark – by force of arms if necessary – the provinces of Schleswig-Holstein in order to drive a canal direct from the Baltic to the North Sea.

In the judgment of Prince Albert, already beset by innumerable anxieties and half off his head with work, this interference was intolerable. The two brothers were very close and had scarcely ever exchanged harsh words, but now Albert let fly at him:

What has that got to do with you [he wrote angrily]. Vicky has racked her brains to help us to find someone [German] but in vain. We have no choice. Bertie wishes to get married soon, and it is also in his interest, morally, socially and politically to do so. What annoys me is, that you spoke to a third person [Stockmar] about such delicate and secret affairs.

Both the Queen and Albert decided to go ahead regardless of this Prussian interference and disapproval, sensibly believing that it would all blow over quite soon. But the success of the plot still depended on the two chief characters, and their reaction to one another. Victoria and Albert waited anxiously for news from Vicky, and even more important from Bertie.

They both wrote to the Queen, independently, from their hotel in Heidelberg.

I see that Alix has made an impression on Bertie [wrote Vicky], though in his own funny and undemonstrative way. He said to me that he had never seen a young lady who pleased him so much. At first, I think, he was disappointed about her beauty and did not think her as pretty as he expected, but as her beauty consists more in the sweetness of expression, grace of manner and extreme refinement of appearance, she grows upon one the more one sees her; and in a quarter of an hour he thought her lovely, but said her nose was too long and her forehead too low.

Bertie himself, writing of 'the young lady of whom I had heard so much', thought 'I can now candidly say that I thought her charming and pretty.' But, he added, 'I must ask you to wait till I see you and then I will give you my impressions about her.'

Neither of them thought it of the least interest to report on Alix's reaction to Bertie.

Vicky returned to Berlin, where, as the Queen had anticipated, hostility to the match had eased somewhat. Bertie returned to England and at once took the train to Scotland, and Balmoral, to do as he had promised. On the following day, 30 September 1861, the Queen wrote in her diary that

Bertie was 'decidedly pleased with Pcss. Alix, and described to me her manners, her pretty face and figure, but seemed nervous about deciding anything yet'.

This sounded all right as far as it went, but the Queen's impatience was evident the following day when she wrote to Vicky: 'Bertie is extremely pleased with her but as for being in love, I don't think he can be, or that he is capable of enthusiasm about anything in the world.' She no doubt recalled her own searing stab of love which had struck her some twenty-two years earlier. Why did her son not feel passion as she had done?

In response to a further letter from her mother confirming Bertie's lack of interest in discussing his feelings about Alix, Vicky wrote on 12 October:

What you say about Bertie is true. I was quite sure it would be so, his head will not allow of feelings so warm and deep, or of an imagination which would kindle these feelings which would last for a long time! I own it gives me a feeling of great sadness when I think of that sweet lovely flower – young and beautiful – that even makes my heart beat when I look at her – which would make most men fire and flames – not even producing an impression enough to last from Baden to England.

It seemed that in everyone's eyes except Bertie's fifteen minutes was quite long enough to make up your mind whether or not you wished to marry and spend the remainder of your life with a pretty young girl. Albert, exasperated and impatient almost beyond bearing, decided to write Bertie one of 'those letters'. The tone throughout reflects his state of mind: 'Your sister and brother-in-law, at great political and personal disadvantages to themselves, succeeded in obtaining an interview with the Princess and her mother. . . . You have come back and given a most favourable report of the Princess.'

Both parties, he told the recalcitrant Bertie, had already been somewhat compromised. What more did he want? All that trouble and still no proposal! If Bertie wished to see her again on home ground, then, all right, this could no doubt be arranged, *but*, his father emphasised,

We must be *quite sure,* and *you must thoroughly understand* that the interview is obtained in order that you may propose to the young lady, if she pleases you on further acquaintance as much as she did at the first.

If he failed to propose, Prince Albert told his son, then he had to say *at once* that the affair was at an end. Delay 'would be most ungentlemanlike and insulting to the lady and would bring public disgrace upon you and us'.

Bertie at length agreed to this condition under the severe pressure, and the first steps were taken to have a second mutual inspection, this time with Queen Victoria and Prince Albert present, to examine, question and see fair play.

Alas, Prince Albert's days were numbered, and he was never to set eyes on the future Queen of England. In ten weeks he was dead.

Bertie had enjoyed ample time on his Middle East tour to think about Alix, and General Bruce had been instructed to bring up the subject of marriage from time to time and to emphasise its delights and advantages. As a consequence Bertie returned home 'most anxious for his marriage', as the bereaved Queen noted with pleasure and relief. But, she asked herself anxiously, would Princess Alix be prepared to accept Bertie's hand when she learned – as learn she must – of his affair at the Curragh?

She considered what beloved Albert would have done under these circumstances, as she was to do on countless occasions for the rest of her life, thus originating 'the royal "we"' as if he were still alive. Once again Vicky was brought in to find the solution. She had recently employed a lady-in-waiting called Walburga (Wally) von Hohenthal, who had married the British minister in Copenhagen, Augustus Paget. Naturally, Wally was very close to the Danish Court, was highly conspiratorial and had, in fact, arranged to send the original photograph of Alix to Victoria and Albert via Vicky. Now Vicky asked her if she would let Bertie's indiscretion be known to the family, while at the same time the Queen wrote to reassure Alix's parents of her confidence that Bertie '*would* make a steady husband. He was very domestic and longed to be at home'; there were similar expressions of recommendation, not all of them entirely true. The Prince and Princess Christian expressed themselves perfectly satisfied. They were in fact excited beyond words at the prospect of their daughter marrying the heir to the throne of the world's greatest power.

The dream of Prince and Princess Christian became nearer to reality when they learned in early August that Queen Victoria intended to visit the scenes of her late husband's childhood at Coburg and would be staying *en route* with Albert's Uncle Leopold at the Belgian royal palace of Laeken. It was suggested that the family might rendezvous with the Queen here.

The meeting took place on 3 September 1862, an occasion that the Queen was more experienced to cope with than the Danish couple, especially because in moments of stress Princess Christian's deafness always became worse. However, the amiable Leopold eased the situation with his charm and *savoir-faire* and the introductions were rapidly completed. The Danes had brought along both their beautiful daughters, and when it was made known that both Dagmar (Minnie) and Alix were present some cynical wags were heard to hint that if Her Majesty did not care for one, then the other might pass muster in her place. This, of course, was ridiculous, for Minnie was much too young at fifteen and Alix had been carefully prepared for the occasion, on the advice of Vicky and Wally Paget.

Prince Christian the soldier, his wife at his side, now took it upon himself to stress privately to the Queen the qualities of his daughter as if advocating a junior officer for promotion. Princess Alix, he emphasised, was 'a good child, not brilliant but with a will of her own', as the Queen later recorded. The Queen nodded assent and approval, adding, 'I hope that your dear daughter will feel, should she accept our son, that she will be doing so with her whole heart and will. They assured me', she continued, 'that Bertie *might hope* she would do so, and that they trusted *he* also felt a like inclination.' Then the first meeting was soon over.

That evening, more importantly, Alix herself was summoned

to the presence of the formidable English Queen. She looked stunning. She was dressed, in deference to Victoria's mourning, in an unrelieved black dress, without jewels, her light brown hair drawn back in front to fall in ringlets to her shoulders. The Queen was enchanted and spoke to her kindly, offering her a sprig of white heather picked by Bertie at Balmoral. 'Alexandra is lovely, such a beautiful refined profile, and quiet ladylike manner . . . the dear child looked so affectionately and kindly at me. How HE [Albert] would have doted on her and loved her.'

Alix stood up to the ordeal sturdily, but also revealed in her eyes and hesitant smile how affected she was by this first meeting with the little woman in black who might soon be her mother-in-law and would in many respects take the place of her own mother. The meeting was as brief as that of the morning with Alix's parents, but for the Queen a more moving and momentous occasion. She had found the parents 'not very *sympathique*' while Alix 'looks as if she were quite different and above them all'.

The Danes returned to their Ostend hotel that evening in a state of some shock and much relief that everything seemed to have gone off quite well. The seventy-five-mile train journey through Bruges took over three hours so there was plenty of time for both meetings to be fully discussed, with Minnie who was not present at either of them listening with enchanted interest. In a few days' time Minnie would be meeting this famous Prince of Wales. What had suddenly happened to their family?

With the death of General Bruce, Bertie had a new governor, General Sir William Knollys, but in deference to Bertie's age, soon to be twenty-one, he was to carry the title of Comptroller and Treasurer. The Knollys family had served in the royal Household for centuries, and Sir William was to be Bertie's friend, adviser and general factotum for some fifteen years. He is 'very fond of *young people*', the Queen assured her son. He was to be 'the person to whom you would go for advice and assistance on all occasions'.

Knollys knew that he had arrived in this new post at a

critical time, and he was excited at the prospect of being at the side of his new charge on his visit to propose to his future bride. The party arrived at Ostend on 5 September, the day after the Queen left Laeken for Coburg. Bertie had received no message from the Queen on how her meeting with Alix had gone off, but Knollys noted that he was buoyed up with pleasure and excitement at what lay ahead.

Alix set eyes on Bertie for only the second time when he called on her at the hotel in Ostend where they were all to spend the night before proceeding to Laeken. Princess Christian had been warned by the Queen to advise care and a measure of austerity in Alix's dress for this occasion. 'Don't encourage too much dressing or smartness,' she wrote. 'Great quietness and simplicity – going to the opposite of loud or smart dress – like our foolish English girls; for God's sake don't try to encourage them to catch the poor Boy by that – fashionable dressing – anything like that.' In spite of the Queen's recommendation, Wally Paget had seen to it that Alix was smartly dressed.

Bertie was more impressed now than the first time he had set eyes on Alix. They greeted one another affectionately, and sat down side by side at the large luncheon table. They talked and laughed together for the entire meal, to everyone's delight, as if they were a couple of schoolchildren. At the end of the meal, Bertie later reported to his mother:

I begged Prince Christian to come to my room, and then I told him how I loved his daughter and how anxious I was that she should be my wife. I told him that I had quite made up my mind, and that I knew that you had told him the same. I don't think I ever saw anybody so much pleased as he was. We [Bertie and Alix] then went out driving. On our return, I saw the Princess Christian and told her the same as I had told her husband. She said she was sure I should be kind to her.

The following morning, the combined parties embarked on the Brussels train for Laeken. It was a strange journey. Everyone knew its purpose. As night follows day, the nice-looking young man, heavyish about the jowls, fair hair centre-parted and with whispy sideburns and modest beard failing to conceal the Hanoverian chin, rosebud lips and kind brown eyes, would shortly be proposing to the beautiful, slender Princess sitting opposite. The precise timing and place of this betrothal were uncertain, perhaps, but the outcome was so predictable that the clatter of wheels on rail was like a roll of celebratory drums.

They chattered among themselves, these royalties and their staff – Bertie's young equerries, his secretary, the grey-haired Knollys – and the 'Danois', as their host King Leopold always called them, sometimes in German, sometimes in Danish, but mainly in English. They noted, and pointed out to one another, perhaps a fine herd of Friesian cows here, children playing in a village street there, the train stopping first at Bruges, then at several larger villages like Hansbeke and Nieuwerken, and at Gent. It was early evening, the shadows were long, the smoke from the locomotive billowed across the fields, and an alarmed pony threw up its head and ran from the sight and sound. It would have been in their nature for the two Danish Princesses, both loving horse-women, to have cried out in sympathy.

Before Brussels, the train wound through forests and devi-ated to avoid the worst gradients. It was almost dark when they halted at the terminus, Gare Centrale, where a string of carriages awaited them, and a crowd, held back by police, cheered their arrival. With luggage following, they clattered off through the fine, well-lit streets of Belgium's capital, north towards the Palais Royal, where King Leopold prepared to greet them.

Uncle Leopold, seventy-two years old now and in frail health but as shrewd as ever, wholeheartedly approved of Alix and considered the match a brilliant one. 'There is some-thing frank and cheerful in Alix's character,' he had written to Queen Victoria. It will, he added, 'greatly assist her to take things without being too much overpowered or alarmed by them. . . . The dear child is very kind to me.' Nothing suited him better than that the sealing of a match between these two families should take place among the extensive gardens or one of the rooms of his great palace at Laeken.

There was no evidence of austerity in Alix's dress at dinner on that evening of 8 September, even if there was little jewellery in the possession of the Christian family. Bertie was seated between Alix and Princess Christian. He did his duty by his future mother-in-law but her deafness was a grave handicap in communication, and it was with relief that he turned his attention to his future bride.

After luncheon the next day, 9 September, King Leopold suggested that they should all take a walk through his gardens, which, although almost in the heart of Brussels, were very extensive with patches of woodland and a number of lakes. As happens on these momentous occasions, the two young lovers lingered behind and the rest of the party strode purposefully forward. Alix was carrying Bertie's sprig of white heather the Queen had given her, and she held it for him to see and thanked him.

I said I hoped it would give her good luck [Bertie wrote later to his mother]. I asked her how she liked our country, and if she would some day come to England, and how long she would remain. She said she hoped some time. I said I hoped she would remain always there, and then offered her my hand and my heart. She immediately said *yes*.

Was she quite sure – completely certain – that she liked him well enough to become his wife? 'Yes, I knew that long ago.' So Bertie kissed her hand and she kissed him.

Bertie continued his characteristically bald account of events, sensibly bringing in the name of his father to please Victoria.

We then talked for some time, and I told her that I was sure you would love her as your own daughter and make her happy in the new home, though she would find it very sad after the terrible loss we had sustained. I told her how *very* sorry I was that she could never know dear Papa. She said she regretted it deeply and hoped he would have approved of my choice. I told her it had always been his greatest wish; I only feared I was not worthy of her.

8

True Love

'What a pearl!'
Queen Victoria of Alix

'I frankly avow to you', Bertie wrote to his mother, 'that I did not think it possible to love a person as I do her.' No one has recorded any public or private expressions of love Alix felt for Bertie at this time. The radiance of the happiness she emanated made words unnecessary. She was aglow with it. Quite aside from Bertie being the most eligible young man in the world, he possessed exceptional charm. 'He turns most ladies' heads,' Vicky had long since recognised. He was also a great sentimentalist, and every woman in his company was drawn to his powerful masculinity.

Considering the narrow range of choice for both Bertie and Alix, they could consider themselves most fortunate. 'A man who can only marry seven women', *Saturday Review* wrote somewhat confusedly, 'may count himself singularly fortunate if one of the seven unites so many recommendations as the Princess Alexandra.' And Hans Christian Andersen, the Christians' family friend and master weaver of fairy tales, would have had to be in an inspired state of mind to have contrived such a plot as this.

All said and done, however, true love could scarcely flower

on one or two hours of acquaintance. That might come later, and there was every promise that it would. But for the present, happiness was enough, and there was no doubt about that. A glance out of a window at Laeken royal palace confirmed it. There the two of them, aged twenty-one and eighteen, could be seen at almost any time of the two days following their engagement, walking and running together, sitting and chatting together, and, time and again, riding together. Alix showed off her skills and fearlessness with horses, Bertie proudly praised her. Indoors in the evenings she played the piano and he sang at her side. The old palace had never witnessed such light-hearted happiness, to the delight of the ailing King Leopold.

I cannot tell you with what feelings my head is filled [Bertie wrote to the Queen in Coburg], and how happy I feel. I only hope it may be for her happiness and that I may do my duty towards her. Love and cherish her you may be sure I will to the end of my life.

May God grant that *our* happiness may throw a ray of light on your once so happy and now so desolate home [he continued with unusual eloquence]. You may be sure that we shall both strive to be a comfort to you.

The satisfactory outcome of Bertie's proposal was confirmed by General Knollys, who told the Queen that it 'was a happy sight to witness the happiness of the young couple in the society of each other'. He judged Bertie to be 'as much attached to' Alix as she was to him.

'He is desperately in love,' wrote General Bruce's widow two weeks later. 'Just interrupted by our "lover" in a state about his bride . . . too tender and so very very dear, a love letter about 12 pages brought forth to be quoted.'

Bertie's sister Vicky wrote in the style of a satisfied aunt rather than a sister a mere twelve months older:

It does one good to see people so thoroughly happy as this dear young couple are. Bertie looks blissful. I never saw such a change his whole face looks beaming and radiant. Darling Alix looks charming and lovely and they both seem so comfortable and at home together. Love has certainly shed its sunshine on these two dear young hearts and lends its unmistakeable brightness to both their countenances.

The official announcement of the engagement had been issued, and all Copenhagen knew of the match by the time the family returned towards the end of April. The excitement was intense and, instead of being merely watched with interest as she and her sister made their way about the capital, Alix was cheered whenever and wherever she was seen. It seemed such a short time ago that she had been a little girl in a plain dress, with ringlets brushing her shoulders, pushing a doll's pram. And now she was to marry the next King of England! In spite of the genuine Danish affection for her, little was known about Alix, or of her brothers and sisters for that matter. The girls were lively and mischievous, it was said, but strictly brought up, and there was little further speculation.

These high spirits, except during periods of sadness or sickness, lasted through her long life – she was eighty when she died. References to her by the hundred bear witness to this. 'The Princess's love of frolic and fun . . .', the Countess de Grey is quoted as saying. 'She was in tearing spirits,' wrote Lord Esher of her in 1901; and again, 'She was in excellent spirits, full of mischief.' Sydney Holland recounts that 'she is always full of brightness and fun, and sometimes with a little spice of mischief'.

Margot, the wife of the Prime Minister, Herbert Asquith, and one of the shrewdest judges of people, wrote of Alix's 'total absence of egotism and the warmth of her manner, prompted not by consideration, but by sincerity; her gaiety of heart and refinement, rarely to be seen in royal people'.

With this light-heartedness, spontaneity and kindness as a frame, the strains of character can be woven to give a picture of a remarkable woman playing a remarkably difficult role with insight and subtlety. She was blessed, first, with an innate toughness, which took her over numerous hurdles and through stressful periods that few would have survived. There is an account of her in the hunting field which exemplifies this on the physical level, where it applied equally for she was always utterly fearless.

The Princess looked very lovely on her horse, 'King Arthur', and rode like a bird. She took the hurdles beautifully; she simply has no sense of nervousness. Returning from the hunting after dark, riding through the woods where these hurdles were, she leapt them again, though both the Prince and Stafford had avoided them.

Even at seventeen her lack of intellectualism was plain to see. She never picked up a book unless she had to, yet she wrote prodigiously, especially letters to her family. Her reluctance to read was widely known when she met the poet Tennyson for the first time. She asked him if he would be so kind as to read the *Ode of Welcome* he had written for her wedding, the only poem she could remember. He did so, one imagines, with appropriate gravity, but before he had proceeded far, the ridiculousness of the situation seems to have struck them simultaneously. The book fell to the floor and they both dissolved into gusts of laughter.

Alix's consideration for others was soon to become a byword, and her servants and suite, from the beginning, adored her, in spite of sudden lapses into thoughtlessness, which included unpunctuality. This became so bad that it later became a perennial royal joke. The lack of money in the family, and sudden affluence when she married, left its mark. 'Prince and Princess Christian have not till quite lately had more than £800 a year pour tout potage and their children tho' *very* well educated have been brought up in the simplest manner,' Clarendon wrote to the Duchess of Manchester at the time of the wedding.

Through all her married life, and even when she was widowed, Alix spent money with carefree extravagance on herself and others. She developed an innocence about the price of things, although on one occasion, recalled by Daisy, Princess of Pless, when Alix was admiring her cloth-of-gold dress and train, Alix surprisingly asked how much it cost. 'I had to confess that the train alone was worth over four hundred pounds. She said she could not possibly afford such a sum.' The Princess mused, 'Bless her, [she] was the only person who ever took the trouble to make me understand that it would be a very wicked thing to pay such a sum.' That was forty-three years after Alix's marriage, when she was an elderly woman, but she had changed little over the years.

Above all, there was her loyalty. Bertie was soon to recognise how deep were her loyalties, and unremitting her antagonisms. Her love for her family and for her country, and her hatred for everything Prussian, were already evident before her wedding and were to lead her into trouble. But this enhanced her attraction in Bertie's eyes, who liked spirit in a woman. He even found her quick temper attractive.

After the engagement the Queen, still borne down with grief and weariness, insisted on doing what she considered her duty by pressing Alix to come to stay with her in order to get to know her better. She also thought it beneficial for her to learn more about England, English Court procedures and, for that matter, the English language. Alix did speak English well but there were refinements to learn and a thick Danish accent to temper. Prince Christian was to escort her to English shores, and then immediately return. Alix's mother was ignored.

Alix put up a spirited opposition to this plan. 'Why should I be placed on approval like this?' she complained. But she had to go and that was that, for three whole weeks. The only concession the 'Danois' achieved was the shortening of the visit, originally five weeks from the beginning of November, in order that Alix could return for her eighteenth birthday. The Queen could hardly refuse. But she continued to insist that she should bring no lady-in-waiting or maid even.

With only her father for support and comfort, they set sail in the British ship *Black Prince*, arriving, lit up blue all over, at Cowes on a foggy evening, 5 November 1862. No provision had been made to accommodate Prince Christian, and he took a train to London from Portsmouth and put himself up at a hotel for two nights, to return home forlornly and alone.

Alix was met at the pier by members of the Queen's suite and by two of the Queen's children, Princess Lenchen, sixteen years old, and Prince Leopold, nine, carrying a bouquet. A faint moon glimmered through the fog. Alix brushed aside any feelings of gloom and foreboding, kissed Lenchen warmly and took the little boy in her arms.*

Osborne House, rebuilt by Prince Albert in the Italianate style, was relentlessly gloomy – interminable cold marble corridors flanked by glowering marble busts on plinths, like bodyless retainers on guard. There was a Horn Room dedicated entirely to the antlers of unfortunate Scottish deer hanging above heavy mahogany chairs and tables. The house – or palace – was approached by a double line of ilexes and cedars and was topped by twin campaniles, a Clock Tower and Flag Tower. The Queen loved it.

For these three November weeks the chill yet suffocating air of Osborne was infused by the fresh presence of Princess Alexandra, who enchanted the Queen, her children and the servants alike. 'What a pearl!', what 'a real blessing to me', the Queen exclaimed of her. She is 'one of those sweet creatures who seem to come from the skies to help and bless poor mortals and to brighten for a time their path'.

Alix, according to Lady Augusta Stanley, showed herself 'anxious to learn the Queen's tastes and interests and to identify herself with all'. She read worthy books, took drawing lessons, worked at her English and wrote endlessly to her beloved. 'The drift of letters is fearful,' commented Lady Augusta. All courtiers and visitors recognised the healing and cheering effect on the Queen. It was said that she smiled and laughed for the first time since Prince Albert had died; and the Queen herself confided to her journal that 'a gleam of satisfaction for a moment shone into my heart. . . . She is so pretty to live with.'

The visit was a stunning success.

We love her [the Queen told her eldest daughter]. She lives in complete intimacy with us and she is so dear, so gentle, good, simple, unspoilt – so thoroughly honest and straightforward – so affectionate; she has been sitting for an hour with me this evening and I told her all about former happy times, our life, a great deal

---

* Leopold was born a haemophiliac and died at thirty-one after a mainly unhappy and hapless life. But he did father Princess Alice (of Athlone), who added colour and light to the British royal family until her death in 1981.

about dearest Papa . . . all about his illness; she showed such feeling, laid her dear head on my shoulder and cried, said how she prayed God to help her to do all she could to help me and comfort me. . . .

The weeks passed rapidly. Possible disputes were circumvented. There was a hint of conflict between Queen and Princess over the suite Alix would bring to England for her married life. There were to be no Danes, the Queen insisted. 'It would not be for the dear young couple's happiness if Alix had a maid to whom she could chatter away in a language her Husband could not understand.' She even tried to persuade Alix to have German ladies-in-waiting and maids, for she was intent on 'Germanising' the couple as far as she was able.

There were two reasons for this. She knew that the Prussians in particular were still furious about the match and suspected Britain was siding with Denmark over German claims to Schleswig-Holstein. Everything, the Queen believed, should be done to neutralise this hostility. Domestically, and not least in memory of beloved Albert, she wanted to strengthen the German connection. 'The German element is the one I wish to be cherished and kept up in our beloved home.' She even pressed Alix and Bertie to write their love letters in German. Happily the outpouring continued in English, until the young couple at last met again.

Queen Victoria put her foot down firmly about Bertie visiting Alix in Denmark, which she recognised (without any confirmation from the Foreign Office) would lead to further Prussian outrage and put Vicky into an even more difficult position. So, after the proposal meeting at Laeken, Bertie followed his mother to Berlin to stay with Fritz and Vicky. Here, at the ducal palace of Coburg, the Queen drew up an announcement for the British press of Bertie's engagement. It was drafted in order to give least offence to her host nation, with strong emphasis on the fact that the marriage was based 'entirely' upon mutual affection and 'in no way connected with political considerations'.

The announcement caused as much rapturous joy and

excitement in England as in Denmark. Lord Granville told Bertie that 'it is impossible to exaggerate how pleased every one in all classes here is with the good news. All accounts agree as to the beauty, the excellence and charm of the person whom your Royal Highness has secured.'

By contrast, according to Albert's brother Ernest, the news fell on Germany 'like a clap of thunder'. He had done everything he could to oppose the match, to the extent of blackening the Danish royal family and hinting of liaisons between Alix and certain army officers. This was only one of the reasons why the Queen considered it suitable for Fritz and Vicky, as well as Bertie, to depart on a cruise. The Queen was against long engagements and this mitigated her other stricture that the future bride and groom should meet seldom or not at all before the wedding.

Then, Prussian politics were chaotic, and Bismarck had been ordered home from the German Embassy in Paris to assume his brutal dictatorial rule in which, as he proudly claimed, 'blood and iron' must settle the great issues of the day – like the imminent invasion of Denmark, and later of Austria and France. Best to be out of the way, the Queen sensibly decided.

It was a happy party of three that set off from Berlin, far different from those boring tours toiling about ruins with General Bruce, followed by Latin lessons. They made their comfortable and leisurely way about Bavaria and Switzerland, then the French Riviera. The *Osborne* awaited them at Marseilles and, with an escorting frigate, sailed the western Mediterranean. They were entertained by the Bey of Tunis and travelled east again to Malta and then Naples. Here Bertie celebrated his twenty-first birthday and wrote, even by his standards, an extra long letter to Alix. British men o'war in the bay celebrated by flag-dressing and firing many-coloured rockets when darkness fell, and the *Osborne* hoisted crowns of evergreens on her masts.

A rendezvous with Alix at Calais had been engineered by Bertie and reluctantly authorised by the Queen. The meeting of the two lovers moved all who witnessed it. They fell into one another's embrace and went off arm-in-arm for a long walk, laughing and talking. Later, they exchanged gifts, Bertie presenting Alix with some bracelets he had bought for her in Italy. They were worth ten times the total value of Alix's jewellery twelve months ago. How times had changed!

Queen Victoria's insistence on a wedding without delay – 10 March 1863 was the date she fixed – left Bertie with little time to make all the arrangements for family life, from preparing homes for his bride to arranging his own Household. The Household when complete consisted of Major Christopher Teesdale, Major Charles Grey and Lieutenant-Colonel Sir Henry Keppel, all old friends, as equerries; Herbert Fisher, Bertie's old Oxford tutor, as Private Secretary. Grooms of the Bedchamber, under the Earl of Mount Edgcumbe, were Robert Henry Meade and Charles Wood, a childhood friend who became Lord Halifax. The head of this establishment, as Comptroller and Treasurer, was General Knollys, to whom Bertie was now as utterly devoted as he was dependent upon him. There were others, like Earl Spencer as Groom of the Stole and (more down-to-earth) Colonel Robert Kingscote, superintendent of the Prince's stables. Altogether, this Household made an efficient and happy team, and there were few mistakes or misunderstandings over the years.

Bertie and Alix's official home was to be Marlborough House in Pall Mall, a Christopher Wren building intended as a gift from the nation for the first Duke of Marlborough. After his death this massive building housed various royalties, the last inhabitant being William IV's widow, Queen Adelaide. On her death in 1849, a parliamentary bill appropriated Marlborough House for the eight-year-old Prince of Wales, who was to take possession on his eighteenth birthday.

Prince Albert, by then already bowed down with overwork and suffering nervous tension, insisted on redesigning the interior of the house himself, but died long before the work was complete. Bertie himself took a keen interest in the last months of the reconstruction, and the final decorations were complete by the end of 1862. The furniture and decoration reflected the taste and style of the time, dark, heavy and ornate. But over the following decades Marlborough House became sparkling and alive, thundering with dinners and balls and summer garden parties for what became known – with a tinge of notoriety – as 'the Marlborough House set'. Only when the family was at Sandringham did a silence descend over the drawing-rooms and dining-rooms, the ballroom and the broad corridors of Wren's masterpiece.

Sandringham, the Prince and Princess of Wales's private and unofficial residence, came into their possession thanks, again, to Prince Albert. By contrast with Marlborough House, Sandringham was a hideous, inconvenient and neglected country mansion, set in 7,000 equally neglected acres in north-west Norfolk. But it was wonderful game country, and shrewd Albert bought it for a knock-down price of £220,000 in the last year of his life.

Bertie set about putting the place in order with terrific zest and enthusiasm. Roads were constructed, hundreds of trees were planted, kennels, stables and cottages were built or renovated. Whenever he had the opportunity, Bertie would take the train to King's Lynn and supervise the work and put in hand more improvements. The development of Sandringham was a lifelong enthusiasm. Thousands more acres of land were added, and later the house was virtually rebuilt from the foundations. Not that its appearance was much improved, but it did enable him to invite guests to shooting parties of the ample size he enjoyed. No one has improved on Harold Nicolson's description of Sandringham and its annexe:

Even when rebuilt, [it] did not prove large enough to accommodate the many guests whom the Prince of Wales delighted to entertain. A small annexe was therefore erected a few hundred yards from the main building and christened 'Bachelors Cottage'*. . . . It was, and remains, a glum little villa, encompassed by thickets of laurel and rhododendron, shadowed by huge Wellingtonias and separated by the abrupt rim of lawn from a pond, at the edge of which a leaden pelican gazes in dejection upon the water lilies and bamboos. The local brown stone in which the house was constructed is concealed by rough-cast which in its turn is enlivened by very imitation Tudor beams. The rooms inside, with their fumed oak surrounds, their

---

* Renamed York Cottage when the future George V inhabited it as the Duke of York.

white over-mantels framing oval mirrors, their Doulton titles and stained glass fanlights, are indistinguishable from those of any Surbiton or Upper Norwood home. [Bertie's] own sitting room, its north window blocked by heavy shrubberies, was rendered even darker by the red cloth which saddened the walls. . . .

During daylight hours, the copses and moorland of Sandringham crackled with the sound of gunfire as if a military invasion from the nearby North Sea was being driven off; and late into the night the lights from the windows illuminated the gardens, and the music of an orchestra on summer evenings could be heard far from the house. For both Alix and Bertie, Sandringham became a haven and retreat as well as a gathering place for all their numerous friends.

All guests loved Sandringham. Mrs Gladstone wrote in a letter to her husband: 'There is really nothing like this royal home – such simplicity and reality and thought for others.' 'It is altogether different here from Windsor,' Lord Esher once wrote. 'No ceremonial at all. Just a country home.' The only duty guests were required to perform was to take an interest in Bertie's latest developments and make a tour in his company. '[He] took me all over his gardens,' recalled the Earl of Sandwich of these early days, 'and I was astounded at his knowledge of horticulture, and the great interest he took in all his works in the garden and farm.' When inviting his old Oxford friend, Dr Acland, to Sandringham, Bertie added to his letter, 'We could look over the cottages together. I have made many improvements which I should like to show you.'

A steady flow of reports on Alix's future homes were included in Bertie's letters to her in Copenhagen (in English) during that winter of 1862–3. It was a strange time for them both, unreal yet with an undercurrent of excitement and anxiety. Alix, it was noticed by her family, was fretful, but her mother recognised that there was nothing especially unusual about this in a young bride-to-be. She rode a great deal, more often alone than with her usual companion, her sister Minnie. Bertie at least had the advantage of being busy, but his mother found him 'a very unpleasant influence in the house'. The Queen remained in full mourning and there was no relaxation at Court. (A letter she received from one of her children was not, in her judgment, edged deeply enough in black, and she was promptly sent a new supply of paper 'which left little room for words!'.) For all her life obsessed by anniversaries, the first anniversary of Albert's death was dreaded by her Household. Bertie 'spent [it] in gloomy converse with his mother and his family at Windsor'. Much against her inclination, Bertie was commanded to preside in her place at the first levee since Albert's death on 25 February 1863. He took this as a first sign of a new regime in which he would take a much greater part in Court affairs and be allowed into the confidence of his mother. It was a false signpost, as he was to discover with increasing bitterness as the years passed.

In this same month, with the opening of the new session of Parliament, the Queen failed to attend and deputed the reading of her speech to the Lord Chancellor rather than to her son. But Bertie, now that he was twenty-one, was admitted a Peer of the Realm as Duke of Cornwall, a county from which he derived a large part of his income. Meanwhile, in the House of Commons the Prime Minister, Lord Palmerston, blessed the forthcoming marriage with these words, carefully calculated to give minimum offence in Germany:

Whereas the common fate of royal marriages has been that persons are contracted together who have no previous knowledge of each other, and with whom political considerations are the guiding principle of union, in this case the marriage may, in the fullest sense of the word, be called a 'love match', while the amiable and excellent qualities of both parties give the fairest promise of permanent and complete happiness.

This reflected the romantic view of the British public, who were excitedly looking forward to the arrival of Alix and the wedding itself, which was regarded as the greatest royal event since the marriage of the Queen and Prince Albert twenty-three years and one month earlier.

During the first days of March the newspapers reported that Princess Alexandra, who was on her way to her wedding, had reached Brussels, where she was staying with King

Leopold. Then it was learned that the royal yacht *Victoria and Albert* with HMS *Warrior*, the navy's first ironclad, was on its way to Flushing. The Poet Laureate, Lord Tennyson, composed and published the poem of welcome, which Alix later asked him to read aloud:

> Sea-kings' daughter as happy as fair,
> Blissful bride of a blissful heir,
> Bride of the heir of the kings of the sea –
> O joy to the people and joy to the throne,
> Come to us, love us and make us your own:
> For Saxon or Dane or Norman we,
> Teuton or Celt, or whatever we be,
> We are each all Dane in our welcome of thee, Alexandra!

If the imminent wedding was not precisely 'joy to the throne' as joy was never again to be acknowledged by the Queen, at least she had to admit that it was 'the only ray of happiness in my life since my husband's death'.

9

The Wedding

'He gives you his blessing.'
Queen Victoria to Bertie and Alix

Princess Alexandra had never seen such a display of jewellery and precious objects, crowned by a superlative necklace, the pendant copied from the thirteenth-century Dagmar Cross, the most famous jewel in Denmark. She was gazing in wonder at some of her wedding presents and at the necklace, which was from King Frederick of Prussia, a kingdom which, ironically, was about to attack Denmark. The date for her departure from Copenhagen had at last been settled: 26 February 1863. This was a great relief for everybody. Relations between the Queen at Windsor and the Christian family at the Yellow Palace in Copenhagen, sticky from the beginning, were steadily worsening.

The Queen had not exercised the courtesy of formally asking the Danish King for Alix's hand, nor was he invited to the wedding. In fact, the only people from Denmark who were invited were Alix's immediate family, the lame excuse being that there was limited accommodation on the royal yacht in which the journey to England would be completed. Nor would there be any spare seats in St George's Chapel at Windsor,* where the ceremony was to take place, instead of Westminster Abbey or St Paul's Cathedral.

The Queen explained to members of her Household who questioned her about this almost unprecedented† choice of venue that it had been Prince Albert's decision before he died. This was as unanswerable as it was unprovable, and because the chapel held only 900 guests, she could exclude all the people she did not like, especially those of a more raffish character like the Hesse-Cassels from Germany and the Duchess of Manchester. Enormous offence was given, and fury raged in London where the citizens were deprived of the pageantry and the excuse for getting drunk.

Alix's journey to England had its ups and downs. The farewell from the Danish people, who so loved their pretty young Princess, could not have been improved upon. 'Every house on the route to the railway station was gay with bunting or flew British and Scandinavian flags'; flowers were flung from the windows at the carriage in which Alix sat with her parents and eldest brother, while the other children occupied a second carriage with Walburga Paget and her husband. Alix 'wore a dress of brown silk with white stripes', Walburga noted, 'with one of those natty little bonnets which seemed to sit better on her head than on anybody else's. Even in those days I was struck by the extreme neatness and taste of her attire.' The streets were thronged and at the station, 'handsomely' – if hideously – decorated, the Chief President delivered a farewell address 'which had all the merits of simplicity and sincerity'.

But the steam vessel in which the party embarked was dirty and its boiler blew up when it reached high pressure, leading to a long delay. Their spirits were low and their appearance filthy when at length they reached Kiel. Alix was reported by Augustus Paget as being 'rather down in the

---

* *Punch* quipped that as the royal marriage was to be held in an obscure Berkshire village, noted only for an old castle with bad drains, *The Times* announcement should read: 'On the 10th inst. by Dr Longley, Albert Edward England KG to Alexandra Denmark. No cards.'
† The last royal wedding at the Chapel Royal was in 1121, when Henry I married Adela of Louvain.

mouth'. But she cheered up at the greeting she enjoyed at the *Schloss* near Kiel where her uncle, the Duke of Glücksburg, resided and was received by 'a bevy of girls all dressed alike in white muslin with rose-pink scarves'.

Blind King George of Hanover was equally welcoming, and then it was on to Brussels, with cheers all the way, where King Leopold, who had done so much to bring about this match, warmly embraced her in spite of his horrible cold. Queen Victoria, he confided to the Christian family, had at first insisted that the entire journey should be conducted in full mourning, 'But I managed to persuade her otherwise.' Uncle Leopold also presented Alix with a magnificent bridal robe of Brussels lace.

Three days later, after a happy rest, some of it for Alix in bed with the cold she had caught from the King, the party was taken in ten state carriages to the railway station, the Grand Marshal of the Belgian Court escorting Alix all the way to Antwerp. Here the last bond with her home country was cut as, with full Royal Navy honours, they boarded the *Victoria and Albert*. Her family might still be with her, but she was now formally under British jurisdiction. The sea was like a millpond, the sun was out and Alix shed many of her anxieties as her journey entered its last stage. At Flushing two more men o'war reinforced the naval escort. The men manned the yards and, in response, Alix walked out on to the *Victoria and Albert*'s paddle box and gracefully bowed.

They were on their way. The stems of the four vessels cleaved through the still waters, funnel smoke rose straight up into the sky. If they had been under sail, they would have been becalmed and their timetable ruined. But the coast of England soon appeared as a blur on the horizon, and by mid-afternoon they had rounded the North Foreland and dropped anchor off Margate. The town's Mayor and fellow dignitaries put off in a boat and were piped on board, and Alix suffered the first of many formal addresses of welcome. The Mayor bowed deeply – what a day it was for him! – presented her with a scroll and departed walking backwards. Without bothering to read it, Alix used the tightly wrapped parchment teasingly to belabour her brother.

The following morning, the *Victoria and Albert* raised anchor and headed up the Thames estuary. The first hint of the welcome to come that day was the boom of the guns from the batteries at the Nore and Tilbury. We can imagine Alix tightly holding the arm of her mother, as if hoping to acquire some of her resolution and strength to face what was to come. She was, after all, only eighteen years and three months old.

Never before had there been such scurrying and such an echoing of children's voices in the corridors and apartments of Windsor Castle. It was the first time that the 'Danois', the German and the English young royalties had met *en masse*, and the competition and even conflict between them were considerable. They ranged in age from the four-year-old Prince William, Vicky's very belligerent son, with his withered arm, and the five-year-old English Princess Beatrice and Danish Prince Waldemar, to Queen Victoria's and Princess Christian's teenage children, including Minnie and Alix herself.

For a Sunday morning the behaviour was decidedly unruly, with parents and nursemaids darting hither and thither to keep a check on their charges. Of the two, the English children and Prince William were the more aggressive simply because they had no measurable standard of behaviour with outsiders, while the Danish children had mixed freely with commoners and were of an easier disposition anyway.

Challenged to do a cartwheel, Alix obliged with amazing speed, which secretly impressed Lenchen and Louise, who could not in the least emulate her. Alix was also crossly challenged by the young English Princesses about her motives for marrying their eldest brother. All she wanted was his rank and wealth, they claimed provocatively. Alix, who only yesterday had been the toast of London, was taken aback by this accusation, but kept her head and responded sharply in her strong Danish accent: 'You perhaps think that I like marrying your brother for his position. But if he was a cowboy I should love him just the same and would marry no one else.'

Much was being asked of Alix. In absurd contrast with these not always seemly nursery revels, within the hour she was making her way on a solemn pilgrimage with the Queen and Bertie to the mausoleum at Frogmore in the grounds of Windsor Castle. This had only recently been completed and contained the elaborately carved tomb of Prince Albert. With her son on one side and Alix on the other, they stood in silence before it, heads bowed. And then the Queen said in a solemn voice, '*He* gives you his blessing.'

The party returned to their carriage and were taken directly to the Castle's private chapel. It was noon and 'the young people' as well as the full Danish contingent were there to listen to the Bishop of Oxford's appropriate sermon on the text 'Rejoice with them that do rejoice and weep with them that weep'. Later, when the Bishop was taking luncheon in the Castle's Oak Room, one of the Queen's ladies-in-waiting, Lady Augusta Stanley, passed on Vicky's compliments on the sermon to the Bishop and made a request for a copy of it on her behalf.

That afternoon Alix's mother and Vicky were among those who were helping to arrange the wedding presents. These were set up in a temporary annexe attached to St George's Chapel for the greater convenience of guests. It was like trying to create a gallery at the Victoria and Albert Museum in a couple of hours. The glitter of silver and gold and the sparkle of diamonds laid out beneath a tall and deeply set window were startlingly magnificent. Bertie's gift was a *parure* of pearls and diamonds. The Queen's gift was a wonder of diamonds and opals, which, as pointedly stated, was from her *and* Albert. The Lord Mayor of London, in spite of his city being scorned as the venue for the wedding, came up with a necklace and ear-rings which were widely known to have cost £10,000.

Some of the Castle guests arrived that Sunday evening, but most of the carriages turned up from midday on Monday, 9 March, or early Tuesday morning, all followed by children to the gates and watched by the local citizens. Lord Combermere was the oldest, having commanded the cavalry in the Peninsular War under Wellington; the Duchess of

Westminster was the richest, with half a million pounds-worth of jewellery on her person.

The Queen had retreated to her private quarters for the day and was said to be in deep distress and lamentation. Someone suggested that in the afternoon all the royalties with their children should go for a grand tour of Windsor and Eton to amuse themselves and the people. It was a great success, everybody behaving in character. Vicky's William snatched his mother's fur muff and hurled it into the crowd. Alix and Bertie waved until their arms ached and Alix once or twice proffered a hand to be kissed.

Some of the Eton boys could not be stopped from giving Alix a personal welcome. 'She came through Eton about four,' one of them wrote, 'and I and about half a dozen other chaps ran with her for nearly a mile by the side of her carriage so I had a stunning view of her. She is very pretty indeed, with a jolly colour, has a beautiful complexion, and looks quite merry, but a little shy.' Another, handing her a bunch of violets, noted that 'she grinned away like beans and so did her mother'.

The English royal children were delighted at this rare chance to be among the ordinary people, and in such a cheerful, crowded state. Princess Beatrice, as Victoria's youngest, was especially excited and observant. Turning to Lady Augusta Stanley, she exclaimed, 'Guska, I *never* thought there were *stays* in shops!'

The banquet that night was strictly for grown-ups, which was a pity because the children would so much have enjoyed the spectacle in the Waterloo Gallery, which was blessed by the absence of the Queen, whose baleful presence would have put a damper on the proceedings. After the 'grand repast' and the speeches, Alix retired to the Tapestry Room to have the guests presented to her. 'She received them and found something to say to each,' Lady Augusta Stanley recalled. 'It was charming and shewed such an advance on what She was able for in Novr. She wore white and mauve. . . . Lovely she looked, and He so proud and happy.'

Thankfully, the last item on the day's programme demanded nothing of Alix. She and her mother, followed by all the diners, proceeded to the state apartments, where they had a fine view of a fireworks display and gigantic bonfire in the meadow below. The Queen was not in the mood for fireworks and was saving her strength for the next day's ordeal. In spite of the gentlest suggestions by her ladies-in-waiting, she was bent on attending the wedding in full mourning, broken only by the purple sash of the Knight of the Garter.

The wedding morning dawned fine and sunny, and the slight mist rising from the Thames soon burnt off. The guests began to arrive soon after 10.30, the haughtier duchesses strolling up and down the nave glancing to left and right through their lorgnettes to check the presence of fellow guests and perhaps relishing the absence of the uninvited, before taking their seats.

The Queen herself was the only reluctant guest. She accepted that it was her duty to attend her eldest son's wedding, but she was determined not to show the world any evidence of happiness about the occasion. In fact, she was so inconspicuous that only those in the choir ever saw her properly. She had earlier put the Castle carpenters to the trouble of building a covered way from the Deanery to the privacy of Catherine of Aragon's closet in the Chapel, which was like the royal box at the opera house. Here she was scarcely visible from the pews below. Benjamin Disraeli was the only guest who made a point of seeking her out with his quizzing glass, and received a withering glance in return for his pains.

The Eton boys were among the first to arrive, for once soberly conscious that they must put on a good show. They all wore white kid gloves 'and a swell favour'.

This was at 10.30, when Lady Frederick Cavendish took her seat, with the certainty of a wait of at least two hours. But there was always something to watch as an overture to the great event, as she recorded in her diary:

About 11.30 the Archbishop of Canterbury, and all the officiating Bishops and clergy, of whom the Bishop of Oxford and the Dean of Windsor were in robes of the Order of the Garter, passed into the choir by the N. transept door and later all the Knights of the Garter, in their splendid blue velvet robes. But all this was only preparing one! . . . We heard 'God save the Queen', faintly, but quite audibly, played over and over again outside the Chapel, and in the middle of its glorious music, which always overcomes me with its pride and pathos – a burst of cheers. That *went through* me, somehow, most of all. Then there was a silence of expectation, till the band quickly formed at the W. door, and the 1st procession came in, preceded by the drums and trumpets.

One of the Eton boys described how the Danish family came first down the aisle, then the English Princes and Princesses. 'The little chaps had kilts on; Princess Helena looked very nice; last came the Princess Royal [Vicky] who got awfully cheered. The next lot was Mayors and Councillors and Sheriffs, with gorgeous footmen; then came the Prince.' He was, wrote Lady Frederick Cavendish, 'in the robes of the Order of the Garter, the blue velvet cloak giving height and dignity to his figure; his face a little pale, but bright, gentle and gracious, in its youth and happiness; his bows right and left full of royal grace, his whole manner beautiful and regal.' Beneath his cloak he wore his uniform as an army general. At the altar he was supported by Vicky's Fritz, Crown Prince of Prussia, and his Uncle Ernest, who had done all in his power to stop this wedding but who could not resist coming over from Germany to play this important role when it was offered to him.

For the second time the Lord Chamberlain went out and, as one Eton boy wrote, 'this time the clang of the trumpets was followed by the organ and orchestra thundering out "The Wedding March" in *Athalie*. . . . At last came the Princess Alexandra. She looked regular nailing. . . .'

Alix's dress was not of the Brussels lace King Leopold had given her. The Queen decreed more patriotic Honiton lace, which was used as a trimming in a pattern of roses, shamrocks and thistles, garlanded with orange blossom. The dress itself was of silver-tissue, the long train held by eight bridesmaids in white crinolines garlanded with pink roses. Lady Geraldine Somerset described the dress as '*trés bon gout*, light, young, and royal, made by Mrs James'. Another guest described the bridesmaids as 'eight as ugly girls as you could wish to see', but that was in a letter to the absent and resentful Duchess of Manchester and no doubt intended to cheer her up.

Alix was ten minutes late, which subsequently turned out to be prompt by her standards for any important appointment throughout her life. Restlessness was just setting in when she came up the aisle on the arm of her handsome father.

The twenty-six-year-old future Lord Redesdale wrote of the 'touching tenderness of her girlish, rosebud beauty and graceful figure, as she passed up the nave, her eyes shyly downcast'. She was, he added, 'like the vision of a Princess in a Fairy Tale'. He was not the only one present to use this simile.

'I never saw in anyone more grace and dignity and aplomb,' Lord Clarendon commented. 'Her eyes and the tip of her nose were a tiny bit red and accounted for by her having cried all the morning.' (This was not true, but there had been a few tears. The serious crying was from Vicky, Alice and their youngest sisters when their brother reached the altar, 'crying and blubbering: but it was only from affection and they soon recovered themselves'.)

The one Arab present called Alix 'a gift of cream and honey specially sent by Allah for the good of the English people'. Lady Frederick Cavendish described 'our pride and hope for whom the prayers of millions were going up . . . her sweet face bent down, her small head crowned with orange-flowers, her step queenly, and her whole look the perfection of maiden grace'.

Little Prince William, sitting near to his mother but with the young English Princes, Alfred and Leopold, in their kilts on each side to keep him in order, chose this moment to reach across and pinch their naked legs. He hurt them, but, much to their credit, they did not protest or retaliate. This was disappointing for the little Prussian, who was bored out of his mind. So he succeeded in extracting the cairngorm from the head of his dirk and then threw the heavy yellow stone across the nave, where it clattered on to the paving among the legs of those sitting there. The two Princes attempted to restrain him and got bitten on the leg for their pains. He had already called the Queen *'Duck'* and continued to do so until his merciful departure.

And now the service began, the Archbishop's sonorous voice was so clear . . . wonderfully striking it was to hear the simple solemn words, which bless quiet marriages in little country churches, spoken here in face of all the splendour and pomp of England. . . . The bride trembled extremely at first, but was heard giving her troth in a clear childlike voice, with a slightly foreign accent. The Prince's *'I will'* was distinct and emphatic.

Prince Albert, no mean composer, had provided a post-humous solemn chorale just for this historic moment, the voice of Jenny Lind heard above all others, the organ notes seeming to rise from the grave. This was almost too much for his widow and children. Then the *'Deus Misereatur'* was chanted and finally the great blessing, 'The Peace of God'.

There was a pause, a silence that not even young William broke, the bells rang out and the guns from the Castle were fired as Alix and Bertie held hands. All in the nave rose to their feet, 'The Mount of Olives Hallelujah' sounded out from the orchestra. The Queen was seen to be still kneeling in prayer by those who dared to steal a glance. The bride and groom led the way down the nave, the glorious music filling the chapel. Alix was looking poised but pale, Bertie smiling with proud propriety.

The Queen disappeared from her closet as unobtrusively as she had arrived and, rather than join the wedding breakfast for both families, she took luncheon alone with little Beatrice and 'Kath', widow of General Bruce. She had earlier greeted the couple at the door of her apartments, 'holding them locked in her arms, and then leading them upstairs with that wonderful grace and dignity we know'. The register was signed, the standing lunch in the Waterloo Room consumed. Everyone was very cheerful and excited, and there was a great deal of milling about, waving and calling of names. Lady Augusta Stanley bustled about in search of a shoe, a minor slip in the otherwise impeccable organisation.

The roar of conversation died when Alix was seen coming downstairs dressed in a white velvet gown, ermine cloak and muff, looking a little pale but smiling sweetly and waving in acknowledgment of the audible sigh, like breeze through grass, rising from the guests. Bertie was waiting for her by the carriage, looking very smart and pleased with himself, bowing before following his bride to the seat. The open carriage moved off and paused beneath the Queen's window. She was seen, a small black figure, responding to their greeting, smiling briefly. Alix looked up at her 'lovingly', the Queen recorded in her journal. After they were gone she was taken to the Frogmore mausoleum, where she prayed alone for the young couple, feeling 'soothed and calmed'.

There was nothing calm about Bertie's and Alix's drive to Slough station. Almost the entire local population and many people from afar were in the streets, many of them drunk, all of them determined to give a great send-off to their future King and Queen. In addition, the Eton boys were out on the streets, demonstrating their royal fervour without restraint. One of them, Lord Randolph Churchill, recorded the anarchy they created:

Nothing stood before us. The policemen charged in a body, but they were knocked down. There was a chain put across the road, but we broke that; several old *genteel* ladies tried to stop me, but I snapped my fingers in their face and cried 'Hurrah!' and 'What larks!' I frightened some of them horribly. There was a wooden palisade put up at the station and we broke it down. I got right down to the door of the carriage where the Prince of Wales was, wildly shouting 'Hurrah!' He bowed to me, I am perfectly certain; but I shrieked louder.

For Alix, the scene was even more frightening than on the drive through London three days earlier, but she remained as calm, seemingly unconcerned and cheerful as before, waving her hand and smiling to left and right. The police managed to regain some sort of order at Slough station, and Bertie and Alix, escorted by members of the Household, walked along the carpet from their horse carriage to the railway carriage of the royal train.

They were to honeymoon for a week at Osborne, at the Queen's insistence. No doubt their youth, love and cheerfulness would counter the dreadful gloom and austerity of this island home. Now the train set off, more or less on time, slowing down so that they could show themselves to the crowds assembled at every station to Portsmouth, once or twice being obliged to halt and receive an address.

The guests' trains for London were a great deal less orderly and punctual. The organisation which so far had been impressive did not extend to the arrangements of the Great Western Railway, which proved quite incapable of delivering 900 guests, most of them of exalted rank, including the Archbishop of Canterbury, the nineteen miles back to London. After the spectacle, majesty and discipline of the morning, it seemed as if a kind of madness seized them, starting with the coachmen driving the carriages through Eton, across the River Thames and for the length of the dusty road to the little town of Slough. Carriages passed and repassed one another, the horses spurred on by freely applied whips.

At the station forecourt, filled with spectators, the carriages disgorged their passengers as if in flight, like refugees from the recent Indian Mutiny. The Duchess of Westminster (with her jewels) found herself crushed by the mob and was thankful to get into a third-class apartment, dragging the Prime Minister's wife, Lady Palmerston, after her. Benjamin Disraeli, fiery politician, future Prime Minister and novelist, was forced to sit on the knees of his wife, the one-time Mrs Wyndham Lewis.

There were shouts and struggles at the train doors, while the police dragged people out from overcrowded compartments. The Archbishop of Canterbury, half suffocated by the press of numbers, cried, 'Policeman, what can I do?'

'Hold on to the next carriage, your grace, it's your only chance.' He did so, finding himself with the newly married Lady Cranworth and William Makepeace Thackeray in a similar desperate position beside him.

Lady Cranworth cried out in relief, 'Oh, I'm so glad to see you, my Lord. I felt so ashamed of my place. Now I am satisfied.'

The last passengers did not reach Paddington until ten

o'clock, only to find a city gone mad with drunken celebrating. There were no cabs on the streets, only mobs of people, shouting and waving flags, while fireworks filled the sky overhead. It was known that St Paul's Cathedral was to be illuminated with *electricity*, but it was quite impossible to reach it. 'We were locked fast by the Illumination crowd for 2½ hours,' complained Lady Augusta Stanley, 'and it was not until 10 that I reached home to find Arthur terrified by my non-appearance.'

At the same time Bertie and Alix were driving up from Cowes to Osborne House. There were fires burning in every grate, and the mistress of the Household and the other servants welcomed them. But the ghost of Prince Albert was everywhere, as he was to be for all their married life as Prince and Princess of Wales, his hat and sticks in the hall, his last papers on his desk.

Above Left Bertie as a young rider at Balmoral. *Right* With his wistful sister Alice, the second of Queen Victoria's daughters to be born and the first to die. Here she is aged seventeen and Bertie eighteen. They loved one another dearly.

Below Left As a young soldier after returning from Canada and the United States. *Right* As a twenty-one-year-old student at Cambridge, where he learned little and hunted a great deal.

Above and *below* Bertie was given possession of Sandringham House in north-west Norfolk in 1862 when he was twenty. He and Alix loved the place for all their lives, developed the gardens, then set about enlarging the house itself. First to be built was a ballroom and then, as can be seen, a wing which dwarfed the original house and could accommodate large parties of guests. A fire in 1891 destroyed thirteen bedrooms, which justified further enlargement.

Facing page, top Bertie embarking in HMS *Hero* at Plymouth for his extensive tour of Canada and the United States. It was a great success and made a new young man of him, although his father, Prince Albert, only cavilled at his popularity. *Bottom* Less than two years later Bertie was engaged to Alix. This is Frith's painting of the marriage ceremony on 10 March 1863 in St George's Chapel, Windsor. Frith lurked in a corner with his sketchbook, the Queen in her gallery 'agitated and restless'.

Bertie and Alix and Prince Eddy, their first child, in 1864. Bertie is twenty-two, Alix nineteen, and Albert Victor Christian Edward about four months.

The Prince and
Princess of Wales
in 1868.

Above Marlborough House, Bertie and Alix's London home. It was by no means the largest private house in London, but for Society it was by far the most notable and was the hub of London social life.

Left In 1870 the marriage was seven years old and five children had been born. Alix had been disabled for life, and made even deafer, as a consequence of rheumatic fever, while Bertie was shortly to be a witness in an unsavoury divorce case.

In December 1871, when he was just thirty years old, Bertie was stricken with typhoid fever, which had killed his father ten years earlier. The son was more robust and fought harder for his life, but lost a great deal of weight, as indicated in this photograph which was probably taken at Cowes in July 1872.

A thanksgiving service in St Paul's Cathedral took place on 27 February 1872 to celebrate Bertie's recovery. Numerous mishaps among the crowds marred the day, but Bertie wrote to the Queen that he was 'gratified and touched' by the people's pleasure and loyalty.

During the winter of 1875–6 Bertie made an extensive tour of India and Ceylon. Between formal occasions the slaughter was formidable. This is Bertie's first elephant.

10

The Acclaimed Couple

'Running about for show.'
The Queen on Bertie and Alix

Bertie and Alix were allowed just two days to themselves before Vicky turned up with Fritz and 'precious little William', as the Queen inaccurately referred to him. Vicky described Osborne as being in 'its greatest beauty and all breathes peace and happiness'; her husband thought it 'one great gloomy vault filled with relics of the Prince Consort'. However, in spite of this rude invasion of their privacy, Bertie looked blissful, his whole face beaming and radiant, according to Vicky, 'while Darling Alix looks charming and lovely'. They both seemed 'so comfortable and at home together'.

By 17 March 1863 the newly-weds were back at Windsor Castle, where, the previous day, the Queen had endured the ordeal of the second anniversary of her mother's death, 'which was the beginning of all our terrible suffering and misery'. However, she had to accept that Bertie looked 'bright and happy and certainly totally different to what he used to be'. The Queen's approval was short-lived. With the sudden relaxation of the ties and disciplines of childhood and the joys of independence, this gregarious young couple accepted the golden mantle suddenly cast about their shoulders – the mantle of leadership of Society.

The monarch and his consort were the natural social leaders of the nation and had been so in the halcyon years of the reign of George IV and Queen Caroline. Since then there had been the brief and drab reign of William IV, with rising hopes of royal patronage of Society in the early years of Victoria's reign. Her marriage had finished all that. Prince Albert disapproved of social gallivanting, of the aristocracy and of Society in general. The aristocracy responded in kind, detesting this prudish German, this gloomy busybody who was always *doing things*, creating exhibitions which interfered with the inviolable cycle of the social round, convening commissions of a boringly earnest nature and being photographed dangling his ever-increasing children on his knee.

The Prince of Wales, the obverse of his father, vivacious, sociable, pleasure-loving, yet supremely royal and now married to a beautiful and equally lively young woman, was the natural inheritor of the crown of Society just as he was heir to the Crown itself. Society, that small group of rich and mostly titled people with their vast estates in the country* and London mansions, knowing one another at least by sight, some more moral than others, all pleasure-seeking, welcomed the Prince and Princess of Wales as their new leaders.

There had never been a Season like that of 1863, when balls and banquets and great dinners followed one another in joyous succession. In those first months of married life Bertie and Alix were, literally, the toast of London, and the young couple loved every minute of it. On 14 June Disraeli wrote in his diary that 'this royal honeymoon of many months is perfectly distracting. Nothing but balls and banquets, and receptions and inaugurations and processions, so that one has not a moment to oneself and lives on in a glittering bustle.'

By May Bertie and Alix had moved into Marlborough House, and from that time they were seen everywhere. While out riding, Lady Frederick Cavendish 'saw a young

---

* In the mid-nineteenth century four-fifths of the land in Britain was owned by some seven thousand people out of a population of twenty-five million.

man riding in front of us, who proved to be the Prince of Wales; only one gentleman with him, and a groom,' she wrote in her diary. 'And near the Marble Arch, a little phaeton with pair of ponies driven by a very pretty young lady, passed us. . . . The carriage looked like a Royal one; and we have nearly made up our minds that the young lady was the Princess.'

This same diary records a drawing-room held by Alix and, a few days later, 'An amusing ball, unlike the general run, at Miss Coutts's. . . .' Then the Christ Church ball – 'we feasted our eyes on the Princess' – and a garden party, also in Oxford, where Lady Frederick Cavendish was presented to Alix, 'who shook hands with me. My curtseys were beautiful, but O dear! I *couldn't* make out what she said to me, with her low peculiar utterance and foreign accent. . . .'

Then, on 26 June,

the great event of the season: the Guards' ball given for the Prince and Princess. It was all on a royal scale; and I shan't soon forget the beautiful effect, when Their Royal Highnesses went away, of the procession streaming through the antechambers and down the flag-emblazoned staircase lined with picked Guardsmen; 'God Save the Queen' going on the while. The Princess looked lovely as if she enjoyed herself, but pale.

And so it went on, week after week. The Queen became vexed and anxious about them, describing them as 'nothing but puppets, running about for show all day and all night'.

On 8 June she wrote to Vicky:

Bertie and Alix left Frogmore today – both looking as ill as possible. We are all seriously alarmed about her – for though Bertie writes and says he is so anxious to take care of her, he goes on going out every night till she will become a skeleton, and hopes there cannot be!! I am quite unhappy about it. Oh! how different poor foolish Bertie is to adored Papa whose gentle, loving, wise, motherly care of me when he was not 21 exceeded everything.

(The Queen might have expressed even greater concern had she known that Alix was three months pregnant. But pregnancy never seriously troubled Alix nor was evident in spite of her tight waist until it was well advanced.)

The Queen's relations with her eldest son were going through another difficult phase. Just as she and Albert believed that, with strenuous and prolonged pressure, Bertie's natural character could be converted to that of his father, so she was convinced that married life and the influence of his bride could make a reformed man of him. This was, of course, nonsense, which took no account of the fact that his bride also loved all this partying, late nights, flattery and fun. It was heady to be at the hub of a Society she scarcely knew existed when she was growing up in Copenhagen.

The Queen's views on the aristocracy were coloured not just by those of 'Albert the Good' but also by her own upbringing in the aftermath of the French Revolution and Hanoverian decadence at home. She firmly believed that the unrest of the 1820s and 1830s, which had a distinct revolutionary flavour, had to a large extent been stirred up by the behaviour at Court and of the aristocracy.

When Bertie, a few years after his marriage, wrote to his mother on the subject of bomb outrages in the capital and the need to take firm action, the Queen replied defensively that these were the work of a few extremists and that 'the country was never so *loyal* or *so devoted to their Sovereign as now*'. The one great danger to the country, she warned her son, was in the conduct of 'the *Higher Classes* and of the *Aristocracy*'. Their example of 'love of pleasure, self-indulgence, luxury, and idleness' was very much like that conducted by the French aristocracy before the revolution. She made no parallel between her position and that of Marie Antoinette before she was guillotined, but she did add that 'the Aristocracy and the Higher Classes must take *great care*, or their position may become *very* dangerous'.

In reply, Bertie defended the aristocracy, 'or Upper Ten Thousand'. While agreeing that 'in many instances, amusement, self-indulgence, etc., predominate . . . I know of so many instances where those of the highest rank are excellent Country Gentlemen, are Chairmen of Quarter Sessions, Magistrates, etc., and the ladies attend to their duties also'. Bertie had no intention of changing his life-style, refusing all dinner and party invitations and restricting their visits occasionally to the houses of two or three high-ranking Cabinet ministers and the very few privileged great houses as his mother wished. On the contrary, he amazed his intimate friends and Household. He would be up at 7 a.m., after retiring at perhaps 3 a.m., fresh as a daisy, signing papers, bustling about Marlborough House or Sandringham (where he would stride round the garden and stables before an enormous breakfast of liver and home-produced bacon or mutton chops). His energy was limitless. 'He regarded the day as eighteen hours long and hated wasting any of it,' Lord Redesdale once commented. 'He is the antidote to every text and sermon that ever was preached upon the pleasure of the world palling upon the wearied spirit,' Mrs George Cresswell wrote in her *Eighteen Years on the Sandringham Estate*.

Redesdale also defended Bertie against the charge that such relentless high living led to neglect of his duties:

However late he might stay up at some entertainment he was up again at earliest dawn to attend a review at Aldershot or take part in a ceremonial in some distant part of the country, where he would appear as gay and as pleased as if he was fulfilling the one ambition of his life.

Bertie was extremely routine conscious, and Alix only too willingly conformed to the annual round of events. The first two months of the year were devoted to Sandringham, which they both loved above anywhere else and where there was almost non-stop entertaining and shooting. In early March the Mediterranean sun called him and, leaving Alix behind, he sped south, first to Paris, his favourite city, where all the pleasures of the world were laid out for him by kind friends. After two or three days he took the train to the Riviera, staying sometimes with friends, but more often on his yacht which was sent ahead.

After three or four weeks of balls and dinners, fêtes and prolonged visits to the casinos, he returned to London, lingering briefly in Paris *en route* again, and was back at Marlborough House in time for the English Season. Ascot, Goodwood, the Derby, balls and receptions, great dinners and

banquets, visits to the opera and theatre, followed one upon
the other. The Season concluded with the regatta at Cowes,
the only time in England spent close to his mother at Osborne
House.

Now there was a brief hiatus, when the great London
houses were closed down until the following May, the rooms
in holland covers, 'even the *tongs* and the *fender* in holland
bags, and smelling sadly of camphor'. 'The glorious 12th'
(August) marked the beginning of the long season of bird-
slaughter. Bertie, however, and many others went on a sort
of pretend penance for the over-indulgence of the London
Season by taking the waters at Marienbad, later his favourite
spa, Baden-Baden, Wiesbaden or Homburg. There he would
arise early, as always, attending to his papers, eating a substantial breakfast – hurriedly as always – before promenading
with his friends sipping a mug of the local water in a token
attempt to reduce weight.

Bertie adored the rich local food and the best that can be
said of his record is that he put on weight more slowly than
usual, probably because he omitted alcohol almost entirely
from his menu. He returned thankfully to London in late
September and would go to a race meeting or two, before
travelling north for the shooting, which lasted a month or
more.

Abergeldie Castle on the River Dee and not far distant
from Balmoral was Bertie's and Alix's base for the month of
October. Women loathed it. It was cold and damp and reputed
to be haunted. The cupola in the single stone tower was
infested with rats, and the rain came down in buckets. The
arrival of the Prince and Princess of Wales created a transformation of the old place.

Within the hour Alix had brought Abergeldie to life with
her darting figure, tinkling laugh and almost non-stop chatter.
Her ladies-in-waiting and personal servants adored her, and
she trailed a light of happiness along the sombre stone passages and public rooms. Guests from the great Scottish
families – the Sutherlands, the Buccleuchs, the Hamiltons –
swarmed in and out, the men big and hairy in kilts or thick

tweed knickerbockers, the women petite but also clad heavily against the weather of eastern Scotland.

Bertie loved deer-stalking above any other shooting, and there was plenty of it on Deeside, while grouse abounded. Soon after the men went out with their gillies in wagons, there would be heard the crackling of fifty or more guns. In the evening, the corpses would be laid out in their thousands for recording, inspection and interment in the Abergeldie larder.

At the end of October, Bertie and Alix and their entire, and ever-growing, entourage moved south again for Sandringham for Bertie's birthday first, then Alix's, and finally Christmas.

From a young bride of eighteen until her death sixty-two years later, Sandringham was 'my beloved home' to Alix, and as always her affection for the place was so transparent that everyone recognised it. As she drove along one day, Lord Knutsford at her side ('she drove very fast – too fast – but very well'),

she pointed out everything. Her love for the place is quite touching and almost childish. I mean she has the same love for the place that a child has for its home. She took pleasure in pointing out her plantations, her single trees, her cottages, the roads they had made, the best stands for shooting, the 'silly names we give' to this or that wood.

But many of her women guests and Household retained a low opinion of the house and its situation. Her Lady of the Bedchamber, Lady Macclesfield (Old Mac), was appalled on her first visit:

No fine trees, no water, no hills, in fact no attraction of any sort or kind. There are numerous coverts but no fine woods, large unenclosed turnip fields, with an occasional haystack to break the line of the horizon. It would be difficult to find a more ugly or desolate-looking place, and there is no neighbourhood or any other countervailing advantage. The wind blows keen from the Wash and the Spring is said to be unendurable in that part of north Norfolk.

Poor Lady Macclesfield had to endure it, none the less, every spring until she died in harness in 1911.

On the other hand, Disraeli wrote of the 'vigorous marine air, stunted fir forests' and 'the splendour of Scandinavian sunsets' at Sandringham. Many lady guests, weather permitting, strolled about the formal gardens admiringly. There was never a word of complaint from the men, who were concerned only with coverts, the great plantation known as Woodcock Wood and where best to shoot partridge.

Alix had become reconciled to cold winds from earliest childhood, and the flat land of north Norfolk reminded her of her homeland. She was happiest here, surrounded by her children and dogs amidst the clutter of her possessions: her knick-knacks, porcelains, portraits, postcards, trinkets and countless objets d'art. While Bertie and his cronies went out shooting early, after a mighty breakfast, Alix would not descend from her apartment before eleven o'clock, when the great house at once began to echo to the sounds of ladies' voices and laughter.

A light luncheon would be taken at 2.30 p.m. When the weather allowed, there would be croquet on one of the lawns, accompanied by sounds of outrage and triumph, and a great deal of laughter. If there was a meet, Alix could not resist taking part, along with some of her more sporting guests. The Queen was appalled when she learned of her hunting, and made Alix promise to desist. Alix learned early how to manage her mother-in-law. She made a great point of following her instructions for a while and then quietly returned to her old practice, as she did with hunting, confident that Victoria would not again refer to the subject.

Alix would always be at the door to greet her men guests when they returned from the shoot. Like soldiers returning from an action, the men were loud in their claims to success as they wiped their boots and handed their heavy coats and tweed hats and caps to the menservants.

A rich and elaborate tea in the hall awaited both the men and women guests. Although Alix was haphazard in domestic matters, and always unpunctual (it was not uncommon for her to keep diners waiting for half an hour, to the near despair of the cook and the dining-room staff, to say nothing of Bertie), she was supremely successful as a hostess. She was one of those women who were tireless in their attention to everyone, no matter how many, while appearing to reserve a special interest in each one. The secret was her lightness of touch, the generosity of her affection and the abundance of her conversation. She might choose the wrong word, quite frequently in her young days, but neither she nor anyone else cared a fig. It was no more than a rather touching little failing.

The men might retire for a smoke and a game of billiards while the women returned to their rooms to prepare for the evening. The guests' rooms at Sandringham were surprisingly small but always warm and comfortable.

Bertie and Alix were equally hospitable and concerned for their visitors. 'His personal attention to his guests was extraordinary,' it is recorded. 'To one he would say, "Have you noticed in your bedroom a picture of the Dartmoor otterhounds which was given to me after I had been out with them?" just to show that he knew where his guests were lodged.'

Dinner for any number of up to forty guests would be taken at 8.30 p.m. according to programme, but according to Alix nearer to 9 p.m. The food was rich and abundant, Bertie finishing each course before anyone else and seldom ceasing from talking to his neighbours, always the prettiest and brightest of his guests. In conversation he was particularly partial to surprising facts and amusing anecdotes, which he would hoard in his remarkably retentive memory and recount to others without acknowledgment at some other time. Thanking Lord Granville for what Bertie called 'a stock of anecdotes', he added frankly, 'I shall certainly endeavour to palm them off as my own.'

Alix would lead the ladies from the room at around 10 p.m., while Bertie indicated by a gesture that the men should close ranks. As the last dishes were discreetly removed, a large mahogany box of cigars and cigarettes was offered to the men in turn, a practice introduced by Bertie who could not wait until later in the evening. He was not a star conversationalist by any means and his second-hand stories had mostly been better told first-hand, and tended to be repeated to the same audience at too frequent intervals. The build-up to the anecdote was given too much emphasis, and he lacked both timing and the light touch. He seemed to recognise his own lack of skill and confidence in holding an audience, even clutching a listener's coat button in his anxiety to keep his attention, although it would have been a brave man who wandered away from the Prince of Wales in mid-story.

But, at table, Bertie did not linger for long, another new convention, for he was anxious to get on with the evening's activities and talk to the women.

Then there would be poker or whist (in later years auction bridge) or another card game, now lost in the mists of time, called chow-chow, for nominal stakes only. Alix hated losing and, when she thought no one was looking, would change a card. 'I won't play any more if your Royal Highness cheats,' she was told indignantly. She 'used to laugh and promise not to do it again which she invariably did'. Alix was usually asked to sing a song or two, accompanying herself. She had a pretty voice, 'like a bird's', but it was not at all strong. She would encourage a volunteer male voice for a duet. Once, when Francesco and Mme Tosti were guests and were prevailed upon to sing, Alix stood up the whole time turning over the pages for the pianist. Dancing took place in the adjoining ballroom for any couple who cared to. If there was no orchestra playing, the music was provided by an ancient barrel-organ, with Alix sometimes putting her arm to the handle.

Some of the more sporting men retired to the billiards room and Bertie would be among them. It was all very masculine here, the air heavy with cigar smoke, while at one end there was a notorious screen featuring photographs of nude women. Bertie thought it amusing to mix among them photographs of some of his guests, including Disraeli, Matthew Arnold, Gladstone and Lord Salisbury. It was not considered good form to complain.

On Sundays a new order prevailed. Everyone went to morning service in Sandringham Church. Bertie and some of his friends cut the preliminaries and arrived for the sermon only, which the vicar was sternly instructed should not exceed ten minutes. (There was a great deal of yawning and restlessness in the pew if he did, although Bertie never actually departed.) The evenings were rather less rumbustious, too, without card games or gambling. Music was permitted, however, and there might be some jolly nursery game like general post or charades.

At around midnight, it was customary for the women to retire, but this did not signal the completion of Alix's duties. She invariably visited all their rooms to make sure that they were comfortable and lacking for nothing. Some items of gossip might be exchanged, but, as far as the hostess was concerned, never of a malicious nature. Alix would give the fire a last poke so that the flames might lull her guest to sleep, and pass on to the next room. 'The Princess might surprise you by coming to your room "to see if you had everything you wanted", but in reality to give a few words of advice, or to offer you sympathy if she thought you needed any,' wrote one guest.

It was as well that Alix enjoyed the packed social life of Sandringham. Bertie's biographer wrote that 'At Sandringham the Prince and Princess practised a continuous hospitality on a generous scale,' adding that 'the Prince's *bonhomie* as host and his cheerful interest in his Sandringham guests were well illustrated by his practice of inviting them on leaving to subject themselves to the test of a weighing machine, the records of which he kept himself'.

Edward Montagu, a near neighbour and contemporary, noted in his diary that he went to Sandringham one 5th of November and 'the guests were Prince Eddy, the Duke and Duchess of Edinburgh, the Landgrave of Hesse, Vicomte and Vicomtesse de Grefuhle, Comte de St Priest, Baron von Holhausen, Captain von Strahl, C. Vivian, C. E. Sykes, Oscar Dickson, Lady Emily Kingscote, Francis and Miss Knollys, and A. Ellis in waiting'.

There was, typically, a shoot almost every weekday: 'Tuesday and Thursday, partridge-driving; Wednesday, Commodore and Dersingham Woods; Friday, Woodcock Wood. Friday night that year was the Prince's birthday, and he received innumerable presents from all sorts and kinds of people, and there was a ball, which lasted until 4 a.m.'

Signifying Bertie's liberated Court and his open mind on

all matters of religion, race and class, some of the leading Jews in the community became close friends and were often invited to Sandringham with their wives. The Queen strongly disapproved, of course, and fellow guests were at first puzzled. Certainly no Court in England within living memory had accepted Jews within the innermost circle. The Irish Bishop Magee, also described as an orator and wit, recalled a visit in December 1873:

I arrived just as they were all at tea in the entrance hall, and had to walk in all seedy and dishevelled from my day's journey and sit down by the Princess of Wales. I find the company pleasant and civil, but we are a curious mixture. Two Jews, Sir Anthony de Rothschild and his daughter [Constance]; . . . an Italian Duchess who is an Englishwoman, and her daughter, brought up a Roman Catholic and now turning Protestant; a set of young Lords and a bishop.

Frequent and equally welcome guests at Sandringham, whose visits with their wives were looked forward to by Alix, were the political protagonists Benjamin Disraeli (the 'ex-Jew') and William Gladstone, GOM ('Grand Old Man') and Liberal leader. Alix held Catherine Gladstone in special affection and liked the way she democratically 'wanted no names or stars for her William'. '*You* don't want your William to be called anything else but Mr Gladstone,' she was once heard to say. '*You* don't care about names and titles and orders. When I think how people trouble and struggle about these things, and what dreadful persons get them, I cannot understand it at all. You are too proud of your William to want him to be anything else or to wear stars.' Once at least she extended her late-night hospitality by helping Catherine Gladstone into bed and then tucking her up.

Demonstrating her inconsistency and anxiety to please all her guests, Alix at dinner one night pointed at Disraeli's chest and remarked on the lack of decorations. 'It is a shame,' she commiserated. 'Here, I will bestow one upon you,' and she pinned the dinner menu to his starched shirt. At another dinner, when Disraeli was attempting unsuccessfully to cut a particularly hard roll and instead cut his finger, Alix immediately felt for her handkerchief and tied it round the wound.

Most people agreed that the social life at Sandringham was novel, and even surprising. No doubt some people were put out by the behaviour of their host and hostess and found it difficult to adjust to some of the arrangements, like all clocks being set permanently half an hour fast to encourage punctuality, and the extraordinary number, and freedom, of Alix's dogs. But no one was ever *bored* and the cheerfulness of the place which affected every guest acted as a tonic for many. 'It is very jolly here indeed,' wrote one guest, 'very unstiff and only a certain amount of etiquette.' It was also a great honour to be invited in the first place; it was, after all, a long time since a Prince and Princess of Wales had led Society, and with such unprecedented style and zeal. Nor did anyone complain about the Wales's table.

At a time of uninhibited interest in rich food, Bertie from childhood had been unrestrained in his appetite. His parents had once expressed concern about how much he ate and observed the first evidence of stoutness well before he was twenty. There was not much the Queen could do about his over-eating when he was a grown, married man, but whenever she saw his doctor she expressed her concern and of his eating told him that she had 'never seen anything like it'. At the opera, which he came to adore, he would be preceded by a chef and six footmen borne down with the weight of hampers of food and gold plate for the ten-course dinner that would be served during the hour-long interval in the dining-room at the back of the royal box.

At Sandringham, as at Marlborough House, Bertie would start the day with a glass of milk in bed, a prosaic overture to a large breakfast and a day of always sumptuous food. Meanwhile, breakfast for his guests would be equally generous, taken either in their rooms or at tables downstairs set for two, four, six or eight persons. Their host made his appearance, dressed in thick tweed and heavy boots for the day's shooting, at 10.30 a.m., and without wasting any time, they would all be off with their guns. An hour and a half later, with the chill Norfolk air sharpening his appetite, there would be a break for hot turtle soup, which would keep him and his guests going until luncheon at 2.30 p.m. precisely.

This meal, held in a large marquee with straw on the ground to keep the feet dry, was always hot: a portable stove producing a fine range of cooked dishes was augmented by more food in fireproof china boxes. It was served by powdered footmen, just as if they were in the grand dining-room. These marquee luncheons posed the problem of divided enthusiasms, for a renewal of the shooting, Bertie's greatest sport, and the consumption of food, his greatest vice. It was resolved by consuming a great deal of hot food in an astonishingly short time. No guest came near to eating half of what their host put down before he was on his feet and issuing instructions about the next covert.

Even in the most distant woods or moors sustenance was usually close at hand. Bertie always found shooting thirsty work and was followed by a boy carrying a basket of champagne bottles covered in ice. When he wanted a draught he would call out, 'Where's the Boy?'*

'The sportsmen generally returned to the house in time for tea,' several of his close friends recorded. 'A delightful meal. It was served in the hall, at one big round table if the party was small, or at several tables if necessary. Scotch scones, little fancy rolls, hot cakes and every sort of sweet cake' were served, along with Bertie's favourite Scotch shortcake. Other favourites of his were *petits fours* and preserved ginger, and he would also consume several poached eggs.

The dinner which guests faced at Sandringham was never of fewer than ten courses, and more often twelve, beginning with oysters. The host would have several dozen, initiating the practice of swallowing them whole accompanied by heavily buttered brown bread. The menu that followed also reflected Bertie's particular fancies, which included great

---

* The fashion soon spread of calling to waiters, 'Bring me a bottle of the Boy.'

He will say that port and sherry his nice palate always cloy;
He'll nothing drink but 'B and S' [brandy and soda] and big magnums of 'the Boy'.

Punch, 1882

sides of Sandringham-hung beef, though he preferred lamb, sizzling legs of which were always on the table. But it was for the richer and more elaborate dishes that he showed the greatest relish. It was not enough for the game to be cooked in an oleaginous sauce; it had to be stuffed with truffles, too. His sole was poached in Chablis, then garnished with more oysters and prawns; his quails were packed with foie gras and garnished with oysters, truffles, mushrooms, prawns, tomatoes and croquettes; his boned snipe was filled with foie gras and forcemeat, grilled in a pig's caul and served with truffles and Madeira sauce. His favourite drink was champagne always preceded by a glass of sherry, though a good vintage claret, from Lafitte or Margaux, was always available. The port was 1811 Comet, 'with a bouquet of violets', and the dinner was capped by a glass of *fin*.

For a birthday dinner, which was not in any way more lavish than usual, the menu was turtle, oxtail or hare soup; *relevés* were filleted soles, fried trout, salmon cutlets, Norfolk perch or East Coast oysters. For *entrées*, veal cutlets, stewed rabbits, stewed lambs' kidneys with fried Norfolk ham and mushrooms were served, which were merely the preliminaries to poultry, roast and game, followed by a multitude of sweets and cheese.

No photograph of a table set for dinner seems to have survived, but we are told that all the glass, china, cutlery and silver were ornamented with the three feathers of the Prince of Wales. The fancy shapes of the table napkins 'so dear to the *restaurateur* and the suburban hostess' were considered rather common, and at Sandringham the linen was simply folded flat. Even in the depths of winter there would be an abundance of hothouse cut flowers at both ends of the table and a magnificent centre-piece. One visitor described the table as 'beautifully decorated with autumn-coloured grape leaves. [Alix] likes high decorations, so they went half-way up to the ceiling in great arches, with bunches of grapes hanging down.'

It says a lot about Alix's sociability that her love for the country, for riding and hunting, for having her dogs about her, in no way compromised her love for London, for London's social life and above all for Marlborough House. When Alix first met Disraeli, in the first year of her married life, she told him that she was 'delighted with our London residence' and that 'when they awoke in the morning they looked out into the garden and listened to the birds singing'. Thirty-eight years later, when she became Queen, she moved to Buckingham Palace with great sadness and reluctance.

Alix loved the spacious garden at Marlborough House with its high brick wall ensuring complete privacy, almost isolation, although the clatter of hooves in the Mall and Pall Mall at the front rarely ceased. There would be at least one and sometimes two garden parties a year, and the garden, it was said, could accommodate the whole of London Society. The same could be said of the vast ballroom. Alix's own apartment of five rooms was very much like that at Sandringham, cluttered, comfortable, cosy, swarming with dogs and a great cockatoo, which frightened some guests.

Visitors were admitted to the entrance hall by a Scots gillie in full Highland dress, who passed them on to two scarlet-coated and powdered footmen, while a hall porter in a short red coat with a band of leather across his shoulders took hats and coats. A page in a dark blue coat and black trousers then escorted them to an ante-room on the first floor next to a drawing-room.

On the way up they would pass a door which led to Bertie's original smoking-room. On hearing that the Queen was due to arrive for her first inspection of Marlborough House, Bertie's friend, the alert-minded Lord Charles Beresford, arranged at the last moment for a sign to be hung on the smoking-room door: 'Lavatory: Under Repair'.

The ante-room, like so many of the rooms in Marlborough House, was panelled in walnut and hung with swords and guns, and the door to Bertie's sitting-room was concealed. He would rise from his big walnut desk, which was invariably covered in papers in no sort of order, and step forward to greet his guest, smiling and with hand outstretched. He exuded benign hospitality, and the visitor would gain the impression that this was the culminating moment of his day.

The only other piece of furniture was a large oak table covered with newspapers like the *Pall Mall Gazette* and *Westminster Gazette* and magazines, *Punch* and the *Illustrated London News* among them, and a great number of documents and other papers. A large blue leather sofa and a number of deep armchairs added to the welcoming element, and several of Bertie's dogs (which were as loved but less numerous than Alix's) attested to the comfort of the sitting-room by lying in these armchairs, acknowledging the visitor with no more than a glance.

Besides numerous paintings of Scottish scenery, naval and military engagements and notable figures of the past hung on the walnut panelling, there was a broad shelf which ran round three sides of the room. Not a single book sat upon it, by contrast with Bertie's smoking-room, which displayed many hundred, all leather-spined and dummies. Instead, there were numerous ornaments, framed photographs of members of his family, his mother and father largest, bronzes and china figures. The large oriental carpet, dominantly blue, matched the curtains of the three tall windows overlooking Pall Mall.

As Sandringham was dwarfed by the aristocracy's great houses, so were there many grander London residences than Marlborough House, yet it was indisputably the dominant social venue in the capital. Several times a week the carriages of the great would roll up, past St James's Palace next door or from Piccadilly and Charing Cross to the east. Formal dinners called for much generalship, and there was nothing that Bertie enjoyed more than dealing with the organisation. The quality and variety of the food and wine was the first consideration, but next was the quality and above all the speed of the waiting. No one appreciated the food more than he did, yet no one wanted the meal to be over more speedily. As a swift eater, this was no bother, but few guests could keep up with him. The waiters were trained to remove plates as soon as the guests had finished and not to await the more usual guidance from the hostess. Bertie's idea of hell was to sit over an old plate while flanked by old bores.

In practice few bores got close to Bertie. His ideal guests

were pretty, clever women, and amusing, clever, well-informed and preferably very rich men. In spite of his chaotic desk, Bertie was particular about organisation, routine and good timekeeping. Dinner was scheduled to last one hour, and no longer, and the men smoked over glasses of brandy for a further fifteen minutes. Then it was whist with the ladies, tables having been set up during dinner; or it might be that the whole party of, say, thirty would go on to a ball.

The editor of *The Times*, John Delane, described a typical stag dinner at Marlborough House to his mother (10 March 1867):

At eight precisely I drove up to Marlborough House, and was received by four scarlet footmen. The hall is very handsome, and I was ushered through the other rooms to the library, where eight or ten people were already assembled. After nearly all had come, the Prince came in, we made a wide circle, and he walked round and shook hands with each. . . . There were twenty in all, and as nearly as I can recollect, the Duke of Cambridge and the Danish Minister, Lords de Grey, Stanley of Alderley, Clanwilliam, Clancarty, Sandys, General Peel, Christopher Sykes, General Knollys, Colonel Keppel, another equerry, Lowe, Quin, Lord E. Harvey, and some men I did not know.

Knollys sat at the top, Keppel at the bottom, the Prince in the middle, and I next to Keppel and Lord Sandys. The table was very prettily decorated with a great abundance of lilies-of-the-valley, the dinner not better than many others, the wine good and abundant, a great many servants and all very attentive.

There was plenty of talking both during dinner and afterwards, and I had my share, and rather more. . . . Indeed, the Prince had so many afterthoughts as I was going away that he actually shook hands with me four times.

These large dinner parties were relatively formal and respectable, though always lively. It was the 'small evenings' that first gave Marlborough House its reputation for raffishness and fast living, and brought about Bertie's head the full tidal flow of Queen Victoria's disapproval. These 'small evenings' would be limited to twelve guests, sometimes fewer, and they would be confined to Bertie and Alix's wilder and younger friends. Just as much care and attention was given to the menu as for the formal dinner parties, but there was no whist afterwards. Instead, there would be parlour games, which sometimes got out of hand, with the casting of missiles and squirting of soda syphons. Tray tobogganing down the stairs was popular. Practical jokes were a special favourite of Bertie and Alix, and these ranged from replacing whipped cream with soapsuds, and a red burgundy with medicine of the same shade, to the more violent taking away of a chair as the victim sat down. 'Their Royal Highnesses like nothing so much as a romp; in more loyal language, they have a great deal of *entrain*,' wrote one guest. 'We had roaring fun,' Charles Carrington wrote in his journal of another occasion, 'and ended by carrying the Prince of Wales in triumph round the house in my Grandmother's sedan chair; one of the old poles snapped in two, and he had a tremendous spill.'

Bertie was quite unable to face an evening without some fun. If there was a gap in his engagement book he looked at it with a sinking heart. A few friends would be summoned to Marlborough House, regardless of their convenience, or a 'baccy' would be set up. Baccarat was prohibited by law because it had been the ruin of so many gamblers, but was played privately and widely among the privileged and rich. Bertie adored it, but it was to get him into terrible trouble.

Alix did not, of course, engage in baccarat, which took place in the smoking-room with everyone smoking enormous cigars. But, when not too pregnant (and sometimes even then), she threw herself into these small dinner parties with great zest and complete informality.

Bertie and Alix had been married only a year or two before word spread through Society, and then to the newspapers and through them to the lower social echelons, of the 'carryings-on' at Marlborough House. Especially in these peaceful days following the Crimea War (1854–6), gossip about the rich and famous was rife. When it touched on the royal family, it was passed on all the faster and it benefited from the telling.

The Queen remained in a more or less constant state of anxiety and exasperation about Bertie and Alix's life-style. When she told Bertie, as she did frequently, that he was 'going about too much', he replied sharply but reasonably,

'What can I do if you go about so little?' 'Going about' in Society, he managed to convince himself without too much difficulty, was a duty because his mother did not even 'go about' in public.

Queen Victoria continued to find the Wales's whole way of life 'unsatisfactory'. Thankfully, Bertie's seedier activities were kept from her. Increasingly, he would go out late at night, using public cabs, to 'shady venues of disrepute' like Evans's Music Hall in Covent Garden where he watched the dancing from a screened private box; and, worse still, to the notorious Cremorne Gardens in Vauxhall, which the local Baptist minister described as 'the nursery of every kind of vice'. A small inner group of cronies together or severally accompanied Bertie on these jaunts. The closest was Charles Carrington, with whom Bertie enjoyed a life-long friendship and with whom he shared a weakness for gambling on horses and pornographic books, which they frequently exchanged.

'As you will probably not be back in time on Monday', Bertie wrote to Carrington on 27 April 1866, 'to settle my Newmarket account at Tattersalls, do you mind writing or telegraphing to some friend to do so for me in *your* name? Our account is I win £300 on Vauban – lose £100 on Plaudit.'

'I think you still have in your possession the 3rd Vol: of "Les Amours de N." and "La Femme de Caesar",' Bertie reminded his friend on 12 July 1865. 'If you have will you kindly send them here tomorrow early.' Then again, in November 1867: 'I find that the 4th volume of "Les Amours de Napoleon" has not yet come out so I send you another French book, which is said to be amusing.'

When Carrington was abroad, Bertie warned him facetiously to behave himself. 'I trust you are enjoying yourself in Paris,' he wrote on 27 April 1866, 'and not committing *too* many atrocities etc. . . .'; and 'I hope you won't go to Baden, as you will only get into scrapes' (19 August 1866).

Their correspondence was conducted in tones of arch masculinity. Earlier, before Bertie's marriage and after he had been persuaded to give up Nellie Clifton, he wrote to Carrington, her next paramour: 'I also trust that you have cut the acquaintance of our friend *N*. . . .' And later Bertie advised his friend: 'You won't I am sure forget those few hints I gave you respecting *certain* matters, and I have not forgotten those you gave me at the same time.'

And again, in reply to what seems to have been an account of a lurid episode in which Carrington participated, Bertie took him to task: 'I am sorry to hear that you went to such a disreputable place as the one you mention in your letter as I hoped that you were conducting yourself better, but I fear that is not the case as I also heard some gossip about you when I was last in Town.'

For Bertie's amusement, Carrington laid on what were described as 'wild parties' at his house, inviting a number of chorus girls from Evans's Music Hall. On another occasion, 'my brother William and I invited the Prince of Wales to supper at 8, Whitehall,' Carrington recorded in his journal; 'we got the "Great" Vance: "Jolly" Nash: and Arthur Lloyd from the Music Halls to sing. We had roaring fun. . . .' *The Times*, in an article, denounced the iniquity of royal patronage being given to such people as Music Hall 'Artistes'.

In the late 1860s 'the Marlborough House set' were acquiring notoriety throughout the country and among all classes. They were also referred to as 'the Marlborough banditti'. Bertie often referred lightheartedly to his 'wicked boys'. 'Now goodbye, my dear Charlie,' he wrote to the 'wickedest' of them, 'remember me to those wicked boys Blandford and Oliver [Montagu].'

More innocent, if more dangerous, were the fire outings, which became increasingly frequent in spite of Bertie's corpulence in middle age. His zest for action spiced with danger was seen most vividly on the fire-engine. He loved fires, the bigger the better. His taste for helping to put them out was acquired from his friend the Duke of Sutherland. George Sutherland, who owned the biggest estate in the United Kingdom, 1,358,000 acres, was also one of the richest men, which encouraged him to enjoy his esoteric tastes. He loved driving locomotives and contributed most of the cost of building the Highland Railway for the benefit of Scotland and to indulge himself on the footplate whenever he wished. For all his life fires fascinated him and when he was at Stafford House, his giant home in London, he had an arrangement with Captain Eyre Shaw, head of the Chandos Street Fire Brigade, to be informed of any interestingly large fire.

When he had made a convert of Bertie, similar urgent news was sent to Marlborough House. No matter what social engagement was in progress, Duke and Prince, and sometimes other friends like 'Charlie' Carrington, would then race to Chandos Street, don firemen's uniform and climb aboard the next fire-engine. All this was kept from the public as far as possible, partly because they were often in danger. Indeed, when the Alhambra Music Hall caught fire in 1882, George Sutherland and Bertie were both on the roof with hoses when part of it fell in, killing two firemen.

11

Idle Hands

'Queen Victoria keeps reigning and will not let the son shine.'
Contemporary quip

Bertie and Alix's first Christmas together was a bitterly cold one. They had dutifully come to stay at Windsor, in Frogmore House, for the second anniversary of Albert's death, quite as appalling an occasion as the first anniversary.* It remained equally cold in the new year of 1864. All lakes and many rivers were frozen over, and there was skating throughout the land. The skating at Frogmore Lake was very lively and there was ice-hockey, too. Alix longed to join in and would have done if Old Mac had not firmly forbidden her from doing so. For Alix was 'seven months gone', and Lady Macclesfield knew all about babies, having had thirteen with three more to come.

On 8 January it was sunny and crisp, a perfect winter's day. A bonfire burned close to the water's edge, a band played all afternoon and there was hard-contested ice-hockey. Alix was pushed about the ice in a sledge chair, and Bertie skated alongside, the crowds cheering the fine-looking couple. The only fly in the ointment for Alix was a feeling of

---

* They carried out this mournful obligation for thirty-seven years, every year of the Queen's remaining life.

discomfort which came and went intermittently. At dusk as she and Lady Macclesfield returned to the house, Alix told her about the pains and their nature. Her Lady of the Bedchamber diagnosed the situation from her own extensive experience and realised that the baby due in March was liable to be born at any time that evening.

Nothing was ready for this occasion. No nurse was on hand, let alone a doctor. Lady Macclesfield sent urgently for the Windsor doctor and, with only Bertie to help, supervised the labour while Bertie gave Alix what comfort and encouragement he could. He was very calm and reassuring. Lady Macclesfield, with only a bowl of hot water and her own flannel petticoat, took the part of midwife with complete aplomb, while Alix kept saying, 'As long as I see your face I am happy.' A tiny male child was born at 9 p.m., weighing only 3¼ pounds.

The local doctor was not as late as the six royal doctors, very busybodyish all of them, but with nothing much to do, which made Alix laugh loud and long. By useful chance, Lord Granville happened to be in the house at the time and he acted as witness to the birth, which was necessary for the nation's future sovereign. It must be a 'n-ice' child declared one newspaper because it was born three hours after the mother had watched an ice-hockey match.

The Queen was pleased to hear of the birth and thought it touching that it had occurred so close to Albert's tomb. But she expressed disapproval at the baby's premature birth, forgetting that her own first child – Vicky – had been equally before her time. She then engaged in the first of many disputes about her grandchildren's names, which she regarded as her prerogative. She fixed on Albert Victor, after the child's paternal grandparents, and divulged this to six-year-old Beatrice, who passed on the news to Lady Macclesfield. 'I felt rather annoyed,' Bertie complained to his mother. A compromise was reached with Albert Victor Christian Edward. In the family, except by the Queen, he was called Eddy for all his life. He shrieked in seeming protest through his christening. 'None of you did,' the Queen commented with a touch of smugness.

Alix recovered from her confinement with what the Queen considered to be indecent haste, and was soon riding about Windsor Great Park and Hyde Park in London, her larger dogs following and gambolling around. Not even the current wave of mother-in-law disapproval dampened her spirits. When alone together the love the Queen felt for Alix seemed unconfined and there was much mutual flattery and kissing. But sometimes on the same day she would write letters to King Leopold or Vicky, or one of her other intimates, complaining about Alix's life-style and the fact that she was gadding about so soon after the birth of her son – which might not have been so premature if she had conducted her life more soberly, she claimed.

'Alix is by no means what she ought to be,' the Queen complained to Vicky. 'I cannot tell you what I have suffered. . . . It will be long, if ever, before she regains my confidence.' The point at issue this time was the proposed marriage of Princess Helena, the Queen's third daughter. Queen Victoria had hoped to keep her at home as a companion for life, but the young woman wanted none of that. She wanted a husband and babies. So, reluctantly, the Queen agreed and chose a German prince from a family actively backing the seizure of Schleswig-Holstein from Denmark. Alix was outraged, and so was Bertie on her behalf. The breach was healed, but the Queen soon found another quarrel to pick with her or Bertie, or both, or with Affie who visited Marlborough House too often for her liking. For Queen Victoria, a day without a quarrel and at least one angry letter was like a day without food or drink for most people.

Alix was delighted that her mother-in-law had not been present at the birth of her son. The Queen was insistent that she should be at the side of her daughters, and later her grand-daughters, when they were in labour, but Alix succeeded in frustrating her when the time came for her second child to be born by telling the Queen a later expected date, so that she was hours away at Osborne when Alix went into labour at Marlborough House. The baby was born on 3 June 1865, just eighteen months after Eddy. 'Mama and everybody fancied it should only be in July,' Affie wrote to his brother, 'but you told me to expect it to happen when it did happen. I am sure you said it was later on purpose.' Affie was right, and the Queen was very cross. 'It seems that *it is not to be* that I am to be present at the birth of your children,' she wrote to Alix, 'which I am very sorry for.' Alix later gave birth to three girls, Louise on 20 February 1867, Victoria on 6 July 1868 and Maud on 26 November 1869, contriving on each occasion to frustrate the Queen's wishes to be at her side.

There was another dispute about this second boy's name. Bertie and Alix wanted George, after the Duke of Cambridge. The Queen thought that too modern: 'George only came over with the Hanoverian family.' The mother and father would not budge, but had to agree to include, once again, the name Albert, so it was George Frederick Ernest Albert – 'Georgie'.

The upbringing of these children was very different from what Bertie himself had suffered. He and Alix both loved them and spoilt them without restraint, to the constant dismay of the Queen. No effort was too great to please them and make them happy. In the royal archives a note from Bertie to Lord Granville survives, apologising for rushing off when the Foreign Secretary was delivering a speech in the House of Lords. It was Louise's sixth birthday and he had promised to take her to the circus at 7.15. 'It is now 6.30. I have not a moment left.'

There is a typical glimpse of these children as they grew up by Princess Mary Adelaide, the Duchess of Teck:

I was delighted with the Prince of Wales's family; the eldest boy is most like his mother, but has not that melancholy look his photographs give him, on the contrary he is very animated. Prince George* is brimming over with fun. The little girls are pretty fair-haired children and take after their father; they were most simply dressed. All were in high spirits and seemed very fond of their nurses, who sat down to tea with them without ceremony. They were easily amused and I never saw such a battered set of toys, and such rickety old dolls. The two boys were very happy over some boats the footmen had made for them.

---

* He was to marry her daughter May in 1893.

In Denmark the birth of every one of Alix's babies was treated as a national celebration, and Alix's mother, who was so maligned by Queen Victoria (and certainly did not wish to be present at the confinements), wrote excited letters of congratulation:

Well, my dear children, you are the most extraordinary pair I know, and I feel so happy as if I were a new-born baby myself. Thank God. His blessing *is* on you, may you never forget how merciful and gracious Our Lord is to you. . . . [And addressing Bertie] How proud you must be, two boys, don't you grow more attached to Alix at every present thus brought to you in pain and anguish?

Queen Louise then asked Bertie what he thought his mother would think about this second 'premature' birth: 'Will she not say it is all weakness in Alix?' she asked, by now having heard of the worsening relations between her daughter and Queen Victoria. As for herself, she thought premature births might be rather a good thing. 'If the children are healthy,' she continued in her broken but confident English, 'they can have any other secret why they want daylight before their time. I only hope it is a good sign for their character to be *before* the time in any good impulse of their life and for every good and noble deed.'

Bertie knew he had to do something about these frequent and exhausting rifts, which so upset his wife. Knowing the matchmaking and peacemaking abilities of his elder sister, he wrote to Vicky in Berlin, citing some of the accusations their mother was making about Alix, like: 'Alix and I never will or can be intimate; she shows me no confidence whatsoever especially about the children.' Alix had 'grown a little grand', claimed the Queen, 'and naughty and frivolous' and (of all things) lacked 'softness and warmth'.

Vicky responded promptly and effectively – she nearly always did. On 9 November 1865 she wrote to her mother at Windsor suggesting that she should invite Alix to come to stay and 'drive or walk *alone* with you'. The Queen took this advice within four days, which says much for the speed of the diplomatic bag by which all letters between them were transmitted. Even swifter was Queen Victoria's transformation from gloomy carping to cheer and delight in her daughter-in-law. On 14 November Vicky was told:

Dear Alix arrived here yesterday with the tiny little boys. She is dear and good and gentle but looking very thin and pale. I was sometime alone with her yesterday and shall take her out alone this afternoon. [And later] I have taken a nice walk and drive with dear Alix and nothing could be nicer or dearer than she is. I never saw a purer mind – it is quite charming to see her and hear her. She looks delicate. I do love her dearly.

These mercurial reflections of Queen Victoria's moods could be coped with, at some cost to her family, who had mostly inherited a fortitude from some ancestor whose genes had missed out the Queen. Her first four children in particular, Vicky, Bertie, Alice and Affie, each possessed more steady common sense (not cleverness) than their mother.

But there was one subject of dispute that was beyond the powers of Vicky to settle in her sensible way. Prussian–Danish antagonism had always been a dark shadow over Bertie and Alix's marriage. Bismarck's rise to power in Prussia, and all the belligerence and nationalistic paranoia that followed, brought Bertie and Alix into the political arena.

In 1863, eight months after Bertie and Alix's wedding, the disreputable King Frederick VII of Denmark died and Alix's father came to the Danish throne as King Christian IX. Within a few months there was an all-out military assault by Prussia, with Austrian support, on the contested provinces of Schleswig-Holstein. Alix was beside herself with grief and anxiety for her beloved homeland and family. She expressed herself forcibly on Britain's refusal to intervene, and Bertie stood loyally beside her. He did more than that. He attended the House of Lords, listened in outrage to the Government's declaration of neutrality, and expressed himself strongly to Lord Spencer, his Groom of the Stole: 'The dreadful war in Denmark causes both the Princess and myself great anxiety, and the conduct of the Prussians and the Austrians is really scandalous.'

A great many citizens agreed with this sentiment. Ten

years earlier, with Prince Albert alive and active, there had been negligible anti-Prussian feeling in Britain. His death and the withdrawal by Queen Victoria from public life, followed by the sparkling entry of the Princess of Wales and her dashing Prince, whose appearance anywhere made everyone feel better, changed all that. Alix's homeland, to which she was so loyal and loving, took on a heroic guise in the public mind, while Prussia and Austria became joint bullies. The dangerous prematurity of Alix's baby was brought about, the public believed, by her concern over her homeland.

The Queen thought otherwise. Victoria's attachment to Prussia was as powerful as her loyalty to the memory of her dead husband, and was reinforced by Vicky's marriage to the Crown Prince. Nothing would ever crack it. The Government, in the form of Palmerston and Lord John Russell, the Foreign Secretary, procrastinated and, it became clear, was not going to support the Danes actively.

Alix cried in her sleep with grief. Bertie pressed for sending the fleet into the Baltic: that would send the Prussians packing and settle the matter. After attending the House of Lords, he wrote to his childhood mentor, Mrs Bruce: 'This horrible war will be a stain for ever on Prussian history . . . and I think it is *very* wrong of our government not to have interfered before now.' Neither Bertie nor Alix made any attempt to restrain themselves in public. At a reception Alix noticed that the Prussian Ambassador, Count Bernstorff, did not raise his glass in a toast to the King of Denmark, and she ostentatiously cut him dead. Bertie loathed Bernstorff anyway (most people did) and made no attempt to conceal this now, so that the Count felt obliged to register a formal diplomatic protest.

On the other hand, so passionate were the Queen's views on Prussia that she even went so far as to ally herself with Bismarck in his support of Russia when it put down the Polish uprising with sickening brutality. As for her own people, she was horrified at their hostility to the land of her lamented husband. 'I am grieved and distressed to say that the feeling against Prussia has become *most violent* in England, and quite ungovernable.' She also, as always, exposed her personal feelings without restraint to her eldest daughter:

What I suffer now, alone without adored Papa, without help or support, or love and protection, living in dread of some false move which may aggravate affairs, words cannot say. My rest disturbed, torn to pieces with anxiety and sorrow, and overwhelmed by the one great abiding sorrow. And then, our worst fears about B's marriage realised – so that there is division in the family!! Oh! it is too much for human mortal to bear, and I hope it may all soon be over for me!

Oh! if Bertie's wife was only a good German and not a Dane!

But Alix *was* a Dane, a passionately patriotic Dane, who was by her nature incapable of concealing her grief at her country's sufferings and her hatred of the Prussians.

When the war ended in inevitable German triumph in July 1864, Alix determined to go to Denmark to see her family and to make clear – if that was necessary – to the people where her sympathies lay. Above all, she wanted to introduce little Eddy to her parents, and to show Copenhagen to Bertie for the first time.

Initially the Queen forbade the visit, fearing a worsening of relations with Prussia, but in the end gave way reluctantly and with numerous conditions, including the obligation to visit Prussia to demonstrate that Bertie was 'not only the son-in-law of the King of Denmark, but the Child of his Parents', as she defined it.

They sailed with a full retinue in HMY *Osborne* and were received rapturously at Elsinore. The Danish people had felt let down by England, but they also knew how strong and public Bertie and Alix's feelings had been. Alix's pleasure to be among her own people was evident for all to see, and she was cheered whenever she appeared publicly, holding up her baby boy. The family went on picnics, played frolicsome games, and behaved just as if Alix was the laughing, excitable little girl of ten years before – and as if there had been no war which had lost Denmark more than half its territory.

For Bertie, after the first excitement of arrival and the sharing of Alix's delight at being back and showing him the scenes of her childhood, the visit soon became a crashing bore. Alix's family were kind and delightful, but they were also very unworldly and simple in their taste for plain food – invariably jelly for pudding. Bertie pined for his rich table and rare champagne, for conversation with the light, irreverent touch, for the gossip and current anecdotes (to say nothing of the evening outings) of his London cronies. The remainder of the journey was tiresome, in one way or another. They went to Stockholm and stayed in the royal palace, which was a great deal more fun than Copenhagen, and they actually went on an elk hunt.

The Queen had specifically instructed that they must travel incognito and stay in hotels, but the best hotels were flea-pits. 'I have not the intention of letting Alix be uncomfortably lodged if I can help it,' Bertie replied sharply. 'Besides the King was immensely gratified by our visit, and what would have been the good of not going to the Palace? . . . If I am not allowed to use my own discretion we had better give up travelling altogether.'

Beside herself with fury at this cheeky response from her errant son, the Queen now reminded Bertie and Alix that she had required the baby to be sent to her at Balmoral on leaving Copenhagen and they had deliberately defied her. Bertie told his mother that Alix would miss 'her little treasure' too much to bear – something which his ultra-maternal mother might perhaps have understood. The Queen had already opposed the visit to Paris after Germany, but had given way on condition that they observed 'a real incognito' and stayed only in a hotel, 'the style of going on there being quite unfit for a young and reputable Prince and Princess'. Now she ordered peremptorily that they must not go to Paris at all, but to make Belgium and Uncle Leopold their last destination on the Continent. 'I have the backing of every member of the Cabinet in my demand,' the Queen further declared, 'except Lord Palmerston.' This was quite untrue. The Foreign Secretary, too, the minister most concerned, suggested that the Queen had been hasty and imprudent.

Meanwhile, the obligatory German visit proved at first boring and worrying to the last degree. At Cologne, Vicky was embarrassed about Prussia having killed so many of her sister-in-law's kinsfolk and occupied so much of Denmark. The situation was not helped by Fritz (of whom Bertie had previously been rather fond) and his ADC appearing always in uniform for social occasions. 'It was not pleasant,' Bertie wrote home to Lord Spencer, '. . . flaunting before our eyes a most objectionable medal ribbon which he received for his *deeds* of *valour*??? against the unhappy Danes.' (In fact, Fritz had been kept out of the serious fighting.)

Bertie's favourite sister Alice had recently married Prince Louis of Hesse and lived in the ducal palace at Darmstadt. This nice couple had disapproved of Prussia's attack and were warmly welcoming. So was old King Leopold. Bertie's uncle was very frail but, as always, full of wisdom and kindness. It was their last meeting, for the King died on 10 December 1865.

The Wales party arrived home on 6 November 1864, Alix as welcomed among her friends as was Bertie by 'the Marlborough banditti'. Eddy had been obediently brought home before them. Alix, pregnant with her second child, greeted the little boy passionately and could scarcely bear to be separated from him.

In their absence, the Queen had written to Vicky about both Bertie and Alix, Bertie becoming 'quite unmanageable' and in the hands of 'that most mischievous Queen of Denmark'; while Alix, 'good as she is, is not worth the price we have to pay for her in having such a family connexion. I shall not let them readily go [to Denmark] again.'

Obediently but with extreme reluctance and anxiety about their reception, Bertie and Alix went down to Osborne. But, once again, the Queen's attitude to the pair altered with near frantic (but none the less welcome) unpredictability. The visit was 'most satisfactory' and Alix was 'a dear, excellent, right-minded soul, whom one must dearly love and respect. I often think her lot is no easy one, but she is very fond of Bertie, though not blind.' As for Bertie himself, he had 'a loving affectionate heart, and never could bear to be long in disagreement with his family'. And later, 'He was affectionate and simple and unassuming as ever. I am sure no Heir Apparent was ever so nice and unpretending as dear Bertie is.'

As for the Danes, the criticism of the Queen faded from sight and sound, and Victoria declared that she was going to make the King a Knight of the Garter – the highest of all honours.

The worst damage Queen Victoria did to Bertie and Alix was to refuse to give her heir anything to do. Long before their marriage, when Bertie was a little boy of six (on 12 December 1847, according to her journal), Victoria recorded that she and Albert had had a family chat about their first two children. Albert had said that Bertie 'ought to be accustomed early to work with and for us, to have great confidence shewn him, that he should early be initiated into the affairs of State. How true this is! [the Queen exclaimed] So wise and right; and the more confidence we shew him the better it will be for himself, for us, and for the country.'

No clearer statement of intention could have been made. So what had happened to bring about the same fluctuations in the Queen's judgment on this subject as on so many others? She did all she could to frustrate Bertie's early and eager desire to participate, however modestly, in state and monarchical affairs, and made certain that Albert agreed with her. Immediately after Albert's death she was in such a dizzy whirl of grief that she could hardly think of anything, and when she began to get a grip on her mind again she clamped down even more firmly on allowing Bertie to take any role at all, excluding him from all royal responsibilities.

Ten years later, on 8 July 1871, Victoria wrote frankly:

After '61 I could hardly bear the thought of anyone helping me, or standing where my dearest had always stood; but, as years go on, I strongly feel that to lift up my son and heir and keep him in his place, near me, is really what is right.

But the failure to implement this resolution was as strong as before. On the very day of his wedding the Queen had instructed Lord Granville that *upon no account* should her son 'be put at the head of any of those Societies or Commissions, or preside at any of those scientific proceedings in which his beloved Father took so prominent a part'. Could there have been a clearer sign of the Queen's intention to exclude Bertie from any activity or responsibility that might encroach upon anything that was related to beloved Albert's work? Better to have him idle than as a shadow of her dead husband. Jealousy of the memory of Albert is equally revealed in an instruction on 9 July 1864 to the Home Secretary:

Her Majesty is very much opposed to the system of putting the Prince of Wales forward as the representative of the Sovereign. . . . Properly speaking, no one can represent the Sovereign but her, or her Consort. There are certain duties and forms which . . . as the Queen is unable to perform them, She can and does depute someone else to perform . . . but Her Majesty thinks it would be most undesirable to constitute the Heir to the Crown a general representative of Herself, and particularly to bring Him forward too frequently before the people. . . .

Every proposal put to her by her ministers and others to grant some useful occupation to the Prince of Wales was peremptorily slapped down. The Prime Minister, Gladstone, was one of the most persistent in putting forward plans for Bertie, and it was unfortunate that as a radical his relations with the Queen were so poor, although no one was more of a royalist. At one time Gladstone thought up the plan of making Bertie a successor to the Viceroy in Dublin, where, every winter, he would learn the art of constitutional sovereignty, while deputising for the Queen at Buckingham Palace in the summer.

This was a very novel notion and a very important one, requiring much foundation work. Gladstone worked at it for two years, building up a strong case and gathering many supporters. But as soon as it came to the official attention of the Queen, it had the same effect as opening a much delayed packet of perishable foodstuff. It was rejected out of hand, and she wrote at once to her Private Secretary, General Henry Ponsonby, that

tho' he may hardly like to believe it, that *she* has felt that Mr Gladstone wd have liked to *govern* HER as Bismarck governs the [German] Emperor . . . she always felt in his manner an overbearing obstinacy and imperiousness (without being actually wanting in respect as to form) wh she never experienced from *anyone* else & wh she found most disagreeable.

At about this same time (1872), Bertie himself pressed for a succession of attachments to the great Whitehall offices – Home Office, Foreign Office, the Treasury and so on – to 'learn the habits of business in general and the work of the Department in particular'. This, too, came to nothing. Worse, the Queen opposed any kind of direct communication between government departments and her son. 'And for close on thirty years she obstinately kept Prince Albert's golden key to the Foreign Office boxes out of hands which seemed to her both grasping and incapable.' At the height of the Schleswig-Holstein war, when both Alix and Bertie were in a fever of anxiety about the fate of Denmark, all Bertie was shown were précis of official Cabinet despatches compiled by Ponsonby for him, and long out of date. When Bertie asked if he could see the original despatches, the Queen told Lord Clarendon that her son must not see '*anything* of a very *confidential* nature'.

From time to time Queen Victoria attempted to justify her order that Bertie should receive no confidential papers by referring to his indiscretion. Certainly, Bertie was a notorious gossip and relished it as if it was his favourite Ayala champagne. These indiscretions which his mother cited were of a trivial and social nature, but because the Queen had never had any confidence in him, she assumed that if he learned of any state secrets, they would be prattled over the dinner tables of Belgravia as if they were tales of infidelities among his friends. The consequence was that the Queen

kept in her own hands every atom of the more solid functions of the Crown, and neither consulted the Prince of Wales on affairs of State or diplomatic relations with foreign countries, nor paid the smallest attention to his views. . . . To open a few docks and bazaars and lay a few foundation-stones was not employment for a mentally energetic man.

By the late 1860s, around five years after his marriage, a conflicting cycle had become established in Bertie's life. The more idle and thwarted he became, the greater grew his feeling of inadequacy and the need to fill his time. By nature he was much too extrovert and bonhomous to become involved in great causes, and in any case an activity that might bring him to wide public attention would not be sanctioned by the Queen. The high living and sometimes disreputable carryings-on were encouraged by his rich and equally idle contemporaries. For a man in his position, there were always those who felt flattered to introduce him to new diversions.

Prince Albert had strongly disapproved of horse-racing, but soon after his marriage Bertie succumbed to its attractions and became a devotee of the turf for the rest of his life. Because of his position, he received the best advice and enjoyed the services of the finest trainers in the land, while Lord Marcus Beresford, the younger brother of Lord Charles Beresford, one of Bertie's closest friends, became his adviser on all racing activities. Against the advice of Knollys, he joined the Jockey Club, and when at Newmarket stayed either at his own private quarters in the club, or with a local landowner. He attended all the chief race meetings and was always received rapturously by the crowd, who knew a real sporting gent when they saw one. His delight when his horses won was appreciated by all the racegoers present – 'Good old Teddy!' they would cry – and his horses were always heavily backed. The Queen, naturally, deplored this racegoing. Once she wrote begging him to attend only the first day of Ascot Races. But nothing was going to deprive Bertie of 'the glorious uncertainty of the turf', and he attended every day, mixing with the crowd, exuding what Sir Edward Grey once called his 'rare, if not unique power of combining bonhomie and dignity'.

Early in his racing career Bertie did bend to the Queen's wishes and raced anonymously, winning the Grand National in 1876 as 'Captain Machall'. But the following year he publicly revealed his colours, purple, gold braid and scarlet sleeves, and after a few meetings every racegoer in the land recognised them.

Rumours about Bertie's gambling began to spread with gossip about his straitened finances and requests for an increase in his allowance. The stakes at whist and baccarat were modest by the standards of many of the rich in the land, no more than a hundred or two hundred pounds winnings or losses, and not much more on horses, but resentful losers sometimes put it about that the Prince of Wales was obliging them to gamble for higher stakes than they wished.

This tarnished his image somewhat, however untruthful it might be, and greatly grieved the Queen. In 1874 it was said that the Prince of Wales had gambling debts of £600,000 and that the Prime Minister was about to ask Parliament to authorise the writing off of this sum. This was quite untrue, but there were older people who remembered with sinking heart the appalling gambling debts of the last Prince of Wales, George IV. The largest known single loss made by Bertie on one race was £600 on the Paris Grand Prix of 1894.

Unsurprisingly, Bertie's friends were from a wide circle and ranged from great landowners like the Dukes of Sutherland and Westminster, Devonshire and Marlborough, to great industrialists and racing figures, and, more surprisingly and to the Queen's distress, actors and Jewish bankers. Bertie loved the theatre and the opera, always welcomed invitations to dine with men and women of the theatre and became the Patron of the Garrick Club, where he frequently dined.

Among the inner circle of Bertie's friends, all of them 'members' of 'the Marlborough House set', were counted the Duke of Sutherland; the sailors Lord Charles Beresford and Prince Louis of Battenberg; Lord Aylesford; Christopher Sykes; Lord Randolph Churchill; Lord Blandford; Harry Stonor; Henry Hastings 'the wicked marquess'; Henry Chaplin (first Viscount) and Sir Frederick Johnstone, both keen sportsmen; Edward Montagu, who had joined him in Canada; and, closest of all, Charles Carrington.

Among his Jewish friends were, first, the Rothschild brothers he had first met at Cambridge, Nathaniel (later Lord) Rothschild and his brothers Alfred and Leopold, who were all strongly addicted to stag hunting – more addicted than Bertie, in fact. Then there were the Sassoons, 'the Rothschilds of the East'. Bertie first met Sir Albert Abdullah Sassoon in India, where he was lavishly entertained by him in Bombay. Sir Albert's half-brothers, Arthur and

Reuben, provided between them equally lavish entertainment in London and the country along with unbeatable shooting and expensive gifts.

Baron Maurice de Hirsch, whose riches were unassessable, became Bertie's unofficial financial 'consultant', to be superseded on his death by Sir Ernest Cassel, the closest Jewish friend. Only the Sassoons took part in the more raffish activities of Bertie's social life, the games of baccarat and whist (their gambling was of a rather different nature and on a somewhat larger scale); nor would they be found on late-night trips to Vauxhall with the Duchess of Manchester, Lady Filmer and one or two other ladies and an equal number of men.

These, then, were the sort of men with whom Bertie surrounded himself, all of them bright and amusing, 'heavy swells' to a man, tending towards the cynical view of life, but many of them engaged in public affairs of great responsibility, rich and patrician in their manner. Charles Carrington, while a steady companion and co-conspirator in Bertie's late-night life, also aroused his conscience about sub-human housing conditions in Britain's cities, and so led him into a notable reforming campaign. Bertie later rewarded him with the Garter.

Others among them – Blandford was one – succumbed to high living and decadent self-indulgence or lost their fortunes. Christopher Sykes, a rich snob, craved for the Prince of Wales's attention and received it at a price. Both in London and in the country Sykes, a superb and extravagant host, entertained Bertie on the most lavish scale, while at the same time acted as the butt of countless practical jokes. These ranged from the commonplace soda syphon in full face to a stab on the back of the hand with a cigar when instructed to watch the smoke emerging from Bertie's eyes. An open bottle of brandy stuffed down the back of his collar, as with all other humiliating 'jokes', called forth peals of laughter from the other guests and from Sykes the solemn and invariable 'As your Royal Highness pleases.'

At Sykes's Brantingham Thorpe there was every entertainment Bertie craved: superb shooting and hunting, and racing at Doncaster not far distant – with ample carriages laid on by courtesy of the host – including the Season's last classic, the St Leger Stakes. Over the years, sycophancy and wild extravagance brought Sykes to a state of near penury. When Bertie was forced to face the truth that he could no longer ask to be entertained for a long week-end in the country, or a dinner in London, he arranged to pay off some of Sykes's worst debts to keep him from the bankruptcy court.

Another close friend, an officer in the Household Cavalry, Charles Buller, was forced to resign his commission when he could no longer pay his mess bills; and Lord Hardwicke, fifth Earl and an army officer of distinction, was also ruined as a result of living, and entertaining, far above his means.

While Bertie's own finances were quite often unstable, and both he and Alix kept aloof from anything as tiresome as economies, the idea that any of his many hosts could not afford to entertain him royally never crossed his mind. To him the fact that they were all so unreservedly enthusiastic about having him to stay was quite enough evidence on that account.

Most of the big landowners were far richer than Bertie and could well afford to have him, Alix and their entourage to stay. A royal visit to Dunrobin, where the Duke of Sutherland's spectacular castle clung to the cliffs of eastern Scotland; or to Badminton with the Duke of Beaufort; or to Chatsworth, where the Duke of Devonshire entertained them; or Eaton Hall, the Duke of Westminster's enormous place; or Welbeck, where the Duke of Portland was host – all these old families, longer established by centuries than the upstart foreign Hanoverians, could absorb the cost of entertaining the Prince and Princess of Wales and their suite without bothering to mark the figures down in their household accounts. All the same, it was quite a business, and when a message arrived from Marlborough House, with the familiar embossed three feathers at the head, asking if it would be convenient for the Duke and Duchess to have the Prince and Princess of Wales as guests between . . . the machinery for doing so had to be put into gear.

It was just as well that the host and hostess were given plenty of notice, for once the dates were settled (and five days was the average stay) later correspondence revealed how many there would be in the party. These included valets, footmen, private secretaries, equerries for Bertie and ladies-in-waiting for the Princess – who had servants of their own – loaders for the Prince's guns and loaders for his gentlemen, police protection of about seven men, a hairdresser and two maids for Alix. There was an Arab boy to prepare the royal coffee, and many more, all to be accommodated. After that the details could be tackled!

These included the submission for approval of a list of proposed other guests for dinners, perhaps a ball, a shoot, a hunt and so on. The reception of the royal train at the local station entailed the provision of a suitable number of carriages not only for the people but also for the immense amount of luggage and favourite dogs. When appropriate a civic reception might be called for, and a lick of paint to the station itself was nearly always needed, as well as the provision of flags, bunting and pots of blooming plants.

The grander houses were kept in such good decorative order that they were fit to entertain a Prince and Princess as they were, but many a host and hostess found themselves having to spend large sums of money re-papering and repainting, and buying bedroom furniture to replace some of the dowdier pieces in the royal suites. Extra staff for house and garden had to be employed along with fresh uniforms for the regular servants. By the day of the royal arrival, with flowers in every room, fires burning in every grate, and the kitchens provisioned for a dozen luncheons and dinners, a small fortune had already been spent, while the host and hostess, to say nothing of the housekeeper, cook, head game-keeper and a dozen more people, had given their minds to little else than the imminent progress for at least a month.

There were rewards, apart from the kudos, to having the Prince and Princess of Wales to stay. Neither Bertie nor Alix appeared much before noon, Bertie attending to his papers and Alix usually writing letters and gossiping and preparing her toilette. Once downstairs after an enormous breakfast taken alone, Bertie expected to be entertained vigorously and without pause. There might be a tour of the stables and the home farm as well as the garden. He had a remarkable eye for any changes and often astonished his host by pointing them out unerringly. 'That is new, is it not?' he would ask in his deep, guttural voice. 'That is much better, Charlie.'

Alix might go for a drive with her hostess and other lady guests if the weather was clement, while the men would take a bowl of soup and a large brandy before proceeding on a shoot, or there could be a meet of the local hunt in which some of the more dashing women – including Alix – would take part. Before darkness fell, according to the season, there might be games. Croquet was one of the most popular outdoor games, but later many country gentlemen laid out nine-hole golf courses, and by the 1880s lawn tennis was becoming popular.

A further convenience to having the Prince and Princess of Wales to stay was that Bertie was a stickler for routine. After a first visit he liked to have the same accommodation next time – the same dressing-room, sitting-room, bedroom and bathroom. He also expected the hours for meals and the entire day's programme to be predictable. He hated surprises and changes; and if he had commented favourably on some rich dish at dinner, he expected it to be served again the next time, and always remembered.

It was, altogether, a great undertaking, but little formality was expected, and as guests they were almost invariably good-humoured and amusing. Some provision had to be made to ensure that Bertie won at competitive games; some allowance had to be made for Alix's notorious unpunctuality. But if they were expensive guests, they were also congenial company.

12

The Accomplice

When the Queen of Denmark had declared that Bertie and
Alix were 'the most extraordinary pair I know', neither this
shrewd woman nor anyone else for that matter knew whether
they were truly in love, or ever had been. That they were
happy to be together none of their friends could deny. Happiness shone through their relationship and it was very rare
for a cross word to be exchanged. Arriving late to the point
of embarrassment, sweetly smiling Alix would be greeted by
Bertie without rebuke, just a faint lifting of the eyebrows and
a barely audible sigh. They laughed at the same things and
they were both intensely interested in people, especially in their
scandals, although neither of them possessed an ounce of
malice and they tended to be generous in their judgments.
Except in their mutual loathing of Bismarck and the Prussians
(and even the Queen was outraged when Bismarck turned
on Austria, grabbing large areas of land without compensation
to the owners, to some of whom she and Alix were related),
they disliked few people. Disapproval was about as far as
they allowed themselves to go.

They never quarrelled about Alix's lack of financial responsibility. Even if they had, Bertie's position would have been ridiculously vulnerable as his expenditure on Sandringham made the sort of sums Alix gave away to people and causes on a whim appear trivial.

Bertie's affairs was a more serious subject. These began indecently soon after their wedding and continued to the end of his life. In her youthful innocence, Alix was at first shocked and surprised, but as it became clear that she could do nothing about them, and that extra-marital relationships appeared commonplace among her friends – with little complaint at that – she became reconciled to them, but not without some reluctance. It was in any case obvious that she could not, on her own, satisfy Bertie's immense sexuality and, as she does not appear to have been much interested in the sexual act anyway, it was something of a relief to have his appetite diverted elsewhere. She knew that many of the wives of their friends had affairs of their own. The lack of discretion at night among fellow guests made clear that the morality of the aristocracy and the rich at this time was not at all high. However, it is quite certain that Alix never took a paramour.

Alix's love for her family never wavered, and through all the 'going out in Society', as her mother-in-law critically described it, her travels at home and abroad, she always found time to write letters to them in her strong, decisive but almost indecipherable hand. Her family became scattered by marriage, and in the case of her favourite brother William (Willi) by being elected King of Greece – as George I. But this did not loosen the ties; it merely increased Alix's travelling.

Alix's brother Waldemar married Marie, a daughter of the Duc de Chartres, and Minnie became engaged to the Tsarevitch, Grand Duke Nicholas.* This young man died suddenly before the wedding could take place, but Minnie found his younger brother, Grand Duke Alexander, equally attractive

* In due course, descendants of the Danish royal family succeeded in completely surrounding Germany as a measure of vengeance for their nation's loss of Schleswig-Holstein. Besides the thrones of Britain, Russia and Greece, they sat on the thrones of Norway, Romania, Spain, Yugoslavia and Belgium.

and became betrothed to him soon afterwards. This was in 1866, and the wedding was due to take place in St Petersburg on 9 November, by chance Bertie's birthday. Alix was too far gone in pregnancy again to make the journey, so Bertie volunteered to go in her place; 'only too happy', he told the Prime Minister, Lord Derby, 'to be the means of promoting the *entente cordiale* between Russia and our own country'.

Leaving aside the strengthening of ties (which, heaven knows, was needed), Bertie enjoyed himself no end in Russia in his own style. The beauty, and willingness, of the ladies of the Court surprised and delighted him, and he was feted wherever he went. He was given the use of splendid apartments at the Hermitage at St Petersburg, and was equally well looked after in Moscow. There were banquets and military parades in his honour, a wolf hunt was laid on specially for him, and he created a sensation by dancing in full Highland dress at the British Embassy ball.

No one could put on a gaudier show than the Russian Court, and Minnie's wedding was even more spectacular than her sister's at Windsor. Of the securing of these dynastic links, *The Times* noted:

King Christian of Denmark has secured for one of his Princesses a Prince of Wales, for the other a Czarevitch. Personal inclination apart, we do not know how much there may be to choose between the Heir of the British Empire and the successor to the Throne of All the Russias; but assuredly since the days of fairy tales greatness by marriage was never thrust on two ladies more admirably qualified to grace the proudest position, yet brought up with more limited pretensions or more sober aspirations than the two Danish Princesses.

When Bertie returned to Marlborough House, he expected to find Alix as radiant as she always had been in the last stage of pregnancy. Instead he was disappointed that she was in poor health, suffering from pains which had nothing to do with childbirth, and a fever. He greeted her lovingly and sympathetically and, after a word with an unworried doctor, took up his programme which was as full as ever. This began with a steeplechase and dinner at Windsor. In his absence, Alix became much worse, and a telegram was despatched, calling him home. Two more, of increasing urgency, had to be sent before he took the train back to London. It was clear that Alix was dreadfully ill with rheumatic fever, and very soon the agonising pain was compounded by the pangs of childbirth. Moreover, she was prohibited by her doctors from taking chloroform in case it exacerbated her illness.

Alix gave birth safely to the first of her girls on 20 February 1867, but the relief was negated by the further onset of the fever, which was so painful that she cried for hours on end and had to be constantly comforted by Lady Macclesfield, who was beside herself with worry. This was more than could be said of Bertie, who possessed to a high degree a masculine distaste for sickness and an equally high ability to delude himself that things were not so bad as all that. His one concession to her, as the days of pain extended to weeks, was to have his desk moved into her room so that he could be near her during the several hours every day when he was writing or reading papers.

But as the fancy took him, he would be off to one of his clubs for luncheon, played whist in the afternoon and found it convenient to be out late at night. Alix would lie awake waiting for him to come in, not wishing to miss a word of good-night. One evening he promised to be back by 1 a.m., but he again failed to do so. Lady Macclesfield recounted that it kept Alix 'in a perpetual fret, refusing to take her opiate for fear she should be asleep when he came! And he never came till 3 a.m.!'

Even from her own mother, Alix at first received little sympathy, and her appeals to her to come to see her were met with a letter to Lady Macclesfield: 'Pray do not humour her too much in giving way to her sensibility but rather cheer her up by advising her to overcome this feeling of depression.' After four weeks of Alix's suffering had passed, her parents were at last prevailed upon to come over from Copenhagen. They were deeply shocked at her appearance. But, according to the Queen in a letter to Vicky, the Queen of Denmark

says (as I did) that she foresaw an illness from the reckless life of fatigue and excitement her poor child has been subject to – and chiefly to please Bertie. She is greatly distressed about it and we must all combine to bring about a great change of system, but God knows it will be months before any activity can be thought of even.

The Queen was right. Spring turned to summer, and Ascot. Bertie arrived every day for the racing as usual, but his reception was highly unusual. Accustomed to being greeted by waving papers and hats and cheers, there was hardly a murmur from the crowds within and outside the paddock. The word was spreading fast that the Prince of Wales was neglecting his wife at a time when she desperately needed him at her side.

Bertie's popularity was indeed declining fast. In May he was in Paris. Normally, the opening of the British section of a great international exhibition would have been sufficient justification for him to go to his favourite city. But not now, especially as scandalous rumour told of his being seen in public cabs with dubious young actresses on the way to supper. With only Christopher Teesdale as equerry and his old friend Charles Carrington, Bertie enjoyed several nights of fun in the shadier corners of the capital before returning to Marlborough House. 'The accounts I subsequently had of this visit were very unsatisfactory,' Knollys complained, 'supper after the opera with some of the female Paris notorieties, etc. etc.' For Alix the physical pain had lessened, but her doctors were certain that her progress would have been swifter if she had not suffered so much mental pain at Bertie's callous disregard for her. No one, through all classes in the land, found it easy to forgive Bertie's behaviour. Lady Macclesfield was heard to remark of him, 'He really is a *child* about such things and will not listen to advice.' Partly due to his secluded upbringing when he had no other standards to observe in his contemporaries, his nature was selfish and his imaginative processes stunted, as is so often the case among royal people.

Bertie would have been devastated and completely lost if Alix had died. He was also an immensely kind young man – he was twenty-five at the time – but his judgment could not encompass the idea that he should adjust his programme and temper his appetites while his wife was in need of him and in such pain. He felt at ease only when not in her discomfiting presence and paid heavily for it. One of her doctors had 'spoken out very forcibly and I fear truly, on the tone people in his own class of society now used with respect to the Prince, and on his neglect of the Princess, and how one exaggeration led to another'.

By early July Alix could be wheeled out on to the terrace of Marlborough House. Visiting her, the Queen found her 'looking very lovely but still, *altered*'. She was indeed altered. Those months of pain had taken their toll. She was tougher in spirit, more resolute and even more obstinate than before. Her spirits still sang, but on a lower note. She knew that her life would never be the same again. Her knee, which had given her the worst of the agony, had frozen and would never flex again. For a young woman of twenty-three who loved dancing, running, skating and riding, this was a terrible blow. Worse still, perhaps, was the secondary effect on her hearing. She had inherited from her mother, who was almost totally deaf in middle age, the disease of osteosclerosis. Until now it had not been a serious handicap, but it had been greatly exacerbated by the months of rheumatic fever.

Alix spiritedly did everything she could to minimise the effects of these two handicaps. She adjusted her movements so that she did all that she had done before, at first clumsily, then more skilfully, but never again with the easy grace and beauty of her earlier young life. The public, too, adjusted to this handicap and in due course it became fashionable to assume the 'Princess Alexandra limp', with bizarre results at large gatherings like garden parties or balls.

Only two years later she was back on the dance floor. Edward Montagu recalled a dance given by the Waleses at Ascot: 'I valsed with the Princess for the first time since her illness. Her knee was stiff, and I remember her saying "If you let me fall, I shall never be able to get up again."'

There was less she could do to mitigate the effects of her deafness, which was not total but bad enough to deprive her of much of the pleasures of the theatre and opera and of her own piano playing and singing. The world of the deaf is an enclosed one, and it is possible only partly to break out of it by learning to lip read, persuading people to look at you and talk clearly and not unusually loudly. Only the deaf can contrive all the cunning tricks to circumvent the handicap. In the course of time, Alix was up to all of them, but they were hard work and necessarily limited in their effect.

When the Queen described Alix as 'altered' she could not have known how profoundly true her observation was. The rheumatic fever of 1867 changed Alix's life in almost every respect and far beyond the onset of her limp and the handicap of deafness, if slow to take full effect. After a while she found the return to a full social life of the kind she had so enjoyed during her first years as Princess of Wales less satisfying than before. However kind and considerate people were, it was exhausting trying to keep track of the conversation of many people about you, of talking herself when uncertain of the drift taken by the conversation, and of the consequent gaffes and solecisms which she risked making.

Gradually, she backed away from the style of life which her mother believed had been her undoing, surrounding herself with her intimate friends, her children and her pets. She did not become simply a domestic figure in her household. She still went about with Bertie and continued to fulfil the duties of her role, but eventually those halcyon years of late-night parties at Marlborough House and about London became a memory.

Bertie's pace of living did not in the least slow down in the aftermath of Alix's illness. In May 1869 he and Alix returned from an extensive tour of the Middle East, which had concluded, as usual, in Paris. This tour had been marked, also as usual, by prickly correspondence with the Queen, who had disapproved of the tour in principle and condemned in advance Alix's inevitable high spending with the milliners and dressmakers of the French capital. ('Dear Mama . . . I have given her two simple [dresses].') Bertie arrived home in a cantankerous frame of mind, with no useful duties assigned to him, and that vile enemy Boredom facing him. On the day following their return to Marlborough House, 12 May, Bertie marched out of the house to meet some of his old cronies at

White's Club at the top of St James's Street. Because of his impatience with restrictions on smoking at White's, which applied at his other clubs, too, he was rebuked, mildly, by one of the senior staff. He at once flounced out, leaving his resignation behind.

There was only one solution, Bertie decided, and that was to set up his own West End club and have total control over the rules. This was done with remarkable speed and ease. The money came from wealthy backers eager for the privilege of founder membership, particularly from 'an old snob called Mackenzie, the son of an Aberdeen hatter who made a fortune in indigo and got a baronetcy,' according to Charles Carrington, another founder member.

The Marlborough Club was built on a lavish scale on a site directly opposite Marlborough House in Pall Mall, and although there was a committee, and a chairman (Lord Walden), Bertie was the President and virtual dictator. No one was elected without his say-so, smoking was permitted everywhere, and the atmosphere was relaxed and virtually without rules. A bowling alley was attached to the back of the Club, but the cacophony of roistering and crashing balls soon led to so many complaints that it had to be closed. Bertie turned it into a large billiards room. He loved billiards and its banter.

Most of the Marlborough's members were dukes, marquesses and lower grade titled men. But the membership also reflected Bertie's wider interest, in Jewish bankers, for instance, the racing fraternity and others who amused him, like William Howard Russell, *The Times*'s war correspondent, and Christopher Sykes. It was a boisterous male community, marked by much gossip, practical jokes and heavy drinking. It was well known among Marlborough Club members that, while the President enjoyed informality, there was a strict limit to the informality with which he could be treated. From time to time members exceeded this limit and quickly found that their membership had expired.

Once, over the billiards table, Bertie felt obliged to remonstrate with Sir Frederick Johnstone. 'Freddy, Freddy,' he addressed him, 'you're very drunk!' At which the misguided fellow pointed at Bertie's stomach and, affecting his guttural accent, countered with, 'Tum-Tum, you're *verrry* fat!' The Prince of Wales at once turned to his equerry and instructed him to see that Johnstone's bags were packed before breakfast the following morning. This episode actually occurred at Sandringham, where Johnstone was a guest, but similar incidents occurred from time to time at the Marlborough.

The Queen, of course, strongly disapproved of Bertie's setting up his own club: it was bad enough that he was a member of others, and she knew that heavy drinking, gambling and other activities inevitably led to the taking of liberties.

Shortly after Bertie's return from the Middle East in 1869, he became involved in a legal case which further damaged his public reputation, and also, coincidentally, again involved Johnstone. An acquaintance of Bertie's, Sir Charles Mordaunt, a baronet who owned land and a great house in Warwickshire, married a young girl, Harriet Moncrieffe – 'such a pretty, pleasant, nice woman; everybody had a good word for her,' Carrington described her. She was also a nervy girl, and when she gave birth to a daughter who was suspected of being blind, her eccentricity turned to insanity. This took the form of a confession to her husband that she had slept with Lord Cole, Sir Frederick Johnstone and others, including the Prince of Wales, 'often and in open day'.

Mordaunt foolishly chose to believe her and went in a rage to his lawyer. As a result, Bertie was among those subpoenaed to appear before a special jury on 23 February 1870. He was fully aware of the dreadful implications behind public cross-examination on an adultery charge, and decided promptly that he must not take any advantage of royal privilege and face up to appearing in the witness box.

Alix was the first to be told and she accepted his entire innocence, supporting him by appearing with him in public and cancelling none of her engagements. Next he wrote with sinking heart to his mother, telling her that Alix had already been informed:

It is my painful duty (I call it painful because it must be so to you to know that your eldest son is obliged to appear as a witness in a Court of Justice) to inform you that I have been 'sub-poenaed' by Sir C. Mordaunt's Counsel to appear as a witness on Saturday next at Lord Penzance's Court.

The Queen stood by her son as stoutly as Alix had done, and wrote him an affectionate letter of complete support. Bertie replied, deeply touched: 'I cannot sufficiently thank you for the dear and kind words which you have written to me. . . . I shall remember all the kind advice you have given me, and hope to profit by it.' But the Queen's real feelings are revealed in a letter to the Lord Chancellor, who had attempted to reassure her that all would be well.

Still, the fact of the Prince of Wales's intimate acquaintance with a young married woman being publicly proclaimed, will show an amount of imprudence which cannot but damage him in the eyes of the middle and lower classes, which is most deeply lamented in these days when the higher classes, in their frivolous, selfish and pleasure-seeking lives, do more to increase the spirit of democracy* than anything else.

Before the case came up Bertie was advised to publish any letters he had written to Harriet Moncrieffe to reveal their innocence. This he willingly did, *The Times* commenting that they were in no way compromising even if 'they were not such as to entitle the writer to a place in the next edition of Walpole's *Royal & Noble Authors*'. But public curiosity remained white hot, and the chance of seeing the Prince of Wales being cross-questioned in an adultery case led to a packed public gallery and hundreds more in the street.

When Bertie entered the box he was observed from the gallery to be a stout, balding, bearded figure, shorter in stature than expected but composed and completely dignified. Lord Penzance, the Judge of Court of Probate and Divorce, first told him that under a recent Act of Parliament he was not liable to answer any question 'tending to show that he has been guilty of adultery'.

Bertie was then questioned on how long he had known the

* A pejorative term in her language.

170

Moncrieffe family: was it before or after Lady Moncrieffe's marriage, had she visited Marlborough House before her marriage, and had he frequently met Sir Charles Mordaunt, with Lady Mordaunt? In every case he answered 'Yes' and admitted to writing to her on her marriage and giving her a wedding present. Several other trivial questions followed, then Counsel more forcefully asked, 'We have heard in the course of this case that Your Royal Highness uses hansom-cabs occasionally?'

Bertie replied, 'It is so.'

'I have only one more question to trouble Your Royal Highness with.' There was absolute silence in the gallery, where everyone knew what that question was inevitably to be. 'Has there ever been any improper familiarity or criminal act between yourself and Lady Mordaunt?'

Bertie replied in what *The Times* called 'a very firm tone': 'There has not.'

There was a burst of applause from the gallery, which the Judge at once repressed. Then, when Bertie bowed to his Lordship and retired, there was another attempt at applause.

But this applause in no way reflected the view of the general public on Bertie. Appearing alone, Alix would be cheered loudly, which made it all the more telling when they were booed when seen together, at the theatre, opera and even at the races. A toastmaster's call for the raising of glasses to the Prince of Wales was echoed by a loud cry, 'To the Princess!' At Ascot races, where Bertie commonly received cheers and waving of hats as he drove up the course, in 1870 he was loudly booed. It so happened that one of his horses won the last race and a section of the crowd waved their hats and cheered him in the royal box. 'You seem to be in a better temper now than you were this morning, damn you!' he robustly called out to them.

This cheerful response did not reflect his feelings. He was deeply hurt and worried by his growing unpopularity and the appearance of scurrilous pamphlets and newspaper articles attacking him. All his life he had known only a cheerful welcome wherever he went. The notorious but widely read radical and anti-monarchist Charles Bradlaugh wrote that 'the Prince of Wales must never dishonour the country by becoming King'.

Some of Bertie's more intelligent friends recognised that the cause of his recent unpopularity could be traced to his 'idle hands', which, like anyone else, led him into mischief and that it was the Queen herself, who was so critical and ashamed of him, who kept him unemployed. Nor was Bertie's style of living the prime reason for the wave of republicanism that was gathering pace all over the nation. The Queen's reclusiveness was a far greater reason. Compounding her folly in giving Bertie nothing to do, she continued to do nothing, publicly, herself. Gladstone, who was secretly in awe and terror of her, occasionally dropped hints about her being seen in public, and in 1869 he did persuade her to leave Osborne a few days early and open the new bridge over the Thames at Blackfriars. She was not best pleased and made it clear that this 'must NEVER be made a *precedent*'.

Bertie did his bit and, by contrast with Gladstone, enjoyed countering her carping with his own: 'If you sometimes ever came to London from Windsor and then drove for an hour in the Park (where there is no [hated] noise) and then returned to Windsor the people would be overjoyed. . . . We live in radical times, and the more the *People see the Sovereign* the better it is for the *People* and the *Country*.'

It made no difference. In Parliament during 1871 Sir Charles Dilke, another radical anti-monarchist, hammered away at the corruption and indolence of the Court. Republican groups mushroomed throughout the nation. The serious and respected *Pall Mall Gazette* wrote on 29 September of 'republicanism of a very revolutionary form flooding in'. A massive republican rally was held in Hyde Park, where twenty years earlier the popularity of the monarchy reached a peak with the Prince Consort's Great Exhibition. Where the Crystal Palace had once stood, 'the mob roared for the end of monarchy'. When the Queen's fourth daughter, Loosy, married the mountainously rich Marquess of Lorne, later the Duke of Argyll, *and* was voted a substantial grant by Parliament, there were rowdy popular meetings in Birmingham and Nottingham condemning this extravagance when so many were starving and out of work. The Franco–Prussian War, ending with the crushing defeat of France, the bombardment and siege of Paris, and the flight of the Emperor and Empress, contributed to the draught which was blowing through the embers of republicanism into flickers of flames.

The year 1871 was a mournful one for members of the British royal family, too, and not only because of the fear of republicanism which was growing among politicians, the respected professionals and the middle classes. What was the purpose of an expensive monarchy that did nothing and was scarcely ever seen? But for the Queen and Alix and Bertie there were grave personal troubles, too.

Early in the year Alix was known to be pregnant again, although, as usual, she did not reduce the pace of her social round, to the Queen's dismay. On 6 April she gave birth to another son, Alexander John Charles Albert, and this time its prematurity was genuine. It was a pathetic, shrivelled baby that could scarcely support life, and on the following morning at 10.45 it was described by the doctors as in 'a very feeble state'. Later in the day 'the Queen received the melancholy intelligence of the infant's death', and ordered the Court into 'deeper mourning than at present for ten days'.

Bertie and Alix were heartbroken, and both cried profusely over the tiny corpse. Bertie himself placed him in a coffin to match the baby's size and arranged the pall and the white flowers. Later, there was a miniature funeral procession, which Alix watched tearfully through her bedroom window, her two boys in grey kilts and black gloves each holding Bertie by the hand.

Elizabeth Longford has written that, 'As far as the Queen was concerned, 1871 was the first, dreadful year in which she stood like one of Landseer's red deer at bay.' But in addition to the usual hazards of a deer's life in the Highlands, mostly from men with guns, Queen Victoria was suffering a number of distresses, the worst of which was the personal attacks upon herself, then the parliamentary questioning of Princess Loosy's dowry and Prince Arthur's annuity. 'Dear Alix's tragedy' had hurt her deeply, too, though she derived compensatory satisfaction from blaming the whole thing on Bertie.

At Osborne the Queen was stung on the elbow while asleep, or so she claimed. She made a great fuss about this sting and complained four days later that it was worse. Gladstone chose this moment to ask her if she would postpone the date of her journey (normally immutable) to Balmoral and instead to prorogue Parliament. He calculated that it would offset some of the outrage in Parliament over the grants to her two children and enable the people of London to see her.

She had not opened Parliament in person since 1852, she pointed out. What more was going to be demanded of her?

What killed her beloved Husband? [she demanded of Lord Hatherly]. Overwork & worry . . . & the Queen, a woman no longer young is supposed to be proof against all. . . . She must solemnly repeat that unless her Ministers *support* her & state the whole truth she *cannot* go on & must give her heavy burden up to younger hands. Perhaps then those discontented people may regret that they broke her down when she might still have been of use.

Pleading the state of her health, and the nation's dreadful fate if she abdicated in favour of the Prince of Wales, she prepared for her departure to Balmoral on 15 August. Gladstone and his ministers knew that the Queen was not only a hypochondriac but also was capable of using the state of her health to further her convenience or for any reason that took her fancy. At the same time, she believed that she was being kept from travelling to the peace and isolation of Balmoral for Gladstone's political convenience. Vicky composed a letter, signed by all the family, warning her mother of the dangers of republicanism, 'which are daily spreading', but delayed sending it. Queen Victoria departed from Osborne as arranged with Ponsonby and the rest of her vast suite, complaining of feeling much worse.

The irony was that she was indeed worse. She was seriously ill. The 'sting' on her arm turned out to be an abscess which would not die down and affected her whole well-being. She had 'never felt so ill since typhoid at Ramsgate', and that was in 1835. The royal physician, Dr William Jenner, thought she might have only twenty-four hours to live, and got her permission to send for Professor Joseph Lister, the famous surgeon. The abscess was lanced, with no immediate beneficial effect. Sometimes she had to be lifted in and out of bed; at others she came down to dinner, her high colour explained by Jenner as 'nervousness'. He also recorded that 'these nerves are a species of madness, and against them it is hopeless to contend'.

It was now widely recognised that the Queen was seriously ill, but this did not in the least stem the flow of invective against her in numerous magazines and pamphlets, only *The Times* apologising for earlier attacks on her. Money was at the root of all the trouble. If only she would make herself evident, in the grandest style, flaunting her wealth, no one would mind; in fact, she would have been cheered to the echo. No one minded extravagance. One writer explained sarcastically that she did not drive about London because she could not afford a new bonnet. A Liberal MP, writing anonymously, totted up the (supposed) figures and decided that she was 'hoarding' £200,000 a year. On 6 November Sir Charles Dilke made a widely reported speech citing the Queen's 'dereliction of duty' and calling for the setting up of a republic.

Bertie and Alix had only recently become aware of the political crisis and the intensification of republicanism at home, having been first in Ireland and then in Darmstadt. They had stayed with Bertie's sister Alice and her family, where Minnie and Alexander from Russia were also guests. This had been an unusually happy time for all of them, and while Alix's deafness could not be ignored, it was never so evident when she was happy with people she knew closely and loved. Later, they took the waters at Kissingen and attended the Oberammergau Passion Play, which moved them both greatly. After their return to England, Bertie observed the military manoeuvres in Hampshire and later joined Alix and the children at Abergeldie. On their way home from Abergeldie, to break the journey to Sandringham, Bertie and Alix stayed the night at Londesborough Lodge near

Scarborough, the home of Lord Londesborough. One of their fellow guests was the young Earl of Chesterfield.

They arrived thankfully, as always, back at Sandringham in time for Bertie's birthday on 9 November. A few days later he complained of feeling unwell and took to his bed. Typhoid was such a widespread disease, and claimed so many lives annually, that the local doctor readily diagnosed it. Bertie now realised that the disease would follow roughly the same pattern that his father had endured, and that it would, more than likely, lead to his own death.

Bertie's sister Alice and her husband Prince Louis were conveniently staying at Sandringham for Bertie's birthday after Alice had helped nurse her mother at Balmoral. Louis returned to Darmstadt, but Alice stayed on to take up again her further nursing responsibilities. While everyone else and especially Alix was devastated by the shock of the diagnosis, Alice took cool command of the situation. The first thing she did was to replace the local doctor – 'not at all decisive or careful', she told her husband – and call for Sir William Gull, one of the Queen's doctors, in his place. This, alone, might have saved Bertie's life.

At first, Alix's anguish was too great for her to be of help. 'At one moment,' Lady Augusta Stanley reported to her sister, 'poor little thing, she ran out in the dark to pray in the Church for a few minutes, to compose and strengthen herself.' She spent almost all day at Bertie's bedside, praying and holding his hand, unrecognised for much of the time, and at night insisted on sleeping – although she hardly slept at all – in Bertie's dressing-room with the door open. From time to time she had to be ordered out of the room, and out of the house, to calm herself and recover in the fresh air.

The course of the illness, with its climaxes of violence and hysterical ravings, was far more alarming to Alix than to her sister-in-law, who had seen it all just ten years earlier. Alice wrote to her husband:

When Bertie was delirious the other day he said to Alix 'I have had a terrible scene *but I gave it one of them well*' – whereupon he hit Mrs Jones – then he said 'that mad woman, I can't stand her any longer . . .' today he said to Mrs Jones . . . 'Do you know who that is – he is a Swedish gentleman I know.' Then he gives orders that all gentlemen are to come in tights 'because I am very particular about dress – and General Knollys must kneel down and give me a glass of water. . . .' He doesn't know Alix, he calls her 'waiter', and says to her, 'You were my wife you are no more – you have broken your vows.'

This accusation, coming from Bertie, was hard for Alix to bear even if it was a mere delirious outpouring; and when, according to Lady Augusta, his ravings became 'very dreadful, and for that cause the Princess was kept out of his room one day, all sorts of revelations and names of people mentioned'. On another day, Bertie suddenly sat up and threw all his pillows at the people about him with remarkable energy and accuracy; and a few days later he conceived a hatred for his chief doctor, shouting 'Gull! Gull! Gull!'

For Alix, drawn-faced and dark-eyed from lack of sleep and periods of tearfulness, the news that both the Earl of Chesterfield, his mother's only son, and Bertie's groom, Blegge, had succumbed to and died from the same fever, intensified her agony. On 29 November the Queen, fresh from her own sick-bed, arrived at Sandringham, her first-ever visit.

I took off my things [she wrote] and went over to Bertie's room, and was allowed to step in from behind a screen to see him sleeping or dozing. The room was dark and only one lamp burning, so that I could not see him well. He was lying rather flat on his back, breathing very rapidly and loudly. Of course the watching is constant, and dear Alix does a great deal herself. Two nurses and Gillet, the valet, take turns in the nursing. How all reminded me so vividly and sadly of my dearest Albert's illness!

It was a day when the patient showed a slight improvement, and she sat at his bedside, holding his hand, while Alix sat opposite her. The Queen's presence seemed to ease the fever, even though 'somehow I always look for bad news & have not much confidence'.

The house was jam-packed with relations, beds were in short supply and Princesses Beatrice and Loosy had to share one. The pressure was eased by the departure of the Queen and her suite, using as an excuse Bertie's improvement. He was certainly conscious much of the time though not making much sense, so that it was as well that Queen Victoria was on the train to London when he began to shout about being King now and 'proposing reforms in the Household'. He had come round to his doctor, and on spotting him approaching his bed roared with laughter and cried out, 'That's right old Gull, one more teaspoonful!'

Dr Gull scarcely had time to feed his patient medicine so busy was he composing bulletins for the outside world. Curiosity and anxiety were widespread abroad as well as in Britain, and the bulletins, issued several times a day, were printed in all the newspapers and pinned on municipal noticeboards. Alfred Austin, the future Poet Laureate, chose this time to compose and publish his own useful contribution in the form of a couplet:

> Across the wires the electric message came,
> He is no better, he is much the same.

The lines were considered to be above his average.

On 7 December the bulletins did suggest that the worst might be over. It was bitterly cold and the flat Norfolk landscape was deep in snow. Alice and Alix suddenly decided to get away from it all for a short time and ordered a sledge. Two grey ponies were harnessed to it and they went for a drive. They returned to find their patient had suffered a relapse.

'The fever had all lighted up and was beginning all over again, as bad as ever, or worse!' wrote Alice. 'Worse and worse,' lamented Lady Macclesfield, 'the doctors say that if he does not rally within the next hour a very few more must see the end. The Princess [Alix] has telegraphed that to her parents. She keeps up heroically.'

For several days Bertie's life hung in the balance, and there was no more ranting and raving as if his last strength was reserved for just keeping alive. At 8.15 a.m. on 8 December the Queen received a telegram from Sir William Jenner, who had been called in some days earlier as chief medical adviser: 'The Prince passed a very unquiet night. Not so well. Temperature risen to 104. Respirations more rapid. Dr Gull and I are both very anxious.' She immediately made arrangements to return to Sandringham, her heart laden with fear that fate would strike down her eldest son on the tenth anniversary of Albert's death, 14 December.

'The Queen was allowed to go up to his bed – he did not quite know her at first – but soon did and he was glad to see her,' Lady Augusta Stanley reported. 'She was in his room nearly the whole day, and sat a long time by his bed holding his hand.' Realistically, Lady Augusta recognised that this was the Queen's 'best self, by being taken out of herself – taken out of doctors and maladies (I mean her own) and nerves and fighting off what Her own righteous conscience tells Her would be right'. 'Lady Augusta', added Elizabeth Longford, 'was one who did not think the Queen mad, but self-indulgent and neurotic, because of a guilty conscience.'

Throughout the country prayers were offered for the Prince of Wales's recovery. Gladstone wrote to the Queen that he did not know 'how either to touch, or to leave untouched, the painful subject, which in the very streets seems to absorb the mind of every passer-by'. Alix attended church like everyone else at Sandringham, but she had a note delivered to the rector reading: 'My husband being, thank God, somewhat better, I must leave, I fear, before the service is concluded that I may watch by his bedside. Could you not say a few words in prayer for my husband before I return to him?'

The recovery was again short-lived, and fearing that her presence excited the patient, Dr Gull ordered her from the room. Not to be outdone, Alix crept in on all fours so that the patient could not see her while allowing her to be close to him. But by this time, after three weeks of the typhoid, she was so exhausted that when she did drop off to sleep, on the floor or in a chair, and a crisis arose, she could not be awakened because the stress had so worsened her hearing.

SANDRINGHAM, 13th Dec. 1871
This really has been the worst day of all. . . . The first report early in the morning was that dear Bertie seemed very weak, and the breathing very imperfect and feeble. The strength, however, rallied

again. There had been no rest all night from the constant delirium. . . . Got up and dressed quickly [continued the Queen's journal], taking a mouthful of breakfast before hurrying to Bertie's room. Sat nearby on the sofa, but so he could not see me. It was very distressing to hear him calling out and talking incessantly quite incoherently. . . .

Returned to Bertie's room, and, whilst there, he had a most frightful fit of coughing which seemed at one moment to threaten his life. . . . Poor Alix was in the greatest alarm and despair, and I supported her as best I could. Alice and I said to one another in tears, 'There can be no hope.'

On this same 13 December, Dr Gull consulted with Bertie's younger brother, Affie – Prince Alfred, now Duke of Edinburgh – as to whether yet another bulletin should be issued stating that the patient's strength was failing. There had been '36 hours of the wildest, loudest, incessant talking, in all languages,' Affie recounted later to Lady Augusta, 'whistling, singing'. This phase was 'too terrible'. Bertie was 'on the very *verge* of the grave', Dr Gull told the Queen, 'hardly anyone has recovered who has been *so* ill. . . .' It was only fourteen hours before dawn on 14 December, and Alix was as conscious as the Queen of the portentousness of the moment. When the worst attack came, 'Only Alix and one of the nurses were there,' the Queen wrote, 'and the doctors were at once hastily summoned. But the dreadful moment passed.'

Miraculously, Bertie slept quietly that night. The Queen crept into his room early when only a nurse was there and was astonished to see him awake and smiling. 'Oh! dear Mama, I am so glad to see you,' he said quite clearly. 'Have you been here all this time?' He kissed her hand in what she described as 'the old way'.

There had been so many crises, so many moments of faint hope, followed by crushing disappointment, that few dared to believe that real recovery was on the way. Alix joined her mother-in-law on the other side of the bed, enjoying a union of spirit she had never before known with this difficult woman. '. . . there is some abatement of the gravity of the symptoms,' Dr Gull announced to the world cautiously. Later in the day Bertie sat up and asked for a glass of his favourite

Bass's beer. The next bulletin was accordingly more cheerful, and in another twenty-four hours fear of a relapse had almost disappeared.

As Alix continued to sit beside Bertie all the next day, a great sigh of relief and thankfulness seemed to sweep through the land. Church bells rang and people accosted strangers in the street in case they had not heard the news. In hundreds of taverns the saving of the life of the Prince of Wales made a fine excuse for getting drunk, while others went quietly to church and knelt down uttering a prayer of thankfulness.

No one could have anticipated the momentous consequences, politically and personally, of Bertie's long illness and then his astounding recovery. Those outside the family who visited Bertie and Alix early in his convalescence noted their changed appearance. Constance Westminster writing to her friend Lord Ronald Gower, the intellectual son of the Duke of Sutherland, noted: 'He is much thinner, and head shaven, but very unaltered in face. . . . She looks thin and worn, but so affectionate – tears in her eyes, talking of him; and his manner to her so gentle.'

13

Recovery

'When, pale as yet, and fever-worn . . .'
Tennyson on the Prince of Wales

A mere four days after Bertie's iron constitution had finally
shaken off the deadly typhoid virus, the Queen was in discussion with the Prime Minister, Gladstone, about some sort
of public thanksgiving. He suggested a procession through
the streets of London and a religious service at St Paul's
Cathedral. Queen Victoria told him that she did not care for
a 'public show'. But Alix, in spite of the exhaustion she still
suffered from her ordeal, shrewdly backed Gladstone and
wrote to the Queen supporting him:

I quite understand your feeling about the public thanksgiving . . .
and I quite agree that a simpler and more private service would be
more in accordance with one's own wishes. But then, on the other
hand, the whole nation has taken such a public share in our sorrow,
it has been so entirely one with us in our grief, that it may perhaps
feel it has a kind of claim to join with us now in a public and universal
thanksgiving.*

The republican movement had been set back on its heels

---

* It should not be presumed that this message and others of special significance quoted in this book were composed by Alix unaided. The hand of
General Knollys may sometimes be discerned.

by the national agony over Bertie's illness. When Sir Charles Dilke moved in the Commons that there should be an enquiry into the Queen's expenditure, it was thrown out 'amid tumultuous applause'. 'What a sell for Dilke this illness has been!' one Conservative Party member wrote to Disraeli. A rally of republicans in Birmingham was a flop. 'The republicans say their chances are up – thank God for this!' wrote the Duke of Cambridge to his mother. 'Heaven has sent this dispensation to save us.' The Russian Ambassador wrote home: 'Incontestably this crisis has produced in England a happy reaction in favour of the monarchical institutions which govern this great land.' The public demonstration of mixed relief and thanksgiving finished off the republican movement, on a serious scale, once and for all.

Deprived of the wedding procession almost a decade earlier, London determined to honour this occasion as never before. Every yard of the procession route from Buckingham Palace along the Strand and Fleet Street to the cathedral, and back by Oxford Street and Park Lane, was decorated with flags and bunting, every lamp-post decked with the royal coat of arms and from every window there hung a Union Jack. At Ludgate Circus before the rise to the cathedral itself a triple triumphal arch was created, every inch of it carved and decorated, engraved with 'God Save the Prince of Wales', surrounded by carved figures and surmounted with a great cross.

On the morning of 27 February 1872, in a bitter east wind and driving rain,

The resources of the great railways were taxed by myriads of passengers from all parts of the kingdom [ran one account], and the inhabitants of the home counties set out at break of day in great crowds along the highways to the capital. . . .

Every window was thronged, every tree, lamp-post, and paling were used as perches, and what was really singular was the way in which the sloping London roofs were somehow converted into standing places. . . .

Precisely at noon, as the procession left the palace, the clouds parted and the winter sun came out for the first time, and remained shining until it set.

Tennyson was to write for the Queen:

> When, pale as yet, and fever-worn, the Prince
> Who scarce had pluck'd his flickering life again
> From halfway down the shadow of the grave,
> Passed with thee thro' thy people and their love,
> And London roll'd one tide of joy thro' all
> Her trebled millions. . . .

The cheers as the nine-carriage procession passed by preceded by cavalry of the 10th Hussars – Bertie's own regiment – could be heard, it was told, as far as the suburbs south of the river. Bertie himself, sitting beside the pinched little figure of his mother and opposite Alix (who smiled and waved all the way), appeared pale and drawn, as expected. But he smiled and acknowledged the cheers, too. These reached a peak when, on passing Temple Bar, the Queen suddenly seized Bertie's hand, raised it and, with a sweet smile, kissed it.

This was certainly Bertie's day, but to see their sovereign again after all these reclusive years, *and* Alix, the most loved woman in the land, set the people afire with enthusiasm unseen since the Coronation of that eighteen-year-old girl thirty-four years ago. Republicanism? Who had ever heard of republicanism?

No one had prayed more deeply and sincerely at the St Paul's service than Alix. Behind the elements of joy and frivolity which she tended to expose to the world wherever she went and whatever her company, religious principles ruled her life. She had prayed so hard and for so long for the survival of her husband, and God had answered her prayers. As the Queen had truly spoken, very few people survived typhoid fever when it struck as venomously as Bertie had suffered it: the hand of God must have intervened.

In a passionate letter to Princess Louise after it was all over, Alix wrote:

Oh dearest Louise, you knew what I suffered and saw my utter despair and misery – you would hardly know me now in my happiness. We are *never* apart and are enjoying our second honeymoon.

Never, never can I thank God enough for all His mercy when He listened to my prayers and gave me back my life's happiness.

This 'second honeymoon' was combined with a convalescent tour on the Continent, beginning and ending, as always, with Paris, and some early spring yachting in the Mediterranean. It also included a happy family gathering in Rome, where they stayed in the same hotel with Alix's mother and father, her younger brother Waldemar and younger sister Thyra. Bertie always became bored within twenty-four hours in Copenhagen, but on neutral ground like this, with plenty of distractions, he was perfectly happy though already itching to return to London's social round. Until he could do so he was amused to witness the first signs of a romance between the young Duke of Cumberland and little Princess Thyra.

The Queen herself thought that Bertie was much changed by his visit 'halfway down the shadow of the grave', but this did not in any way dispose her to offer him serious work. As jealous of her own powers and distrusting of Bertie's discretion and abilities as ever, she rebuffed all overtures of the Government to give him some official role. Gladstone and his ministers had been severely shaken by the outbreak of republicanism and determined to profit by the success gained for the monarchy by the Prince of Wales's illness and the subsequent national rejoicing. 'A worthy and manly mode of life' was desired for the Prince of Wales, but how was this to be achieved in the face of the Queen's implacable opposition? Once again what to do about Bertie became a leading problem for government and family, like a lamenting echo from the past.

Foreign affairs, Ireland, philanthropic work, the army, these and many more occupations were considered and put up to him. But there were three main obstacles, all of them seemingly insurmountable. First, the Queen had no interest in them and the pressure that Gladstone applied she believed to be entirely for political reasons. Second, very few people had any confidence in Bertie's staying power. His way of life appeared to be so restless and frivolous that few trusted him to apply himself seriously to a task for any length of time.

This seemed to be confirmed when, as an experiment, he was asked to sit on some trivial House of Lords non-political committee. Bertie attended the first meeting and then asked if the next could be adjourned for ten days as he had other engagements. Lastly, there was Bertie's own attitude towards a serious role. Because his duties were restricted to the level of foundation-stone laying and the opening of bridges and municipal buildings, when anything more important was offered, so deep was his disillusionment, that he looked on it as a sop or something to keep him out of mischief.

What was needed, as Alix and his more intelligent friends recognised, was the offer of some long-term and important responsibility which would stretch him and offer him a sense of satisfaction. If this were to happen, there can be no doubt that he would relish the challenge and fulfil his duties conscientiously. He was to demonstrate this marvellously the moment when he at last became King.

The idea of employment in Ireland was again brought up by Gladstone, with the Prince of Wales occupying a new royal residence as a non-political Lord Lieutenant and performing all the ceremonial duties. The Viceroy approved, Gladstone approved, but the Queen would have nothing to do with it. By this time, after months of argument and to-ing and fro-ing, Bertie became weary of the whole Irish project.

Exasperated and frustrated, Bertie would instead lay on some enormous and extravagant party at Marlborough House. Fourteen hundred guests were invited to one of these, with Sir Frederick Leighton called in to supervise the decorations. It was strictly a fancy-dress party 'on a scale of splendour greater than any social function that he had yet attempted'.

Lord Ronald Gower, the aesthete, sculptor and son of the Duke of Sutherland, wrote of some of the guests and their costumes:

It was very picturesque and some of the dresses quite superb. Billy Russell looked well in a black cavalier costume, wearing a Shakespearian tuft on his chin. The Duke of Wellington, as a Spanish Hidalgo, wore his father's Order of the Golden Fleece. Poor old

Quin* appeared in a Charles II dress. The Prince looked well, and gained in height in a cavalier's dress, and, as usual, the Princess was the most beautiful and graceful woman in the place; she wore a Marie Stuart dress. The ball lasted all through the night, supper being taken in two vast tapestry-hung scarlet marquees.

After balls like these to mark the end of the Season, Bertie would be off *en garçon* on one of his private visits to France. There, all the delights of Paris would be open to him, and in the summer heat he would drift from château to château, finding agreeable company in bed at Chantilly or Dampierre, Mello or Serrant. All the Ducs and Duchesses loved to have him to stay, and he in turn offered wonderful company with his English and international gossip recounted in his faultless French, which, unlike his English, carried no trace of a guttural accent.

He would take the waters at some spa before returning home to offset – as he thought – the effects of the rich meals he consumed day after day. He would return in time for 'the glorious 12th' for the grouse shooting at Abergeldie, where he greeted Alix and his family fondly, and set about filling in the time before his birthday and then Christmas at Sandringham.

Alix's private pleasures were a good deal less lurid than her husband's, but her hobbies and pets, her sunny temperament, and the long-lasting relief at his survival, kept her happy and amused. Her chief pleasures were her children and her dogs. Pugs and later Pekinese were her favourite indoor dogs. She never entered a room or sat down without dogs around her, and often on her lap. When she played the piano they would be at her feet, and there would often be one lying across her, too. There might be half a dozen of them beside her at any time and, although they looked so similar, she never got their names wrong.

At Sandringham the bigger dogs would be kept in kennels looked after by kennelmaids. 'The dogs most to be envied

---

* Dr Frederick Quin, an eccentric homeopath, friend of Thackeray and Dickens.

in England are certainly those at Sandringham,' wrote Lady Dorothy Nevill after a visit. Lord Knutsford told how the first stop on a tour round the estate and gardens would be the kennels.

She took up a large flat basket of bread [he recounted] and, I must say to my surprise, went right into each kennel. The dogs jumped up on her, and when she was in the kennel with big dogs she was hardly visible. . . . Into each kennel she went. She knew all about each dog, and told us the character of many, and which could be let out together and so on.

The next stop would probably be the stables, where guests witnessed the same knowledge of every horse, its name and merits and demerits and history, accompanied by the feeding of handfuls of oats and the stroking of muzzles.

Alix applied as much love and as little discipline to her children as to her pets. They were for fun and enjoyment, and the fact that they grew up was a matter of surprise and some regret. She liked them to be rolling about enjoying themselves, teasing one another and being loved by her, and by Bertie too who was equally indulgent. Her own childhood had been like this, only nursemaids and, later, tutors applying any sort of order.

Visitors to the house often suffered from 'the wild Wales children' and the more elderly disapproved of their behaviour. There were practical jokes to suffer, too: games of croquet were broken up, the balls disappearing in mid-play. Guests might meet one of their ponies in the house, and once at least a pony was coaxed upstairs to Alix's drawing-room. There was surprise but no protest. 'I was just as bad myself.'

Alix hated to be parted from her five children, and long after it was usual for even a nursemaid to bath them, she would sometimes insist on doing so, urging any guest to help her. Even when they were grown-up she would write them letters in the same (to others rather cloying) style as if they were still six years old.

Queen Victoria could not do with them. 'They are such ill-bred, ill-trained children, I can't fancy them at all,' she once wrote, partly one suspects because they were Bertie's offspring. Eddy was Alix's favourite. She adored him beyond all the others perhaps because he was so slow and unblessed with any intelligence or energy. He was very good-looking and would hang about his mother, an arm round her neck, a cheek against hers, well beyond the normal age for public demonstrations of affection. Georgie was Bertie's favourite boy, which balanced things up nicely, though Bertie applied the only note of dissension in the family by suddenly losing his temper with the lot of them and roaring his disapproval. This scared them out of their wits, but within minutes he was all smiles and affection again.

The three girls were, alas, collectively referred to by friends as 'the Hags', but this was only by contrast with their mother. It was unfortunate that none of them inherited Alix's beauty, though none was disagreeable to look at when a child. Louise, who had been brought into the world in the torment of her mother's fever, was endowed with little spirit, zest or desire to communicate. She really was quite plain, with a long face expressing an inherent sadness. She, however, was the first to marry, to the Earl of Fife, eighteen years her senior, who had been a bit of a rake in his time and was now created a Duke. But he had settled down to running his vast Scottish estate at the time of his marriage and Louise took up salmon fishing, becoming highly expert, and little else. They had two girls, Alexandra and Maud.

For seven more years the other two girls seemed content to remain at home with their mother, who gave them no encouragement to leave. Queen Victoria thought Alix was being selfishly possessive and complained to Bertie about it, who retorted that 'they had no inclination to marriage'. Maud eventually married her cousin, the future King of Norway and naval officer, Prince Charles of Denmark. From then onwards she appeared to be lost to the world in the gloom of northern mists, which reflected her own melancholy. Her only interests were her son, her English garden and her visits to England, which cheered her up somewhat.

Princess Victoria – Toria – was an even sadder case. Like Queen Victoria, Alix was anxious to keep one of her daughters at home as a companion, confidante and general help.

Toria was at Alix's side, running errands that were not always necessary and were sometimes forgotten by Alix before she had returned. There was undeviating affection between mother and daughter, but it was a terrible waste of a life for Toria. She was the most intelligent of the three girls and much wanted to marry and have children. There were three men she would have liked to marry, but two were commoners and were sternly ruled out by Alix. The third was Lord Rosebery, the extremely rich Liberal politician and for a brief time Prime Minister. He was widowed early and would also have liked to marry her. 'We *could* have been so happy together,' Toria lamented, but it was not to be. In later years she became cantankerous and frequently ill.

But in the 1870s, when these girls were still lively and loving children, the future appeared promising: they all adored one another and their parents, they played and rode their ponies and were not much bothered with education.

The harmony between the parents of these young Princesses, which had been enhanced by Bertie's illness and recovery, was for the first time put at risk by a decision he made in the winter of 1874–5. Thwarted in all his efforts to fulfil some useful function on behalf of his country, and as fearful of boredom as ever, Bertie determined to make his mark on the Empire, create for himself an enjoyable distraction and demonstrate his independence by undertaking a grand tour of India.

There was a great deal to be said for an imperial tour. As a result of the mutiny of 1857 and the transfer of power from the East India Company to the Crown, the presence of the heir to the throne would have a settling effect and 'bring home to the native princes and troops the human signification of the sovereignty of the Crown, which for most of them was an abstract rather than a substantive conception'. There had been many murmurs of insurrection since the mutiny had been put down, and Bertie's friend and Viceroy of India, Lord Mayo, had been assassinated only the previous year.

For Bertie's Household, the first hint of his intention was an unprecedented order to his Librarian to assemble all the books on India he could lay his hands on. Soon Whitehall was buzzing with rumours, and Disraeli, the new Prime Minister, Lord Derby, the Foreign Secretary, and Lord Salisbury, the Secretary of State for India, were in turn told of Bertie's plan. Disraeli wanted to know who was going to pay, and the other two ministers expressed doubts about the wisdom of the whole business.

As for the Queen, she would not hear of anything so ridiculous. It was '*quite* against my *desire*', she told Vicky. But Bertie went to Windsor in a very determined frame of mind, exasperated beyond bearing. His ace card was that Prince Albert had included India in an extensive programme of travel for his son drawn up shortly before his death. Bertie also added, not quite truthfully, that the Cabinet had been informed and were in favour, in principle. As a consequence Bertie returned to Sandringham in triumph, but only to face a much more formidable problem.

Alix had, unsurprisingly, got wind of her husband's intentions, resented that he had not taken her into his confidence and was quite determined to accompany him. She had been fired by the mystery of the East on her travels in Egypt and elsewhere, and could think of nothing more enchanting than a royal tour of India.

In vain, Bertie pointed out the difficulties of protocol involved in a sub-continent where the role of women was utterly different from Britain's. But a visit 'to that most beautiful and fairylike country' was what she wanted above anything else, and that was that. The situation by 30 March 1875 was reflected in a letter from Disraeli to Lord Salisbury:

The Indian Expedition!
  It seems that our young Hal kept it a secret from his wife and induced his Mother to give her assent on the representation that it was entirely approved by her Ministers.
  The Wife insists upon going! When reminded of her children, she says, 'the husband has first claim'.
  The Mother says that nothing will induce her to consent to the Princess going, and blames herself bitterly for having sanctioned the scheme without obtaining on the subject my opinion, and that of my colleagues.

For Bertie, it was all like climbing a steep mountain of shale. Just as he thought he was achieving some progress, he was rebuffed and slipped back again. Disraeli defined one of the worst obstacles: 'Where is the money to come from? He has not a shilling; she [the Queen] will not give him one. A Prince of Wales must not move in India in a *mesquin* manner. Everything must be done on an imperial scale, etc. etc. . . .'

At length, despite radical opposition, Disraeli got Bertie £112,000 for his expedition in the form of a supplementary vote. There was rather more fuss and bother about the estimated £60,000 required for Bertie's expenses. This became a long, drawn-out issue and while it was raging, Bertie happened to be at a dinner at Greenwich on 18 July at which his old friend the Duke of Sutherland was present. The Duke was overheard advising Bertie, 'If I were you, Sir, I would not take it. I would borrow the money of some friends at five per cent.'

'Well, will you lend it me?' Bertie asked; and that shut the Duke up, someone observed. As the Viceroy's guest the Indian Government would find a further £30,000, later raised to more than £100,000.

As for Alix, she never quite forgave Bertie for leaving her behind. Much later, when her son Georgie visited India, she wrote to him: 'I do still envy you dreadfully having been there and seen it all when I was not allowed to go when I wished it so very, very much.' Lord Derby was less concerned about protocol problems than of Alix's sensitivities when he wrote: '"Hal" is sure to get into scrapes with women whether she goes or not, and they will be considered more excusable in her absence.'

Having reluctantly and later regretfully given way on the expedition in general, the Queen determined to have her way on the details. She drew up a list of 'dos' and 'don'ts', including what he should or should not eat, bed by 10 p.m., due observance of Sundays, all manner of health advice, and, above all, the company he should keep.

By March 1875 all was settled to the sometimes conditional satisfaction of those involved, and to the dissatisfaction of the Queen and Alix. In an attempt to mollify Her Majesty,

Salisbury wrote to her on the 17th: 'The Indian Council think it will have a highly beneficial influence upon the minds of Your Majesty's Empire in particular.' And in a somewhat belated attempt to show Cabinet approval, he wrote to Bertie of the India Council's 'great gratification at hearing of a determination so advantageous to India and their cordial willingness to make the requisite financial arrangements'.

Remembering only too well the suite imposed upon him for his first important expedition to Canada and the United States, Bertie determined to include a number of his closest friends. These included Charles Carrington, Lord Charles Beresford, Lord Aylesford and George Sutherland; Prince Louis of Battenberg and Lieutenant Augustus Fitzgeorge, the Duke of Cambridge's son, as aides-de-camp; Lord Suffield as lord-in-waiting; and, more formally, Sir Bartle Frere as general controller of the party.

More prosaically, Bertie was to be attended by one page, three chefs, a stud groom and valet, the Duke of Sutherland's bagpiper and twenty-two other servants, besides his favourite French poodle, Bobèche, and three of his favourite hunters from Sandringham. He took the piquant precaution of having the horses taken to the London Zoo in order that they could become acquainted with the wild beasts of the jungle, including snakes, that they might encounter.

The great mistake over the arrangements was that they were so long drawn out, giving everyone, from the Queen to the most radical politician, time to grumble and mock them. The best-selling radical *Reynolds Newspaper* considered the expedition a great folly and mocked any idea of its serious usefulness. 'Albert Edward, the hero of the Mordaunt divorce suit, the mighty hunter,' was in it for 'pig-sticking and women' and nothing else. At the other end of the scale and close to the Palace, Ponsonby was heard to remark realistically that 'the object of the mission is amusement'; to which Lord Salisbury added, 'And to kill tigers.' Also, everyone knew of Alix's chagrin at not being allowed to accompany him, and this, coming so soon after her devoted nursing of him through his typhoid fever, was considered typically selfish of Bertie.

The party was due to leave on 11 October 1875, and as

the day approached both Bertie and Alix, facing the longest separation they had ever endured, became sunk in gloom. At Sandringham Old Mac and the Household were aware of Alix's misery, and when Disraeli came to stay briefly, he noted that she looked as if 'she were about to commit suttee'. For Bertie the misery was not quite as deep because he was, until the last moment, so busy with his arrangements.

On the evening of the day of departure, Alix accompanied Bertie in the train from Charing Cross Station, which reached Dover at 10.50 p.m. In spite of the late hour, the local people were out in their thousands, the Mayor delivered an address and they embarked in the SS *Castilia* amid the sound of the national anthem. At Calais a great crowd greeted them on the dockside, with the self-important Mayor much in evidence. For a moment the Prince and Princess stood side by side together at the ship's gangway, waving and trying to conceal their misery. Then they embraced, the crowd cheered, Bertie walked to the carriage and Alix, with Lady Macclesfield, tearfully returned to their quarters.

That night Paris held none of the attractions that Bertie normally enjoyed. 'He was tremendously low,' Carrington told his mother. 'I had never seen him like this before, and he even felt seriously inclined to return home rather than go on.' Twelve days later Bertie was as depressed as ever. 'We are more like a lot of monks than anything else,' Carrington further remarked. He and the other bloods of the party, like Aylesford and Charlie Beresford, began to wonder if they would not rather return home, too. 'No jokes or any approach to them.'

They were met by their ship at Brindisi. HMS *Serapis* was an elaborately converted Indian troopship, deep carpet covering the decks where once Indian Army soldiers lay panting in the heat of the Red Sea. The portholes had been greatly enlarged and there were fans everywhere. Unfortunately the engines had given trouble *en route* from England, and an Inspector of Machinery had to be rushed out to attend to the boilers. He was a Geordie with a strong accent and a completely unselfconscious manner, but was so important in his role that Captain the Hon. H. Carr Glyn RN treated him with the utmost respect: he had, after all, got his ship to Brindisi on time.

On that first night at sea Bertie insisted that the mechanic from Tyneside should dine with the royal suite. This he did 'dressed in a tailcoat and waistcoat – "me yeller wais'coat" – with numerous buttons (upper half undone to show he was formal), a roll collar and tight sleeves'. Bertie himself was making sartorial history by wearing for the first time a dark blue 'dinner-jacket' with black silk facings and black bow tie. He was exceedingly proud of this invention which he had worked out with his tailor, but did not in the least mind being upstaged by his guest's even more radical departure from formal wear. The two got on exceedingly well and, in addition to repairing their ship's boilers, the Geordie succeeded in dragging the Prince of Wales out of the doldrums. From now on (though Bertie was seasick that night) it was a happy and relaxed party, to everyone's relief.

Bertie and his party were further enlivened by their arrival in Piraeus. He had decided to visit his brother-in-law, the King, and bring to Alix's favourite brother her loving wishes as well as a rather natty steam launch. Bertie was on the bridge admiring the reception awaiting them as they entered the harbour. Ironclads of the British Mediterranean Fleet, including the flagship, were dressed overall, as were the entire Greek Navy and the Greek royal yacht, *Amphitrite*.

All this went to the head of Captain Glyn – or it could have been the luncheon port wine – and he entered Piraeus at twice the advisable speed and lost both his anchors while approaching his billet. In a panic he called for full astern, lost control and collided first with his own attendant royal yacht *Osborne* and then the *Amphitrite*, nearly sinking one and taking away the bowsprit of the Greek royal yacht before coming to. Bertie thought this was a terrific lark, and was in the best of tempers when he met the King, whom he had always liked anyway.

The departure was almost as comic. Just as the *Serapis* was approaching the narrow harbour exit, a French gunboat cut across her bows, her captain in full dress uniform at attention on the bridge. Captain Glyn raced to the bridge and

shouted in execrable French, *'Moosoo, vous êtes un cochon!'*
The captain responded with three bows of uncomprehending
but deep respect before his little vessel disappeared astern.

Even the heat of the Red Sea failed to subdue Bertie. His
secretary, Albert Grey,* wrote home:

He sits mopping away as we steam along with the thermometer at
88 on the bridge at midnight, not complaining like the others of the
discomfort of the heat – but congratulating himself as he throws
away one wet handkerchief after another – 'What a capital thing is
a good wholesome sweat!'

'It was 109° in the sun yesterday,' Bertie wrote home
cheerfully, 'and I went down to the engine-room just before
dinner where it was 118° and in the stokehole 129°!' He was
still in excellent spirits when the *Serapis* entered Bombay
harbour between two lines of British battleships, again
dressed overall.

On this same evening of 8 November 1875, Alix at Sandringham was as aware as Bertie himself that the next day was
his thirty-fourth birthday, and it would be the first time since
their marriage that they had been separated. So she sent him
a loving telegram.

As soon as Alix knew that she was not going to be allowed
to accompany her husband to India, she made arrangements
to enjoy herself as well as she could. That meant being with
her family, and with her own children, who were now
between eleven (Eddy) and six (Maud) years old. To the
clear disapproval of Queen Victoria, Alix invited her parents
over from Denmark to stay at Sandringham. Although King
Christian and Queen Louise were fond of Bertie and certainly
admiring of him, and Alix missed him dreadfully, his absence
lent a relaxed air to the family gathering and an easier tone
to the conversation, games and other activities. For Bertie's
presence was a very commanding one, from his strong voice
with its guttural accent, the cigar smoke which followed him
about like a new-fangled, coal-fired ironclad, to his sheer bulk

---

* Later fourth Earl, who became Governor-General of Canada.

– almost fifteen stone on a mere five feet seven inches. As one of his Household once observed, 'You were never long in a house with the Prince of Wales before you knew he was there.'

From the time the 'Danois' arrived in the country, Queen Victoria implemented a policy of insulting them. First, she invited Alix to stay at Windsor for the christening of the first child of Bertie's younger brother Affie, now Duke of Edinburgh, and his wife, the Grand Duchess Marie, the only daughter of Tsar Alexander II. But the Queen pointedly did not invite Alix's parents, using as an odd excuse that there would be crowding at Windsor Castle – 'an odd way of looking at it', as Ponsonby sharply commented.

As if to underline the insult, the Queen then invited Alix to come to stay at Osborne House, which entailed leaving her mother and father at Marlborough House. Ponsonby, seriously alarmed at this behaviour, which Bertie would never have allowed, wrote: 'Of course the Princess of Wales sees this and will talk about it and if it gets about that the Queen is unkind to her when she is so very popular there will be a row.'

To Ponsonby's horror the vendetta was pursued further. When the time came for King Christian and Queen Louise to return to Copenhagen, Alix planned to accompany them. There was nothing to detain her in London and, of course, she would take her children with her. Queen Victoria said 'No' – not on any account. Finding it hard to restrain herself, Alix pressed her case so firmly that she was told, with the utmost reluctance, that she could go, but not the children. All this travel and change of scene was upsetting for them. Wearily, Alix fought back and at length succeeded in achieving another reversed decision.

But even now the cat-and-mouse game was not yet over. At the last minute before Alix's departure with her entourage of her own suite, nursemaids, the boys' tutor, the Revd John Neale Dalton, nursery footman, Charles Fuller, and others, the Queen informed Alix that she would have to return in time for the state opening of Parliament in February. The Queen had not carried out this duty for years, but now she decided that she would and deemed it essential that Alix, in the absence of the Prince of Wales, must accompany her.

This time Alix exploded with wrath at this curtailment of her visit to her old home, writing in outrage both to Bertie and Disraeli. Bertie, in the throes of some enormous tiger or elephant hunt, or some elaborate ceremonial in the heart of India, wrote a strong letter to his mother protesting at this unreasonable demand. Disraeli consulted the Lord Chancellor, Lord Derby, and Lord Salisbury on the matter, and both agreed that, however inconvenient for the Princess of Wales, it was incumbent upon her to obey the sovereign and return. 'I have the painful duty to communicate this opinion to Her Royal Highness,' Disraeli wrote to Bertie.

Bertie's own letter of protest on the subject had been answered by the Queen thus:

As regards dear Alix's return I have written always in the same strain . . . but I *cannot* be *silent* upon the *one* point of it which, I must say, pains and hurts me, which is yours and dear Alix's treating my reasons for wishing her to return as an *act of unkindness on my part*, and this applies generally to the *so often* repeated *long* visits abroad. It is the very reverse; if I did *not* love you both as I do, or if I did not feel that what I thought and knew to be right on public grounds I would never insist upon what unfortunately dear Alix *never* does view in the *right light*. . . . *Her not returning* and being with me on this occasion, when you were abroad, would have been misunderstood and have done her harm.

King Christian had understood this completely, the Queen insisted, 'but not so the Queen'. Poor, harmless Queen Louise never could do anything right in Queen Victoria's eyes: a Hesse-Cassel was *never* to be trusted!

From Bertie's first night on Indian soil, and his birthday celebrations the next day – parades, illumination of the fleet, fireworks galore – the tour was a stunning success, and Charles Carrington was able to write home to his mother on 13 March 1876:

The Prince has travelled 7,600 miles by land and 2,300 miles by sea [excluding the voyage each way], knows more chiefs than all the Viceroys and Governors together and has seen more of the country in the time than any living man. His health, courage, spirit, tact, and power of memory have been wonderful. He has proved himself a man in 100,000.

Lord Charles Beresford put the success of the tour down to Bertie's 'zeal, ability, tact and indomitable vigour. He gave his whole mind to the entertainment, thought of everything in advance, and set aside his personal comfort and convenience from first to last.'

He could have conditioned this statement by adding that none of them experienced much personal discomfort or personal inconvenience. Princes, maharajahs, governor-generals and residents did everything within their powers to welcome, entertain and provide every comfort for their guests. At Benares, for example, 'a city of tents' had been laid out. Prince Louis recounted that his own tented suite consisted of a double bedroom, sitting-room deeply carpeted and with armchairs and a brick fireplace and coal to make him feel at home, although the temperature was in the nineties, dressing-room and bathroom with constant hand-delivered hot water.

Prince Louis also visited Bertie's suite, the finest of them all, with the tent sides hung with embroideries and shawls, and a young girl of noble birth tucked into his bed every night.

There were numerous hunting adventures, from Ceylon to Kashmir. On 6 December 1875 Carrington described the Prince of Wales's first elephant hunt to his mother:

The Prince of Wales went elephant shooting and knocked one over which lay as if dead and its tail was cut off, till Charlie Beresford got on it and danced a hornpipe. This was more than the beast could stand: so it rose majestically and stalked off into the jungle. Afterwards HRH got another chance and bagged his first elephant. Driving back the Prince's carriage upset, and turned completely over. No one was hurt, but it was a narrow escape.

A few weeks later, on 5 February 1876, Charles Carrington told of Bertie's first tiger, spotted from a 'royal shooting box' (i.e. quite safe) and hit by two successive bullets. The tiger appeared to be mortally wounded, but 'being unused to the sport, we all ran after it and found it dead, a full-grown female 8½ feet long. If she had only been wounded it would have been all up for most of us.' Six more tigers were shot that afternoon, which was not such a famous victory because all these hunts, of tiger, elephant, rhinoceros, buffalo and other wild animals, were organised on a giant scale and to offer the worst shot in the world a near certainty of making a kill. In one double hunt flanking the river dividing Nepal from India, 200 elephants and 2,000 coolies were employed for driving on one side and 1,000 elephants and 10,000 soldiers on the other side.

After the slaughter, Bertie could be sure of a hot bath, a change into his new 'dinner-jacket' and a first-class dinner comparable to anything he could hope for at home.

'Since I last wrote to you,' he told his sons, 'I have had great tiger shooting. The day before yesterday I killed six, and some were very savage. Two were man-eaters. Today I killed a tigress and she had a little cub with her. . . .'

As Charles Carrington's mother wrote to him on 19 April 1876, 'Now you all will chase wild elephants and shoot tigers in your imagination for the rest of your lives.'

Elephant tusks, tiger skins, stuffed and mounted heads of numerous victims of Bertie's shoots, occupied much of the cargo space of HMS *Serapis* on its homeward voyage. Gifts of all kinds from more than one hundred hosts were also space-consuming, especially the live animals and birds. Sir Jung Bahadur, for one, had given Bertie a cheetah and an Arab horse, and in addition, secured below decks, there were seven leopards, four elephants, three large ostriches, five tigers and a Himalayan bear. They all had to be fed and watered, their cages cleaned out, and in turn exercised on deck where they developed amiable relations with the ship's company.

Ponsonby and Lord Salisbury had been quite wrong in their cynical suggestions that all Bertie was going to India for was 'amusement' and 'to kill tigers'. In the course of his long tour, he had established excellent relations with innumerable officials from the Viceroy himself down to the rulers of minor states. Hundreds of British expatriate civil servants and others were cheered by the genuine interest Bertie had shown in their work.

At the same time, Bertie was not pleased with all that he had seen and did not mince his words when he came to report his observations. These caused a great deal of surprise and revealed his unsuspected depth of compassion and determination to seek justice for the underdog. His mother, too, was surprised to receive these early comments on British treatment of the natives:

What struck me most forcibly was the rude and rough manner with which the English 'political officers' (as they are called, who are in attendance upon the native chiefs) treat them. It is indeed much to be deplored, and the system is, I am sure, quite wrong. Natives of all classes in this country will, I am sure, be more attached to us if they are treated with kindness and with firmness at the same time, but not with brutality and contempt.

Lord Salisbury, who after all was the Secretary of State for India, was equally astonished to read of Bertie's comments on 'the disgraceful habit of officers in the Queen's service speaking of the inhabitants in India, many of them sprung from the great races, as "niggers"'.

'Because a man has a black face and a different religion from our own, there is no reason why he should be treated as a brute,' Bertie commented on another occasion.

To bring about a serious reform in the manner and attitude of Anglo-Indian officials was far beyond the capacity of the Prince of Wales after one tour. But it was a start, and Disraeli, shocked by Bertie's findings, had the Resident in Hyderabad 'recalled in consequence of his offensive behaviour'. And the fact that there was widespread resentment among British officials working in India at what they regarded as the Prince of Wales's attempt to undermine their authority, indicated that he might have started them on the road to reform.

All this did credit to Bertie and it was a great misfortune that, before he even reached home, he became involved willy-nilly and innocently in another marriage scandal.

14

Scandals and Tragedy

*'Lily of love, pure and inviolate!
Tower of ivory! Red rose of fire!'*
Oscar Wilde

The greatest scandal to shake the marriage of the Prince and
Princess of Wales took place during the closing stages of his
tour of India, while he was still shooting vast quantities of
game and enjoying the ultimate luxuries of the East. But it
was Alix, having completed her royal duties on the Woolsack
alongside the Queen, and now living quietly at Marlborough
House, who bore the first brunt of the affair.

Some years earlier, and before his illness, Bertie had
enjoyed an innocent flirtation with a sybaritic, pampered and
licentious young woman, Lady Aylesford. He compounded
this folly by writing to her a number of rather silly but uncompromising letters. In the absence of Lord 'Sporting Joe' Aylesford in India with Bertie, the equally promiscuous Lord
Blandford struck up a passionate affair with the lonely Lady
Aylesford. He went so far as to stable his horses nearby and
set himself up in a hostelry, visiting his mistress without
much attempt at concealment every night.

Like everyone else within their circle, the centre of which
was 'the Marlborough House set', Alix had got wind of this

threatening scandal but had no idea that it could involve Bertie, nor that Lord Aylesford, strongly supported by Bertie, who described Blandford as 'the greatest blackguard alive', was hurrying home determined to sue his wife for divorce. Nor did she know that Lord Randolph Churchill, Blandford's younger brother, was equally determined to oppose any divorce, which would be the ruin of Blandford's family. She was certainly unaware of the existence of a packet of letters addressed to Lady Aylesford from Bertie. One afternoon at Marlborough House Alix received a message that Lord Randolph Churchill, Lord Alington and Lady Ailesbury were downstairs and would be grateful for a few minutes of her time. She saw no reason for not seeing them: Churchill was a family friend and she knew Lady Ailesbury and Lord Alington, too.

When the trio entered her drawing-room she realised that she had made a dreadful mistake and had misheard through her deafness 'Aylesford' as 'Ailesbury'. Lord Randolph Churchill, with minimum respect for Alix's rank and in a belligerent manner he would never have dared to assume if Bertie had been present, told Alix that he had in his possession letters of a most compromising nature from the Prince of Wales to Lady Aylesford, indicating her presence as he mentioned her name.

I am determined by every means in my power to prevent the [divorce] case coming before the public, and I have these means at my disposal. I must warn Your Royal Highness that in the opinion of lawyers whom I have consulted, the Prince would be subpoenaed to give evidence if Lord Aylesford sued for divorce, and, if published, these letters would ensure that His Royal Highness would never sit upon the Throne of England.

Twisting the knife in the wound, Churchill added as he left that he was informing the Prince and Lord Aylesford 'about the turn which events had taken'.

Alix was appalled at this brutal threat uttered by one of Bertie's oldest friends, and for a while she remained tearful and nonplussed. Then, inevitably, she called on the wise and mature judgment of Sir Francis Knollys.

The Princess of Wales's drawing-room might have been the stage setting for Act II of some high drama. Just as Knollys entered and before Alix could recite her problem, her favourite cousin, the Duchess of Teck, was announced, leaving Alix with the decision to include or exclude her from her revelations. She decided to take her into her confidence and was thankful that she had done so because the Duchess of Teck at once gave advice with which Knollys agreed: 'Order your carriage, go straight to the Queen and tell her exactly what happened. She will understand and entirely excuse you from any indiscretion. It will be in the Court Circular that you were with the Queen today and any comment will be silenced.'

That was exactly how it turned out. The Queen was beside herself with fury over the threatened blackmail and the general conduct of this second son of the Duke of Marlborough and Member of Parliament for Woodstock; and she was completely understanding of Alix in her wretched situation. 'Her dear name should never have been mixed up with such people.'

Nearly two thousand miles away in Cairo, on his way home, Bertie learned of Churchill's blackmail attempt. He also heard that Churchill was putting it about that he had invited Lord Aylesford to India only in order that Aylesford's wife could pursue her affair more freely. Bertie was thrown into a frenzy of fury and frustration. When he had calmed down a little, he telegraphed to his friend Lord Hardwicke* to ask him to represent his interests. He then despatched Lord Charles Beresford by the fastest means possible to London. He was to ask Churchill 'to arrange a convenient time and place in France for a meeting with pistols', duelling having been illegal in England since 1844. The second step was less wise than the first, but Beresford relished his mission, steamed flat-out to Brindisi in the royal yacht *Osborne* and then took the fastest train to London. In reply, Churchill wrote an insulting letter to the Prince of Wales at his next destination, Malta, refusing the challenge and describing it as 'absurd'.

* His nickname was 'Glossy Top' because he brushed his beaver hat so hard. He liked to see his face in it.

By this time, 19 April 1876, the scandal had spread among the upper classes but had not yet reached the newspapers. Was this going to be another Mordaunt case? people were asking. Would the great dukedom of Marlborough be set against the power of the royal family? What would the Queen's attitude be this time?

The Queen's feelings were made crystal clear in a letter of this same date from her Private Secretary, Lord Ponsonby, to Knollys. First she emphasised her 'perfect confidence' in the Prince of Wales, who had offered to delay his return home to avoid embarrassment, and her belief that the letters were 'perfectly innocent'. All the same, she deeply regretted that the correspondence, 'harmless as it is', should be in existence.

The Queen feels very deeply the pain this matter has caused the Prince of Wales, and had there been any probability of a public scandal into which his name could be dragged by these villains, she would have agreed in thinking it advisable that he should not return until a frank explanation had been publicly made. But, as it is to be hoped that there is no prospect of any such misfortune, Her Majesty hopes that, conscious of his innocence, he will discard all thought on the subject and enjoy the welcome he will find on his return. . . .

The welcome was all that Alix, Bertie and the Queen herself could have prayed for. Alone, Alix insisted on being taken out to sea to meet the *Serapis* as it came up-Channel. Bertie's ship hove to, Alix was helped up the gangway, and they greeted one another with a long and warm embrace on deck before disappearing below to his suite.

That evening the crowds were out on the streets of London as they drove to Marlborough House. 'It did one's heart good to see the Princess's face – she is so glad to have him back,' wrote Lady Knightley. The Queen hoped that they would remain domestically at home that night to recover, but Bertie was having none of that. By 7.30 they were back in their carriage on their way to the opera house with their two boys for a gala performance of Verdi's *Ballo in Maschera*. The packed house was thrilled at this surprise appearance, and the Prince and Princess and their children emerged from their box to wave back to the audience at the beginning and end of every act.

'It seemed as if the demonstrations of welcome would never cease. The Prince bowed and bowed repeatedly till he must have been fatigued with bowing; but the cheering went on,' *The Times* reported.

Further development of the crisis was averted the very next day, 12 May 1876, when it became known that Lord Aylesford was not going to divorce his wife after all: he later separated from her privately. Similarly, Lady Blandford obtained a deed of separation from her husband. Churchill sent a curt note of apology to Bertie, who refused to accept it. Bertie also made it known that he and Alix would never again set foot in any house that offered Lord Randolph and his wife Jennie any hospitality, which meant social ostracism. The Churchills departed for America on a more or less enforced holiday.

Life for Lord Randolph's parents, the Duke and Duchess of Marlborough, had become so uncomfortable, too, that the Duke accepted, with extreme reluctance, Disraeli's offer of the Viceroyalty of Ireland. Here Lord Randolph and his family – including his son Winston – joined them, Randolph in the post of Secretary.

The notorious feud between the Prince of Wales and Lord Randolph Churchill continued for another eight years, in spite of a more fulsome apology being offered and accepted by Bertie.

Meanwhile, Bertie's reports on conditions in India had brought him considerable kudos among senior politicians, some of whom were extremely surprised to learn that there was a serious and responsible side to him. Many people who believed that the Queen was wise to exclude him from employment began to change their minds and, more cynically, recognised that there might be political advantage in backing the Prince of Wales's ardent wish to do something useful and important instead of the never-ending round of speeches and tree-planting and foundation-stone laying. Both Disraeli and Gladstone on behalf of their parties had, they thought, done all that they could to help Bertie become involved in some national social service, but both were frustrated again and again by the Queen, whose obduracy was becoming pathological. Apart from any other consideration, Queen Victoria was becoming an elderly lady and inevitably her son was going to succeed her before long. Yet here he was, edging towards forty, without having seen the contents of the red boxes which were daily read and checked by the sovereign, and without anything more than a superficial knowledge of the workings of government.

It was Gladstone who made the breakthrough in the end. His Liberal Party had returned to power in 1880 and, within twelve months, he had persuaded the Queen that Bertie should become a trustee of the British Museum. No doubt she judged that he could not get up to much mischief in this post because it seemed so wildly inappropriate for her philistine son. In fact, he proved conscientious and interested and soon found himself on the Standing Committee, where he wielded greater power. He shrewdly had his old friend Baron Ferdinand de Rothschild made a trustee, and in gratitude 'Ferdy' presented the Museum with a valuable collection of objets d'art.

In Bertie's liberal eyes it was absurd that the majority of people worked a six-day week while the nation's museums were closed on Sunday. He did not initiate the movement towards Sunday opening, which had been debated before and always defeated by the Sabbatarians, but it was his weight, in the House of Lords, which tipped the scales and led to the Upper House passing a resolution in favour, the House of Commons following suit, though dragging its feet, ten years later.

Three years after this appointment, Gladstone added social neglect to the pursuit of culture among Bertie's responsibilities. Among all the roles he played before becoming King, he was most proud of his work with the Royal Commission on the Housing of the Working Classes. Charles Dickens, who had done more than anyone before him to shame the nation about working-class conditions, had been dead for more than a decade when this Commission was set up in

1884. Two of Bertie's closest friends, Sir Charles Dilke (as chairman and one-time republican) and Charles Carrington, were fellow members and probably had something to do with his adoption.

Although no one cited it as a good reason for including Bertie, it was especially appropriate because his own property included some of the worst slums in London. Bertie's first contribution was to support the liberalisation of the Committee by including, among others, a Roman Catholic in the form of Cardinal Manning, Archbishop of Westminster, an Irish Nationalist, and (previously unheard of) a *woman*, Octavia Hill, who already had half a lifetime of housing reform work behind her. But Gladstone, a political Liberal, obliged the Cabinet to exclude her, which was bigoted and stupid of him.

Even before the first meeting, Charles Carrington and Bertie, participators in so many larks in the past, conspired to join forces on a more serious enterprise. They were keen to learn some of the facts before debating them and, to do this, they decided to view some slums disguised in working-men's clothes. They took with them the Chief Medical Officer of Health in the Local Government Board, and their hansom-cab was discreetly followed by another 'growler' with escorting police.

They made several reconnaissance expeditions, the first on 18 February 1884, which Carrington described:

The first room we went into had no fire, or furniture, and was inhabited by a gaunt, half-starved woman with three little children practically naked lying on a heap of rags in the corner. The landlord asked her where her fourth child was. She answered, 'I don't know, it went down into the Court some days ago, and I haven't seen it since.' The landlord said 'What can I do with her, she can't pay any rent and she won't go.' The Prince was so horrified that he wanted to give her a five pound note. Had he done this, I don't think we could have got out of the Court alive, as the news would have spread like wildfire. . . . B. was very pleased at having been able to see things for himself. . . . We visited some very bad places, but we got him back safe and sound to Marlborough House in time for luncheon.

After this and other visits, Bertie spoke at meetings with the authority of first-hand and recent experience; moreover, he was more assiduous than some members in his attendance, and actually cancelled enjoyable social occasions in order to contribute to meetings. 'The Prince of Wales is most regular in his attendance; he comes punctually at 11 and stays till 1.30 or the break-up of the sitting, coming and going unattended in his hansom,' wrote the Commission's Secretary. 'We should not have had a sitting today [4 November 1884] but for his zeal but he has arranged all his visits from Tuesday night to Thursday night so as not to miss one of our meetings.'

On another occasion this same Secretary wrote that:

. . . he was always ready with apposite questions when his turn for examining came. At times his sense of humour called forth his uncontrollable laughter, which relieved the solemnity of the proceedings. It was my duty to read day by day portions of the draft report for the criticism of members. One sentence on Whitehall began, 'The habits of Jews are indescribably filthy. . . .' This threw HRH into convulsions, as he exclaims, 'What will Ferdy Rothschild say if we don't modify that?'

Unprecedentedly, the Commission's first report was prepared and signed by Bertie within twelve months of its first meeting. As Bertie's biographer recounted, 'The Commission unanimously recommended . . . that local authorities should be empowered to compel owners to keep dwellings in healthy and habitable repair and to supply at their own outlay adequate accommodation. Public interest was quickened, and, unlike many inquisitions of its kind, this Royal Commission early bore legislative fruit.' In fact, and inevitably, procrastination and evasion succeeded in getting round the new laws and more powerful legislation had to be passed five years later to cause a significant improvement. It is safe to say that none of this could have been achieved without Bertie's contribution.

Although many people thought Alix was not very bright, they underestimated the effect of her deafness on her public behaviour and performance. She was profoundly deaf by the late 1870s, often misunderstood what was said to her and, however cleverly she covered up* and however generously people made allowance for it, she was generally judged by Society to be simple-minded: kind, sweet-natured, affectionate, but certainly slow.

Lady Macclesfield and other members of Alix's Household knew otherwise. They knew how wise were her judgments and how sensible her opinions. Lord Esher, a shrewd judge if ever there was one, thought she had 'much of the force of character and a good deal of the sound sense of Queen Caroline. . . . Her cleverness has always been underrated – partly because of her deafness. In point of fact she says more original things and has more unexpected ideas than any of the family.'

It was from 1877, when Bertie adopted the first of his regular and acknowledged mistresses, that Alix's tact was exercised. 'It was the "personal tact" that came to her aid throughout the many difficulties which were to beset her as the years passed,' noted Mrs J. Comyns Carr, 'and which made her so intensely beloved in the somewhat restricted circle of those who had the honour of her acquaintance.'

The period from 1877 to 1890 was a severely testing one for Alix for other reasons. It began with a breakdown in her health in March 1877. When she was better, her doctor ordered her out of the country to convalesce. She chose to visit Greece and the palace of her favourite brother, King George I, where she quickly recovered her robust health and enjoyed a happy and relaxed time. When she returned home, she learned that a woman of great charm, style and self-confidence, Mrs Lillie Langtry, had arrived in London.

Lillie – 'the Jersey Lily' – was the daughter of the Dean of Jersey, the Very Revd W. C. Le Breton. She grew up to be

---

* 'Her manner during dinner was much more vivacious than I had been led to expect, and she wore an expression of interest that belied her deafness, though Lord Cromer told me he did not think she heard a word he said,' wrote Sir Almeric Fitzroy. But the Duchess of Westminster considered that she 'was so deaf that conversation was impossible and we thought her nice but boring'.

striking rather than classically beautiful, her notable features being her golden hair, hour-glass figure and alabaster-like skin. She combined shameless self-confidence with yielding femininity and consummate ambition. In the confines of her island home the best she could do for a husband was Edward Langtry, who had a yacht but not as much money as she thought. He was a colourless, slow-witted, heavy-drinking fellow used by Lillie as a passing convenience to support her planned assault on London Society.

When these two came to London after their honeymoon they knew almost nobody, but Lillie was confident that they would soon meet someone who would 'bring them in', and the wait was a short one. Overwhelmed by her beauty and charm, she found herself first at a tea party, then at an evening party where the guests were mainly artists and actors. John Millais and James Whistler wanted to paint her; the actors, including Henry Irving, to take her out to dinner.

The phrase 'to take London by storm' must surely have been coined for Lillie Langtry. Suddenly, her name was everywhere, her photograph in the shops, and when she went riding in Hyde Park (one of her earliest admirers had bought her a horse), the crowds gathered in great numbers. 'Someone raised the cry that it was I,' she once wrote, 'people rushed towards me, and, before the police could intervene, I was mobbed to such an extent that an ambulance finally conveyed me, suffocating and unconscious, to St George's Hospital.'

Arthur Sullivan wrote:

> Oh, never, never since we joined the human race
> Saw we so exquisitely fair a face

And Oscar Wilde:

> Lily of love, pure and inviolate!
> Tower of ivory! Red rose of fire!

This tall, voluptuous young woman was hardly 'inviolate'. Bertie's young brother, Prince Leopold, laid siege and so did

Moreton Frewen,* the King of the Belgians and the Crown Prince of Austria, the unstable Rudolf.

But none of these, and other, competing paramours could any longer stay the field when Bertie fell head-over-heels in love with Lillie, who became his first recognised and steady mistress – to such a degree that it was all any hostess's standing was worth to invite him without her. While in London he rode in the Park with her almost every day, and she was in and out of Marlborough House as frequently.

As for the Queen, disapproval and curiosity were about equally balanced in her mind, curiosity winning by a short head. So Lillie and her husband received one of those very thick and elaborate invitations to one of Her Majesty's drawing-rooms. There was no longer any question of her acceptability even if, as she complained on being presented, the Queen 'looked straight in front of her, and, I thought, extended her hand in rather a perfunctory manner'.

Sensibly, Alix accepted the 'Lillie affair' without vocal protest. She knew that to complain, privately or publicly, would inevitably lead to loss of dignity for herself as well as for Bertie, and that there was nothing to do but bow to the inevitable. Further she expressed her liking for the woman and gladly had her to dinner at Marlborough House. Bertie openly took her to Paris and let it be known that he would appreciate her being invited, too, to any country house at which he was staying. She invariably was.

For many months, Lillie's standing continued to rise. Society ladies had their hair done in Lillie's characteristic mode, the 'Langtry knot'; at the best milliners, shoe-makers and dress shops they bought 'Langtry shoes', 'Langtry hats', and so on; and they posed for photographs in the Langtry attitude.

It seemed certain that Lillie Langtry would at length overstep the mark with the Prince of Wales, and she did so – resoundingly – at a dinner party at which she had too much champagne and for a joke dropped a lump of ice down Bertie's

---

* A metallurgist who married Lord Randolph Churchill's American sister-in-law, one of the Jerome girls.

213

back. He left at once, puce with rage, and she was not seen with him again for some time.

But Bertie remained fond of his first and amusing steady paramour and used his influence to get her on to the stage. Lacking any dramatic training, she was given the part of Kate Hardcastle in *She Stoops To Conquer* thanks to Bertie's friendship with the actor-manager of the Haymarket, Squire Bancroft, who was also a member of the Garrick Club. His promotion of his one-time lover ensured packed houses. Of the first night of *She Stoops . . . The Times* wrote:

When we say that yesterday's representation of Goldsmith's play was eminently successful, we are paying the highest compliment to the performers who principally contributed to this result. Foremost among these was Mrs Langtry, who, it would be affectation to conceal, was the grand attraction of the piece – the attraction which brought together one of the most distinguished audiences that have recently assembled in a theatre. The house overflowed with rank, fashion, and celebrity, including the Prince and Princess of Wales. . . .

Truth to tell, Lillie was an indifferent, rather wooden actress, but her career prospered, none the less, and she even did a tour in America. At length the parts dried up and she became weary of acting, which had made her quite well off. Bertie remained loyal to her to the end. 'I came up by train at the beginning of the month [January 1890]', he wrote sadly to Lord Randolph Churchill, 'to be present at Mrs Langtry's final performance of "As you Like it". . . .'

Bertie had long since encouraged his friend and relation, Prince Louis of Battenberg, to replace him as a steady lover. The impetus was scarcely needed and their affair, conducted with extreme discretion by contrast with Bertie's, stemmed from genuine love.

Louis, now a Lieutenant RN, had suffered a tragedy which he shared with both Bertie and the Queen. Princess Alice of Hesse and her family had been struck down by diphtheria two years earlier. One of her children had died, and she herself, worn down with nursing them all, had finally succumbed, too. Alice was Bertie's favourite sister, who had so effectively helped him to survive his own dreadful illness. He

The children in 1876. The two good-looking boys are twelve (Eddy standing) and eleven (Georgie). The three girls are (left to right) Louise, Maud and Victoria.

Part of the dining-room at Marlborough House.

Bertie and some of his cronies, 1889. *Left to right:* Christopher Sykes,
Colonel Augustus Fitzgeorge, George Duke of Cambridge, Prince of Wales,
Admiral Adolphus Fitzgeorge, Arthur Sassoon and Colonel Stephens.

The Tranby Croft house party shortly before it broke up on 11 September
1890. William Gordon-Cumming is in the front row between Mrs A.
Wilson and the Prince of Wales. But he had already left and it is clear
that his portrait from another occasion was superimposed on the print to
provide respectability.

Bertie at Baden while taking the waters.

Above Bertie at forty-one, Alix at thirty-eight with Queen Victoria in 1883. The Queen had already been on the throne for forty-six years.

Left Minnie, the Dowager Tsaritsa of Russia (seated), with her sister Alix and Bertie, Copenhagen, 1900. Bertie soon became bored in Denmark and craved the company of his Marlborough Club fellow members.

Some of Bertie's paramours, several of whom were specially accommodated at the Coronation in what wags called 'the King's Loose Box': *Top left* Sarah Bernhardt. *Top right* Lillie Langtry. *Bottom left*, Alice Keppel, Mrs George Keppel, the favourite and longest lasting. *Bottom right*, The Countess of Warwick, previously Lady Brooke – 'the Babbling Brooke'.

Above The new
King and Queen.

The procession,
passing
Guildhall, at
their delayed
Coronation, 9
August 1902.

Admirals in conflict: *Above left*, Sir John (Jackie) Fisher, a favourite of both Bertie and Alix. *Right* Lord Charles (Charlie B.) Beresford, who fell out with both Bertie and Fisher. *Below left*, Lord Esher, wise adviser and *éminence grise*. No one gave *him* a nickname. *Right* Sir Frederick (Fritz) Ponsonby, Bertie's loyal secretary.

The King and his friend and financial adviser, the astute Sir Ernest Cassel, from whom stemmed the mighty fortune of his grand-daughter, Edwina Mountbatten.

was heartbroken, as was her more distant relation Prince
Louis, who later married Alice's eldest daughter Princess
Victoria: their last child became Earl Mountbatten of Burma.

Prince Louis's ardent love affair lasted until Lillie found
that she was pregnant. Louis confessed to his parents in
Germany that he was the father, and they despatched an
aide-de-camp to settle things as tidily and discreetly as possible. Lillie was given a substantial grant and retired to the
country to have her child.* Louis was appointed to a man
o'war appropriately named *Inconstant*, which had orders to
circumnavigate the globe very slowly.

After the triumphant reign of Lillie Langtry, Bertie had a
number of passing lovers in what was coarsely known as
'HRH's virgin band', including a Miss Tennant, Miss Duff,
Julie Stonor, the daughter of Alix's lady-in-waiting Mrs
Francis Stonor, and others. He would have been wiser to
have continued with these temporary liaisons, but as a deep-
dyed sentimentalist Bertie felt deprived when not in love with
his paramours.

The origins of Bertie's long affair with Frances (Daisy)
Brooke should have warned him of the trouble that lay ahead.
Lady Brooke, twenty years younger than Bertie, had married
Lord Brooke in 1881, and Bertie and Alix had attended the
ceremony in Westminster Abbey. She was an intelligent, fascinating, temperamental and classically beautiful woman, rich
in her own right from a fortune inherited from her grandfather, the last Viscount Maynard.

For some years this seemingly well-matched couple lived
a contented life with a large house in London and an estate
at Easton Lodge in Essex, where there was much hunting,
shooting and fishing and indulging in large house parties.

After giving birth to two children, Daisy Brooke tired of
the routine of orthodoxy and sought a lover. She did not have
to look far and engaged in a passionate affair with Lord
Charles Beresford, the notorious philanderer and rake.
'Charlie B's' friendship with the Prince of Wales had already

---

* Lillie's marriage was dissolved and she married Sir Hugo de Bathe, a
twenty-nine-year-old soldier in 1889, and took up racing.

somewhat dimmed since their days in India together. Offered a list of fellow diners for 18 December 1886 by his host, the now reconciled Lord Randolph Churchill, Knollys wrote back on the Prince's behalf:

Perhaps you will not mind my saying to you, of course, quite confidentially, that I think perhaps the Prince would prefer Charles Beresford being omitted. He is afraid among other reasons, that he would try to lead the conversation, which in such a party would be rather a bore.

From about this time and for two more years, this liaison became notorious for its openness and passion, leading to talk of divorce, which would have ruined both of them socially and destroyed Beresford's naval career. It came to an end mutually and almost as notoriously as the affair itself when his wife became pregnant and he discovered that he was sharing the favours of Daisy with others.

Far from showing any shame, Lady Brooke wrote an indiscreet and furious letter to her lover complaining – amongst much else – of his continuing to share his bed with his wife. She did not realise that he was abroad and was certainly ignorant of the fact that he had asked his wife to open his letters. Among the accusations was that one of her children was his (quite untrue), and she instructed him to leave his wife instantly and join her in the south of France.

When she became aware of her howler, Daisy Brooke turned to Bertie for advice on how to get the letter back. She invited herself to Marlborough House and revealed all to a very sympathetic Bertie, describing herself as a 'beauty in distress'. 'He was more than kind,' she recounted to her friend, Lord Salisbury. 'He hoped his friendship would make up in part for my sailor-lover's loss, and suddenly I saw him looking at me in a way all women understand. I knew I had won.'

Bertie had fancied Lady Brooke several times when he had been staying at Easton Hall, or she and her husband at Sandringham. And now, as a 'beauty in distress' indeed, he found her irresistible and eagerly accepted her invitation to tea. Meanwhile, he used his rank without scruple to recover the letter on her behalf, first visiting the solicitor who was known to hold the letter and asking to see it. When he read it, he was described as 'most shocked'. He then hastened to Beresford's wife and, according to her account, became threatening. Finally, she agreed to give up the letter on condition that Lady Brooke absented herself from the London Season entirely for one year.

As go-between, Bertie reported this to his new conquest, who peremptorily turned down the deal, asking him to try again. He did so obediently and Lady Charles Beresford later recounted how 'the Prince came to see me a second time evidently under her influence for he was anything but conciliatory in tone, and *hinted* that my position in Society and Lord Charles's would be injured'. When she again refused, Bertie carried out his veiled threat and struck her off the invitation list at Marlborough House.

Beresford now loyally came to his wife's rescue and, on 12 January 1890, called unannounced at Marlborough House demanding to see the Prince of Wales. Bertie confronted his furious one-time friend in his study, and was himself treated to an outburst of vituperation he had never before heard in his life: 'I demonstrated with some warmth that there was only one blackguard in this case,' declared Beresford. It was said at the time that Lord Charles actually struck the heir to the throne, but more reliably that he pushed up against him causing him to sit down suddenly upon a sofa.

Shortly after this episode, this fiery Irish naval officer steamed off in his cruiser for the Mediterranean. It would have been more sensible for Lady Charles to have joined him at Malta; instead, she found herself socially ostracised in London, as she reported to her husband, whose simmering fury was later expressed in a letter to Bertie, part of which ran:

The days of duelling are past but there is a more just way of getting right done. The first opportunity that occurs I shall give my opinion publicly of Your Royal Highness, and state that you have behaved like a blackguard and a coward, and that I am prepared to prove my words. . . .

Fortunately he was prevailed upon not to send the letter. Instead, he appealed to Lord Salisbury to intervene and use his tact and power as Prime Minister to avert a public scandal which would do irreparable damage to the Crown. Salisbury did his best, but could not prevent a further furious exchange of letters between the two hot-heads.

A point was reached when Beresford, who had given up his command and raced to London to further his campaign, was about to summon the press to his home in Eaton Square. He intended to deal with 'the blackguardly and cowardly behaviour of the Prince of Wales', and describe how he had insulted his wife while pursuing the favours of Lady Brooke. This, coming on top of a gambling scandal in which Bertie had become embroiled recently, was calculated by Beresford to ruin his reputation in the country. As for himself, he would resign his commission and leave the country with his family.

Lord Salisbury, firmly instructed by the Queen to bring about peace, spent an entire week drafting an exchange of letters between the two parties which would be acceptable to them. It was hard work, with numerous and frustrating false starts; but, with extreme reluctance on both sides, a form of wording was at length agreed. The letter that Bertie agreed to sign ran thus:

Dear Lord Charles Beresford,

I regret to find from your letter of 23rd instant that circumstances have occurred which have led Lady Charles Beresford to believe that it was my intention publicly to wound your feelings.

I have never had any such intention, and I regret that she should have been led to conceive an erroneous impression upon the point.

I remain
Yours truly
(signed) Albert-Edward

It was Christmas Eve 1891 and, to his chagrin, Bertie, because of this scandal, had been obliged for the first time since his marriage to be absent from Sandringham while in England. The future Lord Esher, Reginald Brett, accepted that 'Lord Salisbury brought peace – whether with much honour or not may be questioned.' The letter was burnt, but relations remained fragile and continued so for many years, with consequences for Beresford that were professionally very damaging.

For Alix the year 1891 was both eventful and distressing with only one or two moments of pure happiness to touch with colour the drabness of the months. One of these was the birth of her first grandchild. Her daughter Louise, the Duchess of Fife, had a daughter on 17 May 1891. There was no reluctance by Louise to have her mother present at the bedside and, as Alix wrote to her second son Georgie, 'at five o'clock, thank God, I was a happy grandmother and held my little naked grandchild in my arms! It squeaked like a suckling-pig.'

Alix then left for her annual visit to Denmark, as always with her daughter Toria, who had already become a sort of supernumerary lady-in-waiting. These were still the days Alix most enjoyed, especially when her sister Minnie arrived from Russia. The affection between these two women never wavered, and when they were Queen of England and Empress of all the Russias they built themselves in 1907 a private villa in a secluded area on the coast of Denmark. They called it Hvidöre.

It was small and that added to the charm [Baroness de Stock recalled], a pure white marble staircase dividing and then joining once more, the banister was gilt bronze, the carpet bordered with a deep yellow band, a long drawing-room furnished in the softest tints; windows let haphazardly into the walls irrespective of symmetry, only made so that each allowed a different vista framing an exquisite seascape. Another drawing-room with twin writing tables before one of these views, twin bookcases, every article repeated twice, one for the Empress, the other for the Queen. . . . They relived their childhood freedom. . . . No lady-in-waiting, no court official stayed there. The Royal sisters were free. . . .

Rumours of the Lady Brooke affair reached Alix in Denmark, and she decided that she could not face another public scandal. Instead of returning to England on 13 October, therefore, in good time for Bertie's fiftieth birthday, she wrote to him that instead she was going with her sister to Livadia in the Crimea, where the Tsar and Tsarina were about to face another celebration, their silver wedding anniversary.

However affectionate Alix's letters from Russia to Bertie might be, her absence on this occasion, when she knew what store he had set on his fiftieth birthday, badly hurt him. It was, after all, a very public snub. However, he did his best to make light of it, writing to Vicky: 'I get good accounts of Alix from Livadia.' Then, to add to his misery, a serious fire broke out at Sandringham, which gutted the whole of the top floor and also badly damaged the dining-room with its Goya tapestries. Bertie's birthday was celebrated with his children in unaccustomed discomfort.

Three days later, on 12 November, surely a fated month for the disease, Georgie succumbed to typhoid fever. Noting his rising temperature, Bertie took him by special train to Marlborough House, where the best medical attention was more readily available.

A telegram to Alix at Livadia brought her hastening back to London. Alix and Bertie were reunited on 22 November. The fever was approaching its climax, and they recalled Bertie's own condition just twenty years earlier when his life was almost despaired of. Their joint anxiety brought them together again as they sat opposite one another on each side of Georgie's bed, holding his hands and praying aloud. Fortunately, he was a strong, resilient young man, and two days later the worst was over.

The same could not be said of the case of Lady Brooke's letter, but Alix knew where her duty lay now that she was back home. 'She warmly supports the Prince in everything connected with this unfortunate affair,' wrote Knollys on 19 December 1891.

Earlier in the year, Alix had given equally powerful support over Bertie's gambling scandal, which did him more public damage than anything since his neglect of his wife when she was so seriously, and for so long, ill. 'The Tranby Croft affair' was a long, drawn-out, ugly and squalid business which involved Bertie from the beginning as a witness and led to his appearance in court for every one of the days the trial of the accused took place.

Colonel Sir William Gordon-Cumming was a forty-one-year-old baronet, a soldier with a good record, and a land-owner at Gordonstoun in Scotland. He was one of a number of guests at Tranby Croft, the home of the shipowner Arthur Wilson, which was situated near Doncaster and convenient for the racing, including the St Leger, which all the house party had attended on 8 September 1890.

Bertie at this time had given up dancing, which had been a great joy before he put on so much weight, and had taken up the proscribed game of baccarat, which had become highly fashionable. Half-way through the evening's play a son of the house, who was also one of Gordon-Cumming's subalterns, clearly saw his Colonel cheating. On the following evening, when others had been warned, Gordon-Cumming won £225, mostly from the Prince of Wales, who was acting as banker, and most of those present witnessed his use of the sleight-of-hand trick, *la poussette*.

On the third day of the house party, which had become extremely tense, Gordon-Cumming was confronted by his accusers, who were now too numerous for him to deny the charge. A document was drawn up which the wretched Colonel was obliged to sign, accusing him of the charge of cheating and concluding, 'I will on my part solemnly undertake never to play cards again as long as I live.'

The next morning he left Tranby Croft threatening to blow his brains out. He did nothing of the kind: confidentiality had already been broken and many people in Society were discussing the scandal. He instituted proceedings and claimed damages for slander, citing the Prince of Wales as one of the witnesses. It was not until mid-1891 that the case was tried, by the Lord Chief Justice. The publicity was tremendous and highly damaging to Bertie, who acted with dignity but could not deny that he was playing baccarat illegally with a number of disreputable members of the aristocracy at the home of a *nouveau-riche* businessman. Public opinion was heavily loaded in favour of the gallant Colonel against the self-indulgent Prince, and the case became close to a trial of Bertie himself.

The Solicitor-General, acting for Gordon-Cumming, did not mince his words either, claiming that

Sir William was being victimised to save the honour of a Prince who encouraged habitually an illegal game; who had jumped recklessly to a wrong conclusion on bad evidence; and who had ignored deliberately article 41 of the Queen's Regulations for the Army which laid upon all serving officers (including Field-Marshal HRH the Prince of Wales) the duty of requiring any brother-officer accused of dishonourable conduct to submit his case forthwith to his commanding officer.

The Queen was appalled. 'This horrible trial drags along,' she wrote to Vicky, 'and it is a fearful humiliation to see the future King of this country dragged (and for the second time) through the dirt, just like anyone else, in a Court of Justice. I feel it is a terrible humiliation, and so do all the people. . . .'

This time, the Queen was not exaggerating. And although Gordon-Cumming lost the case after nine days (1–9 June 1891), it did infinitely more harm to Bertie than to him. The Colonel may have been disgraced and obliged to resign his commission, but he at once married an American heiress, Florence Garner, the daughter of Commodore Garner of the New York Yacht Club. Then he retired to his Scottish estates, where he was received with acclamation by the local people, and for the remainder of a long and by no means unhappy life shot great quantities of game and collected postmarks, upon which he became a leading authority.

Alix found it more difficult to reconcile herself to Lady Brooke* as her husband's lover than she had to Lillie Langtry, of whom she became genuinely fond. She never trusted the woman and, like many others, believed that it was 'the babbling Brooke' (as the press called her) who had broken the confidentiality of the Tranby Croft business, thus precipitating the Gordon-Cumming case. But it was the love life of her two boys, Eddy and Georgie, which concerned Alix during the years 1891 and 1892.

* She became the Countess of Warwick in December 1893 on the death of her father-in-law.

Although the object of the near-frantic affection of his mother, Prince Eddy had grown to be an inadequate young man, lethargic, indolent and sadly wanting in brain power. The worst that Alix would allow herself to describe him was 'dawdly', but he was really a hopeless case, exasperating Bertie by (among other numerous faults) his failure to be able to apply his mind to anything for more than a few minutes. The boys' tutor, the Revd John Neale Dalton, had given up trying to teach Eddy anything. On the other hand, he was a tall, good-looking boy with a languorous charm that attracted women, even the Queen who thought he was a 'dear good simple boy' but was fearful that he might get drawn into the fast 'Marlborough House set' when he grew up.

Eddy had been sent with his younger brother Georgie to the naval training ship *Britannia*, where he failed to achieve any progress in anything, and had accompanied his tutor and brother on two long voyages, one to the West Indies and the other to Australia. Neither of these expeditions, organised with such care, made the slightest impression on the older boy. After futile attempts to teach him French at Lausanne and anything at Cambridge (though he was given an honorary LLD), the army was resorted to. Here, at least, he became interested, even enthusiastic, about uniforms, belatedly inheriting from his father a keen dress sense.

Alas, the army also led him into dissipated ways. His visits to male brothels in Cleveland Street in London were not always easy to cover up, and on return from a trip to India he looked half dead from debauchery. It was clearly time for him to find a wife. Two attractive German princesses turned him down, which dismayed and distressed the Queen, but pleased Alix. Then he fell in love, something he did quite readily, with Princess Hélène d'Orléans, the daughter of the pretender to the French throne, the Comte de Paris, and of course a Roman Catholic. Without anyone's permission, the two became engaged, and then visited the Queen at Balmoral. This was Alix's idea, reasoning that the Queen's affection for Eddy and romantic nature might lead her to overcome her natural objections. The move worked, too, but when the Comte de Paris learned that a condition of marriage was that the Princess must become a Protestant, he put his foot down and that was that.

The search continued, and during the distressing year of 1891 it seemed as if a suitable bride had been found for the future King-Emperor. Princess Mary (May) of Teck was the eldest child of the Duke and Duchess of Teck and niece to the Duke of Cambridge, himself the C-in-C of the British Army. Her credentials were impeccable, and she was sensible, honourable and good-looking. Most important, she was willing to marry Eddy, who had now been appointed Duke of Clarence. To everyone's great relief the wedding was fixed for 27 February 1892.

It was not to be. By a curious but blessed twist of dynastic fate, soon after Prince George had recovered from his brush with death from typhoid fever, Prince Eddy was struck down with influenza. He had been out shooting with his father at Sandringham and came back shivering with a cold and headache. It was 7 January, the day before his twenty-eighth birthday. He took to his bed and Princess May sat beside him, holding his hand. He came downstairs the next day, looking awful, surveyed his presents and returned to his room. Alix telegraphed the Queen at Osborne: 'Poor Eddy got influenza, cannot dine, so tiresome.' Almost everyone at Sandringham had suffered from 'flu during this cold, miserable winter, and no one was in the least worried about Eddy, at least not until he developed inflammation of the lungs when two royal doctors were telegraphed. They diagnosed incipient pneumonia.

On the morning of 13 January the Prince became delirious and began shouting about his regiment and his brother officers, Lord Salisbury and Lord Randolph Churchill. Unfortunately, within the hearing of his fiancée, he called out the names of some of his past loves, and repeatedly cried, 'Hélène! Hélène!' His fingernails turned blue and his lips became livid.

Alix, now frightened beyond belief, sat holding his hand, fanning his face and wiping the sweat from his brow. No one could believe that he was dying, least of all his father, yet they all gathered about the bed, one doctor kneeling and taking his pulse while the domestic chaplain to the Prince of Wales stood reciting the prayers for the dying.

At 9.30 a.m. on 14 January Eddy called out, 'Something too awful has happened. My darling brother George is dead.' Then, repeatedly until he died five minutes later, 'Who is that? Who is that? Who is that?'

The speed and relentlessness of the disease added an almost unbearable dimension to the shock their son's death inflicted on Bertie and Alix. It did not in the least diminish their grief that he had been a worry to them for all his brief life; rather it added poignancy to the suffering.

In the interval before the funeral, Bertie kept returning to his son's bedroom to gaze tearfully upon his body, just as if he still could not accept the truth of what had happened. Alix took from the room the hat he had doffed and waved at her as he left for that fatal day's shooting and hung it in her own room. She also saw to it that Eddy's room was kept just as it was on the day he died, even to the half-used tube of toothpaste, with a fire burning night and day in the grate.

The whole nation, unaware of Prince Eddy's vices and inadequacies, was utterly shocked by the news. Prince George, as the new heir presumptive, was obliged to give up his prospering and highly enjoyable naval career, something he regretted all his life. It was also appropriate that he should no longer delay his own marriage, and who could be more suitable as a bride than dear Eddy's fiancée? Princess May was inclined to agree. If truth be known, she had experienced some misgivings about Eddy as a husband and had, indeed, expressed her doubts to her mother, who of course had pooh-poohed them.

The Prince and Princess of Wales, the nation was informed, were delighted at the engagement of their surviving son to Princess May of Teck, and they married amidst great national rejoicing on 6 July 1893.

15

The Reconciliation

'Inconvenient friends'
Queen Victoria of Bertie's

For Alix the early 1890s was a period of stress and intermittent unhappiness. Nothing could entirely suppress her natural optimism and extrovertism, and she recovered from any distressing occasion with the same resilience as she had, long before, when she discovered that her husband was having liaisons with other women. But, as one of her friends remarked, 'Poor Alix, she has to put up with so much, and it is not fair that she suffers as well this terrible handicap of deafness.'

Alix freely confessed that she never completely recovered from the loss of her first son. Eddy, like some mongrel dog, might prowl the streets at night, up to no good at all, but at home he was Alix's pretty puppy and she loved to have him near her. There was nothing much that could be called sublime about Prince Eddy, but his relationship with his mother was as close as he ever came to this condition.

She adored her Georgie, too, but not perhaps with the same intensity. He was much less dependent on her than Eddy had been. He had always seemed to be away at sea and now that he had left the navy and married she was no

longer the first woman in his life.* Her daughter Maud had
also just followed Louise into marriage, and their homes were
unhappily distant.

Alix celebrated her forty-fifth birthday on 1 December
1889. Her political judgments remained the same as they
were to continue for all her life. Germany was her great hate.
Like all her political prejudices, this was based on association,
record and instinct. She favoured Greece because her
brother was King, just as she leaned favourably towards
Russia because her favourite sister, her 'darling little Minnie',
was Tsarina. But, above all, it was the land of her birth
that excited her strongest passions, and the slightest hint of
criticism of Denmark or the Danish people, however indirect,
sent her into one of her rare, but ferocious, rages.

Against her wishes Bertie took Prince George to Germany
in the spring of 1890, and she disapproved of almost everything they did. When, for example, she learned that her son
had taken Holy Communion at a Lutheran service, she wrote
to him: 'I am really sorry you should have done so, as with
you it must have been a perfect *farce* as you have often told
me you could not understand a word of German. How could
you suddenly have got so *learned* . . . ?' Alix had been
brought up a Lutheran, but now she associated that religion
with Germany. 'England is not Lutheran but *Anglican*!' she
once exclaimed on another occasion when the Queen, to
Alix's outrage, had sent her Georgie as British representative
to 'a *Luther Fest*'.

Alix was equally incensed when she learned that this same
unfortunate son had been made an honorary colonel of a Prussian regiment – 'my Georgie boy has become a real, live,
filthy, blue-coated, *Pickelhaube* German soldier!!!' She could
not even bear the sight or sound of the German language.
Once, when visiting the laboratory of the famous Dane,

---

* Prince George and Princess May, now the Duke and Duchess of York,
had been given as a country home York Cottage, which was disconcertingly
close to Sandringham House. Alix's visits to the happy pair were more
frequent than May had anticipated. 'I sometimes think that just after we
were married we were not left alone enough,' May wrote in 1894, 'and this
led to many little rubs which might have been avoided.'

Professor Finsen, she was given a pamphlet he had just written. 'Is it in Danish?' she asked. 'No, Madame, in German.' 'Then I will not have it. Give me a Danish copy – why should you write in German?'

There was a rather more profound example of Alix's prejudice against Germany, and one that revealed her strategical prescience. This was the campaign she fought against the agreement between the British and German Governments over the Sultanate of Zanzibar and the island of Heligoland. Under this arrangement Germany would grant Britain its protectorate of Zanzibar in exchange for Heligoland, off the coast of Denmark, which had ceded it to Britain under the Peace of Kiel in 1814, when Denmark had also lost Norway.

But the inhabitants of Heligoland were still all Danish, and the idea of their becoming German against their wishes outraged the Princess of Wales. The Queen, anticipating that there might be a little trouble over this with her daughter-in-law, sent Ponsonby along to discuss the proposal with the Prince of Wales. This was on 13 June 1890. Before they had sat down, Bertie called for Alix to join them, knowing how knowledgeable (and inflammatory) she was on the subject.

This proved to be the case, and Ponsonby returned to Buckingham Palace with words like 'outrage' and 'betrayal' ringing in his ears. On his departure, Alix sat down and composed a long memorandum on the subject. This opened with an historical outline of the island – accurate in every detail – and then, long before anyone had given much thought to it, predicted the threat posed by a future German navy:

Germany has built an important Naval Port in the Bay of Jahde and has begun construction of the great canal from Kiel to the Elbe which will enable her to bring her Fleet, stationed at Kiel, into the Elbe and the North Sea in a few hours' time. But Heligoland dominates the whole of the German coast . . . and can, in time of war, blockade all the outlets from Germany. . . .

In 1914, a century after the signing of the Peace of Kiel, when Germany possessed a fleet second only to Britain's, and was at war with Britain, there was gnawing regret that this deal had ever been concluded and the Princess of Wales's advice ignored.

Meanwhile, with Bertie's encouragement, the memorandum, copied out by hand by Charlotte Knollys and sent to influential politicians by her father, was circulated. For instance:

Sir William Knollys to Lord Randolph Churchill, 3 July 1890
The Princess of Wales feels very strongly on the question of the cession of Heligoland, and she has embodied her idea on the subject in the accompanying memorandum. She desires me to send it to you and to say that she would be glad if you would glance at it.

Everyone who read this document recognised it as the original work of Alix from its style, form and spelling mistakes. Besides, each copy was signed 'By the Princess of Wales'. Lord Rosebery, for one, was mightily impressed by it, not least the final summarising paragraph with its note of irony:

If England cedes Heligoland to Germany, a precedent would at once be created for Spain to claim Gibraltar (another *barren* rock and a very expensive one) and Italy Malta, and there would indeed be but little reason for our retention of Cyprus which Germany might ask for as a convenient Station for her communications with her East African Colonies. At all events the opinions of the naval and military authorities as to the strategical value of Heligoland to England (and to Germany) should be submitted to the Crown before Diplomatic negotiations are completed.

Alix later pencilled in on the copy returned to her, 'I am much flattered by Lord Rosebery's remarks.' But she had to note later that, 'I fear as Lord Rosebery says it is all too late.' Too late it was, but, as Alix minuted, 'Still they might prevent the Germans from *fortifying the Island* which would at any rate be some point gained.' Alas, that was not to be.

It is understandable that Alix's name was reviled in Prussia. For more than twenty-five years, since her marriage to the Prince of Wales, she had made no bones about her dislike of everything, and almost everyone, Prussian. This had not only always concerned the Queen but had also made difficulties with her sister-in-law, Vicky, and her husband, Fritz. The Foreign Office deplored it and leading statesmen were either puzzled by it or wished the Princess of Wales would not flaunt so blatantly her dislike of Prussia.

Matters came to a head in 1888 when the old German Emperor died and Fritz – as Emperor Frederick III – succeeded to the throne. He had been ill the previous year when he attended Queen Victoria's Golden Jubilee celebrations. Vicky, and of course Victoria herself, were beside themselves with worry over his health, and now this giant of a man was dying of throat cancer. After a reign of just ninety-nine days, he died on 15 June.

The Queen, consumed with grief for her daughter, gave instructions that it was not enough for Bertie to attend the funeral; Alix must go with him. Alix refused. She had not been in hateful Berlin for eleven years, and she was certainly not going now. Bertie could go alone and do his best to console his sister. But when the Queen used all her persuasive powers, Alix gave way. 'I am greatly relieved to hear that dear Alix would go with Bertie to Berlin, as I begged her to,' she noted with satisfaction in her diary.

The experience was all that Alix feared it would be. She was fond of bereaved Vicky and feared for her future now 'that young fool William' was on the throne as Kaiser William II. Her concern was justified. Within half an hour of her husband's death, while walking in her garden in the Neue Palais to recover, Vicky became aware of soldiers armed with rifles all about her. As if under arrest, an officer of her son's Hussar regiment took her by the arm and led her inside. Then, before her eyes, this officer and the soldiers began ransacking Fritz's desk and other possible sources of papers throughout the palace, turning out drawers and spilling the contents everywhere. Too distressed to protest, Vicky heard the officer explain that, under the new Emperor's orders, he was ensuring that no important documents left the palace. Worse was to come for the heartbroken woman.

'We arrived here very late last night,' Bertie recounted to his mother, 'after a long and tedious journey as we had a very rough passage to Calais – owing to having a small and slow steamer.' Nor was their reception in Berlin a very warm one: Emperor William gave them a low-grade welcome besides the British Ambassador and his wife. The eventual meeting with William and Dona, his wife and the new Empress, 'was very trying', as Alix agreed. The funeral procession the next day was even more trying. 'Our walk lasted over an hour. The weather was very fine, but it was very hot. . . . Alix is rather tired', Bertie continued, 'after today's emotions, and having to stand so long, and get up so early after our long journey. . . .'

Never was Alix more relieved to return home, to her children and dogs, Charlotte and Old Mac and the rest of her suite, and the ever-comforting disorder of her drawing-room.

On 27 February 1898 the Prince of Wales dined for the first time at the home of the Hon. George Keppel and his wife. George Keppel was like a contemporary caricature of an army officer in *Vanity Fair*, 'every inch a colonel', as Sir Harold Acton described him. He was also a son of the seventh Earl of Albemarle. He had married Alice, a daughter of Admiral Sir William Edmonstone, and it was difficult to imagine a more handsome couple. Alice was twenty-nine when she was hostess at this evening, which was to prove epochal for both her and her guest of honour. Mrs George Keppel was known in Society for her vivacity and wit, her knowledge of what went on in the narrow but fascinating world in which she lived, and her equal capacity for recounting and listening to anecdotes. Well-informed on people and events, she also possessed a nature which prohibited her from uttering an uncharitable word about anyone. There was not an ounce of malice in this young woman, and she was flawlessly beautiful.

After meeting Alice Keppel for the first time some years later, Osbert Sitwell wrote of how, when she opened a conversation, 'she would remove from her mouth for a moment the cigarette which she would be smoking through a long holder and turn upon the person to whom she was speaking her large, humorous, kindly, peculiarly discerning eyes'.

Bertie was immediately attracted by his hostess's wit and her husky voice, her disarming manner and unselfconscious charm, and that single evening led to a relationship which warmed with the speed of a bonfire and lasted unwaveringly to the end of his life. The days of passing liaisons were over once and for all. George Keppel was very good-natured about it, making his own arrangements elsewhere, and the relationship was accepted wherever they were, both at home and on the Continent. Alice was welcome at all but a handful of stuffier houses. In fact, 'Most hostesses were relieved when Mrs Keppel was present to cope with Bertie.' In his last years as Prince of Wales, Bertie's temper had noticeably shortened, although the sun was not long in breaking through again, perhaps the brighter for its concealment. This coincided with an increasing passion for bridge now that baccarat was a forbidden game. Unfortunately, bridge is not the ideal game for people with a short fuse, especially when they do not play very well; on the other hand Alice Keppel, an equally keen player, was also highly accomplished at soothing Bertie's ruffled temper.

He was childishly pleased when he won, and very critical of his partner if he lost. . . . One evening when he was grumbling about bad cards and showing disconcerting signs of temper he suddenly put Mrs Keppel into a high no-trump bid. He was dummy and when he laid down his hand there was scarcely a trick in it. Mrs Keppel had poor cards as well. She glanced at her poor hand ruefully, then remarked in a doleful voice, 'All I can say, Sire, is: God save The King and preserve Mrs Keppel!' The King roared with laughter, and when the game was over paid his losses without complaint.

The qualities and discretion of Bertie's new mistress became widely and rapidly known. Soon she was being frequently used – for instance by the Foreign Office – as a means of confidential communication to the Prince of Wales, whose interest in that department was known and mistrusted.

Another of the subsidiary functions she performed willingly and with grace, style and complete discretion was to act as a kind of liaison officer for Bertie by permitting herself to be seated next to men at dinner in order to sound them out over certain subjects. One of these was the Kaiser at a time when relations were particularly poor between William and Bertie. Count Memsdorff, the debonair Austrian Ambassador in London, an eye-witness but out of earshot, was dying to know 'what sort of report she sent back to Sandringham'.

On this occasion, as at numerous dinners, Alice Keppel's neighbour fell for her charms and she remained on better terms with the Kaiser than did either Bertie or Alix. They met again when the Kaiser was in London in 1907 and Mrs Keppel sent him a picture of herself. The Kaiser responded coyly: 'It is very artistic and also very like you and shows that the picture must be well painted.'

Alix took her usual philosophical view of her husband's new mistress and, while she never came to like her, she by no means found Alice Keppel intolerable and was probably, and unspokenly, grateful that she amused Bertie, eased his perpetual restlessness and kept him happy. Alix, on hearing that her husband, George, was unwell, even took the trouble to write to Mrs Keppel, sympathising: 'I am so sorry to hear of your husband's illness in New York and that you should have this terrible worry. . . .'

But while Alix concealed her irritation, she certainly wearied of Mrs Keppel turning up at some time or another wherever she and Bertie travelled together. Alix particularly enjoyed Cowes Week, which she invariably spent on the royal yacht and for once saw much of her sailor son Georgie. 'How are things going on in general?' May, Duchess of York, wrote to her husband at Cowes. 'I mean, does peace reign or have you had a difficult time?'

It was not difficult to translate the meaning of this question, and Georgie replied dolefully: 'Alas, Mrs K. arrives tomorrow and stops here in a yacht, I am afraid that peace and quiet will not remain.'

'How annoyed Mama will be!' came the reply from York Cottage.

Abroad Mrs Keppel was treated as if she were a member of the royal family and was received with much bowing and scraping. At Biarritz she would stay for some part of Bertie's annual late winter holiday where they enjoyed one another's company in relative isolation, although there would always be political or personal guests for brief periods. Once it was Sir Ernest Cassel, his daughter Maud and a vivacious granddaughter Edwina (later Mountbatten). Admiral Sir John (Jackie) Fisher and Winston Churchill, meeting one another for the first time, were other guests, as was Herbert Asquith, the Liberal Party leader.

Mrs Keppel usually arrived after Bertie and returned home before he did, but they kept in touch with one another by cards and letters:

Hotel de Paris   9 April 1908
Biarritz

My dear Mrs Keppel,
    Before leaving Biarritz, I must send you a line of most sincere thanks for your kind words and wise counsels, which I shall treasure, and (I hope) profit by.
    It was a real pleasure to see you. . . .

Mrs Keppel also contrived to join Bertie at Marienbad when he took his annual cure. They would meet every day at 12.15 for a stroll along the promenade, Bertie, like all the men, carrying a mug of the water and occasionally sipping from it. Then he would return to his suite for luncheon alone, and they would meet again in the evening.

On the relatively rare times when they were separated in England, there would be frequent exchanges of discreet postcards. A coloured one of a game bird when Bertie was shooting them somewhere: 'This woodcock wishes you a happy New Year. . . .' Or at Christmas a postcard from Bertie of a little girl in sepia: 'Another Bonne Année. I think this girl is like dear little Sonia', Alice's daughter.

Peter Quennell was a friend of Alice's elder daughter, Violet, and he recalls a 'big, tumultuous, oddly assorted luncheon party', where he found himself next to her mother, Alice.

Her charm I almost immediately felt [he wrote]. She had the invaluable gift of devoting, or seeming to devote, her whole attention, so long as a dialogue lasted, to the stranger at her side, and of never allowing her gaze to flit around the room, following other conversations and pursuing other enquiries like a modern Madame Verdurin. Thus emboldened, I asked her several questions, which she cheerfully and promptly answered. What, for example, were her recollections of the tragic Czar and Czarina? Well, she had first been presented to them, she said, aboard the imperial yacht at Cowes. The deck was densely uncomfortably crowded . . . the Empress presented a frigid calm. Then [Mrs Keppel] was invited to join the

Empress below; and, as soon as the cabin door was closed behind them, there was a sudden lightening of the atmosphere. Dropping her regal mask, the Empress had at once become a friendly house-wife. 'Tell me, my dear, where do *you* get your knitting wool?' she had urgently demanded.

Alice Keppel remained a prominent figure in English Society for many years after her paramour died, along with her two daughters. Writing of her as an old lady of seventy in 1934, the worldly, sharp Sir Henry (Chips) Channon noted:

Mrs Keppel is grey and magnificent, and young in spirit, but she cannot resist lying and inventing, and saying anything that comes into her Roman head. It is a habit she contracted long ago when, to amuse the blasé King Edward, she used to tell him all the news of the day spiced with her own humour. She is like a worldly Roman matron, but minus the cruelty.

Six years later, there is another glimpse of Mrs Keppel, this time with her husband. After the entry of Italy into the Second World War they had been banished from their villa above Florence, and now could be seen walking arm-in-arm, on their way to luncheon at the Ritz in London, the latter 'a tall and soldierly personage, somewhat slow-footed, how-ever, and stooped by time'. At his side is 'a clear-eyed, straight-backed lady, who wore pearls and a noble air of belonging, unmistakably but unselfconsciously, to an altogether different period'.

Alice Keppel [wrote Peter Quennell] was the only royal favourite I had yet been able to observe; and I knew that, in the delicate role she had played, she had shown exemplary tact and charm; that no previous occupant of the same position had had fewer enemies and critics; that Edwardian statesmen had regularly sought her advice. . . .

The last years of the old century and his last years as Prince of Wales brought Bertie not only his ideal mistress/com-panion, but also other friends whom he came to value and to whom he remained loyal for the remainder of his life. In the same year, 1898, when Alice Keppel had come so gracefully and warmly into his life, he met the banker, Ernest Cassel. Baron Maurice von Hirsch had died in Hungary on 21 April

1896, leaving Bertie without a principal financial adviser. This inconvenience was short-lived. Appropriately at Newmarket, Ernest Cassel was introduced to him amidst the blended aromas of horseflesh and cigar smoke. They matched one another to perfection. Cassel had adopted banking and life in England as a teenage boy, joining the financial house of Bischoffsheim and Goldschmidt and at once revealing an uncanny skill at manipulating money. Between about 1870 and 1890 Cassel accumulated a vast fortune.

Cassel had become a hard bargainer, manipulator, sponsor, promoter, speculator, and venturer of the very highest calibre with the priceless gift of instinctive guidance and feel, sniffing out merit and demerit with equal delicacy. Moreover he got on well with those whom it was important to get on well with. International bankers were his first and closest associates, in Amsterdam and Hamburg, Paris, London and Rome.

Like Hirsch, Cassel recognised the advantages as well as the pleasures of social acceptability, and enjoyed recognition as much as spending vast sums of money on a lavish life-style and the collecting of works of art. In turn, Cassel was recognised by Hirsch for his exceptional prowess in their shared world of international loans, promotions and profits. They became close friends and Cassel was appointed one of Hirsch's executors.

From 1898 until Bertie's death twelve years later, Cassel reigned supreme as chief financial adviser to Bertie as Prince of Wales, and then as King Edward VII. It was a position that brought this financial entrepreneur untold prestige, which he loved, and Bertie a freedom from financial anxiety.

Cassel entertained lavishly in his London house and at Moulton Paddocks near Newmarket, and was a frequent guest at Sandringham and Marlborough House. He hunted and shot and eagerly followed the successes of his own race-horses. He joined the Jockey Club, but much preferred the company of the pretty, clever women, like Alice Keppel, to be found about his patron.

Cassel's charitable donations were prodigious, but like any other deal he expected due requital in the form of honours.

Asked by the Foreign Secretary to grant a loan of half a million pounds to the State Bank of Morocco, Cassel did not question the devious designs of the Foreign Office but stipulated the condition that he should receive the Grand Cross of the Order of the Bath for this favour. On his death in 1921 in his gigantic mansion, Brook House in Park Lane, the Right Honourable Sir Ernest Cassel sported after his name in his obituaries, besides the GCB, a GCMG, GCVO and column inches of foreign decorations.

In startling contrast with Alice Keppel, a woman Bertie met a month or two after that dinner with her became a close friend on quite a different level. She was Miss Agnes Keyser, the daughter of Charles Keyser, a rich stockbroker in the City. Miss Keyser, with her sister Fanny, had founded a military officers' nursing home in her house at 17 Grosvenor Crescent. She was a handsome, selfless, wise and practical woman, who was as efficient at running her hospital as at acquiring donations from those who could well afford them.

Miss Keyser had no hesitation in approaching the Prince of Wales, and when they met a relationship developed as rapidly as with Alice Keppel but on a maternal level, with Miss Keyser as a part-nanny, part-mother and intimate confidante. As sympathetic as she was formidable, Bertie found great comfort in the company of this middle-aged woman, both in her sensible and open advice and her concern with the health and well-being of others. Although no hypochondriac, Bertie had always been deeply preoccupied with anything to do with medicine, the discovery of cures and the conduct of surgical operations. Among many other subjects they discussed, these were Bertie's favourites.

Agnes Keyser was a woman to whom he could open his heart without the intervention of sexual motives, a unique experience for him. He liked nothing better than intimate suppers with this remarkable woman at which she served the healthy dishes of his childhood, like Lancashire hotpot and rice pudding. Nor did Bertie in the least complain at Miss Keyser's nagging about his excessive smoking. At this time, Miss Keyser's services were in great demand due to the Boer War, and it was not difficult for Bertie to persuade men like Cassel and the Rothschilds, Arthur Sassoon, Lord Burnham and others to contribute generously, and also to set up a trust for her. By this time the hospital had greatly expanded and now formed itself in new premises under the name it enjoys today, King Edward VII's Hospital for Officers.

One diagnosis that Sister Agnes and her voluntary doctors could not have made was that of Lord Randolph Churchill's fatal illness. After their famous row, and its somewhat conditional ceasefire, the friendship between the Prince of Wales and this scion of the dukedom of Marlborough had been renewed. It was a public peace-making, *Vanity Fair* announcing the news on 15 March 1884:

A full and formal reconciliation has been effected between His Royal Highness the Prince of Wales and Lord Randolph Churchill MP who have for some years been strangers, on account of differences arising through the attitude respectively taken by them in relation to private matters. The reconciliation was effected last week at a dinner given for the purpose by Sir Henry James MP. . . .

But this detente almost fell to pieces owing to a conditional statement allegedly put out by Lord Randolph. 'It is understood, however,' *Vanity Fair* continued, 'that while Lord Randolph feels much satisfaction at being again on friendly terms with the heir-apparent, he does not propose to become intimate with all the Prince's friends.'

On reading this, Lord Randolph hastened to deny to the Prince that he had said any such thing. Knollys replied soothingly on the same day, 15 March, on behalf of the Prince: 'Perhaps you will be so good as to assure Lord Randolph Churchill that HRH never for one moment entertained the idea that he was in any way responsible for the words that appeared in *Vanity Fair* in connection with the subject to which you refer. . . .'

So all was well and the rising politician and the Prince of Wales, who had been such good and useful friends, renewed their relationship. Dinner parties took place again, Alix was glad to be back on good terms with Lord Randolph's vivacious wife Jennie, whom she had always liked and admired, and she was delighted that Lord Randolph favoured friendly relations with Russia, and moreover converted Bertie to favour Russia.

This dismayed the Queen, who naturally favoured Germany, which was hostile to Russia, and Vicky and Fritz. Alix could visit her sister Minnie with a light heart, secure in the knowledge that Bertie was doing all he could for the cause of Russia.

Bertie followed with enthusiasm Lord Randolph's rocket-like rise in his subsequent political life, congratulating him on his success in the Woodstock election 'with such a large majority in your favour' (3 July 1885), and a year later on his leadership of the House of Commons and on becoming Chancellor of the Exchequer. At the same time Bertie regretted that his old crony Henry Chaplin had not been offered a seat in the Cabinet – 'Will you have a word with Lord Salisbury on this subject?' he asked. (Chaplin was appointed President of the Board of Agriculture within a few weeks and was later made a viscount.)

Lord Randolph kept Bertie in touch with the innermost goings-on at Cabinet level, until suddenly and all too soon after Randolph's elevation, which brought him so close to the Premiership, he committed a fatal, political miscalculation. As Chancellor of the Exchequer and enlightened Tory he had proposed to pare down the nation's defence budgets to £94.5 millions in order to double local government grants for social reforms. He was confident of carrying his fellow radical Tories, but they failed to support him. Arrogantly confident that they would do so if it became a resignation issue, he offered his resignation to the Prime Minister. But Lord Salisbury, weary of the tiresome political conflicts engineered by his Chancellor, shocked him dreadfully by accepting the resignation.

Unfortunately, Lord Randolph had compounded the issue by offering his resignation on headed writing paper from Windsor Castle, where he was staying at the time, failing to inform the Queen and the Prince of Wales of his decision. The Queen learned the news from *The Times*, Bertie from a letter two days later, together with a sheaf of correspondence with Lord Randolph's colleagues.

The Queen was *not* pleased. Bertie, more puzzled than put out, wrote to his mother:

You are, if you will allow me to say so, rather hard on Lord R. Churchill. I do not enter into the question whether he was right or wrong in resigning on the point at issue between him and his colleagues, but he has at any rate the courage of his opinions. . . . Ld Randolph is a poor man and a very ambitious one, but he gave up £5,000 a year in ceasing to be Chancellor of the Exchequer. . . .

To Lord Randolph Bertie wrote from Marlborough House on 23 December 1886: 'I cannot tell you how deeply and sincerely I regret to hear that you find yourself obliged to leave HM's government.' He was taking a train to Cambridge on that day, and was so concerned that he wrote again from it in some agitation: 'What will you do now? Come what may I hope you will now be a thorn in the side of the present Government.'

A thorn or not, Lord Randolph Churchill retained his finger on the Cabinet's pulse through his numerous connections and kept Bertie well informed, better informed than the Queen on many subjects. Lord Randolph slipped him copies of confidential documents, unseen by the Queen, for instance on the Duke of Cambridge's evidence before the army estimates vote in 1888 and Lord Dufferin's memorandum on the Burma War – 'I wish it could be made public,' Bertie noted in praise of it. Lord Randolph also guided Bertie on any important speech he might have to make which required special knowledge – 'Perhaps you could put a few sentences together for an address on Saturday' (2 July 1890).

For his part, Bertie persuaded Lord Randolph to accept an Honorary Degree from Cambridge University (May 1888) and put him up for the Jockey Club. Unfortunately, there was some opposition to this, and Knollys wrote to Lord Randolph asking, 'If you do not mind letting the Prince of Wales know *confidentially* the names of the men whom you suppose to be unfriendly to you in regard to your admittance to the Jockey Club, he will be very glad to see what can be done to "square" them quietly.' Ten days later Lord Randolph's election went through without a contrary vote.

For six years following Lord Randolph's resignation, Bertie continued to encourage a revival in his fortunes and was appalled to learn later that he had given up all activity in the House of Commons. 'I hear you have retired from your Parliamentary duties,' Bertie wrote on 11 February 1890. 'I am feeling very anxious about you.' And in an attempt to cheer him up, he continued, 'I am giving a "Bohemian dinner" on Friday next at the Garrick. Can I persuade you to be one of my three masks?'*

Lord Randolph was feeling low and flat, and there is some evidence that the disease that was to kill him in early 1895 was already affecting him. He had been lampooned in the press, savagely attacked from all sides, and his close political supporters were fewer than they had been. He decided to seek health and recovery in South Africa. He returned home much refreshed two years later.

Bertie was one of the first to welcome him back and was anxious to see him. He took it for granted that his friend would at once plunge back into politics. 'Now to business,' he wrote on 4 January 1892. 'I should insist on the Admiralty and nothing else. The Indian Viceroyalty may be offered to you but I should not accept it. You have everything to gain by taking up public life again and the Government cannot do without you.'

But Lord Randolph found the Government's 'feelings towards myself more bitter and hostile than ever', and he never took office again although he remained a backbench MP and made occasional political forays. The two men, and their wives, remained close friends and Lord Randolph and Jennie often stayed at Sandringham. Bertie and Alix shared with Jennie their grief at the decline in Lord Randolph's health, brought about, according to his doctor, by a form of *delirium tremens* probably caused by excessive dosing of drugs intended to stabilise his nervous system. He died on 24 January 1895. He was only forty-five.

Bertie lost another friend at an early age, Crown Prince Rudolph of Austria. It was the Crown Prince who had first

---

* It was not unusual to invite several guests to arrive disguised by a mask.

introduced the banker Hirsch to him (in exchange for a loan of 100,000 gulden), and the two heirs to the thrones of their countries met often on the Continent, at German spas and in Paris. The Crown Prince had stayed at Sandringham. Alix and Bertie agonised over the young man's failed marriage to Princess Stephanie, the daughter of the Belgian King, but knew nothing of his deep love affair with Baroness Vetsera. After he heard the news of the tragic double death at Mayerling on 30 January 1889, Bertie wrote on 6 February to Lord Randolph about 'this fearful suicide':

Since losing the Emperor Frederick I think the present sad event is the second greatest European tragedy we have had. Prince Rudolph would have been a worthy successor to his father. I knew him well and should have thought he would have been the very last person to take his own life. There is perhaps some dark mystery which will probably come to light. . . .

'If you ever become King,' Queen Victoria once remarked censoriously of 'the Marlborough House set', 'you will find all these friends *most* inconvenient, and you will have to break with them *all*.' These 'inconvenient' friends was one of the chief reasons why, even though her eldest son was well over fifty, she still continued to deny him any serious part in the affairs of state for which the sovereign is responsible. Things had not changed much since 1875, when, while Bertie was actually *in* India, the Queen had herself proclaimed Empress of India, information which he picked up by chance. (He told Disraeli, 'In no other country in the world would the next Heir to the Throne have been treated under similar circumstances in such a manner.') Considering that his mother was in her seventies (from 1889) and not in the best of health, it was highly irresponsible of her to allow her heir to remain almost totally untrained as a future King-Emperor. The Prince was deeply interested in foreign affairs, and a shrewd judge at that, but he saw none of the secret Foreign Office despatches until Lord Rosebery, the Foreign Secretary in 1886 and a close friend, sent him copies without the knowledge of the Queen.

It was not until 1892 that at last the Queen was persuaded

to pass to Bertie the Prince Consort's golden key, which opened the Foreign Office boxes and which had been hidden away since 1861. At about this time he was also sent brief reports on Cabinet meetings. This was at least some advance, but any advice or suggestions on appointments or policy were entirely ignored.

Even Queen Victoria found it hard to disapprove of one of Bertie's closest friends, in spite of his known anti-German feelings. He was the Marquess de Soveral, the Portuguese minister who graced the London scenes of diplomacy and Society for so many years. Soveral was a terrific dandy, which almost made him the best-dressed as well as the most popular man in London, but there was just a hint of raffishness and excess about his clothes. He was certainly the most instantly recognised *boulevardier* with his dark blue suits, prominent buttonhole, blue-black hair and dark complexion. In fact, his nickname was 'The Blue Monkey', which gave him no offence, and he basked in the knowledge that every woman, including Mrs Keppel and Alix, adored him.

Soveral was so bright that he felt it necessary to conceal his intelligence and superb judgment beneath a flippant and highly amusing façade. Bertie found him a particularly rewarding foil to the dour seriousness of Cassel, and persuaded the Queen to make him a Knight of the Garter.

Soveral was a great theatre- and opera-goer, and was often invited into the royal box with Bertie and Alix. Both men felt 'comfortable' with actors and actresses, and Bertie, as Patron of the Garrick Club, mixed freely with the great men of the theatre: Sir Henry Irving, Henry Kemble, W. S. Gilbert, George Alexander, Sir Squire Bancroft, Sir Charles Wyndham, William Kendal, Sir John Hare, Johnston Forbes-Robertson and others. A number of them could thank the Prince of Wales for their knighthoods, which had been few and far between before his time.

As long before as 19 February 1882, Charles Carrington noted in his journal: 'The Prince of Wales who takes a great interest in "The Drama" gave a big "man's dinner" to the leading London Actors. This is a great recognition of the "profession" and will raise them considerably in the social scale.'

Some of the finest actresses of his time attracted Bertie even more keenly. Their social standing was even lower than that of actors, and when Sarah Bernhardt of the *Comédie Française* was observed socially in London, Lady Frederick Cavendish described her as 'a woman of notorious, shameless character'. In the summer of 1881 Bertie asked Ferdinand de Rothschild to give a midnight supper party at his house in Piccadilly in order that his friend the Duc d'Aumâle could meet Sarah Bernhardt. Sir Charles Dilke was a witness to this embarrassing evening, and wrote:

All the other ladies present were English ladies who had been invited at the distinct request of the Prince of Wales. It was one thing to get them to go, and another to get them to talk when they were there; and the result was that, as they would not talk to Sarah Bernhardt, and the Duc d'Aumâle was deaf and disinclined to make conversation on his own account, nobody talked at all, and an absolute reign of the most dismal silence ensued.

As Bertie had shown no interest in reading as a child, so his antipathy towards books lasted all through his life. It was said that he read only one book all the way through, the famous *East Lynne*. Jennie Churchill sent him her son Winston's early books and he claimed to have read at least one of them, though this is very doubtful.

Books and authors smacked of the intelligentsia, a very unreliable and uninteresting body. Sitting still and turning over the pages of a book was not a worthwhile occupation. Bertie could manage state papers, reports and letters all right, but they were *interesting* and kept him informed about the real world. Writers reciprocated in their disdain for this 'corpulent voluptuary', as Rudyard Kipling described him. 'The incomparable' Max Beerbohm exercised on Bertie his second talent of caricature in a particularly savage manner.

Bertie did not even bother to attend the funeral of Lord Tennyson (for which he was much criticised), but took an interest in the Poet Laureateship because it was a royal appointment. He tried to persuade his mother to make

Swinburne Tennyson's successor instead of Alfred Austin. This can be described as his one unerringly correct literary judgment.

Although Bertie attended dozens of theatrical dinners, many with himself as host, his future official biographer, Sir Sydney Lee, did bully him into giving a dinner at Marlborough House to honour the launch of the *Dictionary of National Biography*. Evidently Bertie was simmeringly resentful throughout the dinner, and the shy Sir Leslie Stephen on one side and the heavyweight Lord Acton on the other did not stir up his fire. He did, however, demonstrate an interest in some of his fellow guests and at one point asked, 'Who is the little parson over there? Why is he here? He is not a writer.'

Acton explained that Canon Ainger was 'a very great authority on Lamb'. Flabbergasted, the Prince of Wales put down his knife and fork and cried out in bewilderment, 'On *lamb*!'

Bertie was decidedly more knowledgeable on horseflesh, and the gulf between Lord Acton and Lord Marcus Beresford was as wide as between the London Library (founded in the year of Bertie's birth) and the paddock at Newmarket. Moreover, horse-racing was out of doors, a testing and competitive sport, all of which Bertie relished. He was widely criticised for spending too much time at his stables and at meetings, most of all by the Queen, but he could reasonably retort that, with serious duties denied to him, most rigidly by the Queen, what else could he do?

Then again, he was attacked for his extravagance at racing; this was unjust as well as futile. While other more active sports, even shooting, became less desirable due to his increasing weight and age, racing played a more and more important part in his life. Commensurately, he became more successful.

In 1896 Bertie had thirteen horses in training, including the very difficult but fast Persimmon, which gave him his first Derby win. The crowds shouted their congratulations while they closed about him, waving their hats. It was perhaps Bertie's happiest day. Any disapproval from exalted quarters was offset a thousand times over by his popularity among racing enthusiasts, who probably numbered four out of five of the male population. In 1896–7 his horses won for him £44,000 in prize money alone.

A remarkable three-year-old horse called Diamond Jubilee, named after that splendid royal celebration of 1897, won in succession in one year the Derby, the Newmarket Stakes, the Eclipse Stakes, the St Leger and the Two Thousand Guineas, winning for his owner £28,000 in prize money and a further £31,500 when he was sold. Bertie's enthusiasm for racing never wavered. Between 1886 and the last afternoon of his life in 1910, his stables took over £400,000 in stud fees and stake money – about £16 million today.

In April 1888 Alix had written to her son Georgie, to whom she was always 'Motherdear', 'We are a most happy family and I thank God for having given me such good and affectionate children who are my real comfort in this world.' But for a long time after the death of Prince Eddy the scar of her loss was clearly evident, and it was not until Georgie's wife May gave birth to a fine-looking son* in 1894 that she began to recover. As the Duchess of Devonshire told Lady Paget on 28 June 1894, 'she had never seen anyone so changed as the Princess of Wales since the birth of her grandson. She seems to have thrown off her melancholy depressed air, and to have become quite cheerful again.'

Certainly throughout the last decade of the century, with more grandchildren being born and her Danish family occupying much of her time, and travel, Alix found it easier than Bertie to find responsible work outside her homes and families. It was the Sudan campaign, the loss of Khartoum and the death of General Gordon in 1885 that first realerted her conscience and began her long association with hospital work and welfare, first for the fighting services and later more widely.

In the same month when she heard of the fall of Khartoum, Alix founded a British branch of the Danish 'National Society for Aid for the Sick and Wounded in Time of War'. With complete disregard for the Society's definition, she extended

* David, later Prince of Wales, King Edward VIII and the Duke of Windsor.

its work to all soldiers and sailors, whether or not in need of medical aid. She arranged for collections of books, comforts, games and other amusements to be sent out to Egypt, along with recreational huts for men off-duty. She also raised funds for the despatch of river launches fitted out to carry the wounded down the Nile to base hospitals.

'In no previous campaign have I seen anything like it,' wrote one brigadier, 'and there can be no doubt about the high appreciation the Army entertains for what the Society has done.'

Later, she took up the cause of The London Hospital and founded 'Queen Alexandra's Imperial Military Nursing Service' with herself as President. 'Queen Alexandra's love for "the London" was a real passion,' Lord Knutsford once wrote. 'She wrote of it and spoke of it as "her" hospital, and she made it so. She visited it very often indeed, and her visits were never processions, but were intimate and enjoyed by visitors and visited alike.'

This charity work brought out the autocrat in Alix, too, and she brooked no nonsense or argument. 'It is my wish and that is sufficient,' ended any disagreement that threatened to arise over any point on which Alix had an opinion, and she almost invariably did.

But her warm, generous kindness was always evident, too. When she heard of the tragic case of 'the elephant man', she insisted that he be taken into 'the London'. 'The poor fellow was horrible to look on, but [she] came down to talk to him and to cheer him up, and for years afterwards, until he died, she used to send him Christmas cards, with messages written on them by herself, to show how he was still in her mind.'

There was nothing dutiful about Alix's care for the sick and wounded. Like Florence Nightingale and other great nursing figures, she had that rare talent for personal communication which made each patient feel picked out for special sympathy. Unlike the great Florence Nightingale, she claimed no talent for organisation and practical, detailed work. So long as she was in charge and the ultimate decision-maker, she left the rest to others while she exercised her exceptional talent for the personal touch.

But Alix's nursing duties occupied only part of her time, and in those last years before she became Queen she was mostly at Sandringham living the quiet life of a middle-aged countrywoman, dealing with local affairs, supervising the garden (with many a brush with her head gardener), caring for her horses and dogs, playing the piano, having her children and grandchildren to stay, and keeping an eye on the boys' carving school she had established on the estate. On Saturdays she would choose the hymns for the Sunday morning service, which she attended with her three constant companions, Charlotte Knollys, her daughter Toria and Old Mac.

Apart from visits to her Danish family, and several times to Russia to see her sister Minnie, from time to time she had to travel abroad on more formal business with Bertie. But travel routines for the royal family were much disrupted in 1900. Britain had made itself unpopular in many continental countries on account of the Boer War in South Africa, and the feeling of the people was reflected in hostile newspaper articles and cartoons, especially in France. The Queen cancelled a visit to France and instead went to Ireland for the first time for almost forty years. Bertie cancelled his usual visit to the Riviera and to the opening of the British section of an international exhibition in Paris. Instead, he decided to accompany Alix to Copenhagen, stay with her in the royal palace for as long as he could stand it, and return home by sea.

This delighted Alix, and they left London for Brussels on the first stage of their journey on the morning of 4 April. Bertie's diary austerely records: 'Arrive at Brussels, 4.50. Walk about station. Just as train is leaving, 5.30, a man fires a pistol at P. of W. through open window of carriage (no harm done).'

The single bullet passed between the heads of Bertie and Alix, and before the man could fire again the station-master himself seized the would-be assassin, disarmed him and dragged him away. There were five more bullets in the revolver, so the royal couple had been extremely lucky and probably owed their lives to the quick action of the official. Charlotte Knollys, who was with them in the carriage, recorded: 'There was no time for anyone to be frightened, except the Princess's little Chinese dog, who was terrified by the explosion. The Prince never even changed colour and the Princess behaved beautifully.'

An hour later, in order to allay any fears brought on by reading the evening newspapers, Bertie telegraphed Alice Keppel at Devonshire House, Weymouth: 'As we were leaving Brussels a man jumped on the step of our carriage and fired a pistol at us through the open window. I don't think there was a bullet in it.' When they at length reached Copenhagen, Bertie wrote a number of brief letters making a joke of the affair, adding what a rotten shot the young man had been. He also asked the authorities not to punish the fellow too severely, but he was decidedly put out when a Brussels court, reflecting the anti-British sentiment at the time, absolved the fifteen-year-old anarchist called Spido of criminal intent and released him.

Bertie was also offended that the British Parliament had not passed a vote of thanks for his preservation when they had done so for his younger brother Prince Alfred, who had escaped assassination in 1874. Lord Salisbury replied lamely that, 'It was thought better not to take that course, as it was not then known that the pistol contained a bullet, which the extreme youth of the culprit rendered doubtful.'

This chilly message was more than offset by the reception Bertie received when he returned home on 20 April. The crowds packed the streets from Charing Cross to Marlborough House, waving their hats and cheering their heads off. It was as good as a Derby win, which he was to achieve a few weeks later anyway, and the first thing he did that evening was to compose a vote of thanks to the British nation, which was published in all the newspapers.

When the Queen returned from Ireland a few days later, she welcomed Bertie with much thankfulness and for once there were no exhortations and many enquiries about 'beloved Alix'. But the Queen was not well. On 24 May, her birthday, she recorded: 'Again my old birthday returns, my

81st! God has been very merciful and supported me, but my trials and anxieties have been manifold and I feel tired and upset by all I have gone through this winter and spring.' But there was worse to come in 'this horrible year': the sudden death of her second son from cancer of the throat, and the failure of Vicky to arrive for her regular visit because she was too poorly (she died of cancer, too, soon after her mother's death). Then her soldier grandson, Prince Christian Victor, died of fever in South Africa.

The Queen was almost blind and feeling 'very seedy', according to her grandson Georgie. She survived Christmas and into the new century, but by the middle of January it was evident that she was fading fast, and her multitudinous relations began to assemble at Osborne. Alix left Sandringham on 15 January, and Bertie left London on the same day. The previous evening he had taken the usual plain supper with Agnes Keyser. The Queen's imminent death naturally dominated the conversation. At one point he remarked that he felt quite unworthy to succeed her. Miss Keyser must surely have reassured him, but there were many in the land – including the editor of *The Times* – who agreed with this self-judgment.

16

End of an Era

'A good spring clean . . .'
Bertie of the royal palaces

For sixty-nine years Queen Victoria had never failed to write up her journal. Then on 14 January 1901 there appeared a blank: she had grown too weak to hold a pen. Five days later *The Times* austerely noted: 'The Queen has not lately been in her usual health. . . .' As darkness fell on the following day, her doctors issued a bulletin that left no doubt of her real condition: 'The Queen is slowly sinking.'

In fact, she had already uttered her last word. Bertie and Alix had been at Osborne since Saturday and it was now Tuesday, the 22nd. In the late morning Bertie went into his mother's bedroom alone where she lay looking white and tiny. She opened her arms to her son and whispered the single word 'Bertie'. He put his cheek against hers and wept.

Bertie was followed by the young Bishop of Winchester, Randall Davidson. He had arrived soon after Bertie. A storm had blown up and, by contrast with the solemn silence observed by everyone at Osborne over the following days, the shouting and singing of football fans on board his ferry had been ceaseless between Portsmouth and Cowes. He was joined by the Vicar of Whippingham, and the two men prayed at the Queen's bedside. Then it was the turn of the doctors, though by now there was nothing for them to do.

Osborne House was packed with children and grand-children who had come from far and near, including the Emperor of Germany – the tiresome Kaiser William II – and his wife Dona from Berlin. Every bedroom was full, some with additional beds, and the staff were run off their feet. The Queen had always deplored the gathering of relations about a death-bed. 'That I shall insist is never the case if I am dying. It is awful.' But the eyes of the eighty-one-year-old lady were closed, and she was now past caring at this disre-gard of her wishes. One by one the Princes and Princesses, the Dukes and Duchesses and Lords and Ladies gathered about the bed, in turn kneeling for a moment as if at the outset of a church service.

Last to arrive, at 5·30 p.m., were Princess May and her uncle-in-law, the Duke of Connaught, and his daughters Mar-garet and Patsy. May noted that the Kaiser had appropriated the privileged position, kneeling with his right (good) arm round his grandmother's neck. May could not know that he had been in this awkward attitude for one and a half hours already. She also observed that the Queen's daughter-in-law, Alix, was on her knees holding the Queen's hand with Uncle Bertie beside her. From time to time one or other of the Queen's children or grandchildren spoke their name as if registering their presence for her, and posterity's, benefit. She would not have cared for that either.

At 6·30 p.m., as the Bishop noted, there came 'a great change of look and complete calmness'. The silence in the room was broken by the soft voice of the doctor, who had helped to support the Queen's head with his left arm, announcing that the Queen was dead. 'The Queen looked so beautiful after death,' Princess May noted, 'like a marble statue, & much younger.'

There was a brief service conducted by the Bishop at ten o'clock that evening. It was very simple and not at all mournful. With a relish noted by her Private Secretary, she had arranged everything for her death and funeral in minute detail, and to the surprise of many of her people all arrangements were to be marked by cheerfulness and with no hint of her own morbid preoccupation with death. The woman whose mourning for her husband was a veritable extravaganza of grief, had ordered a *white* funeral. She was to be laid out in her coffin in a white dress, sprinkled with spring flowers, a white widow's cap on her head, her lace wedding veil over her face.

All this was carried out swiftly and precisely, but there was a small, significant hitch over her conveyance into her coffin. The Kaiser took it upon himself to try to lift up her body, but Bertie had had enough of this officiousness. 'This is the right of my mother's sons,' he pointed out none too gently, and with his younger brother Arthur edged aside the German Emperor and raised her little body and placed it tenderly into the coffin. A young child could have managed the task unaided so light was the old lady.

On the following day she was again moved. 'Now she lies in her coffin in the dining room,' Princess May wrote, 'which is beautifully arranged as a chapel, the coffin is covered with the coronation robes & her little diamond crown & the garter lie on a cushion above her head – 4 huge Grenadiers watch there day & night, it is so impressive & fine, yet so simple.'

When the coffin was placed on one of the royal yachts, it was covered with a white and golden pall embroidered with a cross and the royal arms. The vessel steamed across the Solent between lines of a hundred or more warships, British and foreign, their flags at half-mast. This was correct and proper, but Bertie, sharp as always on protocol, noticed that the *Alberta* carrying the coffin had the royal standard at half-mast too. He drew the captain's attention to this contravention.

'But, sir, the Queen is dead,' the officer protested.

Bertie retorted stoutly, 'The King of England lives.'

The Queen had always loathed the sudden crack of minute guns and this was the first voyage she had made when she was unable to hear them, a twenty-one-gun salute. The quayside was packed with people, and Bertie and Alix – no longer Prince and Princess of Wales but King Edward VII and Queen Alexandra – made their presence silently visible.

It was the same all along the slow journey to London in the royal train. Men with their hats off, women and children, knelt not only at the stations but in the fields and roads bordering the railway line. In London the streets between Victoria and Paddington Stations were as packed as for the Queen's Coronation almost sixty-three years earlier. And the route was almost as cheerfully bedecked as on that occasion, with purple cashmere and white satin bows. For music, she had ordered cheerful pieces by Chopin and Beethoven, the only concession to the solemnity of the occasion being a few Highland laments.

The new King and Queen accompanied the coffin on this last short leg of its journey to Windsor Castle. But here at the station there was, for the first time in the day, a hitch. Six Royal Horse Artillery horses had been waiting in the cold – waiting too long, so it seemed, for while they were being harnessed to the big gun carriage which they were to draw up the steep hill to St George's Chapel, one of them reared and broke its traces, leading to violence amongst the others. The traces had to be hastily cut.

Before panic could ensue Prince Louis of Battenberg, commanding the naval escort, ran over to Bertie to suggest that his men should take over to drag the gun carriage. One of his officers had enterprisingly rushed into the train and cut free the communication cord, which served as a supplement to the remains of the traces. Prince Louis then ordered, 'Ground arms and stand by to drag the gun carriage.' The army officers present were outraged to see the navy take over where they had failed, and protested to the King. Bertie was having none of this. 'Right or wrong, let him manage everything,' he ordered, indicating Prince Louis. 'We shall never get on if there are two people giving contradictory orders.' It was a small hint of his new authority.

The shock to the people of Britain of the Queen's death lasted long after the funeral in St George's Chapel and the interment in the Mausoleum alongside Prince Albert. The great majority of the population had known no other sovereign all their lives and one had to be close to seventy years old to remember the funeral of King William IV. Mixed with the shock and grief there was an element of fear. 'God help us all,' Princess May had exclaimed, and this was an expression now heard throughout the land. As at the outbreak of a great war, the future was grey, uncertain and heavy with anxiety. Another expression of the time was, 'Things'll never be the same again.'

Whatever else this bothersome, nervy, spoilt, industrious, dutiful and essentially kind old lady had done for her country, she had willy-nilly created a patina over the land, a style and character, a morality and self-regard, quite different from that of any other European nation, and almost as different as the previous reigns of William and the later Georges. This was bound to have happened anyway considering the length of her reign, the advances in all spheres that had been made in her time and the enormous increase in wealth and standard of living. But the 'little lady of Windsor' had always been there, with restricted power but great authority and influence – influence for the good and authority mainly for the good. As Lytton Strachey was to write of her last days, 'She had become an indissoluble part of [her subjects'] whole scheme of things, and that they were about to lose her appeared a scarcely possible thought.'

If the condition of the nation was one of shock and apprehension, there was also a measure of nervous excitement. Whatever the future held, things were now going to be different. Or, expressed in another way, if this immensely long reign could be compared with a voyage of exploration, 'Land ahoy!' had suddenly been heard and tomorrow would bring the revelations of a new shore to coincide with the new century.

Throughout the land there was also a deep curiosity about how Bertie would comport himself now that he was King. Even among those people who were familiar with his appearance, and had seen him recently, there was an intense need to set eyes on him, almost as if to reassure themselves that kingship had not brought about some sort of metamorphosis. This was widely recognised at Court and arrangements were made for him to be more exposed than in the past.

Coming home from a party given by the Grand Duke Michael of Russia a few months after Queen Victoria's death, with everyone in deepest mourning, 'it was arranged', George Cornwallis-West recalled, that the train should proceed slowly through big stations like Crewe and Stafford in order that the populace might get a glimpse of their new sovereign. He was playing bridge to pass the time, and as the train slowed up at each station an equerry-in-waiting politely reminded His Majesty that it would be as well to show himself at the window, which he did, the cards being hastily put away.

There were plenty of people with grave doubts about the new sovereign, including the editor of *The Times*, who, while admitting that 'he has never failed in his duty to the throne and the nation', also pontificated:

There is no position in the world more difficult to fill than that of Heir-Apparent to the throne. It is beset by more than all the temptations of actual royalty, while the weight of counteracting responsibility is much less directly felt. It must be with a feeling of hopelessness that a man in that position offers up the prayer, 'Lead us not into temptation', but the heir to a throne is followed, dogged, and importuned by temptation in its most seductive forms. . . . The King has passed through that tremendous ordeal, prolonged through youth and manhood to middle age [he was fifty-nine]. We shall not pretend that there is nothing in his long career which those who respect and admire him could wish otherwise. Which of us can say that with even approximate temptations to meet he could face the fierce light that beats upon an heir-apparent no less than upon a throne?

Henry James might have been an American by birth, but he reflected a fair weight of middle-class and intellectual English opinion when he wrote that the Queen's death 'let loose incalculable forces for possible ill', while referring to the new King as 'Edward the Caresser', that 'arch vulgarian'. George Bernard Shaw was much more unsentimentally concerned with the treatment of the Queen's corpse, citing as insanitary and superstitious the delay of the burial by a fortnight: 'The remains of the Queen should have been either cremated or buried at once in a perishable coffin in a very shallow grave. The example set by such a course would have been socially invaluable.'

Doubts were felt in many quarters as to whether the new successor to the throne was fully prepared for his responsibilities [wrote Lee]. Rumour spoke none too well of him, and there were some misgivings even in his own circle as to his fitness for his long postponed vocation. His mother's refusal to delegate to him any of her great responsibilities through her long reign was held in many quarters to have withheld from him information and experience which were necessary for the due performance of the royal function.

Were the doubts about Bertie's fitness really justified? His lack of training in the art of kingship was a severe disadvantage. He fancied himself as something of a diplomat because he had made a study of foreign affairs and got on well with foreign diplomats and ambassadors. He was also virtually trilingual in French and German. But his instincts were those of the common man (in itself sometimes advantageous), and when his nephew, the Kaiser, wrote in 1896 to congratulate President Kruger on his success in defeating the Jameson Raid into the Transvaal, Bertie sided with the common jingo-istic view that the Kaiser should be severely snubbed for his blatant interference. But Queen Victoria, with all her decades of experience at dealing with troublesome diplomatic incidents like this, wrote a 'consummate letter to the Kaiser, which no diplomat in history could have bettered'. Less than five years later Bertie had become King. In the meantime, he had not much applied himself to the art and practice of diplomacy, which would have meant reading, nor been given any serious experience or instruction.

Bertie's great forte was dealing with, and charming, people. Face to face, very few people disliked him. Practically everyone fell victim to his powerful and engaging charm. His memory was prodigious. He never forgot a face, recalled conversations after years and remembered the facts, the tastes and the views of people – especially women – for an inordinately long period, itself flattering. To drag the monarchy out of its long introversion was enough to ensure his popularity. But to do so with such style and gusto, while always retaining his dignity, was a tremendous bonus with which even the disapproving middle classes, especially those in the North, had to agree.

There were many and immense counter-advantages in favour of the new regime. First and most important were the relish and determination Bertie and Alix felt for their dual role. They had waited for almost forty years in the wings and now at last the curtain was up. The country at large required time to absorb the transition. There were never any doubts about Alix's qualifications. The nation had taken her to its heart in the 1860s and had loved her ever since. Her beauty, her simplicity and innocence, and her dignity (especially in the face of her husband's peccadilloes) combined with her generosity of spirit, the time she gave to the poor and sick, and her love of children and of her pets – all these characteristics made her fitness to be Queen Consort unquestioned.

At the same time those close to her did note a new hauteur about Alix. This was signified by the fact that one of the first things she made known was that she was not going to have any truck with the title Queen Consort; she was Queen of England, and that was that. Now that she was Queen she could do exactly as she wished. Her Household noticed the change at once. They were treated with the same kindness and love as before, but Alix now showed herself to be more decisive than ever and she brushed aside advice with a decidedly royal flick. 'As Princess of Wales she was never, so she says, allowed to do as she chose,' Lord Esher not altogether accurately noted. '"Now I do as I like" is the sort of attitude.'

The Baroness de Stoeckl noted at the end of one dinner at Sandringham that one of Alix's Greek nieces and her daughter Toria made

a sudden movement to rise from the table, whereupon the Queen, who had not finished her coffee, looked around and in a clear firm voice said: 'Wait!' Such was the power Her Majesty exercised over her children and Household that not another word was uttered about our leaving although time was flying past. She drank her coffee slowly and only when she had quite finished did she rise from the table with a satisfied smile.

It was so long since a Queen Consort had been crowned that records and precedents about dress were searched for in vain. Alix pooh-poohed the whole business. 'I know better than all the milliners and antiquaries,' she declared. '*Basta!* I shall wear exactly what I like and so will all my ladies.' And no longer would she have to travel down to Windsor to beg, not always successfully, to be allowed to stay in Copenhagen with her family. She would travel to where she wished when she wished.

The freedom was heady and for a while she became drunk on it. It also led to strong differences of opinion with Bertie. Alix wanted nothing to do with Windsor Castle with its cold stone and lack of intimacy. She wanted to stay within the familiar confines of Marlborough House and Sandringham, where she had enjoyed all her happiness with her children and pets. When she lost the battle with Bertie over Windsor, she determined to occupy the State Apartments: if she was going to have to live some of the time here, she wanted to do so in style. Bertie preferred the old family apartments and again thwarted Alix.

As for moving into Buckingham Palace while in London, Alix flatly refused and indicated that she was prepared to become besieged in her old home. What little she knew of Buckingham Palace, for Queen Victoria had been so seldom there, she disliked intensely, if only because of its vast size. But inevitably the siege was broken. Buckingham Palace was the royal palace and it was their duty to move into it. Mourning Marlborough House, Alix wrote to her son Georgie that she thought this move would 'finish' her: 'All my happiness and sorrow were here, very nearly all you children were born here, all the reminiscences of my whole life are here, and I feel as if by taking me away a cord will be torn in my heart which can never be mended again.'

Nevertheless, Queen Alexandra embarked on her new role with joy in her heart and a certain belief that she would make a success of it. Queen Victoria's subjects had seen little or no colour, beauty or pomp associated with the monarchy for all their lives. Alix began the new reign with the immense advantage of being able to supply these in abundance, and the pleasure she experienced in filling this role 'by her own radiant light' was wonderful to behold.

Sarah Bernhardt wrote at this time of 'that adorable and seductive face – with the eyes of a child of the North, and classical features of virginal purity, a long, supple neck that seemed made for queenly bows, a sweet and almost timid smile'. Her 'indefinable charm' made her 'so radiant that I saw nothing but her'.

There is no happier chance in royal history than that the

Queen Consort who ascended the throne in January 1901 perfectly reflected the period of her reign. She was the ideal Edwardian: short on intellectuality, long on larks, rich in trivial and mainly innocent gossip, childish, unworldly, reprehensibly prejudiced and hide-bound. It was a brief age of mediocrity between the enormous advances and achievements of Victoria's reign and the massive destruction of men, cities and morals during the Great War of 1914–18.

If the Edwardians were generally second-rate – compare Henry Campbell-Bannerman with Gladstone or Disraeli, Laurence Binyon with Tennyson or Browning – nothing was more appreciated than a beautiful woman, and here again Alix not only conformed but also remained peerless for a woman of her maturity – she was fifty-six when she became Queen. Margot Asquith, not an easy woman to please, wrote of her at this time as 'making every other woman look common beside her'. Another, as if writing of Princess Diana today, declared that she was 'so beautiful with her sly sideways look'. It was almost unfair that God had not only blessed Alix with these peerless looks but also with an almost ageless quality.

In 1903, two years after her accession, Lord Knutsford, describing her at dinner in Copenhagen, wrote: 'Our Queen was in grey, diamond necklace, and one large diamond in her hair. She looked about the youngest in the room, and dashed about from person to person, laughing with everyone.' And on her visit to Berlin, six years later, Lord Hardinge commented waspishly: 'She was looking particularly well at the time, and had a useful foil in the German Empress, who was much younger and looked old enough to be her mother.'

A final advantage was that she not only possessed an infallible dress sense but also the money to exploit it. On the night before the wedding of Princess Alice of Battenberg and Prince Andrew of Greece (Prince Philip's parents) in 1903, Alix was 'in a dress embroidered with mauve sequins, and wearing a tiara of diamonds and amethysts, looking lovelier than ever'. And George Wyndham, a noted connoisseur, left this portrait of Alix at Court in Dublin on 26 July 1903:

Her garter ribbon brought out the blue of her eyes. Her chamoise train was hung to her shoulders by great jewels of dropping pearls. She had a high open-work lace collar, a breastplate and a gorget – you may say – of diamonds and ropes of round pearls falling to her lap. And she is an angel.

Georgina Battiscombe quotes from the Macclesfield family papers that, soon after she became Queen, Alix remarked to Old Mac that while all she ached for was privacy and peace, 'with a heavy heart I have to lead this new life with all its many responsibilities'. This was either a tease or a joke which Lady Macclesfield would recognise, more likely the former. Alix as Queen lost none of her love of fun and certainly laughed no less than before. But the throne did have the effect of toughening her up and leading her to insist that she received the recognition to which she was entitled.

In a subtle way, becoming Queen affected her relationship with Bertie. Now that her husband had assumed the dignity and rank of King-Emperor, she considered that the infidelities she had become reconciled to when he was Prince of Wales should now cease. They did not and this angered her. Alice Keppel was as much at his side, and as much a dominant influence in his life, as ever: off to Biarritz, and treated as if she were Queen; off to Mrs Willy James* at West Dean Park, to the Savilles at Rufford Abbey (for the Doncaster racing),

---

* Hilaire Belloc composed an unpublished ballad on the subject of West Dean. This is an extract:

> And there is that when the dryads ope
> Their young enchanted arms to grasp the Spring,
> There comes a coroneted envelope
> and Mrs James will entertain the King!
>
> There will be bridge and booze till after three,
> And, after that, a lot of them will grope
> Along the corridors in *robes de nuit*,
> Pyjamas, or some other kind of dope.
>
> *Envoi*
> Prince, Father Vaughan may entertain the Pope,
> And you may entertain the Jews at Tring,
> But I will entertain the larger hope,
> That Mrs James will entertain the King!

(Tring was the seat of Lord Rothschild.)

and to the Grevilles at Reigate Priory. The King was always with Mrs Keppel, his little white terrier, Caesar, at heel, and rarely with Alix.

It never occurred to Bertie for one moment to restrict in any way the pleasures and life-style he had enjoyed as Prince of Wales. And yet, anachronistic as it may seem, he remained profoundly loyal to Alix. This was reflected in his strong opposition to the plan to send Georgie and May, still the Duke and Duchess of York, on an Empire tour. This had been proposed, and largely arranged, while Queen Victoria was still alive. It was to embrace South Africa, Australia and Canada, its main purpose being to inaugurate the first Parliament of the new Federal Commonwealth of Australia, and also to acknowledge the Canadian and Australian contributions towards the war in South Africa, where many lives had been lost.

Alix had been miserable at the thought of losing her son for the eight months this tour would occupy and pleaded with Bertie with his new authority as King to have it cancelled. Much against his better judgment, Bertie, on the third day of his reign, attempted to do this, using the death of the Queen as the reason.

Lord Salisbury, as Prime Minister, consulted with his colleagues, who unanimously agreed that it would give great offence. Arthur Balfour, as Leader of the House of Commons, drafted a letter to the new sovereign which made clear where the King's duty lay. He was, one section of the letter ran,

no longer merely King of Great Britain and Ireland, and of a few dependencies. . . . He is now the greatest constitutional bond uniting together in a single Empire communities of free men separated by half the circumference of the globe. All the patriotic sentiment which makes such an Empire possible centres in him. . . .

Bertie had no need of this instruction from one of his ministers and had received it only because of his kind but ill-conceived attempt to spare Alix the misery of separation from her beloved son. The old Queen would have been outraged at this interference in state affairs and the episode exemplifies Alix's selfishness and new imperiousness as Queen. Her selfishness had been accepted for years, and her surviving son once wrote to his wife, May: 'Mama, as I have always said, is one of the most selfish people I know.'

In the event, Alix derived a great deal of happiness from looking after Georgie and May's children while their parents were away, spoiling them outrageously. These York children suffered from a regime which was closer to Victoria and Albert's rather than that of their grandparents. Bertie and Alix were never happier than when romping with their grandchildren, whose discipline and education relaxed while their parents were carrying out their royal duties around the world. It was a particularly fine summer in 1901 and the gardens of Sandringham, which more usually echoed to the sound of deep male voices discussing the day's shoot, or women's voices gossiping and admiring the flowers, were now filled with the cries and laughter of four young children.

Set against this summer jolliness was Alix's concern about Bertie's health. Since acceding to the throne, he had become increasingly tetchy and inclined to fall into black periods when only the grandchildren could make him smile. As if in search of relief from depression, he began eating even richer food even more swiftly and in greater quantity than before. Normally a moderate drinker – a glass or two of champagne during dinner, a single brandy with his cigars afterwards – he began drinking wine more liberally. Georgie and May had noticed this increased irascibility before they had left in March, and Georgie had bossily written to his mother that 'you must do all you can to help him and insist on him having a rest this autumn'.

But trying to get Bertie to rest during the first months of his reign was hopeless. After so many years of frustration and inactivity, he fell on his duties like a starving man. Thousands of army and navy commissions had accumulated, unsigned, during the Queen's last months. He tackled the task manfully and actually succeeded in signing 6,600 army commissions before he had to accept defeat and have a rubber stamp made. Even then, he insisted on wielding the stamp himself to give his signature some sort of royal authority.

Bertie also, at first, opened his morning post, about four hundred letters on average daily, but this took several hours and left him no time for his boxes. The red boxes which he had so ardently wanted to open for so long now accumulated at frightening speed. The first Baron Redesdale,* an old friend, called on the King late one night:

I found him in his private sitting-room all alone, and we sat smoking and talking over old times for a couple of hours. Towards midnight he got up and said, 'Now I must bid you good-night, for I must set to work,' pointing to a huge pile of familiar red boxes. 'Surely,' I said, 'your Majesty is not going to tackle all that work tonight!' His answer was, 'Yes, I must! Besides, it is all so interesting,' and then gave me one of his happy smiles.

In addition to the everyday burdens of office, which had kept his mother busy pretty well all day and every day except Sunday, Bertie took on with happy enthusiasm the engagements she had failed to carry out for decades: not just the opening of Parliament, but also countless civic ceremonies, the laying of foundation-stones and celebrating city anniversaries – all the minor duties he had carried out for so long as Prince of Wales and understudy for the Queen.

However, Bertie did not work at such depth as his mother, who might write out several drafts of a letter before she was satisfied and then worked on a final, fair draft. He hated writing, which was just as well as few could read it, and simply dictated a single draft. It may not have been so carefully thought out as his mother's rendering would have been, but it got the work done more speedily. And speed was a prime requirement – speed, decisiveness, endurance. One of those closest to him for so many years gives a graphic picture of him at work:

The scene at Marlborough House during the first weeks of King Edward's reign was in sharp contrast to everything to which we were accustomed. He himself was accessible, friendly, almost familiar, frank, suggestive, receptive, discarding ceremony, with no loss of dignity, decisive but neither obstinate nor imperious. . . . He permitted those who had access to him to smoke in his presence. He stood with his back to the fireplace, while one or two of us sat

---

* Besides eight children of his own, he sired four more by his sister-in-law, including Clementine Hozier (later Churchill).

at tables arranged for our use. He passed from one to the other, going minutely into every question as it arose, and giving decisions in short and concise sentences. You were told to enter the room unannounced, and if you desired to do so you left the room with a bow to the King, and returned when you wished. He was still questioning, dictating, deciding. His memory never seemed to betray him. The slightest slip in the instructions he had given was detected at once. The impression he gave me was that of a man who, after long years of pent-up inaction, had suddenly been freed from restraint and revelled in his liberty.

To Alix's relief they remained for many months at Marlborough House while Bertie was giving Buckingham Palace 'a good spring clean' – one might say, almost a reconstruction. Because Queen Victoria had been so rarely at Buckingham Palace and did not much like change in even quite small things, it was almost an historical relic. There were one or two water-closets and even a fixed bath or two. There was a telephone but with lines only to her Private Secretary and herself. There were rooms which had hardly been penetrated since the Prince Consort's death. There were rooms full of junk and piled up with paintings. It would be hard to imagine a more inefficient and inconvenient palace.

Bertie tackled these 'Augean stables'* like some latter-day Hercules with Caesar at his heels, a Homburg hat on his head, silver-topped stick in his hand and a cigar in his mouth, followed by a retinue of staff, a secretary and often Lord Esher. The sacred suite of his father was treated like the rest, to be redecorated and refurnished: a bath here, a basin there, old pictures to be removed, new ones to be hung . . .

He lost no time in decision [his Surveyor of Pictures recalled]. I found it useless to ask the King if I should hang this *here* and so on. . . . 'Offer it up,' he would say and when 'offered up' he would come to see and perhaps put his head on one side, all with a twinkle in his eye, and say, 'That is not *amiss*'. . . . He enjoyed sitting in a room with the men working about him, and liked giving directions himself as to the actual position of pictures.

---

* Most of the actual stables were converted into garages for the growing fleet of royal and guests' cars.

The refurbishing was even more radical at Windsor Castle, of which Esher became Deputy-Constable and Lieutenant-Governor. The plumbing had been improved since Albert had died as a consequence of the drains' inadequacy, but it was now the twentieth century and residents and guests reasonably expected running hot water and a sufficiency of lavatories. The old Queen's ornaments, bric-à-brac, special pictures and much else were stacked away in the capacious Round Tower, along with enough furniture for every house in the town of Windsor. However, with special relish, letters, papers, busts and statues of John Brown, the Queen's tiresome, intrusive, liberty-taking Scottish gillie, loathed by all but the Queen who became unhealthily dependent on him after she was widowed, were summarily destroyed. The same fate was handed out to anything relating to the sly, toadying Munshi, the Queen's closest servant for many years. (On his return to India and his subsequent death, his widow tried to blackmail the Queen over a bundle of letters she had unwisely written to him.)

Alix had hated Osborne House as strongly as Bertie and agreed that she would never voluntarily visit that chill, marble, mausoleum-like island home, so beloved of Queen Victoria, who had made it clear that she wished it to be retained in the family. Bertie was inclined to act at once and on his own to hand it over to the nation for conversion into a naval college and convalescent home for naval officers. Part of the domestic quarters of the Queen and Prince Albert would be preserved, but that was all. Alix, on the other hand, wisely counselled restraint and consultation with his sisters, Helena, Louise and Beatrice, Vicky being too ill.

Bertie reluctantly agreed and contrived to persuade the three of them to meet at the house in August 1901. It was an odd gathering. Clever, artistic Loosy was closest to her brother and did not care tuppence about Osborne. Helena – Lenchen – the closest to Alix was not much interested either. For Beatrice it was different. As the youngest child, an afterthought, she had been closest to her mother, had been married from Osborne and her husband was buried in the church at Whippingham.

The King withdrew with his sisters to a secluded part of the grounds and a discussion took place between them in German, so that their respective suites could not understand what was being said. Sir Lionel Cust [Gentleman Usher to the King] related, 'The King returned after some time flushed, but with a happy smile on his face.' He had convinced – or coerced – his sisters, who could not have presented a united front.

Of course, the Kaiser had to have his say later. 'Osborne,' he wrote to Louise, 'what became of this heavenly, holy quiet spot so dear to me!!' The question was rhetorical and mischief-making. As Elizabeth Longford reminded the readers of Louise's letters, he knew perfectly well what had happened to it.

No one cared what Bertie did to Balmoral. This massive pile of Scottish granite was disliked by all the family except Bertie, who enjoyed the shooting but not much else. Alix loathed it. From earliest childhood Queen Victoria's children dreaded their visits, the only comfort lying in their unanimity and the retelling of their dreadful experiences.

In one department, however, Alix claimed total autocratic control, and that was decorating and furnishing. Bertie could have his lavatories and baths and, with his Surveyor of Pictures at his side, could deal with the choice and hanging of the royal picture collection, which even then was the finest in the world. Alix's taste was not particularly adventurous, but it reflected the best at the time, which meant a revolutionary transformation of Buckingham Palace in particular which had not been tampered with since the dark, heavy, musty days of Prince Albert.

Buckingham Palace became full of bright chintzes and William Morris wallpapers. Out went marble and black walnut, mahogany and ebony, and in came furniture from the schools of Richard Norman Shaw, Edward Burne-Jones and the like, all introduced by the up-to-date designers of the day. They would have preferred to be rid of the knick-knacks, the objets d'art and the countless photographs which had cluttered Alix's rooms since her marriage, but she was having none of that.

The conversion was comprehensive at Windsor and Buckingham Palace, but Alix had neither the heart nor the inclination to deal with Balmoral. She expressed her feelings about this Scottish pile to Old Mac:

I dreaded very much at first coming up here without our beloved Queen, whose favourite home it was; one misses her at every step and corner and it seems almost like sacrilege sitting here writing at *her* table and living in *her* rooms with all her things about me. I will not have any of her things and treasures touched here, all shall remain as she placed them herself.

Bertie's new royal Household preoccupied him during the first weeks of his reign and he freely discussed candidates with Mrs Keppel, whose advice he sought on almost everything, which made Alix very cross because she was never asked. He did not make any immediate appointments and let it be known that his mother's Household would be retained for six months. Yet all Queen Victoria's officers knew that their jobs were at risk and that the King was likely to remain loyal to most of his own, long-serving staff. Among these was Sir Francis Knollys, Bertie's Private Secretary for over thirty years, a man who understood the workings of his mind, and whose advice and guidance had been thoroughly proven. Almost as long-serving was General Sir Dighton Probyn, and no one could match the length of his grey beard and density of his side-whiskers. Before he entered royal service he had had a distinguished career, earning the VC in the Indian Mutiny. Probyn was not only honourable and wise, but as Bertie's Comptroller and Keeper of the Privy Purse had shown a remarkable talent for handling the Prince's financial affairs, which always needed a steady, firm hand. He was now made a Privy Councillor, Keeper of the Privy Purse and extra equerry.

Also concerned with finances were the Master of the King's Household and his deputy, Lord Farquhar and Colonel Charles Frederick, who at once set about dealing with the extravagances which had accumulated over the past decades. Balmoral, for example, was absurdly overmanned and here at times it was difficult to find a sober servant. At shoots, for example, it had become traditional that gillies and beaters were issued with a bottle of whisky to keep out the cold if

the weather turned inclement. If it did not, they were supposed to return them. Naturally, the definition soon became
hazy, like the heads of these Scotsmen as they put down
their whisky even on sunny October afternoons. 'The amount
of whisky consumed by the servants was truly stupendous,'
Sir Frederick Ponsonby noted. 'A drunken man was so
common that no one ever remarked on it.'

Old friends of around Bertie's own age, men who had travelled with him, shot with him and dined with him for decades,
were favoured with appointments. For instance, Charles
Harbord (now Lord Suffield), who had been Chief of the Staff
on Bertie's tour of India in 1875–6 and his Lord of the Bedchamber for nearly thirty years, now became Permanent
Lord-in-Waiting. As military and naval ADCs were two
remarkable men of their time, General Sir Thomas Kelly-
Kenny and Admiral Sir John Fisher.

Fisher, an ebullient, entertaining, charming but tricky naval
genius, had for long been a favourite, and Alix adored him.
A typical report from Fisher to his friend, Lord Esher, runs:

Ponsonby sent me 3 letters and 2 telegrams about going to see the
King, so I had a sort of presentiment there was something amiss!
I had 4¼ hours alone with him, and he was most kind and cordial,
and took me to the station finally and saw me off, and told me at
parting how much he had enjoyed my company!

With Alix, Fisher had a steady correspondence and a most
cordial relationship. He was often on the royal yacht with her
and they chatted away merrily for hours, occasionally breaking into a music-less – a hum sufficed – but energetic dance
on deck in spite of his years and her lameness. She addressed
her letters to him 'Dear Admiral "Jack"'. When he telegraphed her on her sixty-second birthday, 'May you live till
you look it is the fervent wish of this humble admirer,' she
replied, 'In your kind telegram you wish me too long a life. It
would take me 300 before I could look 62 by your reckoning. I
am delighted with the lovely Mecca stone.' 'I treasure the
remembrances of all her kindnesses to me as well as that of
her sister, the Dowager Empress of Russia,' Fisher wrote

in his memoirs. 'The trees they both planted at Kilverstone [his seat in Norfolk] are both flourishing. . . .'

The relationship between Fisher and his King was of immense importance to both of them. They were born in the same year and had a great deal more in common. Fisher was the Royal Navy's great reformer, even before he became First Sea Lord in 1904, and made many enemies in part because he did not suffer fools gladly and knew that war with Germany was inevitable (he correctly predicted in 1908 that it would break out in the late summer of 1914). His most ferocious adversary was Lord Charles Beresford, by this time a very senior admiral. Bertie had absolute faith in Fisher and took particular pleasure in backing him against his own one-time enemy.

In another book of memoirs, Fisher devoted almost the whole of the opening chapter to the King. 'King Edward, besides his wonderful likeness to King Henry the Eighth, had that great King's remarkable attributes of combining autocracy with almost a socialistic tie with the masses,' Fisher wrote. He also told of a meeting with two admirals:

I mention another excellent illustration of King Edward's fine and magnanimous character though it's to my own detriment. He used to say to me often at Big Functions: 'Have I missed out anyone, do you think?' for he would go around in a most careful way to speak to all he should. Just then a certain Admiral approached – perhaps the biggest ass I ever met. The King shook hands with him and said something I thought quite unnecessarily loving to him: when he had gone he turned on me like a tiger and said: 'You ought to be ashamed of yourself!' I humbly said, 'What for?' 'Why!' he replied, 'when that man came up to me your face was perfectly demoniacal! Everyone saw it! and the poor fellow couldn't kick you back! You're First Sea Lord and he's a ruined man! You've no business to show your hate!' and the lovely thing was that a man came up I knew the King did perfectly hate, and I'm blessed if he didn't smile on him and cuddle him as if he was his long-lost brother, and then he turned to me afterwards and said with joyful revenge, 'Well! did you see that?' Isn't that a Great Heart? and is it to be wondered at that he was so Popular?

Bertie, with Alix lovingly behind him, supported Fisher through almost six years as First Sea Lord when the navy built the first *Dreadnought* battleship and then a fleet of them, and the navy's efficiency improved a hundredfold.

The third of what Lee defined as Bertie's 'nucleus of the new court' was Charles Hardinge, later Lord Hardinge of Penshurst. Hardinge was high in the Foreign Office for almost the whole of the King's reign, and was the only figure in that office whom Bertie totally trusted. When Bertie, on his own initiative, planned a tour of Europe in 1903 which was to have historic consequences, to the outrage of Lord Lansdowne, the Foreign Secretary, he arranged to take Charles Hardinge, then an Under-Secretary, and no one else. The two men saw eye-to-eye on every aspect of foreign policy, and Bertie depended heavily on Hardinge's superior knowledge of foreign affairs. At the end of the 1903 grand tour, Bertie told his son that Hardinge had been 'invaluable in every respect'.

Lord Esher can only be described as a special case. There was no one quite like him in political or royal circles. He was forty-nine when Bertie came to the throne, and with little to his record. He had been an invaluable Private Secretary to Lord Hartington and a trusted confidant of Queen Victoria. An undoubted genius, Esher preferred to work behind the scenes as a manipulator and, in this role, sometimes made himself unpopular among staid bureaucrats. A fellow old-Etonian, Lord Rosebery, did however persuade him to accept the post of Permanent Secretary to the Office of Works, or 'Master of Lavatories at Buckingham Palace' as someone rudely called it. He was in fact responsible for the upkeep of all royal property, and this included the organisation of the 1897 Diamond Jubilee celebrations. It also brought him deep into Court circles, and to the admiring attention of the Prince of Wales, as Bertie then was.

Esher was a 'fixer', devious by instinct, handsome in looks, aesthetic by nature, with beautiful handwriting for composing numerous lucid memoranda and enormous correspondence. As a reformer, he was a match for Fisher, and the two men were devoted to one another: 'My Beloved Esher', the Admiral always addressed him. After the wretched performance of the army in the South African War, Esher sought to bring about reforms of a radical nature at the War Office which were strongly opposed by the established cabal, which included the Secretary of State for War. Bertie backed him all the way, the reforms were introduced, and, like the navy, the army was better prepared for war in 1914 than it would otherwise have been. Esher was the ultimate patrician, wandering in and out of the royal palaces without notice, perhaps bringing to the King some scraps of inside information from the last Cabinet meeting which the minister concerned might fail to pass on, letting his wishes be known and invariably having them satisfied, putting in a word for some promising official and hinting that another was unfit for his responsibilities.

Esher could read Bertie's mind and anticipate his wishes and responses as no one else could, and with the same intimate charm that had conquered the old Queen he was even closer to the King than his innermost circle of advisers and confidants. Esher made only one notable error of judgment during Bertie's reign and that was a personal one. Cassel had observed with admiration Esher's silent progress through the corridors of power and how he discreetly got things done without seeking credit. At the end of the first year of Bertie's reign, Cassel offered Esher a most attractive proposition as a consultant in his firm at the rate of £5,000 (close to £200,000 in today's money) a year, plus commission on any successful negotiations he might complete. It was for a trial period of three years 'in case we don't get on'. Esher warned Cassel that 'I might seem dull in perception of great financial and economic problems for a while!' He told his friends that he took on this very part-time job for the benefit of his beloved younger son Maurice* and confided from the outset, 'I don't know how long it will last.' It did not last the full proposed term, Esher deciding that he was 'unfitted for the City business'. These two men were worlds away from one another in background, tradition, ethics and too much else for any such arrangement to prosper, and Esher's private papers reveal evidence of dispute and distrust.

* He became a professional soldier, with a predilection for actresses, later marrying Zena Dare.

Both men were far too wise to become enemies, but Esher made plenty of them elsewhere, notably Sir John Brodrick, the Secretary of State for War, who fiercely opposed the Esher–Haldane* reforms. Brodrick claimed with some justice that 'by the time any decision had come to the point when the Cabinet could lay it before the Sovereign, the issue had been largely pre-judged on the incomplete premises of an observer who had no official status'.

But Esher never crossed swords with Knollys, by far the most important figure in the Household as far as he was concerned. Knollys knew how useful Esher was to his master's well-being and satisfaction with life. With his internal knowledge about almost everything that went on in politics and the social world, he could keep the King amused for hours on end, to the relief of those immediately around him, who sometimes despaired of winning 'the perpetual battle against fatigue and irritability' which rose to new heights during the first demanding year of Bertie's reign.

Charles Carrington, now a viscount and prominent Liberal politician, gives us a brief glimpse of Esher in action when

the door opened and in came Esher. He certainly is an extraordinary man and has a wonderful footing in Buckingham Palace. He seems to be able to run about it as he likes and must be a considerable nuisance to the Household. He is a clever, unscrupulous man, who might be dangerous; and he is not trusted by the general public, who look on him as an intriguer.

The year 1901 was sorrowful in many respects, but it was also momentous and eventful. For Alix there was much anxiety, as well as the joy of having her grandchildren with her for most of the time.

As the winter of 1901–2 approached, she became increasingly worried about her role as Bertie's Queen. He was as affectionate and well-disposed to her as ever, but with Alice Keppel beside him for so much of the time, and so publicly, she felt the distance between them growing. Now that he had the power and responsibilities, and the inside knowledge

* Richard Burdon, first Viscount, liberal statesman, who, as successor to Brodrick, remodelled the army and founded the part-time Territorial Army.

of affairs of state, of which he had been deprived for so long, Alix expected him to share some part of them with her, just as she rightly imagined that the old Queen and Prince Albert discussed contemporary events and took mutual advice. But Bertie remained as unforthcoming about state secrets as his mother had been with him. If that was hard to bear, the offence was compounded by the knowledge that he took constant advice from Alice Keppel and confided in his daughter-in-law, May, as he never would in her. Once when showing some boxes to his son he added, 'You can show them to May.'

'But Mama doesn't see them,' Georgie exclaimed.

Bertie replied, 'No, but that's a very different thing.'

The truth was that Bertie did not trust Alix's confidentiality, any more than Queen Victoria had trusted his. Dear wife though she was and always would be, he tended to regard her, as he always had done, as a bit of a light-headed flibbertigibbet. They were never heard to exchange cross words, but Alix got her own back in small measure by becoming more unpunctual than ever. If reminded by an equerry, possibly several times, that the King was waiting for her, she was heard to say, 'Keep him waiting; it will do him good!'

One of the most time-consuming duties of Bertie and Alix was the receiving of deputations with addresses. It became standard practice that on certain days Bertie would begin receiving addresses at 10.30 a.m. and Alix would join him at midday.

But when it came to twelve o'clock [Sir Frederick Ponsonby recalled] there was no sign of the Queen. Meanwhile the second deputation arrived and then the third, fourth, and fifth, which upset all the arrangements. In order that they should not get mixed up, a different room had been allotted to each, and soon every room was filled with eminent men in uniform, but in spite of repeated messages there was no sign of the Queen. The King in full uniform sat in the Equerries' room drumming on the table and looking out of the window with the face of a Christian martyr. Finally at ten minutes to one the Queen came down looking lovely and quite unconcerned. All she said was, 'Am I late?' The King swallowed and walked gravely out of the room.

Alix took refuge and comfort in her Household, especially in her new acquisition, her six Maids of Honour. They were young and pretty and there was genuine mutual love on a maternal basis. Alix would listen enchanted to their gossip and tales of their love affairs, and she would tell them about her life in Denmark as a child, contrasting it with her early married life and conditions at Balmoral and Osborne back in the 1860s and 1870s. Two of these young women were the Hon. Dorothy and Hon. Violet Vivian, 'my heavenly twins', daughters of the third Lord Vivian. When Dorothy became engaged to the future Field Marshal Earl Haig, then a promising young cavalry officer, Alix insisted on the wedding being held at Buckingham Palace. And it was one of her own shoes which, at the last minute, she tied to the back of the happy couple's car.

Because Alix was never allowed (until 1907) on any of Bertie's trips to Paris – always *en garçon* – where he liked to renew his friendship with past hosts and lovers, nor to Biarritz, when he was always accompanied by Alice Keppel, Alix quite reasonably made her own travels. What's more, she gave the shortest feasible notice of when and where she was going, though it was nearly always to Denmark, or to Greece to visit her brother, when she customarily ordered up one of the royal yachts and arrived in Piraeus by sea.

No one could claim that this was an ideal marriage, and they were hardly ever known to be alone together for a meal under the same roof for Bertie's entire reign. It was not a close marriage like that of Georgie and May, but there was genuine warmth between them and an understanding unblemished by bad feeling.

17

The Crisis

'The Coronation must proceed as planned.'
Bertie's futile instruction

Bertie was an early enthusiast for motoring. His friend, the future Lord Montagu of Beaulieu, introduced him to it in 1899, and Alix was soon as keen as Bertie. They were sometimes to be seen, usually in an open Daimler, being driven along the dusty roads of north Norfolk, wearing hats, scarves, goggles, Alix heavily veiled. They would each have a dog on their laps, whose fur was flattened in the wind and whose noses savoured the ever-changing smells. Villagers would recognise them, for there were very few cars about when they became King and Queen, and bow or drop a curtsey as they passed. But Edward Hinchinbrooke noted mixed reactions when out motoring with Bertie from Sandringham: 'It was amusing to see the various receptions accorded to the King on the road. We passed brewers' vans and were vociferously jeered at, and on the other hand ladies jumped off their bicycles and curtseyed.' Then again the royal car was dented by stones hurled by jeering urchins, who did not realise that their target was the King of England.

Bertie and Alix together was not a common sight for, as in much else, they had completely contrary views on motoring.

It was, simply, that Alix could not tolerate speed above that of a fast walking pace in case they hit a dog, while Bertie was always urging on their sorely tested driver. Alix would tap him on the shoulder when she thought they were going too fast, while Bertie, especially if there was another car in sight, urged him on – 'Faster, faster!' His Daimler was never known to be overtaken and he enjoyed few greater pleasures than overtaking another fast car, dust and cigar smoke streaming behind like a destroyer's funnel smoke.

From time to time, when alone and on the open road and far from dogs, Alix would emulate Bertie's practice of driving flat out, ordering the surprised chauffeur to put his foot on the accelerator as hard as he could. Toria, sitting beside her mother and not enjoying herself in the least, would see a smile of utter contentment beneath her motoring veil.

In April 1901 Esher told his son of Marcus Beresford's motoring experience: 'On Saturday he drove with the King to Newmarket, in the latter's new motor car, 50 miles in 2½ hours. Not bad. He says the dust was something portentous. They were white as millers.' It is quite likely that Bertie was the first man to drive at 60 mph on the Brighton road.

Mr Charles Stamper, the 'King's Motor Mechanic', sat in front, beside the driver, bag of tools at the ready to deal with punctures, of which there were many, and breakdowns, of which there were few. At the conclusion of a long drive and when he had been helped out of his seat, Bertie would comment, 'A very good run, Stamper. A very good run indeed!'

Charles Stamper was an intelligent man, who had the good sense to put down his reminiscences of five years in Bertie's employ. Stamper told vividly of the King's reaction when he lost the way and had to halt the car and get out the map. He 'would gravely deplore the manner in which misfortune singled him out for her victim', settling himself 'gently in his corner as if resigning himself to his fate. In his countenance there was written a placid acceptance of the situation and a calm expectancy of worse to come. The listless way in which he heard my apologies was inimitable. Of such gentle irony the King was a master.'

As if the royal Daimler's speed were not enough to terrify the villagers, their horses and their stock, Bertie had fitted to his cars a four-key bugle which had impressed him in the Kaiser's Mercedes. The noise it made was cacophonous. However, he remained strongly opposed to motor-racing, which began during his reign and was conducted on the same lines as horse-racing, owners and drivers having their colours and the pit area called the paddock. But some of his own experiences matched those at the headquarters of motor-racing, Brooklands, which opened in 1907. One day, *en route* to Newark and no doubt travelling at twice the legal speed of 20 mph, the car's front wheels struck a drainage culvert with a fearful crash. 'Stop! stop!' exclaimed the King. 'Do you want to kill me?' But he was more put out by the state of his brown bowler, which had been heavily dented while protecting his royal skull from the roof.

The King's cars were painted claret colour, carried the royal coat of arms on the side and had no number plates. Their bodywork was never flashy and, although comfortably fitted out, there was, as a reflection of Bertie's taste, nothing ostentatious about them.

Three of Bertie's cars were always despatched to Biarritz for his annual holiday there, and Stamper and drivers went, too. Alice Keppel's daughter Sonia tells in her memoirs how Bertie loved to go out in the cars for a picnic somewhere in the surrounding country or by the sea.

On Easter Sunday [she writes], Kingy, ourselves and a host of others set forth for a mammoth picnic. Kingy liked to think of these as impromptu parties and little did he realise the hours of preliminary hard work they entailed. Kingy spied out the land for a suitable site and, at his given word, we all stopped. . . . For some unfathomed reason Kingy had a preference for picnicking by the side of the road.

On other occasions he liked dropping in for tea at a café. Stamper recalled how

he would stop on the [out]skirts of a village and send me to see if I could find a café clean and fit for him to enter. . . . I would order the tea and then return to the car. By the time the King arrived at the café, the tea would be ready, and he would enter the house and

281

sit down to it like an ordinary customer. When he had finished he would leave me to pay the bill. . . . Once or twice I have known him call for the bill and settle it himself.

Bertie's cars gave him the opportunity to mix informally with ordinary people, and sometimes when abroad without being recognised. On another occasion, when driving near Bayonne, the car burst a tyre. Stamper at once busied himself changing the wheel. Meanwhile,

after picking a few primroses, His Majesty sat down and began to talk to a French peasant, who had come out of his hut to see what was going on. They spoke together until the car was ready, when the King rose and said he must be going. As the car moved off, he raised his hat to the poor man, who did the same, quite unaware of His Majesty's identity.

At Marienbad, where he took the waters during his reign, he sometimes hired cars locally. Haldane tells of one trip out into the country when he was the companion:

He proposed to me one day that we should go in plain clothes as though we were Austrians, and drive out in a motor into the country and have coffee somewhere, because, he said, Austrian coffee was always admirable, and you could tell when you had crossed the frontier into Germany, because of the badness of the coffee. The first thing he did was to make me buy an Austrian hat, so as to look more like a native.

As we were passing a little roadside inn, with a wooden table in front of it, the King stopped and said, 'Here I will stand treat.' He ordered coffee for two, and then he said, 'Now I am going to pay. I shall take care to give only a small tip to the woman in case she suspects who I am.' We then drove on to a place the King was very fond of – a monastery inhabited by the Abbot of Teppel – where we had a large tea, and where the King enjoyed himself with the monks very much, gossiping and making himself agreeable. . . .

Bertie was not only a pioneer motorist; he made motoring acceptable. Queen Victoria, along with most respectable people, regarded motor-cars as filthy, noisy, anti-social objects owned only by the fast set. Now anyone could drive without losing their reputation and the motor-car manufacturing trade received a great boost.

* * *

Bertie had been introduced to yacht-racing at the age of nine and on an historic occasion, when the schooner *America* won the first ever America's Cup in 1851. He was on-board the royal yacht *Victoria and Albert*, with Queen Victoria and Prince Albert, when they saw the American schooner double the Needles and enter the last leg of the race towards Cowes. Bertie kept in close touch with yacht-racing over the next twenty-five years, but did not start racing himself until 1876, after his return from India, when he bought a small schooner-yacht and entered her for the Queen's Cup. He had no luck, but scored his first victory later in the season, and from that time he became increasingly enthusiastic about the sport.

Yachting at the level at which Bertie practised it was a horribly expensive business, and in the early 1890s he spent tens of thousands of pounds annually on it. He looked forward keenly to the two or three weeks of Cowes Regatta at the end of July, after the racing at Goodwood. He was not only Commodore of the Royal Yacht Squadron and the Royal Thames Yacht Club, but also President of the Yacht Racing Association, bringing enhanced status to this sport. Alix, too, enjoyed the Regatta and the sea air at Cowes, though she did not often go cruising.

Bertie's halcyon years of ocean-racing began with the completion, at vast expense, of the *Britannia*, a racing cutter of 300 tons and with a crew of twenty-eight. For four years, this beautiful boat won almost every race for which it was entered, much to Bertie's satisfaction, especially as his other racing – his horse-racing – was running through a bad patch at the time.

The Kaiser watched his uncle's successes with envy and determined to beat him at his own game. At the same time, he persuaded himself that, politically, it would also act as a recognition signal of Germany's imminent challenge to British naval power. In 1895 Kaiser William arrived off Cowes in his mighty royal yacht *Höhenzollern*, with his brand new racing yacht *Meteor 1*, accompanied by two equally new and impressive warships, both named after victories in the Franco–Prussian War. With characteristic bombast, he made provocative speeches, strode about the grounds of the Royal

Yacht Squadron as if he owned the place, and complained insistently about the handicapping and the rules. Bertie dubbed him 'The Boss of Cowes' and feared the worst. His fears were well-founded. Soon the German Emperor became the Pest of Cowes.

Finally, when the Kaiser ordered from the King's own designer of the *Britannia* an even bigger racing yacht, *Meteor 2*, Bertie decided to withdraw and never raced again. 'The Regatta at Cowes was once a pleasant holiday for me,' he complained, 'but now that the Kaiser has taken command it is nothing but a nuisance, with that perpetual firing of salutes, cheering and other tiresome disturbances.' He sold *Britannia* to the man who invented Bovril, John Lawson-Johnston, but bought it back again for sentimental reasons when he became King.

In fact, if he could somehow avoid the presence of his nephew, there still remained a lot to enjoy at Cowes and he never missed a year. One of the friends he always met there, Sir Alan Young, was widely known to have one of the best chefs in the country who specialised in some of Bertie's favourite dishes. Coming on-board his yacht, Bertie would grumble teasingly, 'I don't suppose we shall have anything decent to eat, nothing but ship's biscuits as usual?'

Because of his weight, now seventeen stone on a stocky frame and forty-eight inches round the waist, and his loss of flexibility and mobility (several falls did not help either), Bertie's sports and pastimes became more restricted during the last decade of his life. He had tried tennis in the 1880s and did not much enjoy it. He regarded golf as a futile competitive sport and fishing a lonely and boring business. He still enjoyed his shooting, but was confined to a low, specially built pony trap, which was not very satisfactory, or the back of a pony, which was better. Unlike his son, Georgie, he never became a crack shot. 'Never a good shot at taking birds in front of him, King Edward used to make some marvellous long shots at birds behind,' wrote his friend, George Cornwallis-West.

In these last years the pleasures of shooting began to

decline with his mobility and he enjoyed horse-racing more in proportion. There was nothing better, on a fine day at Ascot or on Epsom Downs, than taking his party into the paddock to see the horses saddled and to chat encouragingly and in subtle technical terms to the jockey wearing his colours. The camaraderie, the mixing of all classes, the bookies shouting the odds, the build-up of excitement of both crowd and horses – all this was highly pleasurable.

Bertie had thirteen horses in training for 1901 and he was looking forward to another good year. Unfortunately, with the death of his mother, Court mourning prohibited him from racing, and he leased all his horses to the Duke of Devonshire, who incidentally had foul luck all season.

The return in November of Georgie and May from their long tour was a time of great joy for Alix, even though it also meant that she would now have to yield responsibility for her grandchildren, who had been delightfully spoilt in their parents' absence. Also, there was suddenly a great deal to do. Georgie and May were to be made Prince and Princess of Wales on Bertie's birthday in eight days' time, 9 November 1901, which meant a lot of preparation and rehearsal.

At the same time Alix found increasingly that life in London, that is to say with Bertie, had become irksome. After the Christmas festivities she removed herself more or less permanently to Sandringham. May, who loved her mother-in-law and felt increasingly responsible for Court conduct now that she was Princess of Wales, deplored both her long absences and the reason for them:

. . . alas when she once gets *stuck* at Sandringham, it is difficult to move her [she wrote to her aunt, the old Grand Duchess of Mecklenburg-Strelitz], I had so hoped that in her new position as Queen all this would have improved, & I do feel that it is very important that one should take a lively interest . . . in anything connected with the good of one's country. . . . It does not look well either for her so constantly to leave *him* alone as she does.

By chance the Grand Duchess had the opportunity to see Alix a few days later and had 'a long talk with her'. She told May:

She says, *he* does not permit her taking [her position] as he takes everything to himself [and] lets her do nothing in the way of carrying out her duties; for instance, he did not even let her give the Prizes for the Red Cross which she has done hitherto; he says he is in an exceptional position and must take all the honours to himself.

Life in London for Alix was also tiresome because of Bertie's increasing ill-temper and the manner in which he almost flaunted his closeness to Alice Keppel. 'The King has been making a good many "Mrs George" dinners lately,' Charles Carrington noted. Moreover, he was still seeing Lady Warwick, although not, it was believed, sleeping with her. Alix had never liked either woman, but she cared even less for Lady Warwick and now determined to put an end to the affair. She wrote a polite letter herself and then persuaded Lord Esher to follow it up. 'He told me with charming courtesy and frankness', Lady Warwick wrote, 'that he thought it would be well for all concerned if my close connection with great affairs were to cease as it was giving rise to hostile comment which distressed Queen Alexandra.'

In April 1902 Alix travelled once again to Copenhagen, in company with Georgie and May, to celebrate the old King's eighty-fifth birthday. It was a great family reunion, but only a brief one, and by the end of the month Alix was back in London. Thanks to Esher, Buckingham Palace's renovations and redecorating were complete, and everyone was talking about and preparing for the Coronation on 26 June. The route had been published as early as January, and soon 'the main streets through which the procession would pass took on that backstage air inseparable in London from the erection of wooden stands, barricades, flagpoles and Venetian masts'.

In the early days of June, the first foreign dignitaries began to arrive in London – Indian princes and maharajas and colonial leaders from all parts of the empire, royalty from every kingdom in Europe and from Russia, and Arab and Turkish grandees – packing the big London hotels. In every city, town and village throughout the land preparations were being made to celebrate the Coronation locally with bonfires, pageants and processions. By happy chance it became a double celebration because peace had come at last in South Africa.

The Corporation of the City of London came in state to Buckingham Palace to present an address of congratulation on this peace to the King, to which Bertie replied, 'It is my earnest hope that by mutual co-operation and goodwill the bitter feelings of the past may speedily be replaced by ties of loyalty and friendship, and that an era of peace and prosperity may be in store for South Africa.'

A week later Bertie and Alix, with their daughter Toria and Georgie and May at their side, travelled from Buckingham Palace to St Paul's Cathedral by open carriage 'to return thanks to Almighty God for the restoration of peace. . . . It was a memorable service, memorable not only for the event which it celebrated, but also for the vast gathering of all that was best and noblest in the kingdom within the walls of the great cathedral,' ran a contemporary report.

The party of five returned to continue work on the preparations for the Coronation. Bertie was depressed and irritable from overwork quite unnecessarily brought on by attending to endless detail, down to the design of new liveries for his servants. With this daily fretting, after being heir to the Crown for more than sixty years, he almost seemed to be attempting self-destruction. If that were so, he very nearly succeeded.

On 14 June Bertie and Alix travelled to Aldershot to review 40,000 troops on Laffan's Plain. It was bitterly cold for the time of year and the rain was bucketing down when, that evening, they witnessed from the Royal Pavilion a great torchlight tattoo. That night Bertie complained of pain and feeling unwell and went to bed. He wrote in his diary: 'The King rather ill with severe chill. Unable to dine.'

It was noted the next day, a Sunday, that he did not appear at church as arranged. Sir Frederick Treves was called in, and it was thought advisable to issue a bulletin to assuage public anxiety: 'His Majesty the King is unable to leave his room today owing to an attack of lumbago caused by a chill.' The press was not convinced and later never forgave Treves for deliberately misleading them.

Rumours began to fly when Alix took over Bertie's responsibilities the following day at the Coronation review of the troops. She was already under great strain, understanding only too well that Bertie's condition was serious and that the Coronation might have to be postponed. At least she had the support of Georgie, who rode behind her carriage, but it was still pouring with rain and the march-past and presentation of colours to the 2nd Highland Light Infantry lasted two and a half hours.

Alix was nearly sixty, no longer a young woman even if she looked it, and she said later that she did not know how she got through the ordeal. But she put on a brilliant perform-ance from her open carriage, returning to the Pavilion to see if Bertie was any better. He was not. He was certainly not fit to travel, but somehow he had to be got back to Windsor the next day. He looked awful and there could be no conceal-ment on a train journey; nor could a car journey, with all its bumps and vibration, be considered. So two coaches, with blinds drawn, were rapidly prepared; Bertie and Alix sat alone in the leading coach, while four doctors travelled, well con-cealed from the public eye, in the second one. It was only twenty miles, but it seemed like two hundred at the pace at which the anxious coachmen drove.

On the following day, 17 June, Bertie and Alix were due at Ascot for the first day of the race meeting, an event Bertie never missed. But this time there was no question of his attending. His doctors absolutely forbade it. Again Alix stood in for him, and when she was seen alone in her carriage on the ceremonial drive down the course, the crowds knew that the King must be seriously ill. Not a cheer broke out; only the silence of sympathy greeted her as she waved to right and left, smiling courageously until she could disappear into the royal box.

Esher was one of the very few people who knew how serious Bertie's condition really was. Having learned that Treves was 'very uneasy', Esher went to see Bertie on the morning of the 19th, when his temperature was 102. 'He received me in bed,' he recorded in his journal that day. 'He was looking feverish and flushed, but was quite cheerful. He was lying in his charming bedroom, very bright and gay, overlooking the East Terrace. Jack, his terrier, was lying on the bed, and when I kissed his hand, growled at me. . . .'

Still only bland bulletins were issued from Windsor Castle: 'Lumbago . . . a rather persistent chill. . . . The King intends to rest for a day or two to prepare himself. . . .'

But day by day his condition deteriorated, although the patient insisted on getting up and dressing, while his temper became shorter and shorter. On Sunday, 22 June, he was due to give a pre-Coronation luncheon to a number of friends, including Mrs Keppel, and to everyone's consternation he turned up, looking grey and drawn and obviously in pain. Afterwards, instead of retiring to bed as everyone pressed him to do, he insisted on taking his guests on a sightseeing tour round the Castle. 'The more fervently they begged him to stop and rest, the farther and faster he walked with the result that by the end of the afternoon the guests were almost more exhausted than their host.'

That evening his temperature shot up, and Sir Francis Laking and Treves agreed that Bertie was suffering from appendicitis and that peritonitis had set in. Rumours were now widespread in London, and when his office issued a denying statement – 'not a word of truth in the report . . .' – the press no longer believed it.

The following day Bertie and Alix were due to return to Buckingham Palace, driving in semi-state from Paddington Station. Alix, already beside herself with anxiety, declared that this was ridiculous and out of the question. But the idea of disappointing the crowds who were already gathering along the route was also, to Bertie, out of the question. His wishes prevailed, and Alix became committed to the worst hours of her life.

At Paddington the Captain's Escort of the Household Cavalry was waiting to accompany them down Praed Street and Edgware Road to Marble Arch, and then down Park Lane and Constitution Hill to the Palace. It was for once a fine day, the Coronation decorations were already in place, and so dense were the crowds that it might have been the Coronation itself.

In the carriage, Alix sat very upright as always, looking impressively regal, smiling all the way, waving to right and left, but not once turning towards Bertie, which might be interpreted as a sign of anxiety for him. He did as well as his pain and high fever allowed, attempting a smile, even giving a feeble wave from time to time, and trying not to slump too deeply in his seat. Twenty minutes later their carriage turned into the Palace's forecourt, where a Guard of Honour was drawn up. There were faces at every window – the faces of some of the two hundred guests, all due to attend a banquet that night, followed by a reception.

This time Bertie was forced to agree that he was unable to preside, and once again Alix stood in, putting on a peerless performance, just as if she heard every word spoken and was not tortured with worry. Meanwhile, the doctors gathered about Bertie, looking to him like assassins closing in for the kill: Lord Lister, Sir Thomas Smith, Sir Francis Laking, Sir Thomas Barlow and Sir Frederick Treves, a great bevy of beards and side-whiskers, smelling of a mixture of antiseptic and cigar smoke.

Bertie told them repeatedly that there was no question of postponing the Coronation. 'No matter how ill I may be I cannot disappoint everyone,' he kept saying, 'even if I die in the Abbey.'

'Sir, we have a room ready for an operation. We must operate or you will die.'

'A room has been prepared for the operation, sir. Sir Frederick will operate in the morning.'

'The Coronation must proceed as planned,' Bertie exclaimed again in high wrath. Then, 'Laking, I will stand no more of this. I am suffering the most awful mental agony that any man can endure. Leave the room at once.'

Laking indicated that the others should leave, but he remained behind to plead further with Bertie. He succeeded at last, convincing him that he certainly would die and that a postponed Coronation was better than no Coronation. Bertie gave in with the utmost reluctance and agreed to see Treves, who would conduct the operation.

Knollys managed to get a message through to Princess Toria concerning the outcome of the doctors' examination. She had been, as always, at her mother's side all through the crisis, and now let it be known first to Alix and then to others at the banquet that 'Dear Papa is very ill.'

Somehow Alix struggled through the rest of the evening, but it was not until after midnight before she felt able to leave her guests. Bertie had been given a sleeping draught, and she learned from one of the doctors who had remained that Bertie's life depended on the success of the operation to be performed the following morning.

Early on 24 June Laking and the others issued a signed bulletin:

The King is suffering from perityphlitis. The condition on Saturday was so satisfactory that it was hoped that with care His Majesty would be able to go to the Coronation ceremony. On Monday evening a recrudescence became manifest, rendering a surgical operation necessary today.

Never since Alfred Austin had composed those baleful lines about Bertie's condition with typhoid – more than thirty years earlier and the last time when he had been at death's door – had public anxiety risen to such a pitch. Crowds in thousands gathered about the Palace, silent with dismay. They knew that if 'a surgical operation' was necessary, his condition must be very serious. In 1902 a surgical operation had far worse connotations than in later years. An operation was something you were lucky to survive.

I have never felt anything like the physical and mental oppression of the day in London [wrote Lady Lygon to Lady Ampthill]. It was hot and airless and muggy – the decorations flapped about in an ominous manner – and gloom and consternation were in every face. The King's age etc. is much against him – but he has a wonderful constitution which may carry him through. . . . I was very sorry for the Prince of Wales, for everything had to be decided by him; and besides his *great* devotion to his father – the feeling that at any moment he might find himself King of England must have hung like a horrible nightmare on him. He does not like responsibility and though he has aged much in the last eighteen months – one could wish for him another two or three years of respite and preparation.

Apologising for the state of his favourite old dressing-gown, Bertie walked into the temporary operating theatre just after noon, his terrier Jack banned, and resentful about it, at the last moment. Alix was at his side, and Treves noted her serenity. With matching calm, Bertie allowed himself to be helped on to the operating table, and the anaesthetist at once applied the chloroform. When it began to take hold and Bertie started to flail his arms, Alix helped to hold them down and calm him. He began to go black in the face and was soon wholly unconscious.

Treves waited for Alix to leave so that he could begin his work. 'I was anxious to prepare for the operation,' he told later, 'but I did not like to take off my coat, tuck up my sleeves, and put on an apron whilst the Queen was present.'

There was an awkward silence, broken by an anxious question from Alix, 'Why don't you begin?'

To his horror, Treves realised that the Queen expected to be at his side while the operation was being performed.

'Ma'm, I think you should leave now.' Whether or not she heard what was said, she understood that she should not be there and left at once. Forty minutes later the operation had been completed, the last stitch secured. Treves removed his apron, put on his frock-coat and went into the next room where Alix, with Georgie and Toria and others, were waiting for news. He told her that the operation was all over and a complete success. As soon as the nurse in charge reported that the King had regained consciousness, Alix was allowed back into the room. Bertie was just demanding in a clear ringing voice, and rather tactlessly, 'Where's Georgie?',* and fell into a deep sleep.

The relief was universal, the disappointment among those thousands who had come from far away for the Coronation was very great. All the foreign royalties and delegations returned home, except the Abyssinians, who realised that they would lose serious face if they returned home without witnessing the Coronation and remained in London. The financial losses were colossal. The Ritz, Claridge's and all the other great hotels were empty within days. The railways

---

* The newspapers, relying on a report from the Palace, declared that his first words were 'Will my people ever forgive me?'

which expected to bring tens of thousands of people to London for the day were instead deprived of tens of thousands of pounds. The *Ode for the Coronation* composed by William Watson sold few copies, and from his humble abode he complained of lost royalties. It had some admired lines in it, too:

> Time and the ocean and some fostering star
> In high cabal have made us what we are.

M. Menager, the Palace head chef, contemplated in deep gloom the banquet he had prepared for 250 guests on Coronation night. The menu was to be of fourteen courses, and now he had left on his hands 300 legs of mutton, 2,500 quails and other tasty birds, masses of fish, sturgeon, caviare, foie gras, asparagus and strawberries. Orders were finally given by the Masters of the Household that the food must all be packed up and distributed among the poor of the East End.

A less elaborate, and perhaps more digestible, menu had long since been arranged, 'The King's Dinner for the Poor'. This was to benefit half a million citizens and was pronounced a great success. Included in the contributions from manufacturers were 27,827 gallons of ale by the brewers Bass and 72,000 gallons of soft drinks to be served at the 'temperance tables' provided at every dinner. Rowntrees, the famous Quaker-owned chocolate company, ordered 600,000 tin boxes with the King and Queen's portraits in colour and filled them with silver-paper-wrapped chocolates. It took twelve railway trucks to carry the forty-five-ton load from York to London.

Another satisfactory compensation for all the disappointment was a service of intercession in St Paul's Cathedral on the day the Coronation should have taken place. Before going home all the foreign royalties, delegations and individuals attended this miniature Coronation without the crowning. It was described as 'an act of supplication to almighty God for His Majesty King Edward VII in his sickness'.

The prayers were answered by what the doctors called 'an unusually rapid recovery'. On the following morning Georgie 'found him smoking a cigar and reading a paper. The doctors and the nurses say they never saw such a wonderful man'. Alix, who prided herself on her nursing skill, sat at his side eager to perform the most menial task. She even tried to dress his wound, but Treves would have none of that and asked her to leave the room while the nurse attended to it. The only thing that hurt Bertie was talking loudly. Quite often when he heard that Alix was coming to see him, he pretended to be asleep.

'I saw the Queen today [14 July],' wrote Esher to his son, 'who was perfectly sweet, pale and affectionate, and tender about the King.' Gentle and tender as she was, Treves saw another side of Alix's nature when he casually referred to the postponed Coronation as being on 9 August. She may have been told but had not heard, or Knollys had unforgivably forgotten to tell her. Alix exploded with righteous wrath at this second-hand information. She was being crowned, too, she would have them know. How dare a date be fixed without reference to her, and while her husband still lay on his sick-bed, his well-being in doubt? This was a subject still in the hands of God!

She was just in time to stop an official bulletin from being issued. A compromise was reached, and it was now announced that if the King was sufficiently recovered, the Coronation would take place on a day between the 8th and the 12th of August.

Meanwhile, Bertie improved every day as the frequent bulletins testified. But when Lord Kitchener returned to London to a hero's welcome for winning the Boer War, Bertie was still in bed. He wanted nevertheless to receive the famous soldier, who was brought to Buckingham Palace on 12 July. Kitchener entered the bedroom, knelt beside the King's bed and kissed his hand. Then Bertie took up the ribbon and insignia of the newly instituted Order of Merit and hung it round his neck. Alix found the whole scene too emotional and burst into tears.

Sea air was what their patient needed, Treves and his fellow doctors agreed. This suited Bertie and Alix perfectly, and the convalescence was completed on-board the *Victoria and Albert* in the Solent with Georgie and May for company, Soveral as a sort of elegant and refined court jester, Randall Davidson, Bishop of Winchester, for his charm, amusement and the occasional offering up of prayers, and Esher for his gossip as well as his wisdom. Esher wrote of spending two hours with Bertie on 27 July:

He is very comfortable, dressed in his yacht clothes, with a white cap and looking wonderfully well. He *sits* up now – in a huge chair specially constructed – and he reads and writes all day, quite happily, not a bit bored. He is on a very sparse diet – hardly anything – and he is proud of a reduction of 8 inches round the waist, and a loss of certainly 2 stone in weight. His face is improved – and grown younger – much fined down. He is to be allowed to stand up on Tuesday, just five weeks from the operation. . . .

(Esher omitted to mention that his beard had changed from grey to pure white, another improvement, many people considered.)

To break up the days the royal yacht made a number of short cruises to sea, once to Brighton where the royal party came in close to the shore to attract the attention of their son-in-law, the Duke of Fife. They also attracted the attention of hundreds of holidaymakers on the beach, who cheered and waved until they sailed away.

There was one duty call which Treves persuaded Alix to make. The royal surgeon, now a baronet, had been deeply angered by the standard of treatment of wounded soldiers from the Boer War at Netley Military Hospital on the shores of the Solent, and wanted Alix to make a surprise visit so that she could see conditions for herself. On one of the last days before they all returned to London, Alix and Treves led a party in a launch to the landing pier in the hospital's grounds and walked ashore. Lying about on the lawn were limbless and dreadfully mutilated soldiers. They at once recognised Alix, who approached them in turn asking their names and where they lived and how they were wounded. This was the sort of thing she did with consummate tact and gentleness, and her hearing appeared to improve miraculously. She was particularly amused by one wounded soldier who addressed her as 'Miss'.

But there was one great Highlander who was unable to recognise his Queen because he had been blinded. Treves led him up to Alix, who held the man's hand and exclaimed, 'Dear man, I am so sorry, so sorry. How terrible it is! What can I do to help you?'

The Highlander, standing so tall beside Alix, found her heartfelt sympathy too much and burst into tears. They stood together, both weeping profusely, for some time, and then Alix led the man back to the bench on which he had been sitting, asking if there was anything she could do for him. Later, she accompanied Treves round some of the wards of the hospital so that she could see conditions for herself while she talked gently to many of the patients.

The royal party was back at Buckingham Palace on 6 August, and the doctors issued a final bulletin to reassure the public that Bertie was now well able to face the rigours of the Coronation. There was no feeling of anti-climax or *déjà vu* in the air. The flags and bunting still appeared fresh, the stands were still in place as if held in a time-warp, like the enormous Canadian arch which stretched clear across Whitehall: 'CANADA – FREE HOMES FOR MILLIONS: GOD BLESS THE ROYAL FAMILY'.

On the eve of my Coronation [ran the King's 'message to my people'], an event which I look upon as one of the most solemn and important in my life, I am anxious to express to my people at home and in the Colonies and in India my heartfelt appreciation of the deep sympathy which they have manifested towards me during the time that my life was in such imminent danger.

The postponement of the ceremony owing to my illness caused, I fear, much inconvenience and trouble to all those who intended to celebrate it; but their disappointment was borne by them with admirable patience and temper. The prayers of my people for my recovery were heard; and I now offer up my deepest gratitude to Divine Providence for having preserved my life and given me strength to fulfil the important duties which devolve upon me as a Sovereign of this great Empire.

Edward R. & I.

On the night of 8–9 August 1902 tens of thousands of people were on the streets of the West End of London. It did not rain but seemed as if it might at any time. Of the dawn May wrote: 'Fine but dull and cloudy. At 10.45 we started in state for Westminster Abbey. . . .'

The skies of London [ran one report] were of a sober and neutral grey, yet touched at times with a quiet, softened and silvery beauty. Sometimes rain seemed about to fall, and an autumnal coldness came upon the air, but the dark, heavy, sagging clouds sailed slowly over the streets, instead of showering down on the metropolis. . . .

Lord Rosebery described the postponed Coronation as having 'something of the character of a family festival'. It certainly lacked some of the international grandeur that would have characterised the June event. Only closely related royalties from the Continent were present this time including, to Alix's delight, her sister from Russia, who stayed at the Palace.

As a tribute to the sub-continent she knew that she would now never see, Alix's dress was of golden Indian gauze, embroidered in India. The gold, the diamonds and other precious stones were dominated by the replica of the Danish Dagmar Cross, and her long train was of violet velvet. Because the Archbishop of Canterbury, Dr Frederick Temple, was so frail and aged, it was thought that he might not stand up to the double ceremony of crowning both Bertie and Alix; the Archbishop of York was therefore deputed to crown Alix. The Most Rev. William Maclagan was seventy-six himself, but was reasonably strong and fit and did, in fact, outlive Bertie.

For two reasons, Alix wished to see the Archbishop before the Coronation. Firstly, she wanted to discuss the service and ceremony with him, and to learn something about him. Alix was treating the event more from the religious angle than Bertie, being a great deal more religious than he was. Secondly, and related to her depth of feeling, was the more prosaic business of her toupee. Many women of Alix's generation supplemented their sometimes thinning hair with a toupee, and she worried that the holy oil with which she would be anointed might not reach her skin through it. She therefore asked the Archbishop to make sure that he poured enough oil so that it reached her forehead. He promised to do so, and afterwards she always called the Scotsman 'My Archbishop' and had his signed portrait near her bed.

Bertie looked so magnificent in his Coronation robes that he sent for his grandchildren. They stood in a row, stunned into silent awe. 'Good-morning, children,' he greeted them. 'Am I not a funny looking old man?'

Two long processions, each of many impressive carriages, set off from the Palace, first the family procession and then the Prince of Wales's procession. The King's procession was heralded by the firing of a sixty-two-gun salute, which could be heard all over the centre of London, alarming some old people so soon after the end of the Boer War, and setting hundreds of dogs off barking and pigeons flying.

The gorgeous procession slowly moved through London, a broad stream of scarlet and gold. Headed by the band of the First Life Guards in their glittering State uniforms, came the cavalcade of Royal Horse Guards [ran one account] . . . with the King's Barge-master and twelve Watermen, who formed in their quaint livery a pageant of mediaeval picturesqueness. . . .

There was contingent after contingent of richly uniformed soldiers from all parts of the Empire; then Lord Kitchener in his carriage 'with his bronzed face and steadfast eyes', who received 'the first full-throated cheer of the day'. After that, at last, drawn by eight cream horses, 'a coach that seemed to have come from fairyland appeared behind the dancing plumes of the Guards. . . .'

In the Abbey, among the sights provided for the packed congregation, none drew greater attention than what was lightly called 'The King's Loose Box', a special reserved pew arranged by Bertie for a number of ladies with whom he had been, or still was, associated. Among them were Lady Warwick, Lillie Langtry, Sarah Bernhardt, Jennie Churchill, her sister Leonie, Princess Daisy of Pless and Mrs Keppel: 'a bevy of ageing loveliness'.

The American-born Consuelo Vanderbilt, Duchess of Marlborough, one of four Duchesses holding the canopy over Alix, recounted later how, the trumpets were blaring, the organ pealing, and the choir singing the triumphant hosannas that greeted the King and Queen. The long procession was in sight [she continued] – the Court officials with their white wands, the Church dignitaries with their magnificent vestments, the bearers of the royal insignia, among whom was Marlborough carrying the crown of King Edward on a velvet cushion, the lovely Queen, her maids of honour holding her train, and then the King, recovered, solemn and regal. I felt a lump in my throat and realised that I was more British than I knew.

Lady Jane Lindsay wrote:

When the Queen appeared [in the Abbey], it was like a vision coming through the dark archway of the screen. I never saw anything more beautiful. Her left hand was supported by the Bishop of Oxford in a wonderful gold and white cope, the Bishop on her right in a dusky red damask. During the slow progress the opening anthem 'I was glad' was sung by the choir, broken by the ringing cry of the Westminster boys, 'Vivat Regina'. Then came the King. . . . After the oath the King moved to the Coronation Chair for the anointing. . . .

The Archbishop of Canterbury was demonstrating that the authorities had been wise to limit him to the King's Coronation. He was keeling about as if he might fall at any minute. Randall Davidson, Bishop of Winchester, soon to succeed him, had secreted meat lozenges in his gown and offered one to his master. 'What's the good of that?' Temple responded roughly. 'My trouble's in my *legs*, not in my stomach!' When the moment came to place the crown on Bertie's head, his hands were trembling so much that no one believed he would complete the task. When he did succeed, it was back to front and Bertie had to turn it round. He later leaned heavily against Bertie through the long service, which put a considerable strain on the King, who had not completely recovered his strength. And when it became necessary to rise to his feet after prayers, the Archbishop was quite unable to do so without Bertie's supporting arm.

Alix's crowning went off without a hitch, the four Duchesses, each with sustaining bars of chocolate secreted about their person, holding the canopy. The Duchess of Marlborough looked down on Alix's bowed head, 'her hands meekly folded in prayer'. She watched the shaking hand of the Archbishop 'as, from the spoon which held the sacred oil, he anointed her forehead. I held my breath as a trickle escaped and ran down her nose. With a truly royal composure she kept her hands clasped in prayer; only a look of anguish betrayed concern as her eyes met mine and seemed to ask, *"Is the damage great?"* '

The most moving and beautiful event in the whole ceremony, most people agreed, was immediately after Alix's crowning. The Peeresses put on their coronets, all at the same time as if long-rehearsed, each face framed by white-gloved arms. Equally memorable, and less happily for all the women present, including the coroneted Peeresses, was the distressing shortage of lavatories. Understandably, the need for them was great at the close of the service, but the way to them was temporarily barred by a line of Grenadier Guards across the steps at the end of the choir to prevent anyone leaving until the royal party was well clear of the Abbey.

The 'Double Duchess' of Devonshire, so called because of her marriages to two successive Dukes, and also noted for her hauteur, attempted without success to break through this line. But, as if at Ramillies or Malplaquet, the Grenadiers stood their ground, with the result that the Duchess lost her footing and took a tremendous purler down the stone steps:

She fell heavily forward and rolled on her back at the feet of Sir Michael Hicks-Beach, who was just leaving his stall [wrote one eye-witness]. Her coronet fell off and struck the stalls at some distance from the spot. . . . Willing hands, directed by the indefatigable Soveral, at last restored the illustrious lady to her legs, Mrs Asquith secured her coronet and placed it on her head, and after some little attention to her ruffled hair she was permitted to proceed.

18

Entente Cordiale

'Our near neighbour, and, I hope, always a dear friend.'
Bertie of France

When President Loubet agreed to make a visit to London, a diplomat in the French Embassy provided him with telling and authoritative pen sketches of some of the people his President would meet. Of Alix he wrote:

Queen Alexandra will reach her sixtieth year next December. She is surprising, and preserves her looks with meticulous care; she might be taken for a woman of thirty-five. She is deaf and one cannot make oneself heard by her, but when one pronounces words clearly she grasps everything. She is said to be narrow-minded, but that is a rumour spread by the King's woman friends, who hate her, though wrongly, for she is very indulgent towards them and shows them much forbearance. She is more receptive and cultured than is supposed; she talks freely on all subjects and does not hide her feelings. She is sensitive to the impression she is making, and likes to read admiration in the eyes of those to whom she is talking.

The brief summary cannot be faulted, and this anonymous diplomat could not be expected to know that Alix's character, too, had changed little since she was thirty-five. The closest of her long-serving Household, like Charlotte Knollys, recognised a new firmer authority in her stance, and an even greater degree of obstinacy. She determined to have her way in all things and invariably succeeded, yielding only to the superior authority of Bertie.

Alix remained as playful and lively as she had been when she left Denmark back in 1863, although there was nothing coquettish about her and her childish, romping behaviour was so uncontrived that it never seemed ludicrous or in poor taste; rather it was like the sweet froth on a sustaining beverage.

Esher probably got it right when he accounted for this unique blend of character as 'living with such a *garçon éternel* as the P. of Wales'. He also recounted an anecdote about Alix and Randall Davidson during Bertie's convalescence on-board the *Victoria and Albert* in July 1902:

One source of amusement was the fascination which the Queen exercised over the Bishop of Winchester, when she led him so far from the paths of virtue, as to make him smoke a cigarette with her. . . . When we were at Osborne yesterday, she took him alone up to the room where the Queen died, and they had a little service at the bedside together.

Sir Frederick Ponsonby, Bertie's Assistant Private Secretary, noted an evening at Chatsworth with the Devonshires when they remembered that it was Twelfth Night. 'We had a sort of Christmas dinner with crackers and paper caps. Queen Alexandra was wonderful at this sort of thing and made everyone play up so that the fun became fast and furious.'

In the brief period when Bertie was persuaded that he would enjoy golf and that it would benefit his figure, a course was actually laid out at Windsor. He played only once or twice, but Alix was sometimes seen on the greens having a lovely time. Once she and Ponsonby had a four with Toria and Francis Knollys. Ponsonby recalled:

The Queen seemed to confuse it with hockey, and was under the impression that one had to prevent the opponent putting the ball in the hole. This usually ended by a scrimmage on the green. She also thought that the person who got into the hole first won it, and asked me to hurry up and run between the strokes. It was very good fun and we all laughed.

But contemporaries always returned to her looks, even the steely-eyed, contentious Margot Asquith:

My heart beat when I looked at her [she wrote in her autobiography]. She had more real beauty, both of line and expression and more dignity than anyone I had ever seen. . . . Queen Alexandra had a more perfect face than any of those [other contemporary beauties] I have mentioned. It is visible now, because the oval is still there, the frownless brows, the carriage and, above all, the grace both of movement and of gesture which made her the idol of the people.

Even when she had been Queen for more than five years, Daisy, Princess of Pless, another woman of her time who was not easily pleased, exclaimed,

It really seems *quite* impossible! She does not look a day older than fifty, and has a lovely figure and a straight back, and fresh red lips that are *not* painted, as one sees that they are always moist. And I have seen her at Cowes in the pouring rain, and she is certainly not enamelled – and all that nonsense as the people say.

Alix's courtesy and generosity of spirit – sometimes over-generous with gifts of money – were as marked as ever in her late middle-age. Lord Frederic Hamilton recalled an occasion when Alix was staying with him at Barons Court:

There are not many people in Queen Alexandra's position who would have taken an eight-mile drive in an open cart on a stormy and rainy April afternoon in order to avoid disappointing a dying child, of whose very existence she had been unaware that morning.

Lord Knutsford, who ran The London Hospital in which Alix had such a close interest and visited so frequently, once wrote:

She gives to everyone who asks; she cannot refuse; she has intense sympathy for anyone who has done wrong. . . . She never sends for me without apologising for troubling me, and generally ends every interview with 'It's a shame to bother you, you are such a busy man.'

Lord Knutsford probably did not realise it but he was not as busy as his King. With his complete recovery after his operation, certainly by mid-September 1902, Bertie filled his days with work. Those closest to him, notably Knollys, Dighton Probyn, Arthur Davidson, Frederick Ponsonby, Soveral and Carrington, all noted the new vigour and enthusiasm, just as if, snatched from the jaws of death, he felt duty-bound to make up lost time and to redouble his efforts to fulfil his responsibilities. He considered that he owed that much to his people, who had prayed for his recovery and then given thanks for it. His interests were widespread and embraced matters of defence, law and order at home, the plight of the poor, housing, agriculture, the health of the nation and especially his own King Edward VII Hospital Fund and King Edward's Hospital for Officers under Sister Agnes Keyser.

But, as in his mother's time, it was foreign affairs that still interested him most, and for which he thought he could do most. There were many reasons for this. Bertie was by nature a cosmopolitan man, a linguist with charming and persuasive manners, who loved negotiation and the interplay of power. He was a shrewd judge of people, enjoyed exchanging views, and had a low opinion of the Foreign Office and senior diplomats, believing that the wars of his lifetime – from the Ashanti campaign to the Crimean War, the Zulu Wars to the Boer War – could have been avoided by negotiation. Far, very far, from being a jingoistic King, Bertie believed that war was the ultimate international crime. He determined that if he was going to be remembered for anything, it was as a peacemaker. There was no riper time for the exercise of peacemaking powers than the first decade of the twentieth century, and no more difficult time in which to sustain the peaceful process.

There was one good augury for Bertie in that the longed-for peace in South Africa almost coincided with his Coronation. Bertie certainly regarded that as a promising omen. But the times were not favourable. After the solid Victorian decades of the *Pax Britannica*, when Britain's power was scarcely challenged and wars had been relatively few and minor, the challenge to British military power and industrial dominance, chiefly from a unified Germany, first under Bismarck and then Kaiser William II, were early-warning signals that Britain's splendid isolation was becoming increasingly untenable.

At the turn of the century two sets of alliances held sway over Europe, the Triple Alliance of Germany, Austria and Italy, and the Dual Alliance of Russia and France. There were any number of sources of antagonism between these two alliances, the worst being the French resentment at the loss to Germany of the provinces of Alsace and Lorraine, the price France paid for losing the war of 1871. Britain distanced itself from the heat of these burning resentments for many years, but began to feel it itself on the outbreak of the Boer War. Almost every Continental nation had opposed Britain, and very vocally too, during this war against the Boer republics: the big imperial bully against struggling Boer farmers, as it was seen on the other side of the Channel.

There was for a while a real fear that the two great Continental alliances, resentful and jealous of British power, might forget their disputes and turn on Britain. For the first time for almost a century Britain needed allies. As early as November 1899, just after the outbreak of the Boer War, the Colonial Secretary, Joseph Chamberlain, declared that 'the natural alliance is between ourselves and the German Empire' and proposed 'a new Triple Alliance between Germany, England, and the United States [which] would correspond with the sentimental tie that already bound Teutons and Anglo-Saxons together'.

This was hardly a proposal that appealed to Alix, still Princess of Wales at the time; and luckily for her the Prime Minister, Lord Salisbury, could not summon up any interest in it. Bertie could see the advantages as well as the difficulties of an alliance with Germany. The dangers lay in the instinct for military aggression and expansionism within the Prussian character. Germany already had the greatest army in Europe – in the world for that matter – and had proclaimed, none too quietly, that it intended now to 'ultimately dispute sea-power with the British'.

As soon as he became King, Bertie found it convenient to visit Germany, ostensibly to see his sister Vicky, who was dying of cancer. But at this early stage in his reign he was also anxious to test the water in Berlin. On 25 February 1901 he left England and, with only Ponsonby and Laking, was met at Homburg by the Kaiser and Sir Frank Lascelles, the British Ambassador. There was at the time a comparatively minor dispute between the two countries about their trade relations in China, which was discussed briefly between the two monarchs but without acrimony. On the whole, it seems to have been a pleasant enough occasion.

The trouble came later, after Bertie's return home, and after he had received a memorandum from Lascelles reporting on a less friendly conversation in which British ministers concerned in the China dispute were referred to as 'unmitigated noodles'. This made Bertie very cross and led him to call for the Secretary of the German Embassy, Baron von Eckardstein. According to this official, the King was sitting at his desk with two letters in front of him when he arrived, one much longer than the other. He read passages from both of them. The Kaiser had written to confirm his friendship with England, at which the King muttered sarcastically, 'I hope that is so.' Then from the Ambassador's letter he read the passage about 'unmitigated noodles' and, putting down the letter, asked, 'What do you think of that?'

Eckardstein recounted that he thought about this and then suggested that the King should treat the whole thing as a joke. Bertie laughed and replied, 'Yes, you are quite right. I must treat the thing as a joke. But unluckily I have already had to put up with many of these jokes, and even worse than this one, too, and I shall have to put up with many more.' He continued with the obvious question:

Whatever would the Kaiser say if I allowed myself to call his Ministers such nice names? As you know I have for years had the greatest sympathy for Germany, and I am still today of the opinion that Great Britain and Germany are natural allies. Together they could police the world and secure a lasting peace. Of course Germany wants colonies and commercial developments. And it can, after all, have as much as it wants of both. Only we can't keep pace with these perpetual vagaries of the Kaiser. . . .

Bertie, it seems, continued on these lines, and Eckardstein later commented that 'throughout the conversation the King was more irritated than I had ever seen him before'.

In spite of a long *tête-à-tête* conversation between the King and the Kaiser in Germany in August, after Vicky's death, relations declined further. It seemed that nothing could please the German Emperor, neither the rumour (which proved true) that Britain was negotiating a treaty of friendship with Japan, nor another rumour (which proved untrue) that the island of Malta was to be given its independence.

It was not until after Bertie's operation and the subsequent Coronation that he could make another personal attempt to mend fences with his nephew, and Germany. This time he invited the Kaiser to the celebrations at Sandringham of his sixty-first birthday on 9 November 1902. The Kaiser accepted the invitation eagerly and arrived with the Empress and a large suite in the *Höhenzollern* the day before. Everything had been done to amuse and entertain the German party, including, tactfully, a rendering of Conan Doyle's *A Story of Waterloo*, with Sir Henry Irving, the last occasion when Germans and Britons had fought on the same side. There was also a show by a famous illusionist, which might have been less appropriate, and comic songs were sung by Albert Chevalier.

There was nothing comic about the shooting parties, however. The Kaiser sported an extraordinary sort of military uniform, and some of the escorting military officers who accompanied him were inclined to draw their revolvers from time to time to take pot-shots at hares.

The Emperor demonstrated all his most unattractive characteristics, self-righteousness and bombast, tactlessness and arrogance. He could be a great charmer when he so wished, as at the death and funeral of his grandmother, when he had left the country under the bright light of public approval. But not on this occasion. His sententiousness reached a peak and completely puzzled Bertie when he asked his uncle, 'What oil do you use in your new car?' Bertie had no idea. He left that sort of thing to Stamper. 'Petrol perhaps?' persisted William. 'I use potato spirit myself. It is much the best.'

Before his nephew left Bertie was surprised to see on a table in the hall a newly arrived array of bottles and substances as if he were being encouraged to take up amateur chemistry. It transpired that the Kaiser had ordered them posthaste from Germany in order to prove the merits of potato fuel. Bertie was at a loss for words and wondered if his mercurial nephew had finally lost his reason.

Although the Kaiser met the Foreign Secretary and most members of the Cabinet, no attempt was made on either side to discuss relationships between Germany and Britain on a serious level. It can be assumed that at one time or another – perhaps more than once – the German Emperor referred to Germany's new navy, the building programmes on which it was engaged and the superior merits of the men o'war, the design of which he often sketched out himself. In spite of Bertie being almost pure German by descent, there was no meeting of minds between the two monarchs. Politeness was maintained throughout the over-long visit, but nothing that could be described as warmth was evidenced.

King Edward's heart, as well as his mind, had always inclined towards that republic across the Channel rather than the kingdom across the North Sea. In his search for lasting peace and for an ally in these dangerous years when it became increasingly clear that a European war would be a worse catastrophe than had ever been known, Bertie's instinct and intellect was for an alliance with France, a grand *entente cordiale*.

Relations with France were not in the least cordial in 1902. By nature and tradition *perfide Albion* had been perfidious for decades, and there was a strong element of jealousy in French feelings towards Britain. The Boer War had greatly intensified France's hostility, and newspaper comment and cartoons in particular had become so strong and coarse that the Foreign Office had instigated formal protests.

On the morning of 2 April 1903 the *Victoria and Albert*, royal standard gleaming in the sun, entered the Tagus and made its stately way up-river to Lisbon. Her escort, in gleaming

Mediterranean Fleet white, was two identical 5,600-ton protected cruisers, with twin tall funnels and armed with a multitude of six-inch guns on each broadside and fore and aft. This was the first port of call of the King's first ever state visit, organised privately and with no reference to the Government. Even his suite knew only the broad outline of the itinerary. It was due to Soveral, who was on-board the royal yacht, and to the traditional friendship with 'Britain's oldest ally', that this tour began in Portugal.

The spectacular city of Lisbon rose up in terraces on the hills north of the river, the Moorish citadel of Castelo da São Jorge, the cathedral and the church of São Vicente de Fora, standing proud above the teeming streets, and to the west, in the lower town, was the royal Palace of Necessidade, where the King, Don Carlos, would be entertaining them.

The British vessels dropped anchor with simultaneous precision in mid-river, the Embassy staff came on-board the *Victoria and Albert* and the Portuguese royal party followed soon after. It was a wonderful sight, 'just like the Middle Ages', Ponsonby commented, for the state barge was ancient, in gleaming gold and green, and was rowed by eighty men in red uniform. King Carlos was resplendent in formal admiral's uniform, like his son, the Duke of Oporto, beside him.

Bertie looked grand, too, but very peculiar. Long ago he had been made an honorary colonel of a Portuguese cavalry regiment and had chosen to wear the appropriate uniform, but it was designed for slim horsemen not a stout monarch. The coat was very short and therefore 'showed an immense expanse of breeches'. They greeted one another like long-lost brothers, and then presented their respective suites by name, a prolonged process accompanied by much bowing.

The idea for this extensive Portuguese and Mediterranean tour had germinated in Bertie's mind in the first weeks of the new year. He confided in no one, not even Knollys or Alix, and when it became necessary for practical reasons to inform his Household, he swore them to secrecy. Ponsonby was intrigued and puzzled:

Everything was in water-tight compartments, so that the person who was responsible for the orders to be given to the yacht knew nothing about the telegrams and letters that were being sent to foreign capitals. Beyond the fact that I was to form one of the suite, I knew nothing at all about the arrangements.

Among those in Bertie's suite were Major-General Sir Stanley Clarke, Acting Master of the Household, an equerry, Captain the Hon. Seymour Fortescue, the King's physician, Laking (now a baronet), and Charles Hardinge. The Foreign Office was greatly put out, not only because of the junior rank of Hardinge (the Foreign Secretary thought that *he* should have been included), but also because they were deprived of early notice of the King's itinerary. Arthur Balfour, the Prime Minister, was also displeased. He did not wholly trust the King and feared that he would put his foot into it somewhere.

The welcome ashore at Lisbon was all that the British party could have hoped for, tedious though much of it was. Guns boomed, addresses were exchanged, crowds cheered and officials by the dozen had to be shaken by the hand. 'We were then all conducted to gilded coaches amidst more cheering.'

These coaches were not unlike that which Cinderella had, to take her to the ball, with exquisitely painted panels in the style of Boucher, but they were so old and cracked that I feared lest the floorboards . . . should give way and we should have to run inside the coach [Ponsonby recalled]. The first four coaches were each drawn by six white Arab ponies and the last two by black English horses, while a large body of cavalry formed the escort.

Over the following days, between the inspection of a convent, a visit to a bullfight 'robbed of its murderous features', a gala performance at the opera house and much else, the suite gradually became aware that Bertie had a card up his sleeve, and an ace of trumps at that. Instead of returning home direct from Italy, as planned, the King let it be known – he had to by now – that he intended to make a state visit to Paris. The cypher telegrams began to fly.

Bertie had scarcely ever been known to return from the

The
faithful-unto-death
Charlotte Knollys,
Woman of the
Bedchamber to
Alix for fifty-five
years.

Sister Agnes
Keyser, founder of
the King Edward
VII Hospital for
Officers and
confidante of
Bertie as Prince of
Wales and King.

Above The King abroad: Bertie in Paris, his favourite city, on the epochal occasion in 1903 which led to the *Entente Cordiale*. He is flanked by the British Ambassador and the French President.

Left Walking in Biarritz with the Marquess de Soveral.

Kaiser William and the Kaiserin, Dona, the former Princess Augusta Victoria and daughter of Duke Frederick of Schleswig-Holstein-Sonderburg-Augustenburg, arriving at Waterloo Station for the disastrous visit of November 1907.

The 1909 return visit to Berlin led to little communication between the two monarchs.

Edward VII, always a dog lover, with his last terrier, Caesar.

Bertie was a keen motorist, but not quite as avid as the Kaiser, who was, as always, free with his advice to his uncle.

Facing page Alix with Georgie and May's children, whom she loved and spoilt outrageously. *Left to right:* Mary (later Princess Royal and Countess of Harewood); George (later Duke of Kent) in Alix's arms; Henry 'Harry' (later Duke of Gloucester) between Mary and David (later King Edward VIII and Duke of Windsor).

Above and below Successive and handsome Queens: Queen Alexandra and her daughter-in-law, Queen Mary.

Bertie's last visit to Russia in June 1908. For security reasons no one could go ashore. Bertie, in his Cossack uniform, with Tsar Nicholas, reviews the boys of one of the Russian battleships.

Two years later Bertie's body lies in state at Buckingham Palace.

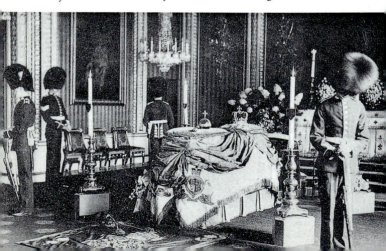

Continent without a few days in Paris. But then in the past he had been the Prince of Wales, out for a good time, visiting some of his favourite ladies and one or two places of not quite sanitised repute. It soon became clear that this was serious, but did he realise just how hostile his reception from the public was likely to be? No longer jolly Prince Hal, as King he would be the embodiment of the English Boer-bullies.

Meanwhile, this grand tour went off according to expectation, with sunny, calm cruising in the Mediterranean, the usual junketings, a pony ride up Gibraltar's rock, a dreadful opera at Valletta, Malta, but also a marvellous reception by the Mediterranean Fleet, which had not been inspected by a reigning monarch in living memory.

For some reason no one could understand, it had been arranged for the King to travel from Malta to Naples incognito. 'It seemed rather absurd,' Ponsonby reflected, 'as no other human being in the world could come with eight battleships, four cruisers, four destroyers and a dispatch vessel.'

However he might travel, Bertie was certainly not treated incognito in Italy. No Italian cared tuppence about the Boer War, and King Victor Emmanuel III had the highest regard for the British royal family and people, one reason being that so many rich and elegant Englishmen had come to live in his country. Britain and the British were loved and admired, especially in Naples where Nelson had first seduced Emma Hamilton. And now, here was the British Fleet again! As at Lisbon, the moment the *Victoria and Albert* dropped anchor the local dignitaries and notabilities came on-board: Sir Francis Bertie, the British Ambassador, the Duke of Abruzzi, several generals, Consuelo Vanderbilt (Duchess of Marlborough) and Lady Lowther.

The Italians thought that Bertie should see some of the Neapolitan museums and on the next day, 25 April 1903, he was taken ashore with his suite. As it was only three years since the previous King of Italy had been assassinated, strict security was imposed, and Bertie found himself tightly escorted. He also learned that the museums were all being closed to the public for the day.

Bertie had always considered security arrangements as a

reflection on his manliness and at home pooh-poohed them. At first he was to have had a close escort, but when he absolutely refused, two of his suite were asked by the police to walk closely behind him, 'no doubt with a view to guarding him from bullets and knives'. This made Bertie very cross and he immediately dispersed them.

After three days of junketing at Naples, including an interminable lunch at Lord Rosebery's wonderful villa at Posillipo, they took the royal train to Rome to stay with the King at the Quirinal. The trouble about visiting Rome was that the Pope lived there, too. King Victor Emmanuel was on cool relations with the Pope, but in the ordinary way he was quite happy for his guests to visit the Vatican. On previous visits, as Prince of Wales, Bertie had always called on the Pope, and there had been no unfortunate repercussions at home. Now that he was King, it was different. If he did not pay a visit to the Vatican, his Roman Catholic subjects, led by the Duke of Norfolk, would be greatly offended. If he did, it was thought that there might be a counter-reaction from non-Catholics at home.

Telegrams had fluttered to and fro on this vexed subject ever since they had been at Gibraltar, with inevitable intervention by politicians and church leaders of both persuasions. At length, after Bertie had argued that 'not to see the Pope when in Rome would look an affront', the Government agreed to the King paying 'a private and informal visit'. When all the formal state functions were over, this is just what Bertie did. As in earlier years, the ninety-seven-year-old Pontiff, Pope Leo XIII, and the sixty-one-year-old King of England got on famously, chatting about the state of the world, the relief at the conclusion of the Boer War and the need to keep the peace in Europe.

'And now,' as Lee has written, 'facing one of the most critical episodes of his life, King Edward went to Paris.' The earlier part of this grand tour was merely an overture to the visit to France, no more than a blind, as Balfour and his Cabinet had recognised when they belatedly were informed of this addition to the original itinerary. Sir Edward Monson, the British Ambassador in Paris, was not at all enthusiastic about the visit. He feared a hostile reception, and believed that the King had not realised what a change of heart there had been in the French capital, brought about not just by the Boer War but by colonial conflicts in Morocco, the Sudan and the Far East. He hastily arranged to meet Bertie's train at Dijon in order to have a few hours with him before he reached Paris.

The royal train was met at the Paris station in the Bois de Boulogne by 'all the great dignitaries of the state' and the President. It was a beautiful, warm, spring day, with Paris looking at its incomparable best as Bertie and his suite took their seats in the waiting carriage and clip-clopped away with heavy cavalry escort up the Avenue Bois de Boulogne and down the Champs-Élysées to the British Embassy. Monson had been right. The reception was *not* warm. There was intermittent muted cheering but also booing and cries of '*Vivent les Boers*', loud enough to embarrass the French Prime Minister, M. Delcassé.

In the state carriage an equerry remarked, 'The French don't like us,' and Bertie replied crisply, 'Why should they?' Others in the party thought philosophically that a visit that began as badly as this could only get better.

The process of healing began that very day. After he had rested from his journey and changed from his fine scarlet uniform into a suit, Bertie addressed the British Chamber of Commerce. He began:

It is hardly necessary for me to say with what sincere pleasure I find myself in Paris, which, as you know, I have very frequently visited in the past with a pleasure that continually increases, with an affection strengthened by old and happy associations that time can never efface.

That this was not just a delivery of the standard bromide was made evident later, with its clear hint of a diplomatic rapprochement.

A Divine Providence has designed that France should be our near neighbour, and, I hope, always a dear friend. There are no two countries in the world whose mutual prosperity is more dependent on each other. There may have been misunderstandings and causes of dissension in the past, but all such differences are, I believe, happily removed and forgotten, and I trust that the friendship and admiration which we all feel for the French nation and their glorious traditions may in the near future develop into an attachment between the peoples of the two countries. The achievement of this aim is my constant desire, and, gentlemen, I count upon your institution and each of its members severally who reside in this beautiful city and enjoy the hospitality of the French Republic to aid and assist me in the attainment of this object.

There was no sign of breaking ice at the opera that evening. It included a selection from Saint-Saëns' *Samson and Delilah*, and both he and Massenet were presented to the King. During the interval Bertie went down on his own to the lobby to mingle with the crowd, 'much to the terror of the police', according to Ponsonby. By happy chance he caught sight of a distinguished actress and at once approached her. 'Oh Mademoiselle,' he greeted her, holding out his hand, 'I remember how I applauded you in London. You personified there all the grace, all the *esprit* of France.' He spoke to her in his perfect French, and the effect of his words was electric as accounts spread among the *haut monde* of Parisian society at their usual pace. The ever volatile French were already undergoing a great conversion of spirit about *les Anglais* and their monarch.

On the following morning Bertie and most of his suite were taken by carriage and with formal military escort to Vincennes to the inevitable and tedious review of no fewer than eight thousand troops. There was nothing much that he could do to cement relations on this duty except to wave to the crowds in the poorer parts of Paris through which they drove. A better opportunity occurred in the evening, when he was due to make a speech at the Hôtel de Ville. As usual, and in whatever language, Bertie used no notes, spoke clearly, with seeming spontaneity and from the heart, and looked the embodiment of regal authority. These were his words:

I should like to say how much I am deeply touched by your kind words [he told his audience in French]. It is sad that while passing through your beautiful city, it is not possible for me to stay in the Hôtel de Ville. Very sincerely, I thank you for the welcome you have given me today. I shall never forget my visit to your charming city, and I can assure you that it is with the greatest pleasure that I return each time to Paris, where I am treated exactly as if I were at home.

Hardinge was among members of the King's suite who were present, and later wrote: 'These few words produced an electric impression throughout Paris, which was felt during every succeeding moment of the King's visit.'

This was the shortest speech Bertie made during this state visit, but its effect was immense and historic.

Ponsonby, who was also present, noted:

That last phrase went home, and as he sat down he received a tremendous ovation. He seemed to have captured Paris by storm. From that moment everything was changed wherever we went. Not only the King but all of the suite were received with loud and repeated cheering. It was the most wonderful transformation. . . .

To make Bertie feel further at home, the French Jockey Club invited him to Longchamps for an afternoon's racing, followed by a state banquet at the Élysée. At this magnificent occasion – gold plate, glittering glass and silver, hundreds of footmen with powdered hair – 'The Sun King' himself might have been the host, though he would have done better than President Loubet. When it was time for the speeches, Loubet stood up in an obviously nervous state, holding in his hand a speech prepared by the Protocole. He could not easily read it, so he resorted to propping it against the nearest candle, requiring him to lean forward to read it in a mumbling voice.

Bertie then stood to his feet and in a clear voice, in faultless French, addressed the diners, again without a note, praising Paris and the French, repeating his assurances of eternal friendship, and concluding, 'Our great desire is that we may march together in the path of civilisation and peace.'

It was Sunday, 3 May 1903. When Bertie and his suite left by train for Cherbourg, Anglo-French relations had enjoyed a metamorphosis without a single communication between the Élysée and Whitehall. The cries from the crowds of 'Vivent les Boers' had changed to 'Vive notre Roi.' Delcassé wrote a special article for the *Figaro* emphasising the importance of the visit to future relations between the two countries, and Monson broke protocol and added words of his own.

A more neutral view was expressed by the Belgian Foreign Ministry in a widely distributed report. It concluded with these words: 'Seldom has such a complete change of attitude been seen as that which has taken place in this country . . . towards England and her Sovereign.'

One of Bertie's oldest friends wrote after his death: 'Frenchmen looked upon him as a true friend, and in society he was said to be "*le plus Parisien des Parisiens*"; a leading Royalist once said to me that if ever he is tired of his job in England, we will take him by acclamation.'

It was not in the interest of the Foreign Office or the Foreign Secretary that undue credit should be given to the King for his part in bringing about a détente by his visit to Paris. But everyone else at home and abroad recognised what sturdy foundations he had laid and that if he had not 'called in at Paris on his way home from Rome', there would have been no conversations two months later between Delcassé and Loubet and Lord Lansdowne, the Foreign Secretary, on the subject of a formal *Entente Cordiale*, which was eventually signed in 1904. Many years before, Gambetta, the French revolutionary, had said of Bertie, 'He loves France gaily and seriously, and his dream is an Entente with us.' By his own initiative that dream was about to come true.

There was never any suggestion that Alix should accompany Bertie on his 1903 tour though she would have loved the spring cruise through the Mediterranean, and would have been an extra asset in Paris, an icing on the cake of rapprochement. She spent almost all those weeks of separation at Sandringham, leading a quieter life than she would have chosen, much as she loved the place. But now suddenly, on Bertie's return from Paris, without any preliminaries she was told that she would be accompanying him to Ireland. She would rather it was Copenhagen.

The discontentment of his subjects in Ireland had always worried Bertie, just as on earlier visits he had seen something of the poverty of the people. As a boy he had learned of the potato famine of 1845–7, when a third of the population had died of starvation. He had intended to visit this part of his kingdom earlier in his reign but the hostility of Nationalist MPs to the Boer War (in the House they cheered Lord Methuen's defeat in one battle) deterred him from doing so.

By 1903 conditions were more favourable. An Act of Parliament, the Irish Land Purchase Bill, provided landlords with encouragement to sell their land to their tenants, and before Bertie left a supposed account of a conversation between the King and his Under-Secretary for Ireland was widely spread:

THE KING: 'Are the Irish disloyal?'
SIR ANTONY MACDONNELL: 'No, Sir, but they are discontented.'
THE KING: 'What do they want?'
SIR ANTONY MACDONNELL: 'They want education and they want security in their land.'
THE KING: 'I shall come to Ireland with an Education Bill in one hand and a Land Bill in the other.'

And so he did, metaphorically. But Bertie was already popular with the Irish people. They recognised his sympathy with them and they liked his robust style, and especially his interest, and success, in horse-racing. In spite of the hostile reception Bertie and Alix had received on an earlier visit in 1885, Alix as an individual was extremely popular in Ireland, which was another good reason why Bertie insisted on her accompanying him. Toria came, too, making three royal assassination targets for the extreme nationalists.

The first omens were not favourable. On 3 July at a meeting of the Dublin corporation, the Lord Mayor's proposal that a municipal address of welcome should be presented to the King on the party's arrival was voted out. But there was no sign of hostility on their arrival on 21 July, none of the demonstrations they had suffered eighteen years earlier. One reporter wrote: 'The old woman who rushed through the line of soldiers and seized the Queen's hand, made a more impressive figure than the Lord Mayor of Dublin.'

It is eleven miles from Kingstown, their port of arrival, to Viceregal Lodge, Dublin, and they were greeted all the way by cheers from a vast crowd, who had earlier decorated the route with flags and bunting. No matter what the Dublin corporation thought, there were no fewer than eighty-two deputations each with an address of welcome, and nothing could have been more Irish than the conduct of what was usually a staid and formal occasion. George Wyndham, the Chief Secretary for Ireland, stood beside the King and Queen outside St Patrick's Hall.

I stood on the steps and presented each of the 82 deputations. *They* were to present the addresses. But they did anything but that; shook the King's hand and marched off with address under arm. . . . The Queen was very naughty and did her best to make me laugh, so that my next was delivered in quavering tones. Yet the Queen did this in such a way as to make everyone, including the culprit, feel comfortable and witty. I cannot adequately express the kindness and coolness of the King. He coached them in a fat, cosy whisper 'Hand me the address,' and then accepted it with an air and gracious bow, as if gratified at finding such adepts in court ceremonial.

By convenient chance, the old Pope died the following day allowing Bertie the politically advantageous opportunity to send a message of condolence to the College of Cardinals in Rome. That went down very well. But he felt in need of a message of condolence himself for there had been a domestic tragedy during the night, as Bertie noted in his diary: 'The King's faithful Irish Terrier Jack dies suddenly at 11 p.m.'

Under tight security controlled by the Royal Ulster Constabulary, the party of three went through the inevitable rituals of inspecting troops in Phoenix Park under the command of Bertie's brother, the Duke of Connaught. Then things suddenly got out of hand in an entirely unexpected way, to the terror of the security police. The crowds had gathered in such numbers, and the noise became so intense, that the cavalry began to have trouble with their horses. George Wyndham wrote of what followed to his sister Pamela:

The stupendous cheering and surging of the crowds drove the horses out of their senses. A Lancer's chestnut horse put his fore-feet almost onto my shoulders. The [mounted] King paced on and lit a cigarette, bowing and smiling and waving his hand to the raga-muffins in the branches. That finished me and now I love him. When we dismounted he laughed, thanked us all, and beamed enough to melt an iceberg.

The one bright spot, which amused them by its unexpectedness, was the display by the priests at Maynooth College of a large picture of Bertie's famous horse Persimmon decorated with ribbons of his racing colours. Meanwhile, Alix spent an hour at a hospice for the dying, the sort of ordeal she was always ready to face.

A more predictable warm welcome greeted them at Belfast, and from there, with much relief, they boarded the *Victoria and Albert* and completed their tour by water, making several landings along the north, west and south coasts of Ireland. At Leenane it was decided that they should make a brief motor tour of the beauties of Connemara. The unfrequented roads – no more than tracks really – posed security problems when a sufficient number of cars were finally assembled for this unscheduled trip.

Word rapidly spread round this remote part of Ireland, and small crowds of villagers gathered to take advantage of the exciting break in their hard and humdrum lives. Sir Henry Robinson, one of the party, recorded that

we suddenly found ourselves in the midst of an amazing mob of horsemen: farm horses, cart horses, ponies, donkeys, of all sizes and descriptions, mounted by men and boys in rags and tatters, black coats, flannels or home-made stuffs. Some had saddles, others none, some had reins, some had straw ropes. There they all were waiting on the high ground up the mountainside to see the arrival of the cars, and the moment the cars came into sight they were off down the mountainside like an avalanche, yelling, cheering, laughing, knocking each other over and leaping over the ditch on the road with a speed that sent most of them on to the bog on the other side.

Before they left, the oldest inhabitant of Leenane was deputed to lead the cheers. Bertie and Alix wondered just how old he must be when they heard him call out to the townspeople, 'Three cheers for King Henry VI and his Quaine!'

Whatever reservations Lord Lansdowne may have had about the wisdom of Bertie's visit to Paris, he was delighted

by the success of the Irish tour. 'It is impossible to exaggerate', he wrote to the King, 'the effect produced upon the
simple people of this glen [he was staying at Derreen] by
the kindness of your Majesty's demeanour; they refer to it
constantly and always in terms of goodwill and admiration.'

Alix was glad to get home from Ireland to Sandringham with
her dogs and horses and ponies, which remained one of the
first pleasures in her life. For her the year 1903 improved
further with the passing months after the disappointment of
being cut out of the Mediterranean cruise and the visit to
Paris. So far neither of her daughters had produced a son,
but now at last Maud, Princess Charles of Denmark, gave
birth to a male heir,* Alexander, 'my little Hamlet' as she
called him.

Second to the births of her grandchildren, Alix enjoyed
most a family wedding. On 5 October 1903 she left London
with Toria and Charlotte Knollys, and without Bertie, for
Darmstadt. Her nephew Prince Andrew, son of her beloved
brother, King George of Greece, had fallen in love with eighteen-year-old Princess Alice, the beautiful elder daughter of
Prince and Princess Louis of Battenberg. Alix thoroughly
approved of the match, having a particular liking for Alice,
who shared in a milder form the deafness from which she
suffered.

The Hessian Grand Ducal palace at Darmstadt, and the
Battenberg *Schloss* Heiligenberg nearby, formed the centre
of a web of royal dynasties, crossing not only frontiers but
also religions. On 7 October, one more securing pin in the
Hessian dynasty, this time with the Danish–Greek connection, was put into place. The Tsar and Tsarina were there
as well as the Queen of England, the King and Queen of
Greece, the Emperor of Germany's younger brother and his
wife, and Queens-to-be like Ena Battenberg (Spain) and the
bride's younger sister (Sweden). Grand Dukes and Duchesses, Queen Victoria's youngest daughter Beatrice and
favourite grand-daughter Victoria (Princess Louis), and a vast

* Later to become King Olaf of Norway.

selection from the *Almanach de Gotha* swelled the number to 260.

Everything about this wedding might have been contrived to please and make Alix happy. The weather was perfect, the setting incomparably beautiful, the company compatible and anxious for this to be a light-hearted occasion. There was an enormous banquet on the night before the wedding, then dancing until 4 a.m., with Alix sweeping about the floor as if she were still in her thirties and had forgotten her lameness.

The next day there were three ceremonies, a civil one to conform with local law, another in the palace's Protestant chapel, and finally the third in the Russian Orthodox chapel. Much champagne was consumed in between, and more when they were all over. The bride had arrived in one of the old Hessian state carriages, and the couple left in a new Wolseley motor-car, the Tsar's wedding present.

The whole proceedings, including the part played by Alix, were recounted later by Mark Kerr, a friend of the bride's mother and grandson of the Marquess of Lothian:

It was more like a Bank Holiday on Hampstead Heath than a Royal ceremonial. I was given the bridegroom's overcoat and hat to hold, and was standing next to the Grand Duchess Vera when Prince George of Greece seized the hat and put it on his aunt's head, knocking her spectacles off and damaging her coiffure. . . . She could not see who was the aggressor. However, she pulled the hat off and started to hit me over the head with it. Queen Alexandra . . . found the opportunity for having a little joke, so she went back to find my sister [Nona], and told her, 'Your brother has been so funny. He has put his hat on the Grand Duchess Vera's head and knocked her spectacles off.' My sister evidently thought the champagne had been too much for me, and hurried forward to reprove and, if necessary, remove me. I don't think she quite believed my statement of innocence until she heard a chuckle, and looking round saw Queen Alexandra laughing heartily.

Bags of rice were hurled at the couple as they drove off, followed by a crowd of Darmstadt citizens. The Russian security officers thought that the bags were bombs, adding to the drama, and could scarcely credit their eyes as they watched the Queen of England and the Empress of Russia in hot pursuit, too, followed by most of the hierarchy of Europe, shedding tiaras, ribbons and stars, while the bride was seen leaning out of the car and beating the Emperor over the head with the shoe, which he had just thrown at the couple.

19

A Difficult Nephew

'King Edward is a devil.'
Kaiser William II of his uncle

One of the clauses of the 1904 *Entente Cordiale* called for the adjustment of boundaries between British and French overseas possessions. France was granted a total of 14,000 square miles of British territory in Nigeria, which would give her 'uninterrupted access from her territories on the Niger to those on Lake Chad'. The minutiae of some of these clauses make absurd reading today, dealing as they did with respective predominance of interest in certain valleys of Siam, for example. However, after prolonged but unacrimonious discussion, the Convention was signed in London on 12 April 1904.

Bertie was in Copenhagen with Alix at this time, suffering the boredom of the Danish Court, and he telegraphed his congratulations to Lansdowne on 14 April. But he then heard that because Parliament was not sitting (Easter recess), the approval of the House of Commons would be invited in the form of a Bill later.

A Bill? Bertie asked himself. A Parliamentary Bill, the terms of which included the ceding of British sovereign territory? He knew that was not right and telegraphed the Prime Minister, Balfour, the following day:

Have not seen newspapers but understand that you stated in House of Commons that consent of Parliament was necessary in connection with Anglo-French Agreement. Constitutionally power to cede territory rests with the crown. Should be glad to hear from you why this statement was made as feel sure you would be careful to safeguard my rights.

Balfour had not safeguarded his King's rights, and *The Times* was certain that the Prime Minister had failed to do so deliberately. 'It was no casual slip,' *The Times* insisted. 'Mr Balfour repeated it when the leader of the Opposition called attention to the words in the preamble that the plenipotentiaries made the agreement subject to the approval of their respective Parliaments. . . .'

Bertie complained to Knollys that the Prime Minister, whatever his motives, had treated him 'with scant courtesy', and that if he was wrong he insisted that Balfour must '*admit*' it. But in the end, Bertie had to climb down, losing for the monarch one of the last remaining royal prerogatives. As a result, the Foreign Office gave Bertie no credit for bringing about the climate which made the *Entente* feasible, while the Prime Minister's office slapped him in the face by radically reducing his powers. Bertie showed no sign of being aggrieved and ascribed the whole unfortunate business less to Balfour's doubts about Bertie's capacity as a diplomat than to Balfour's shiftiness, laziness and patrician arrogance.

Bertie continued to feel complete confidence in his own diplomatic knowledge and wisdom. The Foreign Office – i.e. Lord Lansdowne – had deluded itself that the agreement with France led to no unfortunate reaction in Germany. It was misled by pronouncements by Count von Bülow, the German Chancellor, that no objection was to be made to the *Entente Cordiale* and seeming to dismiss it as of no importance. Bertie knew otherwise. He was certain that his fractious and capricious nephew, whose mind he read so well, was feeling thoroughly paranoid about the agreement.

As early as December 1903 Bertie had put out feelers to

the German Government about a visit to offset any offence given as a result of his recent trip to France; and in a private memorandum to the Kaiser, von Bülow had suggested that 'In my opinion we have no political reason for dodging this visit.' It was not until the summer of 1904, because of an illness suffered by the Kaiser, that it took place.

It turned out to be very much a naval occasion, which was appropriate because Anglo-German relations were more bedevilled by naval rivalry than by the recent Anglo-French accord. German shipyards were hard at it building battleships in a determined attempt to rival Britain at sea, and (though Germany did not yet know it) Jackie Fisher, who was shortly to become First Sea Lord, had conceived a revolutionary battleship which would make all others obsolete, the *Dreadnought*. And, finally, Bertie had insisted on bringing Prince Louis of Battenberg with him as a sort of superior ADC.

Prince Louis, whose promotion to rear-admiral occurred while he was away at Kiel, was one of the most highly regarded RN officers besides being a cousin by marriage of the King. Although German-born, Louis had left Darmstadt at the age of fourteen to train for the Royal Navy. He became a great favourite of Queen Victoria's, before marrying her grand-daughter, but had to overcome much prejudice to succeed in his career.

He was particularly reluctant to accompany the King because it would be a public reminder of his German origins, something he wanted to put behind him. Also his sister-in-law was married to the Kaiser's younger brother, Prince Henry, a particularly fervent Prussian naval officer. On hearing Bertie's command, Louis wrote to Knollys:

It is very unpleasant for me to go to Kiel at any time in an official or semi-official position. My relationship to Prince Henry, my German name and origin, my position at the Admiralty – all combine to make it awkward for me. I very much doubt if the Emperor [Kaiser William] would appreciate meeting me there.

But the order stood, and Louis became one of the party who boarded the *Victoria and Albert* and sailed for Kiel, escorted by four cruisers and a full flotilla of destroyers, on

23 June 1904. Everyone was very polite, and each social event and serious conversation was marked by many bows, salutes, heel-clicking and (in the Kaiser's case) moustache-stroking. There were banquets and a regatta, there were even informal breakfasts – the table laden with a tremendous range of sausages – and, of course, there were speeches, some of them inordinately long.

The tone of Bertie's responses to the drinking of his health was quite as warm as in France the previous year: 'May our two flags float side by side to the most remote ages even as today, for the maintenance of peace and the welfare not only of our own two countries, but also of all other nations.' But on both sides there was never any hint, as there had been in Paris by Bertie, that these conversations might lead to a treaty of friendship. There was tough talk about Russia, and it was generally agreed that she was getting all that she deserved in the Far East from the Japanese army and navy.

Probably the most frank and uncompromising statement was made by the Kaiser in private discussion with Prince Louis, justifying Bertie's decision to bring him in spite of his protests. In a report to the First Lord of the Admiralty, he wrote: 'Now that the clay feet of the Colossus over the Eastern border have been disclosed (the Emperor's actual statement to me) there will be no more coquetting with France.'

On all sides the visit was described as a success, if in muted tones. One German report put it: 'The meeting of the two monarchs has produced no concrete arrangements on any particular point, nor any change of direction in the line of policy of their countries.'

If peacemaking was the most important, and successful, activity of Bertie's reign, when at home his life was still governed by the battle against boredom which was as ceaseless as the Hundred Years War. The two most effective and time-consuming weapons were racing and staying in other people's houses, where he could be sure of food to meet his mountainously high standards, occupations to fill the day, and half the night, and congenial company.

There had never been any shortage of welcoming country

houses with adequate shooting; indeed, there was fierce rivalry among aspiring hostesses, and venomous jealousy of those who regularly received the King and Queen. Two of these were the Grevilles and Saviles, who became known in Society as 'Grovels' and 'Civils'.

The cost of having Bertie and Alix to stay for a long week-end was colossal. But because by now the landowners with whom they stayed were prodigiously rich, that was not a serious consideration. What hosts and hostesses suffered – however gladly – was worry, inconvenience and disruption.

For example, from 11 to 14 May 1904, soon after Bertie's return from Paris, he and Alix found it convenient to stay with the Duke and Duchess of Buccleuch* at their gigantic Dalkeith Palace, outside Edinburgh. But the entourage was so numerous that the Duke and Duchess found it necessary to move themselves discreetly to their agent's house.

Later that year, after Bertie's return from Germany, they stayed with Lady Savile at Rufford Abbey for Doncaster race week. The preparation and disruption involved can be assessed by the numbers in the suites, which included for Bertie a sergeant footman, a brusher, an Arab boy to prepare his coffee, two telephonists, a valet and a valet each for his two equerries, two chauffeurs and Stamper. When Alix accompanied him and there was shooting, there would be two loaders and a loader each for the equerries; and for Alix probably four ladies-in-waiting, a hairdresser, and two or three personal servants. Reasonable standards of accommodation were expected by this entourage. This took no account of fellow guests to help entertain the royal visitors, who would also bring with them two or three servants of their own.

As to luggage, it took a regiment of servants to carry in anything up to thirty trunks and hat boxes containing forty suits and uniforms and thirty pairs of boots and shoes for everything from dancing and dining to shooting. Since becoming King, Bertie required extra services and a study in which

* Their third daughter Alice is today Duchess of Gloucester, widow of Queen Elizabeth II's uncle Henry, Duke of Gloucester.

to work. A steady stream of messengers arrived with the red boxes for him to work on, and with documents for immediate study and signing.

There was not a hostess in the land expecting to entertain the King and Queen who did not have a good idea of Bertie's preferred dishes. Alix was not in the least choosy about her food and was constantly appalled by Bertie's taste for rich food and the quantity he put down. They knew that if he was going shooting in the morning he would, in rapid succession, require for breakfast platefuls of haddock and chicken as well as plenty of bacon and at least three eggs.

Our hostess would remember that hot turtle soup as well as bottles of champagne would be required to keep His Majesty going until lunch at 2.30 p.m. sharp. Whether this was taken out in the woods or on the moors, it would have to be a hot, rich meal of several courses to sustain him until tea. On Sundays, as a token act of austerity, he demanded a less rich luncheon than on other days, just a plate of roast beef and Yorkshire pudding. By teatime he would have changed out of heavy tweed into an abbreviated dinner-jacket and black tie. Dressed thus, and in a sunny humour if he had shot well, he would expect eggs and *petits fours*, hot and cold cakes, scones and rolls, and his special favourites, Scotch shortcake and preserved ginger.

Our hostess would remember that there was just one dish that the unfussy Alix liked best of all for dinner and that was crayfish cooked in Chablis. For dinner there would normally be twelve to fourteen courses. Everyone knew how much Bertie fancied stuffed food with rich cream sauces. But contrary to popular belief, and hostile foreign cartoonists, Bertie was not a heavy drinker, not in later life anyway. The only wine he liked was champagne, which he had with meals, but he rarely drank more than two glasses. After dinner he might have a brandy, or perhaps two if he played cards.

However, Bertie's smoking was as excessive as his eating. He tried to limit himself to a cigar and two Egyptian cigarettes before breakfast, but for the rest of the day he would smoke twelve or fourteen enormous cigars, and at least twenty cigarettes in the brief gaps between them. He was badly affected bronchially by early middle age, and smoking finally killed him, as it was to kill his son, George V, and grandson, George VI. His favoured cigars were Corona y Corona, Uppmanns' and Henry Clay's 'Tsar'. Ponsonby once tried to get him to take up pipe smoking, which even then was considered less damaging. He persuaded Bertie to accept, and use, a pipe with a covered lid, which would be so much more convenient while shooting. The experiment was short-lived as the pipe seemed to go out before Bertie had time to shut the lid.

Regular guests at Sandringham were comforted by the immutable daily timetable, just as in the days when he was Prince of Wales. But guests still had to remember to advance their watches by half an hour to conform with Sandringham practice. It was more difficult to remember to adjust their watches back again at the end of their stay, and this fad of Bertie's led to much confusion, especially over railway timetables.

Bertie's frequent Continental travels had the effect of liberating Sunday guests from the stifling atmosphere and routine of the average Victorian and Edwardian British household. First-time guests were surprised, or even shocked, by the relaxed air of Sandringham on Sunday, when the King and Queen seemed as happy and cheerful as on any other day. Everyone went to church, and carriages were always available for anyone wishing to worship at any other church. Thereafter on Sunday there might be found a laughing party of croquet players in the garden, just as bridge would be played in the evening.

There would, however, be no shooting on Sundays. The King and Queen had breakfast in their own room, and anyone else could, too, if they so wished. Luncheon was served at two big tables presided over by Bertie and Alix, only the seats next to them being reserved.

It was a good deal more formal at dinner, guests being placed according to rank, and decorations were worn. Conversation was very free and easy and plenty of laughter always rang out. Guests who recalled dinner at Windsor in the old Queen's time said that it was like a children's tea party compared with lunch with Trappist monks.

There were two things that guests must not do: in the case of the Queen, there was to be no malicious gossip; and no one must bore the King. Otherwise the conversation ranged widely from contemporary politics, especially if personal relations were involved, to the current theatre and opera, and events of the day, especially if scandalous – but out of Alix's hearing, which was not difficult.

Tsar Nicholas of Russia only once came to Sandringham and that was in 1894, shortly before he succeeded his father, Alexander III. He was totally confused by the place, never mind the time being out of joint. The place was full of Jews. And all the men who were not Jews talked about nothing but horse-racing and horse-dealing. He wrote to his mother (the Empress Marie, Minnie, Alix's sister) that the house party was 'rather strange. Most of them were horse dealers, amongst others a Baron Hirsch!' He might have been further upset if he had known that Hirsch was not only about the richest man in the world, but was also on the point of launching a charity to support oppressed Russian Jews. The Empress Marie never could understand how her brother-in-law actually appeared to enjoy having Jews in his house, and she never received a satisfactory explanation from her sister.

Bertie thought the Tsarevitch Nicholas a nice enough young fellow, but hardly fit to become Emperor of all the Russias. Bertie's eleven-year-old niece Alice – his brother Leopold's daughter – told of a conversation she had had with the Tsarevitch a few days earlier while driving round Windsor Park with his fiancée:

I remember him saying – and it was typical of him – 'I really dread becoming Tsar because I shall never hear the truth again.' Isn't that defeatist? I never forgot him saying it. What a dreadful thing to say! . . . You would think that he would stand up to these people who would never tell him the truth and say, 'I'm not going to have them around me when I am Tsar.'

But Princess Alice and all other members of the royal family who met and entertained the Tsarevitch that summer were touched by the handsome young man's evidence of being in love. His fiancée was Princess Alexandra (Alicky) of Hesse, the youngest of the Hesse children. 'We all loved her,' Princess Alice also recalled. 'She was so delighted and happy.'

In November of that same year, 1894, Nicholas became Tsar, opening a reign scarred by war, pestilence, revolution and finally assassination of his entire family.

When Bertie became King more than six years later, Anglo-Russian relations were almost as bad as they had ever been. The British liberal element was appalled at the relentless autocracy practised in Russia, imposed by the young Tsar partly out of fear and mainly under the influence of his dominant and already fairly mad wife. Then came the Russo–Japanese War. Britain was uncompromisingly on Japan's side and nearly went to war itself when a Russian fleet sailing to the Far East from the Baltic fired on British fishing vessels. An opportunity to mend fences with Russia did not occur until 1906, a year after Japanese victory and peace.

The revolution of 1905 had been cruelly snuffed out, and it was not until the next year and the replacement of the Russian Prime Minister with a more liberal leader that the Foreign Office felt able to consider negotiations on a treaty of friendship. There remained countless impediments, however: the hostility of the British public, the suspicion of the Indian Government and the Viceroy over Tibet and Afghanistan, Russian pressure on Persia, among them.

Bertie kept in close touch with his ministers and the Foreign Office in particular about developments, eager for some sort of breakthrough. When he heard that the Russian Foreign Minister was in Paris in October 1906, he telegraphed Charles Hardinge (now Permanent Secretary of State at the Foreign Office) from Scotland, eager as a schoolboy: 'The great M. Isvolsky is at Paris. . . . I would give anything to see him . . . as there are so many important matters to be discussed. How is this to be managed? I leave here tomorrow [20 October] and shall be in town by 7.'

Alexander Isvolsky was so flattered to learn that the King of England was coming to London from Scotland in the hope of meeting him that he at once took a train and steamer and was soon talking to him at Buckingham Palace. The two men covered every aspect of British–Russian affairs, and, according to Hardinge, 'helped materially to smooth the path of the negotiations then in progress for an agreement with Russia'.

The success of these talks led to a happy domestic outcome, too. For political reasons it had been unacceptable for the Empress Marie to visit her sister Alix in England for the past thirty-four years. Now relations had warmed sufficiently for Minnie to undertake the journey, which she did in high glee in March 1907. Alix was also beside herself with excitement and, after taking Minnie round Buckingham Palace, whisked her down to Windsor.

Minnie wrote to her son, Tsar Nicholas:

How happily we are all living together! We spent Sunday at Windsor. It was the 44th anniversary of Aunt Alix's wedding! We went by car. After lunch we went over the Castle – I have no words to describe *how magnificent* it all is. Aunt Alix's rooms are remarkable beautiful and cosy – I must say they are the same here, at Buckingham Palace. Everything is so tastefully and artistically arranged – it makes one's mouth water to see all this magnificence!

I do wish you, too, could come over here for a little, to breathe another air. How good for you that would be! I myself feel as if I were a different person – and *twenty years* younger!

Such exclamations from a woman who had spent almost all her life in extravagant Russian palaces! The visit lasted nearly three weeks, and Alix was able to take her sister to the theatre and the opera, to London's picture galleries, and to hospitals and orphanages particularly close to her heart.

Bertie was fond of Minnie and enjoyed her company, which pleased Alix, who had another treat in 1907: Bertie took her to Paris! She could hardly believe her ears when he first made this suggestion in January 1907. They were to travel *in quasi incognito* as the Duke and Duchess of Lancaster, as if that would fool anyone in Paris of all places. They would 'do' the theatres, operas, restaurants and studios, and stroll along the *boulevards* arm in arm, dropping into *les grands magasins*, buying whatever took her fancy just as many of her friends, unburdened by the weight of her rank, had always done.

Bertie and Alix and their suite took over the entire British Embassy, where Alix occupied the bedchamber of Napoleon's sister Pauline Borghese (and unchanged since), and the Ambassador, his wife and the entire staff put up at the Hotel Bristol.

Alix told everyone that she had never enjoyed herself so much. In the evenings they dined with aristocratic friends of Bertie of whom she had previously only heard, like Victorien Sardou. They dined at the Café Voisin; the new Prime Minister, Georges Clemenceau was presented to them; the shy and self-effacing Madame Jean de Reszke sang for them; and, of course, they saw Sarah Bernhardt on and off the stage. Bernhardt was performing in the play, *Les Bouffons*.

That evening they had a little dinner party so an equerry was sent to ask Sarah if she would start the play a little later as the Queen particularly wanted to be there before the curtain rose, and Sarah, who knew no half measures, would have postponed the *trois coups* till midnight to please Queen Alexandra whom she adored as ever.

The crowds had always collected to see Bertie since the *Entente Cordiale* and in earlier days when he was Prince of Wales. But now he had brought his oh so adorable, *'belle et magnifique'* Queen Consort, ran the ecstatic newspaper comments, and the whole city, ignoring the supposed informality of the occasion, went *en fête*.

The only unfortunate consequence of this Parisian triumph was the displeasure it caused in Germany. A typical caustic comment in the press was *Reichbote's*, 'The King of England wants to see for himself what is taking place in his branch establishment in Paris.' Bertie was unusually displeased at this show of hostility and protested that he had visited the French capital entirely for the pleasure of his wife and for no political purpose whatever. None the less, that enjoyable time for the visitors and for the host nation did have political consequences, just as any visit anywhere by the sovereign of the most powerful nation and largest empire on earth had its effect.

This same year of 1907 marked the peak of Bertie's endeavours to keep the peace in Europe, at least in his own time. The degree of influence of the King in helping to keep the peace and in achieving the highly satisfactory emergence of England from anxious isolation is impossible to assess with any accuracy. Too many prejudices were at work at the time both within the Foreign Office of the Conservative Government of 1904 and the Foreign Office of the Liberal Government of 1907. Nor was it in the interests of either Lord Lansdowne for the Conservatives or Sir Edward Grey for the Liberals to give more than token credit to the King for helping to bring about these accords.

As for Bertie, it would have been quite out of character and in the worst possible taste to make any public claim as a peacemaker. But his work in helping to bring about a climate of friendship with France and Russia after decades of coolness if not hostility – and a war in the Crimea – gave him more satisfaction than anything else he achieved during his reign. It also hints, retrospectively, at what he might have done while still Prince of Wales. He had very few negotiating skills, but his charm and friendly demeanour, his reasonableness and persuasiveness, backed by the weight and dignity of his rank were incalculably valuable in the run-up to detailed negotiations.

The negotiations with the Russians, following the Paris jaunt, to cement relations with an Anglo-Russian Convention, were as drawn-out and tortuous as with the French in 1904. This time there was the additional handicap of the suspicion, if not the enmity, of the British public, who remembered all too clearly the 1905 'Bloody Sunday' shooting in St Petersburg and other outrages against the people. To help offset this, Bertie did a clever thing. Entirely on his own initiative, he arranged for a Russian Navy squadron to visit Portsmouth. Every Englishman loves a sailor, and when the sailors were invited to London in hundreds and flooded the streets, they enjoyed a rapturous reception.

The British Ambassador and M. Isvolsky decided that it would be appropriate for such an historic document as an Anglo-Russian Convention to be signed by the two sovereigns themselves, and Bertie enjoyed the utmost satisfaction when he inscribed his slanting signature on 23 September 1907.

Despite German protestations of indifference to this Anglo-Russian Convention, Bertie recognised that it was going to make relations with Germany, and his own relations with his nephew, even more difficult. Ever since that surprisingly successful visit by the Kaiser to Britain in 1899, the deterioration had been steady. Anglophobia was constantly whipped up by the press, with diabolical cartoons of Bertie, by hostile speeches which referred to the encirclement of Germany by Britain and by almost hysterically anti-British figures like Admiral Baron von Senden and Bibran and Alfred von Tirpitz, head of the *Kriegsmarine* and inspiration behind the German naval expansion.

During the course of Bertie's visit to Kiel in June 1904, both von Bülow and the Kaiser expressed absolutely no dismay about the *Entente Cordiale*, which, among numerous other clauses, contended that British primacy in Egypt was to be matched by an acceptance of French primacy in Morocco. William even went out of his way to disclaim any interest in Morocco, a country in which France had keen trade links. Then suddenly nine months later the Kaiser, while cruising in the Mediterranean, landed at Tangier, where he proceeded to make a bombastic and near-paranoid speech claiming Germany's 'great and growing interests in Morocco', and declaring that the Sultan of Morocco was 'absolutely free' and that all powers could be 'considered to have equal rights under his sovereignty'. From claiming to have no interest whatever in Morocco, Germany now demanded an international conference on the future of the country.

The first purpose of all this was to attempt to drive a wedge between Britain and France, the second to pose a military threat to France from the south, and the third to set up a naval base where Germany had never had one before. This, the Kaiser knew, would be unacceptable to Britain as in time of war it would threaten its trade through the Mediterranean and in the North and South Atlantic.

It so happened that Bertie was cruising in the Mediterranean, too, and anxious messages were soon flashing between the *Victoria and Albert* and Whitehall about this startling and dangerous development. From Morocco, the Kaiser had cruised to Gibraltar, where he had met Prince Louis of Battenberg. Prince Louis reported the burden of his conversation to Bertie, who was at that time in Palma, Majorca (which Alix thought the most beautiful place in the world), and passed on the message to Lansdowne:

I have received from Prince Louis of Battenberg notes of conversation which he had recently with German Emperor at Gibraltar. So interesting and important that I send them to you. . . . The Tangier incident was the most mischievous and uncalled for event in which the German Emperor has ever been engaged in since he came to the Throne. It was also a political theatrical fiasco, and if he thinks he has done himself good in the eyes of the world he is very much mistaken. He is no more nor less than a political 'enfant terrible' and one can have no faith in any of his assurances. . . .

Nevertheless, so belligerent were German utterances to France, with strong implications of outright war, that they forced the resignation of Delcassé (in spite of Bertie's intervention and encouraging words) and the holding of a conference on the future of Morocco.

Up to this point, honours had gone to Germany, although Britain had remained tightly loyal to France throughout. But when the conference was convened, Germany hopelessly mishandled its case, which got nowhere, except to renewed antagonism between Germany and the new Western partners. Verbal abuse did not help either. 'King Edward is a devil. You can hardly believe what a devil he is,' the Kaiser told 300 guests at a Berlin banquet.

To give cheer to the French, who thought that they had been on the brink of war with Germany again, and to demonstrate to the world the unimpaired solidarity of the *Entente Cordiale*, Britain invited the French Fleet to Portsmouth, where the matelots were welcomed so vociferously that the whole world knew about it. And, later, a British squadron was welcomed with equal warmth in France.

The Morocco crisis had been resolved, but the bitterness

left behind, and the clear signs of British accord with France and Russia, had all added to German suspicions. Time and again the Kaiser and German ministers referred in speeches to the encirclement of Germany.

Bertie's private feelings about his nephew were known within the Foreign Office. Lansdowne had once written that the King 'talks and writes about [the Kaiser] in terms that make the flesh creep, and the official papers that go to him, whenever they refer to His Imperial Majesty, come back with all sorts of annotations of a most incendiary character'. Two years later, under a new Liberal administration, with Grey as Foreign Secretary, both the Foreign Office and the King agreed that a formal state visit by the Kaiser to Windsor later in 1907 might mend some of the broken fences as a result of the Morocco crisis and the new accord with Russia. It says much for Bertie's sense of duty that he should encourage such a notion because it was not something he could look forward to, while Alix found the prospect too distasteful to contemplate. She not only shared Bertie's dislike of his nephew but loathed William's wife Dona, who was one of those big, difficult, self-righteous, bossy and sanctimonious Prussian ladies, as different from Alix as it was possible to be.

These first talks between Hardinge and Bertie were in April, but in the succeeding weeks the attacks on Britain, and on Bertie personally, in the press and on public platforms, became so virulent that it became inappropriate to advance the idea of a visit. After complaints to the German Ambassador in London, the savagery diminished, and by June the air had sufficiently cleared for Bertie to open negotiations at an informal level.

Bertie's letter of invitation was responded to promptly and eagerly on 20 June 1907 by his nephew: 'We are most thankful to you and Aunt Alix for the kind invitation. . . . It would give us real pleasure to come over. . . .' He followed with a suggestion that Bertie should come and visit them on the way to Marienbad 'to talk the visit over together . . . ever your most affectionate nephew WILLIAM'.

Bertie should have learned by now that you could not just

'drop in for a chat' with Kaiser William, and he was stupefied to find 50,000 troops lining the streets of Cassel, their rendezvous. Behind this rigid, colourful line-up, the entire population of the city appeared to have been ordered on to the streets to wave and call out a vehement welcome. The Kaiser and von Bülow with a numerous suite had met them at the station, and now at the Palace of Wilhelmshöhe the entire Cassel Army Corps under the Duke of Würtemberg had assembled for an interminable march-past. Bertie hated this sort of thing, declaring it to be the usual bombastic show-ing-off which his nephew loved to engage in. On this scale it was simply ridiculous!

However, there was nothing Bertie could do about it, and he looked forward to an informal chat over dinner, encour-aged by the suggestion from the Kaiser that there would be no speeches. But in the middle of the meal, the host reneged on this agreement, stood up and began a long, carefully pre-pared speech, in German, espousing the cause of peace, goodwill towards all men, and other unlikely pleas. He then indicated that no reply, of course, was expected, but, as Bertie wrote to Ponsonby later, his nephew had effectively forced him into the position of making an impromptu speech in German or refusing the implied challenge.

The Kaiser, however, had not reckoned with Bertie's skill at impromptu speeches, nor his facility with the German lan-guage. He rose to his feet, and to the occasion, delivering one of his fluent masterpieces and falling down on only one obscure word, promptly provided by von Bülow. There was no political discussion between King and Kaiser during this brief visit, that being left to Hardinge and von Bülow.

Bertie was thankful to get away the next day, and thankful, too, for the modest and friendly reception by the Emperor Franz-Joseph when he arrived in Austria: no ceremonies, no military, just a collection of amiable arch-dukes and arch-duchesses, and a pleasant banquet in the evening, chatting away to the old, rather disappointed and sad Emperor, who found the Kaiser as difficult a neighbour as Bertie found him a nephew. The next day, Bertie travelled to Marienbad, look-ing forward to his three weeks of socialising, taking the waters and deluding himself that he was losing weight and gaining health.

On Bertie's return to London the arrangements for the visit by the Emperor and Empress were put in hand and rapidly completed, strictly supervised in detail by Bertie himself. Then the blow fell: six weeks before their arrival date of 11 November, Bertie was at Newmarket when a long telegram arrived for him from his nephew. The Kaiser complained that he had suffered a nasty attack of 'flu, which had quite 'upset my constitution. I venture to enquire whether my eldest son would be acceptable to you accompanying his mother as my *remplaçant* or whether you deem it better to have the visit put off.'

If ever there was a diplomatic illness, this was it. There had been no reports from the Foreign Office of German displeasure at anything that the host nation had done to cause this embarrassing retraction. 'The German Emperor has placed me in a most difficult and dangerous position,' Bertie declared and asked Grey, the Foreign Secretary, to make urgent enquiries. It seemed that there could be three reasons for the cancellation. Firstly, offence might have been taken at British hints that it would be inconvenient for the Kaiser to arrive in Portsmouth with an escort of huge battleships. Secondly, the Kaiser feared a cool reception on account of an impending trial for homosexual offences (more than ever abhorred since the Oscar Wilde trial) of the Kaiser's crony, Count Philip Eulenberg.

Bertie ascribed the sudden change of plans to his nephew's fear of unfavourable comment in the Anglophobic German press, which did not like to see their Emperor ingratiating himself with his evil uncle. 'He dare not "face the music" and has practically been told he will get a bad reception in England.'

Grey and Knollys suggested a let-out for both host and guest in a postponement. Bertie, believing that his nephew would give in if pressed, told Knollys that a change of date 'would be most inconvenient and lead to endless confusion. Still hope that strong recommendation not to put off visit will have its effect.' And so it did. Great diplomatic pressure led to the Kaiser agreeing to come after all.

The Kaiser and Dona arrived at Portsmouth, without heavy escort, in the *Höhenzollern* on 11 November 1907, eleven years to the day before the Germans put down their arms on defeat in the First World War, with two million young men dead. But for the present all was sweetness and smiles, and Alix did her utmost to make welcome at Windsor two of the relations she disliked most in the world.

At the state banquet the following night Bertie could not resist making an oblique reference to his nephew's recent 'illness':

In welcoming their Imperial Majesties the German Emperor and Empress to British shores, let me express, on behalf of the Queen and myself, the great pleasure and satisfaction it gives us to entertain them here at this old and historic [Windsor] Castle. For a long time we had hoped to receive this visit, but recently we had feared that, owing to indisposition, it would not take place; but, fortunately, their Majesties are now looking in such good health that I can only hope that their stay in England, however short, will much benefit them. . . .

The whole speech went down very well, and the Castle itself was at its most impressive, floodlit and flying the flags of the two great nations, courtiers and guards in their colourful uniforms. Strolling along the ancient stone corridors, or listening to the orchestras after the banquet, were not only the Emperor and Empress and their dazzling court but many more royalties from other parts of Europe – the popular Queen Amelie of Portugal, the King and Queen of Spain, Queen Maud of Norway, numerous members of the French Bourbon and Orléans families from France here to celebrate the marriage of Charles of Bourbon to Princess Louise of Orléans. It was the last and surely the most spectacular and moving gathering-together of the most illustrious royal and aristocratic families of Europe before the curtains were drawn across the stage in 1914. When they were drawn aside again, there were few members of the cast who had not died, been killed or deposed.

However, the show went on for those few days in a very

lively style. Bertie took William out shooting, Alix was super-humanly courteous to Dona, Georgie and May did their bit with the German party, and at a ceremony and banquet at the Guildhall, the words flowed graciously. The Lord Mayor presented the Emperor with an address of welcome in a gold casket, and the Kaiser gave one of his peace-to-all-men speeches: 'The main prop and base for the peace of the world is the maintenance of good relations between our two countries, and I shall further strengthen them as far as lies in my power. Blood is thicker than water [much clapping]. The German nation's wishes coincide with mine.'

Once again, it had been agreed between Bertie and William that the discussion of politics should be confined to the professionals on both sides. But as before at Cassel the Kaiser 'was temperamentally incapable of excluding high politics from his conversation', even when out shooting. The foremost source of friction between the two nations at that time was the construction by Germany of a direct railway to Baghdad. This was seen by Britain as a provocation, a challenge to British interests in Persia, and an arrow aimed at India. But to the Kaiser the Baghdad railway was sacrosanct, and moreover his own idea, he claimed. Under the mellow influence of all this hospitality, the German diplomatic representatives agreed to certain concessions which eased difficulties over this subject.

Bertie was more sceptical than his ministers about these assurances, and his caution was justified only a few weeks after the German party had returned home when the German Foreign Office effectively dismissed earlier promises, opening up again this running sore.

To outsiders the German visit had seemed to have been a resounding success. The crowds in the streets had cheered lustily and German flags had been waved. The newspapers had commented favourably. But Bertie was deeply depressed by it. His nephew had appeared to be madder than ever, informing all and sundry, especially generals he met, that they owed it to him that they had won, albeit belatedly, the Boer War. It was his advice, and his advice alone, which had led the British army to alter its tactics, thus leading eventually to the Boers' capitulation.

On a more personal level, Bertie was very put out by his nephew's cruel and tactless comments about the Jewish people. Like many Prussians, William had always tended towards anti-Semitism, but he had become much more virulent and, while knowing of his uncle's numerous Jewish friends, spoke of them with the utmost hostility. Like the late autumn dusk on the evening of the Germans' departure, nothing it seemed could lighten the skies over Europe.

20

A Threatening Sky

'A splendid hour with the King . . .'
Admiral Sir John Fisher

In the contribution he made to bringing about treaties of
friendship with France and Russia Bertie could reasonably
claim not only to have helped end British isolation but also
to have increased the chance of a lasting peace in Europe.
At the same time he was no subscriber to the fashionably
radical belief that armaments increased the chance of war –
not as far as Britain was concerned anyway. With the return
of a Liberal government under Campbell-Bannerman in 1906,
there was a powerful swing of policy towards expenditure
on social services, housing, and care for the poor and
unemployed.

Bertie had no quarrel with the idea of improving social
services, and especially housing, the improvement of which
he had worked for many years. But he was suspicious of the
Prime Minister's attitude towards defence, and also towards
lesser matters like women's suffrage, of which Bertie and
Alix strongly disapproved. He did not like Campbell-
Bannerman's soft Liberal approach. At the time of the second
Hague Peace Conference in 1907, the new left-wing weekly,
The Nation, published its first issue. When Bertie's attention

was drawn to the leading article by his Prime Minister, he did not care for his message about 'The endless multiplication of the engines of war in 1898 [the year before the first peace conference]. . . . It was desirable then to lighten the burden of armaments; but that consummation is not less desirable today when the weight of the burden has been enormously increased.'

Bertie was also concerned at the Liberal Party's clear intention of reducing the powers of the House of Lords so that it could no longer impede Liberal legislation. 'Between ourselves,' Knollys had written to Esher a year earlier, 'I don't think the King will ever like C-B [Campbell-Bannerman] politically. I do not believe the latter understands him, any more than Mr G [Gladstone] understood the Queen. I have just heard from the King who says, "I hope the PM will not abolish the House of Lords before I return [from Biarritz]."'

No matter what Bertie thought of Campbell-Bannerman politically, he and Alix were concerned when they heard that he was seriously ill. Before going off for his six-week sojourn with Alice Keppel in Biarritz, Bertie called on the Prime Minister at Number Ten. By entering through the garden gate from the Horse Guards he hoped that his visit would not be noticed. Campbell-Bannerman was much moved by his sovereign's attention, as he was by flowers from Alix, who wrote on the card: 'A few violets I brought back from Windsor in the hopes that they may cheer the poor patient. With heartfelt wishes for a speedy recovery.'

That the Royal Navy was Britain's first line of defence had been a truism for centuries. Since the Battle of Trafalgar a century earlier there had not been a serious challenge to British domination at sea, even if there had been a few scares about the French; now, almost exactly coincident with Bertie's accession to the throne, the German threat had become real. For the length of his reign it increased year by year, until by 1909 some authorities predicted that in five more years the German *Kriegsmarine* would be stronger than the Royal Navy.

By 1905 Admiral Fisher had been the navy's leading reformer for about ten years. His career reached its summit on 21 October (Trafalgar Day) 1905, when he became First Sea Lord. No two people could have been more pleased at this appointment than Bertie and Alix, who loved him personally and admired him professionally. But he was not everyone's cup of tea, and he had as many deep enemies in the service as he had loyal supporters. Fisher was an assertive figure, who brooked no opposition to his plans and labelled people who stood in his way as dastardly enemies – for life, too. He was the most unforgiving of men and his methods caused divisions which would eventually lead to his downfall. He was also a genius who, at a cost, did more for the service for which he lived than any other man.

Fisher knew everybody in the seats of power, could manipulate with Machiavellian skill, and could spot brains and leadership from miles away. He was also a prodigious worker. Every morning he would be up by 5 a.m., prayed in Westminster Abbey on the way to his office, and was at his desk before the cleaners, seven days a week. Bertie once felt impelled to order him, 'Admiral Sir John Fisher is to do *no* work on *Sundays*, nor go near the Admiralty. . . . By command. Edward R.'

He was gifted with two great assets of the born administrator [Professor Arthur Marder has written]: an exceptional memory and the 'pertinacity of a debt collector' in the pursuit of a goal. Noteworthy, too, were his unparalleled powers of persuasion, a product of his knowledge, sincerity, and forcefulness of speech and writing. When he became First Sea Lord, the heads of big ship-building, engineering, and ordnance firms, professors, and many other great and clever men always seemed anxious, ready and willing to carry out his views, and with despatch. No person could get big things done quicker than could Fisher.

The biggest thing that Fisher did most swiftly was to complete HMS *Dreadnought* in 1905, from laying down to readiness for sea in fourteen months, instead of the usual 2½–3½ years. Bertie launched her and the Kaiser was very put out.

Bertie was as close to his First Sea Lord as he was distant from his new Liberal Prime Minister. The sailor's colourful, dogmatic style suited him perfectly, and rich laughter punctuated their conversation, which from Fisher was always full of ripe anecdotes, appropriate quotations from the Bible (enormous chunks of which he knew by heart), proverbs and popular poems. Quite early on in their close association, in October 1904, Fisher wrote to his wife:

I had a splendid hour with the King yesterday. He is really most wonderfully kind to me, and we never ceased talking (or rather I did not!) for a whole hour, and he seemed intensely to enjoy it and kept on saying 'Bravo! Bravo! That's right! Of course you're right,' etc. etc. It really was very interesting and delightful.

Not surprisingly, Fisher valued the friendship and support of Bertie above all others. Here he writes to his son Cecil after going to the races with the King in July 1907:

The King has asked me to his rooms at the Jockey Club at Newmarket. . . . He dines at Cassel's the night before, but he said he shouldn't have a chance of talking to me much there, so I had better come to him the next day. I couldn't help thinking it a strange thing that the head butler took me into the room next [to] the King's bedroom, and said, 'The King will come to fetch you to breakfast himself' . . . and the thought passed through my brain: '53 years ago you slept in the outfitter's attic at Portsmouth and didn't think then you'd come to a King fetching you to breakfast'.

If ever Bertie felt his anxiety about the growth of the German fleet cooling, Fisher would stoke up the fires again, even going as far as suggesting on two occasions a preemptive strike against the German Fleet in its base, as the Japanese had done at the outset of war with Russia in 1904. On the first occasion, shortly after the Japanese action, the King, outraged, answered, 'My God, Fisher, you must be mad!' The second time this suggestion was made, when German belligerence was getting out of hand, Bertie appeared to be more receptive.

Fisher, who always claimed, 'War is HELL!!!', meant what he said and believed it would be a life-saving act. He once told his First Lord, Viscount Cawdor, 'Sir, if you want to smash up the German Fleet, I am ready to do so now. If you wait five or six years, it will be a much more difficult job.' Esher did not necessarily approve of this extreme notion, but as one of his greatest admirers he was there behind

Fisher all the way. By 1906 Esher believed that war with Germany was inevitable and (like Fisher) told the King so: 'There is no doubt that within measurable distance there looms a titanic struggle between Germany and Europe for mastery,' he wrote. 'She has 70,000,000 of people and is determined to have commercial pre-eminence. To do this *England* has to be crippled and the Low Countries added to the German Empire.'

J. L. Garvin, editor of the *Manchester Guardian*, a disciple of Fisher and one of the best-informed men of his day, put the contemporary (October 1907) situation in a nutshell in an article in *Fortnightly Review*:

Germany has challenged the naval supremacy which is the life of our race. That is why we have been so urgently moved to settle our outstanding differences with the rest of the world. This is why we have been brought in the last seven years to view in a totally altered light our relations with the Third Republic [France] and the Empire of the Tsars. That is why we have made the real but sensible sacrifice of minor interests to major interests.

For every year that he remained in office, Fisher made more enemies at home as well as in Germany. On 17 December 1906, when he had been in office for a mere three months, Fisher had cause to write to Knollys about a meeting with the British naval attaché in Berlin, Captain Dumas:

He tells me I am the most hated man in Germany! I think that proves we are doing the right thing in the British Navy and I accept it as a compliment. I am not sure I am not the most hated man over here as well! but so long as the King gives me the splendid support His Majesty has so consistently done, my position is impregnable and the fighting efficiency of our Fleet and its instant readiness for war gets no check. I simply say the *sincere* truth, and I think you know it, that His Majesty's gracious and kind confidence in me really means everything!

The reasons for Fisher's half-facetious suggestion that he was 'the most hated man over here' stemmed not only from his autocratic manner and divisiveness, his unforgivingness and cocksure manner. There were many in the service, and not just empty-headed traditionalists, who disagreed with his reforms in detail and his policies in general. The building of the *Dreadnought* itself was condemned by one of the brightest admirals of his time, Admiral Sir Reginald Custance, who thereby became an enemy of Fisher's for life. The anti-*Dreadnought* school contended that because she made every battleship in the British as well as the German fleet obsolete, with her superior speed and greatly superior heavy gun fire-power, Germany would start level in the coming battleship-building race. Fisher's counter, supported by the King, Prince Louis of Battenberg and many others, was that Britain had gained a great start and, because of its superior shipbuilding capacity, had ten *Dreadnoughts* built or building before Germany had completed one.

The second main contentious issue was the reduction of the Mediterranean Fleet to no more than eight battleships and the withdrawal for scrapping of countless obsolete men o'war from distant stations, like China, South America and the Indian Ocean, where they served only 'to show the flag'. In typically acid tones Fisher referred to the 'frightened or gunboat-desiring Consuls, who one and all pine for the prestige of the presence of a man o'war within signalling distance of the consular flagstaff and for the consular salute of seven guns!' What a waste of money, he would exclaim. Every penny must be spent on preparing the Fleet for fighting the Germans in the North Sea. That was all that mattered.

Georgie, Prince of Wales, an ardent but very conservative navalist, remained – unlike his father – unconvinced by all this withdrawal from Britain's far-flung Empire. Fisher therefore drafted a letter intended to persuade the Prince of Wales that his was the right policy, and showed it to Bertie for approval. (He approved.) 'Our only probable enemy is German,' was the core of his argument. 'Germany keeps her *whole* Fleet always concentrated within a few hours of England. We must therefore keep a Fleet twice as powerful concentrated within a few hours of Germany.' Then, quoting his great hero Nelson: 'Your battle ground should be your drill ground.'

It was most unfortunate that the Commander-in-Chief of the Mediterranean Fleet, the most prestigious of all sea-going commands, was none other than Fisher's, and also Bertie's, enemy number one, Admiral Lord Charles Beresford. Already stinging from Fisher's appointment as First Sea Lord, which he regarded as his own sinecure, Beresford was transferred to command of the Channel Fleet and then forced to resign a year early. He gave up the rest of his active career to revenge and the destruction of Fisher.

Beresford was a man with powerful connections and would stop at nothing. He split the navy down the middle between the Beresfordites and Fisherites and did everything he could to hinder Fisher's crusade. Bertie remained loyal to Fisher throughout this unseemly and debilitating struggle, but was constrained as a constitutional monarch from showing it publicly. When the opposition argued for smaller, slower, cheaper, mixed-armament battleships, Bertie stuck by Fisher. When Fisher promoted his 'two keels to one' (i.e. double the German rate of construction), the King supported him. And when Fisher called the Cabinet a pack of cowards for not sacking Beresford, Bertie concurred. But the Prince of Wales now thought Fisher had gone too far in the humiliation of his enemy and was anxious about the consequences. 'He will probably agitate for a Parliamentary enquiry into the Navy and God knows what,' was his all too prescient speculation.

Earlier in that same year of 1908, Bertie and Alix received the shocking news from Lisbon that the King and Crown Prince of Portugal had been assassinated on 1 February. The Queen, in the carriage with them, had thrown herself across her son in an attempt to protect him, but to no avail. Heartbroken at this loss, Bertie and Alix attended the memorial service in the Church of St James, Spanish Place, the first time since James II's reign that a British sovereign had attended a Roman Catholic service.

No one attacked Bertie for this, but when he committed the only constitutional gaffe of his reign a few weeks later he attracted a lot of criticism. During the winter his bronchial condition had worsened. His coughing became alarming as he fought for breath, while never for one day reducing his consumption of cigars. When the time came for his regular stay at Biarritz, with Alice Keppel as usual, Laking instructed him to remain there for at least six weeks, the warmth and sea air giving relief to his poor abused lungs.

Unfortunately, his time in France coincided with a political crisis at home. The Prime Minister was very ill and weakening swiftly. Campbell-Bannerman wrote to Biarritz and told his King that he would have to resign. But the appointment of a new Prime Minister required the presence of the sovereign on British soil and Bertie did not wish to cut short his visit, neither for the sake of his health nor for the premature loss of Alice Keppel's company. So, when Knollys telegraphed from Buckingham Palace that the Prime Minister 'will probably resign end of week', Bertie expressed his wish 'that he should not resign till Easter vacation', when he would have returned.

This led to much embarrassment and confusion. Business was being held up because Campbell-Bannerman was unable to conduct it, and in fact died three weeks later. It was finally agreed with Herbert Asquith that he would come out to Biarritz, arriving on 8 April, in order to go through the ritual of kissing hands with his King and presenting for his approval the names of his proposed Cabinet. 'We were quite alone for an hour and I went over all the appointments with him. He made no objections to any of them,' Asquith recalled, 'and discussed the various men very freely with a good deal of shrewdness.' But it lost Asquith five days in his frantically busy life, and Bertie was strongly attacked for his breach of tradition and possibly of the law. *The Times* thundered, but such was Bertie's popularity that the incident was soon forgotten.

In spite of his weakening health, Bertie did more travelling in 1908 than in any other year of his reign, as if determined to pack in as much work for international friendship before what he suspected was to be his imminent death. After returning from Biarritz he was soon off to the Baltic, intent on making that sea one of peaceful co-existence between the nations with coastlines upon it – particularly Denmark, Sweden and Norway, the last two of which were on poor terms. Anglo-Swedish relations were not good either, ever since Norway's assertion of its independence of the Swedish crown, with British encouragement. A healing hand was sorely needed, and Bertie and Alix embarked on a visit to these three Baltic states, the first-ever visit of a British sovereign to Stockholm. Here they were greeted by a state banquet which resulted in greater harmony between the two countries, thanks entirely to the charm and graciousness of both Bertie and Alix. Finally, on 20 April 1908, they embarked for Denmark and Norway. In Oslo they were greeted by almost the entire population of the capital, in which every street was decorated. The outcome of these visits was all that Bertie and the Foreign Office had hoped for: the signature of a Baltic and North Sea agreement.

Within twenty-four hours of his return to London Bertie was discussing with Asquith a state visit to Russia in June, the following month. Hardinge was convinced that the visit 'will be productive of great good', but the plans were kept secret for as long as practicable 'to avoid questions from extreme members of the House of Commons', meaning men like Keir Hardie and other Labour members whose hostility to anything Russian was widely known.

But in the end the news of this first-ever British sovereign's visit to 'this tyrannical state' (Keir Hardie) to meet that 'common murderer' (Ramsay MacDonald) had to be made known. There was an inflammatory debate in the Commons, which infuriated Bertie because, as he could reasonably claim, his mission was entirely in the cause of peace and family solidarity.

Alix was especially looking forward to this visit. She loved the sea, loved sailing in the royal yacht and loved the idea of seeing a part of the Baltic she had never before visited, quite apart from the joy of seeing her sister for a few days. Her one wish was that they would see as little as possible of Germany and the Germans, though she knew that this was not altogether avoidable as they were going to pass through the new Kiel Canal, built through the stolen Danish territories of Schleswig and Holstein.

The company in the *Victoria and Albert* promised well, too.

Besides the inseparable Toria and Charlotte Knollys, Jackie Fisher would be among them, and his army counterpart, General Sir John French; Bertie's groom-in-waiting and equerry, Sir Archibald Edmonstone and Seymour Fortescue, as well as *his* inseparable lord-in-waiting, Lord Hamilton of Dalzell – all of them good company – and Alix's own lady-in-waiting, Louisa, Countess of Antrim.

On Saturday morning, 6 June, the royal party embarked on-board the *Victoria and Albert* at Portsmouth. It was a beautiful early summer day and everyone was in the highest spirits; the scene was delightful with the big armoured cruisers *Achilles* and *Minotaur* and a flotilla of destroyers as escort. Soon after noon they passed through the Straits of Dover, the French and English white cliffs clearly visible. But the horizon ahead was black with cloud and the barometer had dropped like a stone. The North Foreland was still in sight when the sea suddenly became turbulent and an hour later they were in the centre of a considerable storm.

The royal yacht was notorious as a poor sea boat and always took on a corkscrew action in heavy weather. Those who had been enjoying themselves on deck went below either to lie down or to fetch their overcoats. Fritz Ponsonby found everything in his cabin already in chaos.

I determined to remain on deck [he wrote] and then I came across the Queen, who was a first-rate sailor, and didn't seem to mind the rough sea at all. . . . I determined to face tea, which I thought might help. I went to the dining-saloon not feeling very strong. The Queen came in and sat down as if everything was as usual. She had Charlie Hardinge next to her, when suddenly the yacht gave a bad lurch and she was thrown, chair and all, into the corner, while the teapot and kettle came flying after her and only just missed her. All the tea things were smashed and there was a real mess, tea-cake, biscuits, bread and butter, sugar, etc., all collected in a heap. Charlie Hardinge persuaded her to have tea brought to her elsewhere, and she retired still laughing as if it was a good joke.

Even Jackie Fisher almost succumbed, but suffered 'a horrible sick headache, which was worse,' he reported later to his wife. Finally it was too much for Alix. 'The Queen lay on deck like a corpse!' he continued, 'and Princess Victoria beckoned me to her . . . and said she had been continuously sick and could not keep down a biscuit.'*

The storm scarcely abated until they were almost at the entrance to the Kiel Canal, which they reached during the few hours of darkness. The German authorities, though well aware of the yacht's timetable, made known no formal arrangements except the authority to pass through the canal. But the Kaiser was not going to miss this opportunity to impress his uncle and his party with the military and naval might of the German Empire. Brightly lit and dressed overall were the five new battleships of the *Braunschweig* class, and numerous earlier battleships, the armoured cruisers *Prinz Adalbert* and *Friedrich Karl* and a host of smaller vessels. As the Kaiser had intended, this reception 'gave food for reflection upon the recent naval programme of construction, while the intricate evolutions of the torpedo flotilla,' ran Hardinge's report to the Foreign Secretary, Grey, 'which excited the admiration of all the naval officers on board the royal yacht, served as a useful object-lesson of the efficiency of the German Navy'.

Alix entirely ignored all this showing-off and was content to remain in her cabin. Bertie, on the other hand, after learning that the Kaiser had sent his younger brother, Grand-Admiral Prince Henry of Prussia, to greet him, was obliged to go ashore. His party reluctantly followed him, from the warmth of the yacht to the cold and dark of the quay. 'I was conscious of the presence of troops on the quay,' Ponsonby recalled. 'As my eyes got accustomed to the darkness I became aware that there were masses and masses of men drawn up. Prince Henry led the King through a labyrinth of troops and it was a most impressive sight.'

The morning was as beautiful and warm as the dawn at Portsmouth had been. Alix still remained in her cabin, curtains drawn, while Bertie summoned Fisher for company over breakfast – 'He usually does this and we talked away of everything.' Then the *Victoria and Albert* cast off and entered the

---

* Later that year Bertie and Fisher drew up plans for a replacement royal yacht, which remained in service until the Second World War.

canal that linked the Baltic and North Sea. They were escorted for the entire journey by German cavalry in splendid uniform, elaborate headgear and much shining brass, trotting fast along the towpaths to keep up with the yacht, and to everyone's relief were rested at half distance for others to take over. None of this colourful activity was seen by Alix, who had decided that the poignancy of seeing her beloved homeland in German hands would be too much for her. She emerged only when they were well out to sea again and the German coastline had faded astern.

On the last morning of their passage across the Baltic, Bertie summoned Sir Arthur Nicolson, his Ambassador to Russia, for a final briefing on Russia's current policy on a host of subjects, and especially on relations with Germany and about Peter Stolypin, the Foreign Minister, with whom he would be doing most of the talking. Then, dressed in a uniform of the Kieff Guards, he went up on deck in the afternoon and joined Alix as Reval (now Tallin), 'a picturesque little town on the southern entrance to the Gulf of Finland', came into sight. Almost the entire Russian navy which the Japanese had not sunk at the Battle of Tsu-shima and earlier defeats at sea was there to greet them.

Admiral Lambton* pointed out the relatively modern flagship, the battleship *Tsarevitch*, several tall-funnelled armoured cruisers, a number of destroyers and submarines, all flying the white ensign as a courtesy to the visitors, and dressed overall as the German fleet had been.

The recent fog had cleared, the sun shone from a cloudless sky and, in spite of the high latitude, it was very hot. Last to come into sight as they proceeded between the two lines of men o'war, answering the gun salute, were the two Russian royal yachts, *Polar Star* and the bigger, beautiful twin-funnel *Standart*. Ponsonby recorded:

It was properly the duty of our King to pay the first visit to the

---

* The Hon. Sir Hedworth Lambton was no longer commander of the royal yacht but accompanied the King as Extra Equerry. Three years later he changed his name to Meux as a condition of inheriting the brewery fortune of that name.

Tsar, but the Tsar, being the nephew, insisted on coming on board the *Victoria and Albert* first. The King gave orders that the ladder and the steam launch were to be got ready as soon as we anchored, but of course we had no chance as the Tsar's boat put off and was almost alongside before we could lower the ladder. He came on board and greeted his uncle and aunt affectionately.

The Tsar left a few minutes later, and Bertie and Alix and their entire party followed them in two shining launches to the *Polar Star*. Nicolson had briefed Bertie on the reception he would receive, so he was ready for the guard of honour lined up on deck and addressed them according to custom. 'Good-morning, my children!' he said in Russian, and remained standing as the guard called out, 'God save the King,' also in Russian. The whole British party was then offered caviare sandwiches and a glass of kirsch, which, according to Ponsonby, tasted like boot polish. Any lingering taste was soon washed away, however, by the fine champagne accompanying the lunch that followed below, everyone talking English now.

The band played all afternoon with hardly a break. With all these pretty young women present, including the Tsar and Tsarina's four daughters, and the Tsar's twenty-six-year-old sister, the Grand Duchess Olga, the temptation for Jackie Fisher to dance was irresistible. He was seen to bow to Olga while they were all seated on deck and offer his arm. As they swung round to the music, 'I said to my sweet partner, "How about Siberia for me after this!" which sent her into hysterics.' Later and again with the Grand Duchess Olga he asked the orchestra to play 'The Merry Widow' waltz. They 'danced with their hands behind their heads', according to one eyewitness, 'with all the brilliant company standing round the dancers until they were tired. Then "Jackie" went on deck, and by requests which were demands he brought down the house by dancing a hornpipe in approved nautical fashion.'

Fisher himself wrote to the new First Lord of the Admiralty, Reginald McKenna: 'The Grand Duchess Olga felt herself like Herodias's daughter [Salome] as they formed a ring round us while we danced! and my head wasn't wanted on a charger!' But the King, enjoying himself as much as anyone, did call out to Jackie, 'Just remember, you aren't a midshipman any longer!'

Fisher was 'the life of the party', and Alix, who felt a certain proprietorial pride in him, loved to see him so lively and popular. 'He even succeeded in achieving the impossible by bringing a smile to the face of the Empress of Russia.' The Grand Duchess later wrote to Fisher that everyone was 'delighted with you, as you brought such an amount of frolic and jollity into their midst'.

The Empress of Russia, Alicky, Bertie's niece, was already becoming deeply neurotic. After giving birth to four daughters, she at last had a boy in 1904 who turned out to be a haemophiliac. He bled internally at the smallest knock and was a constant anxiety. This condition fuelled Alicky's deep neuroses, and Hardinge was not the only member of the British party to find her 'nervous and distraught'. On that first evening when he went up on deck for a breath of fresh air, he found her sitting on a deck-chair in a corner sobbing uncontrollably. When asked if there was anything he could do, she shook her head, said that there was nothing anyone could do and asked to be left alone.

On the second evening at Reval the Emperor hosted a grand banquet on-board the *Standart*, and Bertie made one of his impressive off-the-cuff (or seemingly so) speeches calling for close friendship between the two nations, and the Tsar answered it, briefly and less impressively. Then Bertie, without notice or preamble, asked the Emperor if he would do the honour of accepting the rank of Admiral of the Fleet in the Royal Navy. Nicholas II beamed with delight. No greater gift could be offered to him, he said.

No one went ashore from the yachts during the whole meeting for security reasons, secret police officers manned every gangway day and night, and no vessel of any kind was allowed within 1,200 feet of the yachts. Nevertheless, the meeting was a triumph. When it was all over Fisher told McKenna:

The visit has been a phenomenal success. Private. The Emperor said, for instance, 'The whole atmosphere of feeling has altered. . . .' The Emperor is simply like a child in his delight at being made an

Admiral of the Fleet. . . . Princess Victoria, who is his bosom friend, told me that he had said to her how grateful he was. The King has just surpassed himself all round. Every blessed Russian of note he got quietly into his spider web and captured! The whole lot of them are all now dead-on for the Emperor coming to England.

Quite simply, in less than three days, Bertie had extended the *entente* with France into a triple *entente,* and the last lingering hints of acrimony between Britain and Russia had been dissolved. Unsurprisingly, the Kaiser was highly displeased at the outcome; surprisingly, at least to Bertie, Asquith and the Foreign Office were also put out. There were two reasons for this. Asquith had been tepid about the visit for political reasons because so many of his supporters in the Liberal Party as well as the entire Labour Party loathed the oppressive regime. The whole notion of strengthening the ties with 'this barbaric nation' was still anathema to millions of people in Britain.

But what seriously piqued Asquith was Bertie's offer to the Russian Emperor of the honorary rank of Admiral of the Fleet without consulting the Cabinet and himself first. 'Without, for the moment, giving any opinion as to the wisdom or otherwise of this proposal,' the Prime Minister wrote to Knollys, 'I feel bound to point out that it would have been more in accordance with constitutional practice, and with the accepted conditions of ministerial responsibility, if before His Majesty's departure, some intimation had been given to me and my colleagues, that it was in contemplation.' What he really meant was that his *amour-propre* had been deeply dented. Asquith, clever as he was, never understood Bertie's mind and methods. Of course he was not consulted before departure. Nor were Ponsonby or Nicolson informed before the speech because, as so often in the past, Bertie had sensed the tone of the occasion and judged that the effect of the offer would be out of proportion with its triviality.

As for the Kaiser and his ministers, they drew the conclusion that Bertie's visit was one more twist in the encirclement of Germany. William could not have believed for one moment that the hated Fisher had danced the hornpipe and taken part in no naval discussions with his Russian counterpart, and that it was almost entirely a family occasion which undoubtedly resulted in greater friendship between the two Empires but no military treaties.

A mild comment in the *Illustrated London News* was typical of British press reaction: 'The meeting which took place between the King and the Tsar . . . and its political issue, have aroused a good deal of comment in Germany, where perhaps, both meeting and result have been taken a little too seriously.'

Bertie and Alix enjoyed every minute of their brief Russian visit. As for Fisher, when he returned to his duties at the Admiralty, he wrote to Ponsonby: 'These last days the happiest I ever spent.'

The close proximity of York Cottage to 'the big house' at Sandringham could have led to difficulties between the two generations occupying them. Fortunately Bertie was so fond of his only surviving son and Georgie so loving towards his father, and Alix and May as mother-in-law and daughter-in-law so attached to one another that – at least while Bertie remained alive – domestic contentment reigned.

May, Princess of Wales, was a kind-hearted and intelligent woman, even if she was stiff, shy and pathologically incapable of relating to her children. Blessed with a loyal, loving if stodgy husband, she appreciated what Alix had been through in her married life. Her Georgie had never hankered after the bright lights of Paris or felt the need to take long holidays abroad with a mistress. A rough shoot and a couple of hours with his stamp collection made an ideal afternoon and evening for Bertie's son. Georgie never cared for gambling, was exceedingly unlikely to appear as a witness in a divorce case, and would have been constantly at May's side if she were sick.

May understood well that fortune had not always been kind to Alix, whose most beloved son had died in the fullness of young manhood, another child in infancy, while her own poor health and disabilities were an additional burden. Fragments of surviving letters between the two women confirm the very real affection between them, and the mutual help enjoyed by

Queen and Princess of Wales. On the closeness between their houses in Norfolk, Alix writes: 'You know well, my sweet May, what pleasure it is to have you near me. . . .' And again, 'You know well *how* fond I am of you, my dear child.'

Following some occasion when Alix's hearing let her down, to May's distress, Alix wrote:

You, my sweet May, are always so dear and nice to me, and whenever I am not quite *au fait* because of my *beastly ears* you always by a word or even a turn towards me make me understand. I am *most grateful* as nobody knows what I have to go through sometimes.

This fond relationship even survived Georgie's and May's tour of India in 1905, though it was sorely stretched. Since Bertie's refusal to allow her to accompany him back in 1875, Alix had conceived an obsession about the sub-continent, read all the books on which she could lay her hands, and even collected a wardrobe of Indian clothes and saris. India remained 'the *one wish* of my heart to see'. It was especially hard for her to wave good-bye to Georgie and May on 19 October 1905. She was wretchedly envious and hated to be separated from Georgie in particular. As in 1901, however, she would enjoy having all six children to herself: David, Bertie, Mary, Harry, George and John.*

A little more school work was done by the children than in 1901, but not much. The gravel drive between York Cottage and Sandringham House echoed to the crunch of running feet, often until quite late in the evening, to the exasperation of the boys' tutor, Henry Hansell, and the younger children's nursemaids. Bertie romped with 'the little darlings' when time allowed. Alix participated in every aspect of their daily lives except the older boys' lessons, admiring and encouraging Mary's increasing skill as a horsewoman and the boys as bicyclists; playing games in the evenings; helping them paint

---

* In order of birth, David became King Edward VIII and Duke of Windsor, Bertie King George VI, Mary Princess Royal, Harry Duke of Gloucester and George Duke of Kent. John, mentally handicapped, died before reaching manhood. Their ages at this time ranged between eleven years and three months.

when the Norfolk weather was at its worst; and bathing the younger children.

As foster-grandmother, Alix kept the children's parents fully informed about day-to-day happenings and their general condition. David 'has grown and such a sturdy, manly-looking little fellow, and little Mary also grown a good deal and sweet Bertie my particular friend'.

In 1905, while Bertie was deeply immersed in his campaign to improve relations between the nations of Europe, and Britain was convulsed in an economic slump, Alix visited Portugal on her own. She might be denied India, but no one was going to prevent her from visiting friends and relations in Lisbon, a foreign city she loved only after Copenhagen and Athens.

In early April Alix with her suite embarked on-board the *Victoria and Albert* at Portsmouth and headed down Channel in fine weather, enjoying the early spring sunshine. The notorious Bay of Biscay treated her courteously, too, and everyone was in high spirits as the graceful yacht steamed slowly up the Tagus to Lisbon. The welcome from the Portuguese was even warmer than on the visit Bertie had made two years earlier. The crowds seemed stunned by her beauty, grace and evident pleasure that she was being greeted so warmly. The newspapers extolled her virtues under great headlines about the wonderful Queen of our oldest ally.

Wherever Alix went, to state luncheons, evening banquets, museums and the cathedral, the crowds packed the pavements and overlooking windows. In her forty years as the centre of attention wherever she went, neither she nor Charlotte Knollys could remember anything like it. Sir Maurice de Bunsen, the British Ambassador in Lisbon, wrote of Alix:

The Queen sent for me before she left, and I had a quarter of an hour with her alone in her sitting-room at the Necessidades Palace. She was charming, full of impressions of the visit, which was enthusiastically received by the people, usually so quiet and undemonstrative – and especially the night of the Opera, when they simply went mad with delight at seeing her.

The next port of call on Alix's solo cruise was Gibraltar for the usual reception, inspections and other formalities, but she also took time off to visit her godmother, Queen Isabel, who lived in retirement in Seville. Touring Europe by land or sea, Alix was seldom far from one or other of her widespread family.

But at this time, news from home told of Bertie being unwell. Once again, he had been laid low with bronchitis, and Alix telegraphed the suggestion that, as soon as he was fit enough, he should make his way to Marseilles and cruise in the warmth of the Mediterranean with her. This entailed cancelling her usual spring visit to Copenhagen, but she shrugged this aside and prepared for Bertie's arrival. She found him 'very unwell and dreadfully pulled down', and they then embarked together on the cruise that led to their involvement in the Franco–German Morocco crisis.

Having done what he could to counter the Kaiser's mischief, and recovered his health in the sun and sea air, Bertie returned to Marseilles and arranged to take a few days on his own in Paris on the way home. Alix knew what this meant and also knew that there was nothing she could do to stop him even though it would probably undo all the good that the cruise had done for him.

Now that she had 'lost' her spring holiday in Copenhagen, Alix decided to visit her brother and his family in Athens before returning home. As for her elderly father, her later visit to Copenhagen was the last time she saw him alive. On 29 January 1906 the old man, once the dashing soldier whom Alix had hero-worshipped as a child and loved all her life, suddenly collapsed and died within the hour in his palace. Alix was heartbroken and inconsolable. 'The old King was quite well till luncheon,' Esher wrote to his son of this occasion. 'He had a pain in his chest, and lay down and died quite quietly. The Queen, of course, feels the break up of her Danish home, which she cared for much more than anything else. I don't think she is very intimate with the brother who succeeds.' He was quite right. They were not close in age or temperament, Alix and Freddie, and his wife Princess Louise of Sweden was eccentric to the point of dottiness.

Following the funeral, Alix retired to Sandringham. 'After all that sadness and terrible grief and sorrow for my beloved Papa, I must bury myself for a little while quite away from the world and its noise and bustle,' she wrote to her son. Bertie was just off to Biarritz with Alice Keppel so Sandringham this year provided a double consolation.

The death of King Christian of Denmark coincided by chance with the virtual demise of the British Conservative Party in its greatest defeat at the polls since 1832. Bertie wrote to Georgie on 19 January 1906 that 'the Radical wave had simply swamped' the opposition. The Liberals had inherited an economic crisis of such seriousness that unemployment had driven many of the working class close to starvation. That winter, shortly before the death of her father, Alix's conscience, always easily aroused, led her to set up an appeal for gifts for the unemployed. During the old Government's last days, Balfour's brother Gerald wrote from the Board of Trade to the Prime Minister: 'I hope you will be able to say something to dissuade the Queen from trying to interfere with the delicate machinery of administration. So far as I can judge her only idea of assistance to the unemployed is by way of doles.' (No wonder the Conservatives lost so heavily!)

Alix knew nothing of any attempts to discourage her charitable work and would have disregarded them anyway. Ironically, she was dismayed at the outcome of the general election, not realising in her naïveté that the Liberals were about to lay the foundations of the welfare state. 'Anything so ungrateful I have never seen,' she wrote of the Prime Minister losing not only the election but his own seat. As for Lady Warwick, who had become a socialist since ceasing to be Bertie's mistress, Alix asked Georgie rhetorically, 'What do you think of that charming Lady Warwick mounting a waggon at the corner of the street and addressing her "comrades", the scum of the labourers, and then taking off her glove to shake and feel their horny hands!'

Alix also agreed with Bertie about the new Prime Minister, Campbell-Bannerman, and was thankful when Herbert Asquith replaced him two years later. Asquith's second wife, Margot, who admired Alix so ardently, she found intellectually intimidating, as many people did. 'Too clever by half!' she might have said of her.

Although scarcely a year went by when Bertie and Alix did not visit friends and relations abroad for social or political reasons – sometimes twice in one year – the routine of their lives at home scarcely changed at all. Like many people with great power and responsibility, Bertie had long since succumbed to the comfort of routine, and the more elderly he became the more strictly he conformed to it. He liked to be awoken at the same time of eight o'clock every morning by his Austrian first valet, M. Meidinger, who had already been with him for eighteen years when Bertie came to the throne. The curtains were then drawn back and a glass of milk to start the day placed beside him, when Bertie would return the greeting 'Good-morning', and follow with the invariable question, 'What's the weather doing today, Meidinger?'

At Sandringham as elsewhere only the faces seemed to change as the years rolled by. Bertie's oldest friend, Charles Carrington, noted in his journal shortly after Bertie became King and invited him to stay:

I could hardly realise that the Prince of Wales was King. He seemed so entirely himself, and with all the old surroundings it seemed as if the old days were back again. The Queen walked out alone after dinner, and the King remained in the dining room and smoked as he used to do. . . . When the Queen retired we all went into the smoking room which was the same as ever. The Leech pictures, the same furniture, the table where the Equerry wrote the stable orders for the morning, the bowling alley next door, and the whole thing brought back memories of Blandford, Oliver Montagu, Christopher Sykes, Henry Calcraft, Bowmont, Andrew Cockerell, Charlie Beresford, Charlie Dunmore, and old Quin.

All the servants at Sandringham and the other residences were aware of Bertie's and Alix's need for an unchanging routine, although Alix's unpunctuality continued to wreck timetables. Most of the staff remained to the end of their working life, when they were given a generous pension, accommodation if they had none of their own, and received a card on their birthday. Unlike Queen Victoria's, Bertie's Household included few Indians. Not that there was any prejudice against their race – quite the contrary – but several, including the notorious Munshi, had proved unreliable. But there were many foreigners, French, Italian and Spanish, among them, and Bertie's courier was a Swiss man, M. Fehr. He had the heavy responsibility for all the travelling and accommodation arrangements, ensuring that carriages met trains, that there was adequate but unostentatious security, and that the right people would be ready at the right time everywhere. The detailed work involved was minute and exacting, but he never slipped up.

Lee tells of another of Bertie's 'faithful servants, almost a friend':

H. Chandler, the Superintendent of the Wardrobe. When the King was suffering from acute irritation and wanted to 'let himself go', he would retire to his room and send for Chandler, upon whom the vials of his wrath could be expended. Chandler was fully prepared to meet any such storm, and when this was over King Edward's one desire was to make amends to anyone whose feelings might have been hurt during these occasional outbursts.

The routine of the seasons was as predictable as the daily routine Carrington had witnessed at Sandringham, and as it had been in the 1880s and 1890s. Marienbad had replaced Wiesbaden and Homburg as a favourite venue for the cure, and that was about all. At home favourite hosts and hostesses could expect a heavily embossed letter from Buckingham Palace asking 'if it would be convenient' . . . and giving proposed dates for a visit: Carrington, of course, at Daws Hill, Mr and Mrs James at West Dean Park, the Crewes at Crewe Hall, Lord Rosebery at Mentmore, and so on.

In London, Bertie and Alix continued to support the theatre and opera, at least once or twice a week. If he was alone, Bertie liked to take a late supper at the Garrick Club, where he might have the opportunity of congratulating Sir Henry Irving and others on their most recent performance.

Bertie and Alix both had a close interest in The London Hospital, and Alix's service to the nursing profession never ceased. Shortly after he became King, Bertie was presented with a cheque for £200,000 by Sir Ernest Cassel to create a new charity entirely at Bertie's discretion. He did not hesitate in his choice. Tuberculosis had killed Cassel's wife after a brief marriage, and he had been devastated by the loss. Bertie had also once looked over a tuberculosis sanatorium, close to the hospital where his sister Vicky died, and saw what wonderful work it did.

Cassel was delighted, and Sir Felix Semon was placed in charge as co-ordinator. Bertie's long and detailed brief began:

What we require is a Sanatorium for the poorer middle classes. Rich people can avail themselves of private sanatoria, the really poor ought to be provided for by municipalities and institutions of public benevolence, but between these two classes is a stratum of educated yet indigent patients, such as clergymen, teachers, governesses, clerks, young officers, persons skilled in art, etc. They cannot afford the big sums charged by private sanatoria, whilst they are too proud or too bashful to avail themselves of public charity. . . . They are to pay a *small* sum and this for two reasons: they are not to be degraded into paupers, and the institution is to be self-supporting. . . .

A committee was formed, including Sir Francis Laking and several venerable and knighted authorities on tuberculosis and sanatoria. Like any good administrator, Bertie now let them get on with it, checking on progress intermittently and not as often as he would have liked owing to the multitude of other commitments. So it only gradually became clear to him that the committee was bungling things horribly. Months passed and they still had not fixed finally on a site. When this was chosen at a spot near Midhurst, in Surrey, and the building almost completed four years later, Bertie had begun to lose interest. But disillusion turned to anger when he learned that the committee had taken poor advice about the water supply, leading to the necessity of constructing at great cost, some distance from the sanatorium, a reservoir and pumping station.

Summoning Semon, Bertie gave him a piece of his mind: 'I will tell you something: you doctors are nearly as bad as the lawyers, and God knows that will say a great deal!' Semon, according to his own account, then burst into laughter instead of showing contrition, and in a moment the King was laughing, too. Semon was a vain man and may have been making the best of a bad situation. But it is indisputable that Bertie took no more interest in Midhurst after appointing Esher to clean up the Augean stable, and in the end it filled a great need and saved many lives.

Instead, Bertie concentrated his charitable work on London, on the Keyser sisters' King Edward VII's Hospital for Officers (still flourishing today), The London Hospital and King Edward's Hospital Fund. He had set up the Fund in 1897 as a source of support for other hospitals in the London area, providing money, equipment and advice. The distribution, which was a modest £500,000 in 1901, increased 200 per cent during Bertie's reign and doubled again ten years later.

In 1908 Bertie wrote to his old friend and saviour (as he regarded him), Sir Frederick Treves: 'My greatest ambition is not to quit this world till a real cure for cancer has been found, and I feel convinced that radium will be the means of doing so!' Treves had just returned from Paris, where he had visited the Radium Institute. 'We must indeed have one in London,' Bertie had agreed.

One reason for Bertie's determination was his own experience when he had suffered recently from an ulcer on his face, which was believed to be malignant and had been treated successfully with radium. But towering above this minor personal experience was the haunting memory of the long, drawn-out and agonising deaths from cancer of his eldest sister Vicky and, earlier, of his brother-in-law, Fritz. If only, Bertie would often lament to Alix, Fritz had been spared, his dreadful and dangerous son would not now be Emperor of Germany, driving Europe towards war!

Bertie selected as candidates – or victims – for the funding of a London Radium Institute two of the wealthiest men he knew, Lord Iveagh, the brewer, and Sir Ernest Cassel. There was no slackness, inefficiency and suspected jobbery in the creation of this charity.

21

A Monarch in Decline

'Their hearts went out to him . . .'
The Derby crowd

Towards the end of 1908 Alix confessed for the first time that she was beginning to feel her age of sixty-four. This was probably brought on by the news that Bertie was going to Berlin in February and that she was to accompany him. We can almost hear him saying, 'I know, I know, it is the last place I wish to go. The weather will be dreadful, my nephew will be tiresome, to say nothing of Dona. But I must make one more attempt to solve some of the problems which bedevil relations between our two countries.'

Alix accepted the truth of this and the need for her presence in order to represent family solidarity. But the effort asked of her was very burdensome, and how she wished it was Russia they were visiting when she could again be with her sister and those charming Grand Duchesses, the daughters of Nicky and Alicky.

In January 1909 she was feeling decidedly poorly and it certainly crossed her mind, with a flash of anticipatory relief, that she might be too ill to travel on the date of departure, 8 February. Her daughter-in-law, May, shared these thoughts. Alix, she said, was suffering badly from neuralgia and depression. 'I only hope she will be all right for Berlin for she ought to go there if she possibly can.' Any last minute failure to accompany Bertie would certainly be taken as a slight, no matter what the doctors said.

But the doctors were seriously worried. Alix had now contracted influenza and it was becoming so bad that no one, not even her closest family, was allowed to see her for several days. Towards the end of the month she was showing signs of recovery, and with her usual courage and resilience let it be known that she was perfectly well again. In fact, it was Bertie who gave the greater cause for concern. He was petulant, impatient and thoroughly difficult during the last days before departure, succumbing to unusually long fits of coughing with accompanying struggles for breath. But for this wretched duty to which he was committed, he would be off now to the sun and warmth of Biarritz and the tender, amusing company of Mrs Keppel.

For what was to be their last state visit together – or alone for that matter – they brought with them a suite almost as extravagantly vast as the Emperor and Empress of Germany's on these occasions. After the undeniable success of earlier state visits, especially those to France and Russia, the Foreign Office, in the shape of Sir Edward Grey, now accepted that the planned conversations between the King and Kaiser could significantly improve relations. The Colonial Secretary, Lord Crewe, was to serve as Minister in Attendance, while the King insisted that Charles Hardinge (whose mind Bertie was attuned to) should accompany him, too. To represent the navy, a service which Bertie was determined his nephew must discuss this time, he took Admiral Sir Day Bosanquet rather than the abrasive Fisher, and to represent the army Field Marshal Lord Grenfell. Also present were Lord Althorp as Lord Chamberlain, Lord Howe as Lord Chamberlain to the Queen, Fritz Ponsonby as Private Secretary, Commander Charles Cunninghame Graham as groom-in-waiting, Sir James Reid as physician, and assortments of ladies-in-waiting and equerries.

A royal train packed with all these people and a truly phenomenal pile of luggage ran from Charing Cross to Dover, where everyone boarded the royal yacht *Alexandra*, which, unlike the *Victoria and Albert*, could comfortably be accommodated in Calais harbour.

The trip began with a contretemps [Lord Grenfell wrote later]. The King was much excited at seeing the Royal Standard flying on the flagstaff at Dover Castle, the regulation being that only one Royal Standard should ever be seen, and that only above the house, public building, or ship actually occupied by the King. It had been hoisted when the King stepped on to the royal yacht. He desired me to report the error, which I did, by telegram to the General commanding at Dover and by letter to the War Office.

Having vented his spleen, the twenty-three-mile voyage continued uneventfully. By landing in France they had to suffer the formalities of welcome and presentations by the local big-wigs, so that Bertie had to wait with his usual appearance of suffering patience until 2 p.m. for his luncheon on the German train.

For the rest of that day their train made its way across the north German plain. At 8 p.m. they all proceeded to the lavishly equipped restaurant car in the centre. By this time, Alix, refreshed as always by a sea voyage, was in characteristic form, chattering away and hearing little. 'When the train lurched,' Ponsonby recorded, 'and a footman upset some quails on her, actually leaving a quail hanging on her hair [toupee, in fact] she kept us in roars of laughter describing how she would arrive in Berlin *coiffée de cailles*.' Later in the meal the waiters (who seem to have been untrained for these conditions) upset a carafe of claret across the table.

There were more mishaps on arrival for the *Freundliche Verhattnisse*. At Rathenow, on the Brandenburg frontier, where there was a guard of honour and band to greet them, Bertie for once kept them all waiting for ten minutes, during which the band played 'God Save the King' over and over again, 'till we all nearly screamed'. His valet had got the time wrong, which greatly displeased his master. But there, at last, he was in German Field Marshal's uniform, which emphasised his corpulence, and looking not at all well. There was a guard of honour and a regiment of guards to inspect, and now anxious to recover lost time Bertie 'went at a brisk pace and was very much blown in consequence', according to Ponsonby, and was still breathless when he tried to deliver an address to the municipal authorities.

The reception and formality were ten times greater at Berlin, and so were the mishaps. A misjudgment led to the red carpet and the entire family of the Emperor and Empress, with all their entourage, being 100 yards from the point on the platform where the royal carriage halted. With unseemly haste, William and Dona and their Princes and Princesses ran to resite themselves, skirts like luffing yachts' sails, swords held tight for fear of disaster. No one present had seen anything like it.

Alix watched this display of Teutonic inefficiency with great satisfaction before the two families greeted one another with a fine show of affection. 'There was a great deal of embracing between the royalties,' according to Lord Grenfell. Then with much German bowing and heel-clicking they and their entourages disposed themselves among the waiting line of carriages, the two Kings first, then Alix and Dona, and the rest behind.

The decorated streets were lined with thousands of troops, with many thousands more Berliners behind them. 'The sun shone intermittently and lit up the curving line of bayonets', and it was agreed that the city had seen nothing to compare with this for years. Unfortunately, the leading carriage made its way alone in stately isolation and there was no sign of the Queen and Empress, nor of their children, nor of their suites. William ordered his carriage to halt, and in a moment a breathless minion, bowing deeply, explained that the second carriage's horses had refused to move, no doubt from pique at being kept waiting too long. Alix was rightly confident that she could have coaxed the four horses into action; on the other hand, she was greatly enjoying the embarrassment of her hostess.

The Kaiser was furious at being kept waiting, too, and beside himself with mixed shame and anger at the disruption. A mile behind them everyone had to be reshuffled in accordance with the order of precedence. Later Ponsonby overheard the Kaiser telling the Master of the Horse that he 'wouldn't have had it happen for the world before the English, who were all good horse-masters'. Ponsonby comforted the unfortunate fellow by saying that 'we at least knew enough about horses to understand how unreliable the most perfectly trained animals are when frightened by the cheering and waving of flags'.

From their arrival at the Palace, and for the following three days of packed activities, the organisation worked with Teutonic efficiency and the Kaiser's wrath was appeased. The only disruptions were caused by Bertie's health. His cough had turned into full-scale bronchitis, he was feeling awful and should have been in bed. But there was nothing that either Alix or Sir James Reid, doctor in attendance, could say to persuade him to cancel any of his engagements. Henry Bruce, the third secretary at the British Embassy, described Bertie as 'looking very seedy, poor old dear,' and told of the worst experience he witnessed during the visit:

My most poignant memory is of the awful moment after a huge official lunch at the Embassy when his eyes shut, his mouth fell open and, with a rattle in his throat, his head dropped forward on his chest. We all thought it was the end.

He had been talking to one of his oldest friends, Princess Daisy of Pless, and she, too, thought Bertie had died suddenly. Many of the guests panicked as they were hustled from the room, Sir James Reid was called and Alix ran to Bertie's chair, undoing his collar. He came round from his faint a few minutes later, puzzled at all the fuss. When the guests were recalled, they found him sitting up, smiling a greeting and puffing at a newly lit cigar.

But Bertie was very poorly again when Ponsonby went to see him about the important question of decorations to be given before their departure. This was a subject which was usually discussed with the utmost seriousness, but this time Bertie wearily waved it aside and Ponsonby had to distribute them himself.

Both Bertie and Alix were looking forward to the gala performance at the opera house, especially because it would mean an evening without obligations and offer Bertie a complete rest, which he desperately needed. The first part of the entertainment was organised by the Kaiser himself. It consisted of a series of ever more spectacular scenes accompanied by songs and ending with a representation of the funeral pyre of Sardanapalus. By this time Bertie was fast asleep and woke up only when the tongues of flame burst into a mighty conflagration, with clouds of smoke filling the auditorium.

He looked about him in amazement that no one was sounding the alarm and began to rise from his seat. It was with the greatest difficulty that the Empress could convince him that it was all part of the spectacle. With the doors open and the smoke clearing she explained that it was the custom for guests of honour to mix with the most distinguished people in the crowd – those in the *Almanach de Gotha* – during the long interval.

Alix quickly realised that this was far beyond Bertie's powers while in this condition and insisted that he should be allowed to rest, and that she undertake it herself. 'She went round,' Ponsonby observed, 'not hearing a word that was said in reply, and charmed everyone with her manner. I have never seen anything better done.'

Bertie's weakness and the evidence he gave of failing health were observed by thousands, though they were tactfully not referred to in the press while he was in Berlin. The Controller of the Kaiser's Household later wrote:

The King of England is so stout that he completely loses his breath when he has to climb upstairs, and has to save himself in many ways. The Emperor told us that at the first family dinner he fell asleep . . . but he eats, drinks and smokes enormously.

But the overall impression Bertie made in Berlin was favourable, while Alix by her charm, grace and beauty captivated the Berliners. His greatest success was at the *Rathaus*, where he was received by the Burgomaster. Lord Grenfell wrote of this occasion when Herr Kirschner asked the King to receive a cup of German wine from the city of Berlin out of the hands of a citizen's daughter:

The King then drank from a golden goblet filled with Rhine wine, which Herr Kirschner's little daughter presented to him, and, speaking in clear terms in German, expressed his appreciation of the splendid reception accorded him, and his desire that the relations of the English and German peoples should always be the best. He then drank to the townspeople assembled in the galleries, and finished by a charming speech to the pretty little girl who had presented the goblet to him. This last touch brought down the house. It was a triumph of tact, eloquence, and courtesy, and the King was enthusiastically cheered.

On the last morning before they left by train, Bertie made a final effort to discuss the one most critical issue between the two nations: naval competition. During the time that had been allowed for farewells between hosts and guests, and as the King-Emperor strode up and down the platform, this conversation took place:

KING EDWARD: 'We are in a different position from other countries. Being an island we must have a fleet larger than everyone else's. But we don't dream of attacking anybody.'

KAISER WILLIAM: 'I agree that it is perfectly natural that England should have a navy according to its interests and to be able to safeguard them.'

KING EDWARD: 'And I perfectly understand it is your absolute right to have a fleet according to your needs. Nor do I for one moment believe you are designing anything against us.'

KAISER WILLIAM: 'This [naval] bill of ours was published eleven years ago; it will be adhered to and exactly carried out, *without any restriction*.'

KING EDWARD: 'Of course that is quite right, as it is a bill voted by the people and their parliament. I know that cannot be changed.'

KAISER WILLIAM: 'It is a mistake on the part of Jingoes in England that we are embarking on a building race with you. That is nonsense. We only follow the bill.'

KING EDWARD: 'Oh, I know that is quite an absurd notion, the situation is quite clear to me and I am in no way alarmed; that is all talk and will pass over.'

This had been neither the time nor the place for a serious discussion, and Bertie let the subject remain there. It was, in any case, time to board the train.

With this useless exchange in mind, Ponsonby commented:

'The effect of this visit was nil.' On a general level he thought that

one felt that a few charming men really liked us, but with the majority I derived the impression that they hated us. The Germans never forgave the King for having, as they imagined, isolated them from the rest of Europe. . . . The Emperor seemed to do all he could to make the visit a success,* but he was never at his ease with the King. There were always forced jokes, and the whole atmosphere when the two were together seemed charged with dangerous electricity.

The journey home was a depressing business after the high hopes and spirits of the outward journey, and they were all thankful to get back to Buckingham Palace. Bertie and Alix dined alone at 9 p.m. She was concerned at how awful he looked, pale and drawn and lethargic, coughing uncontrollably every few minutes and nodding off occasionally towards the end of the meal. If only something had been achieved in Berlin, perhaps he would not now be so cast down. But from this time he knew in his heart of hearts that war with Germany was inevitable, that Fisher and Esher and many others were right, and that all his efforts to leave as an inheritance of his reign a stable and peaceful Europe had been in vain.

While Alix made her way to Sandringham the next morning, Bertie faced three days of tiresome business and appointments in London before he could get away to Biarritz. On the last of these days he had to fulfil the onerous duty of opening Parliament.

The year 1909 was almost unprecedented in its degree of domestic civil strife, crisis and disorder. The split in the Royal Navy between traditionalists and reformers, personified by the increasingly bitter conflict between Beresford and Fisher, was reflected on a vastly bigger scale in the country, where the Conservatives were fighting the Liberals, who were in power and determined to push through their social legislation

* He saw to it that pictures of Danish rustic scenes were hung in Alix's rooms and famous British naval victories in Bertie's.

at the cost of higher taxes. In addition, labour strife, which was to lead to the dreadful strikes of 1910–11, was boiling up; and the suffragettes in their struggle for votes for women were becoming increasingly violent. Added to all this contention were the internecine conflicts within the campaigns. There were naval officers who approved of Fisher's reforms but not with his method of implementing them. There were Liberals, like Lloyd George and Winston Churchill, who were prepared to limit naval expenditure to pay for old-age pensions, better state education and improved housing for the poor. Even the suffragettes were divided between the militant and violent Women's Social and Political Union and the more moderate Women's Freedom League.

It was hard for the King, weary and bronchial and feeling his sixty-seven years, to have to suffer all this sound and fury, but it was not to be escaped – except for those few weeks at Biarritz and in the Mediterranean, and even here not completely. Cassel was only one of Bertie's numerous friends and advisers who warned him of coming political and even constitutional uproar. At Biarritz, the weather was foul and cold and he remained unwell. He had learned some months earlier that if the (unelected) Upper House threw out the budget, he would be approached by Asquith to create some two hundred new peers in order to redress the anti-Liberal disparity in the House of Lords.

The Upper House had already sent back (i.e. refused to pass) or substantially watered-down a number of Liberal bills, but it had been an established practice for more than two hundred years not to throw out a complete budget; instead, mere amendments in detail were made. If the peers were to do so with this budget and the Prime Minister came to the King with his request in order to force it through, the King would be left in a hideously difficult situation that must end with the undermining of the power and standing of the monarchy.

Bertie loathed everything about the political scene, the bitter division of the nation over what came to be known as the 'People's Budget' and the inflammatory speeches* made by entrenched Conservatives and radicals alike.

The Harmsworth newspapers in particular whipped up outrage against the threat of socialism and even revolution in the land. But the Liberals were able to depict the peers and the brewers and big industrialists as rich men twisting and turning every way in an effort to avoid paying their fair share to the cost of running and defending the nation. It was an unanswerable case. Lloyd George and Asquith were on the winning side all the way and they knew it. Lloyd George stomped the country, exploiting his Welsh energy, oratory and sense of ridicule which no one could match. However outrageously he spoke, Asquith backed him to the hilt.

Bertie succumbed to near despair. He protested weakly to Asquith at the 'mean' and 'improper' language of some of his ministers, and declared that politics had never been so bitter. Everything tended towards the Government 'inflaming the passions of the working and lower orders against people who happen to be owners of property'.

He was equally disenchanted with the Lords and begged them to pass the budget, which had gone through the House of Commons (379 to 149) on 4 November 1909. But their folly and their arrogance proved as great and decisive as Asquith had predicted. It was rejected by them on second reading by 350 to 75. Within two days Asquith moved and carried a resolution in the Commons, 'That the action of the House of Lords in refusing to pass into law the financial provisions made by this House for the service of the year is a breach of the Constitution and a usurpation of the rights of the Commons.'

Just one more inevitable measure remained to be taken: an election in January 1910. Bertie was devastated. He had done all he could to bring about a compromise, and dreaded an election fought on the issue of the rights of the House of Lords. It seemed to him that the nation he had served as Prince of Wales and King for almost fifty years was breaking

* Lloyd George upset Bertie, and many Conservatives, and even shocked some Liberals by declaring at one public meeting that a peer cost more a year than two *Dreadnoughts*, and could not be scrapped.

up about him, and not for the first time he contemplated abdication.

In the last days of April 1909 Minnie arrived in London from Russia and the two sisters, Queen of England and Dowager Empress of Russia – now sixty-four and sixty-two years – fell into one another's arms. As always they had much to talk about, mainly family affairs, although Minnie, it is certain, wanted to hear all about the horrors of Berlin, while the state of Bertie's health, being Alix's chief preoccupation, would also have been discussed.

Early in May 1909 the two sisters, with Toria and their suites, travelled by royal train to Dover and across France to Marseilles. The country was looking at its best, and the sunshine always lifted Alix's heart, easing the anxiety she felt about Bertie's condition when she met him.

The meeting took place on-board the *Victoria and Albert* soon after she arrived. He looked as bad as she had feared, and it was evident that Biarritz had not had its usual restorative effect upon him. He was in no better temper than he had been when he left England, and had good reason to vent it within a few hours of leaving the French port.

Bertie had decided to visit his brother the Duke of Connaught, who was living on Malta as High Commissioner, and ordered a signal to be sent informing the authorities, duplicated to London. To his fury and amazement he received a reply indicating that the entire Mediterranean Fleet had been 'ordered off to make a demonstration' on the day before he was now due to arrive. He felt this to be an outrageous insult and tossed the telegram at Fritz Ponsonby. 'I've a good mind to order the Fleet back to Malta,' he shouted, working up his fury to an even higher pitch.

Ponsonby did all he could to placate Bertie, pointing out that the Fleet could only have been ordered to sea for some urgent need, and to cancel the demonstration would attract adverse comment at home. After a while the King began to cool down, only to suffer a second rise in temperature when Ponsonby pointed out that the real culprits for this mix-up were Reginald McKenna, First Lord of the Admiralty, and

Asquith, both of whom had been told of the royal yacht's destination and had not had the courtesy or sense to inform the King in advance.

Telegrams to be sent in cypher were dictated. 'I went to my cabin and softened down the messages,' Ponsonby wrote later. 'It was a bad start to a cruise that was intended to please the King and grant him a real rest in the sun.'

Everyone cheered up when they met the King and Queen of Italy, who were on-board their royal yacht at Baiae. To the music of the yacht's orchestras they lunched and dined together, dancing on a deck illuminated by the moon. Everybody remarked on the cordiality of the occasion, which certainly failed to hint at Italy's supposed friendship with Austria and Germany in the Triple Entente. One of the Italian ADCs confided in Ponsonby that the pact was 'drawn up by Kings, Emperors and Governments, whereas the whole of the Italian people were mad keen to fight the Austrians'.

From Naples the English party was given a train to take them to the base of Vesuvius, where donkeys awaited them for the ascent, if they so wished. Bertie did not, but Alix and Minnie were game and managed to get more than half-way up over the steep indented lava. Then Bertie, furious and bored out of his mind, had the train's whistle blown, more than once, until he observed distantly that the party was on its return journey. Never had Alix known his temper to be so short and sharp.

As in earlier years, Bertie returned to London leaving Alix to cruise to Athens to stay with her brother Willi (who had become almost as fat as Bertie) and his family at the royal palace. For a few days only, in warm spring weather, Alix basked in the company of her brother and sister, talking of the old days in Copenhagen when they had been so poor yet so happy together before four of them became kings, a queen or an empress.

Bertie returned to innumerable troubles in England, but also to a triumph which gave him one of the happiest moments of his life. Alix had also arrived home in time for the 1909 Derby. On the morning of 26 May they travelled to Epsom Downs and made the traditional carriage drive down the course, with Georgie and May beside them. Esher recorded how when Bertie 'raised his hat to the immense concourse of his people, his salutation reached the heart of every man and woman. . . . The fact is that, just as their hearts went out to him, his heart went out to them, and they knew it.'

Marcus Beresford had twenty-three horses in training for the King that year, and a colt called Minoru had already shown exceptional promise, winning the Greenham Stakes and the Two Thousand Guineas Stakes while Bertie was away. The crowd had taken a special fancy to Minoru.

'But danger was believed to have arisen from another quarter,' wrote Alfred Watson, the King's sporting historian. 'Mr Louis Winans had given 15,000 guineas for an American-bred colt named Sir Martin, who had won as a two year old some of the principal races in the United States.' There were other threats to Minoru, including Louviers and Bayardo.

The flag fell to an even start; Minoru held a sufficiently good place, and was just where his jockey wished him to be when more than half the distance had been covered. Here, however, a disaster occurred. Sir Martin either crossed his legs or struck into another horse – precisely what did happen has never been clearly stated. At any rate the American colt fell, and some of those who were banked behind him necessarily suffered. . . . Most fortunately Minoru escaped. . . . The purple and scarlet jacket was prominent at Tattenham Corner, with Louviers in close attendance. . . .

It was neck and neck to the finishing line with the crowd roaring and Alix hanging on desperately to Bertie's and Georgie's arms. No one knew who had won until the numbers were hoisted, indicating a royal victory. Bertie was beside himself with delight, Alix burst into tears, and never had there been such a roar from an Epsom Downs' crowd as those around the finish surged towards the unsaddling enclosure.

Bertie also made his way there, at first comfortably, and then with increasing difficulty, although half-a-dozen policemen did their best to clear a way for him. 'Good old Teddy! Good old Teddy!' the crowd shouted, and Bertie, beaming, called out in his deep, guttural, authoritative voice, 'Make way for the King!'

Herbert Jones, the King's jockey, had had almost as much difficulty as his master in reaching the enclosure, where he dismounted. Some of the crowd were singing, tipsily and well out of tune, 'God Save the King', hurled hats fell from the air with no one caring; and in the royal box Alix was kissing everyone around her.

Minoru's leading rein was buckled on, and Bertie, cigar between his teeth and with an occasional pat at the colt's sweating neck, led him away. Odds had been 7:2, and it was a bad day for the bookies – but no one else.

When Bertie returned to Epsom for the following day's racing, he was greeted again by repeated cheers. Then, in a brief lull, a voice called out, 'Now, King, you've won the Derby. Go back home and dissolve this bloody Parliament.' He roared with laughter but made no comment. The 'People's Budget' crisis was at its height, but it was another six months before Parliament was dissolved. The general belief was that, based on the outcome of by-elections, the Conservatives would be comfortably returned to power. These predictions did not take account of the electors' revulsion at what they considered to be the unconstitutional machinations of the House of Lords. The Conservatives recorded a net loss of 100 seats. But the crisis was not resolved by these figures, especially as the Liberals still depended on the support of forty Labour and eighty-two Irish Nationalist members.

Bertie had prayed that his beloved son would inherit a calm political climate at home and a peaceful and stable order in Europe. The Prince of Wales was not to be vouchsafed either of these conditions.

Minoru's Derby victory was a prelude to a mainly satisfactory last summer for Bertie. Alix also enjoyed herself for much of the time and was relieved at Bertie's improvement in health and temper. The high point, in spite of the disapproval of radical elements, was the visit of the Tsar and his family to Cowes in August.

Long before the Tsar's arrival on 2 August 1909, the Labour Party declared that the King's proposed reception 'was an insult to the good name of the nation', and claimed that the royal visit to Reval the previous year 'had made the Russian domestic situation worse than before'. On the very day of the Russian arrival a letter was published in the newspapers protesting against the official reception. It was signed by seventy MPs, several peers and church leaders. But Bertie agreed with Sir Edward Grey that good relations with the British ally in the east was far more important than this minor left-wing political outrage. It was certainly difficult to imagine a larger and more enthusiastic welcome from the crowds on both sides of the Solent when the mighty and beautiful imperial yacht *Standart* arrived from France, where the Tsar and his ministers had been talking to the French President and ministers.

The Royal Navy put on a spectacular show, which rubbed salt into the wounds of German pride. Not only had three of the latest *Dreadnought* battle-cruisers (Germany had not yet completed its first) escorted the Russian yacht from Cherbourg, but the reception in the Solent consisted of twenty-four battleships, sixteen armoured cruisers, forty-eight destroyers and fifty more assorted men o'war. They were dressed overall, Royal Marines' bands played and a twenty-one-gun salute rang out as the Russian vessel dropped anchor close to the *Victoria and Albert*.

For three days there was much friendly to-ing and fro-ing between the two royal yachts, and breakfast was the only unshared meal. There were almost as many cordial speeches as cordial toasts, the Grand Duchesses enchanted everybody, and the poignant little Tsarevitch melted all hearts, though he shyly rebuffed friendly advances made by Bertie. There were fireworks and dancing in the evening, Jackie Fisher being much in evidence, dancing with everyone – Olga, Tatiana, Marie and Anastasia in turn, and with his favourite partner, Alix, most of all.

The Russian secret police were everywhere, and as at Reval there was no question of going ashore, at least not on the mainland. The Isle of Wight was declared to be safe enough, however, and under close escort the Russian imperial family were taken to Cowes by steam launch. Bertie and Alix took the Tsar and Tsarina to Osborne House to guide them through Queen Victoria's suite, kept just as it had been on the day she died. They talked fondly of that hot summer of 1894, when Nicky and Alicky were engaged and deeply in love, the last time when they had been unrestricted and carefree and everyone had loved the romantic couple.

Georgie and May's first child had been born when they had been in England that time, and now the boy, Prince Edward (David), aged thirteen and in the uniform of a naval cadet, proudly took them round the college he was attending. When the party returned to Cowes, the Russian children were playing on the beach. They had bought postcards and rock, which they ate with relish and offered to their parents. Their time on British soil had been only one hour but they remembered it with pleasure for the remainder of their short lives.

The next day, when the *Standart* sailed away east into the morning sun, the five children and the Tsar and Tsarina waved farewell from the poop deck until Bertie and Alix, Georgie and May were out of sight on the bridge of the *Victoria and Albert*. They never saw one another again.

The English royalties split up after Cowes, Bertie leaving straight for Marienbad, Alix for Balmoral, Georgie and May for Bolton Abbey and the Duke of Devonshire's grouse moors for 'the glorious 12th'. After the pleasures of Cowes Week and the Russian visit, Alix felt flat and lonely in the great stone castle. She wrote to Georgie:

I do miss you my darling boy so dreadfully at times. Really on board the yacht at Cowes seems the only time we ever sleep under the same roof which makes me quite low and unhappy when thinking of how formerly we were so much together and to each other. Of course I know it cannot be helped but that does not make it better. If I had not my darling Toria with me I should indeed be quite miserable and lonely as Papa is always so much away now from home.

Alix's letters became more cheerful when later in the month she joined her sister at Hvidöre. She was also relieved to hear that Marienbad seemed to have done Bertie a lot of good and that he was shooting grouse in satisfactory numbers from Balmoral. The two came together at Sandringham as usual in November for the celebration of their birthdays.

After a beautiful summer the weather had turned cold and stormy, like the political climate. On the very day of Alix's birthday – 1 December – Esher wrote to Bertie, through Knollys, about the Prime Minister's threat to ask the King to create some two hundred peers to thwart the present House of Lords's threat to throw out the budget. It would be 'an outrage on the common sense of the country', he wrote. '. . . But the graver aspect of the question is, that the Prime Minister wishes to obtain a promise from the King *before* the General Election.'

No such promise was forthcoming. Although it was generally assumed that it had been given, which heightened the political crisis still further, Bertie, supported by Esher and other advisers, refused to give in to Asquith's pleas. Nor did he relent when, after Christmas in London, he contracted 'flu and felt so weak that it seemed as if he would yield to any appeal. His doctors longed for him to be off to Biarritz. So did Alix and, independently, Alice Keppel and Mrs James. But Bertie would not leave the country at this critical time and agreed only to going down to Brighton, for the sea air, to stay with the Sassoons.

'We had very difficult dinners at first,' Ponsonby recounted, 'because the King sat silent, and this rather chilled the conversation. Mrs Sassoon was quite wonderful and, realizing that the King did not want to talk, kept the ball rolling with me and Seymour Fortescue [equerry].'

When Asquith found it necessary to talk to Bertie, he was thankful that, this time, he did not have to take the four-day journey to Biarritz and back. Ponsonby met him at the station on the morning of 11 February and drove him to the Sassoons' modest house. Here the Prime Minister was closeted with Bertie for a long time.

At length Asquith emerged, saying nothing, except that he would like to go for a walk with Ponsonby. It was pouring with rain and blowing a gale along the esplanade, and there was an inconveniently large crowd which had learned that both the Prime Minister and the King were in their midst.

As they walked, bent double against the gale, Ponsonby, referring to the House of Lords question, asked, 'I suppose you have come down to talk to the King about the guarantees?'

'Oh dear, no!' Asquith replied, and began to talk about the political situation generally. Recalling that uncomfortable walk the King's Private Secretary wrote: 'It seemed to me incomprehensible that Asquith should take the trouble to come down to Brighton from London to tell the King that the political situation was very difficult.'

In fact, the House of Lords was not discussed. Asquith 'finds himself in a very "tight place"', Bertie reported to Knollys, who had remained in London. That was no news to anyone, but the Prime Minister wanted also to inform him of proposed Cabinet changes, and of the difficulties he was having with the Irish MPs.

Bertie returned from Brighton, and Alix from Sandringham, in time for the opening of Parliament on 22 February. Unlike his mother, Bertie had not omitted this duty since he ascended the throne and, weak and ill though he was, he was certainly not going to fail in this important year.

In a strong, clear voice which had become so familiar to members, Bertie informed the House, on behalf of the Government, what Parliamentary business would be conducted. There were references to the Prince of Wales's imminent trip to South Africa and India, and to the provisions of the last budget 'to which effect has not yet been given', and then a crucial paragraph referring to 'the undivided authority of the House of Commons over Finance, and its predominance over Legislation'.

With his duty completed for the time being, Bertie felt able to meet the wishes of Alix and his doctors and at last leave for Biarritz. Esher agreed that it was the right thing to do, not just for the sake of his health but because 'there was much to be gained by his not having any personal intercourse with any of his ministers just at present'. Alix, for her part, left with equal eagerness to join her brother and his Greek royal family on Corfu.

As if suspecting that he might not see again some of his

closest and oldest men friends, Bertie invited a number of them, including Redesdale and 'Charlie' Carrington, to a farewell dinner at Buckingham Palace on 6 March. They were all surprised to find him in such excellent spirits; it might almost have been one of those happy-go-lucky dinners he used to give as Prince of Wales at Marlborough House. Nor had his appetite diminished. Bertie, eating at his customary high speed, had turtle soup, salmon, chicken, mutton, then (best of all) snipe stuffed with foie gras, asparagus, ices and a savoury.

After dinner, Redesdale related:

. . . he went the round of his guests, as was his wont, and chatted gaily with each of them. As he was leaving the room he stopped for a moment to talk to me, and spoke with all his natural cheerfulness, like a boy before a holiday, of his journey which was to take place on the morrow.

That evening somehow provided Bertie with a merciful remission from his bronchial torture. But the reality of his condition was confirmed when he reached Paris the following night. He was suffering from the usual shortness of breath and had a sharp pain close to his heart. But he insisted on going to the theatre as arranged, to the Théâtre Porte St Martin, where Rostand's *Chantecler* was playing and where he caught a cold.

On the way south in the train the cold worsened and inevitably turned into bronchitis. Sir James Reid, doctor in attendance, put him to bed as soon as they arrived and attempted to conceal his serious anxiety from the others in the party who had assembled to share the King's holiday. Among them were Alice Keppel and her two daughters, Mrs James and Cassel's grandchildren, Edwina and Mary Ashley. Edwina was Bertie's god-daughter, an enchanting eight year old to whom he was devoted. The days passed and the King remained confined to his room, although there was a steady flow of boxes in and out of his suite. At last there was word that he was better. On 21 March he appeared in a chair and was wheeled on to the hotel's lawn. There he chatted and played with the little Ashley girls, who in turn played with Caesar, Bertie's brown and white fox terrier.

There was bridge in the evenings, Bertie and Mrs Keppel playing Mrs James or Arthur Davidson and Soveral, who was present in anticipation of the arrival of the King and Queen of Portugal. Ponsonby arrived later to relieve Davidson. He was astonished to hear how seriously ill Bertie had been, the bulletins having been bland and reassuring, but noted how improved he was from his condition when in London.

On the evening of 25 April 1910, the town put on an elaborate farewell to Bertie, who was leaving with his party the next day. They certainly owed him a great debt for making the town fashionable, quite apart from the money he and his suite, and their friends, had spent there. There were fireworks and parades and dancing in the streets to bands.

'I shall be sorry to leave Biarritz,' Bertie commented, adding significantly, 'Perhaps it will be for ever.'

22

'The King is Dead . . .'

*'. . . turned into stone, unable to cry, unable
to grasp the meaning of it all . . .'*
Alix on Bertie's death

Alix was still in Corfu when Bertie arrived back in London,
his train entering Victoria Station at 6 p.m. on 27 April 1910.
For the only time he could remember he had not stopped off
at Paris, so anxious was he about the political situation, which
seemed to have reached a total impasse over the House of
Lords, and other delayed business. There was nothing that
he could do that evening, but, as it had been for all his adult
life, the prospect of empty hours looming ahead was not to
be countenanced. *Rigoletto*, one of his favourites, was playing
at the opera house, he learned, with Campanini conducting
and Melba and McCormack heading the cast. So he ordered
his carriage.

His old friend Redesdale was in a stalls seat that night.

The King came in and sat down in his usual corner place [he wrote].
I noticed that he was looking very tired and worn. He sat through
one act, all alone. Then he got up, and I heard him give a great
sigh. He opened the door of the box, lingered for a little in the
doorway, with a very sad expression on his face – so unlike himself

– took a last look at the house, as if to bid it farewell, and then went out.

For the next two days Bertie worked with scarcely a break. The choice of a new Viceroy of India required appointments – long ones, too – with Asquith, Lord Althorp, Kitchener and others; the obduracy of the House of Lords was still another major subject, and there were dozens of other less important issues to be aired.

One visitor, looking at him in some alarm, begged Bertie to desist and take to his bed. 'No, I shall not give in – I shall work to the end. Of what use is it to be alive if one cannot work?'

On Saturday, 30 April, like his ministers, Bertie went to the country. He had earlier given orders for a number of things to be done on the Sandringham gardens and he was anxious to see how they were proceeding. He took with him only his old friend, Comptroller and Keeper of the Privy Purse, Sir Dighton Probyn, three equerries and Ponsonby. A doctor would also have been appropriate.

The staff greeted him with their usual warmth, but they all noticed the great change in him. 'He was normally quick-tempered, insisting on things being done at once, ever kind but accustomed to being obeyed. Now, on the contrary, they found him so quiet, so gentle, so unlike his impulsive nature.'

Regardless of a foul east wind and intermittent driving rain, Bertie went out after divine service the following morning to supervise the planting of some saplings. Inevitably, in his weakened condition he contracted a cold and was feeling decidedly seedy when he returned to Buckingham Palace on Monday evening, 2 May. He was having only brief relief from bronchial coughing, his face changing with frightening speed from dead white to black.

As at other critical moments in his life, he craved for the company and comfort of Sister Agnes Keyser, and now in spite of his condition he invited himself to supper with her. She would certainly not refer to his condition or fuss over him. She would be her usual brisk, level-headed, kindly self and would not comment on his loss of appetite.

When he returned to Buckingham Palace, and to bed, he slept badly. In the morning Laking came and examined him. Bronchitis had definitely set in and the doctor concealed his anxiety while attempting, unsuccessfully, to confine him to bed. Bertie was looking forward to a visit from 'Teddy' Roosevelt, ex-President of the United States, soon and was due to discuss the itinerary with the American Ambassador, Whitelaw Reid.

It was an awkward meeting. The American had no idea that he would find the King in such low health. 'Our talk was interrupted by spasms of coughing, and I found that he was suffering from a good many symptoms [of] bronchial asthma. . . . It seems to me that these attacks are coming on more frequently within the last two years, and that they are becoming harder to shake off. Still,' he added, 'he is a man of tremendous vigour of constitution, and of extraordinary energetic habits.'

That evening Alice Keppel and Mrs James were invited for dinner and bridge, the fourth being made up by Ponsonby. Bertie ate almost nothing, but remained cheerful enough and suggested that they start playing early because the game saved his voice, which meant less coughing.

The next morning, though clearly worse, he insisted on rising and dressing in his formal frock-coat to receive delegations and visitors, none of whom was allowed to be turned away: a member of the Japanese royal family, the new agent-general for Queensland, the new Governor and Commander-in-Chief of New Zealand, and others.

Ponsonby had suggested to the Prince of Wales that his mother should be recalled from Corfu, and he agreed. But, fearing to alarm Alix, the message did not suggest great urgency and Alix and Toria even discussed remaining in Venice for a while on their way home. Thankfully, they continued their journey, and at Calais another message from Georgie awaited Alix:

His cough troubles him very much and he has slept very badly the last nights. I cannot disguise the fact that I am anxious about him. . . . I know Laking is writing to you and I will say no more but thank God you are coming home tomorrow to look after him. God bless you, darling Motherdear.

It was the first time that Alix had arrived home without being greeted personally by Bertie at the station. Nor was she to receive the customary welcome from the Household and the Officers of State at the grand entrance to the Palace. Georgie who had met the train with his entire family thoughtfully decided that 'Motherdear' would prefer to go straight to her husband and arranged for her to enter by the garden gate. When she failed to make an appearance at the grand entrance, the entire welcoming party rushed through the Palace in order to intercept her. But the Master of the Household, anticipating this, held them up at the end of a corridor.

Alix and Toria saw that Bertie was in a much worse condition than they had anticipated, and they found it hard to conceal their alarm. Bertie, for his part, tried to make things seem as normal as possible, asking after their journey and telling them that he had ordered the box to be ready for them to go to *La Traviata* at the opera house that evening.

Shortly after they left, Ponsonby was summoned to the King's study. It was at once evident that Bertie intended to carry out his duties until it became impossible any longer to do so. 'I found the King sitting at his writing-table with a rug round his legs, and I was rather shocked at his appearance,' Ponsonby recalled. 'His colour was grey and he appeared to be unable to sit upright and to be sunken.' He was having great difficulty in breathing, as if he had unduly exerted himself. But he managed to control it enough to say that he would sign whatever Ponsonby had for him.

Ponsonby opened the first of the boxes he had brought and handed Bertie a document, which he placed on the desk in front of him. 'They were merely routine submissions, and he signed these one after the other and seemed to like the work.' Ponsonby held back other papers which would call for a discussion, but gave the King some Foreign Office telegrams which he read. He had not missed one since he became King. After this Ponsonby tried to leave, but Bertie wanted to chat. They exchanged a few awkward words about an inspection of Boy Scouts, and then Bertie said, 'in a gasping voice', 'You managed so well at Biarritz. I hope everyone was thanked. Especially the press.'

'I thanked them all, sir,' Ponsonby assured him.

'I feel wretchedly ill,' Bertie confessed. 'I can't sleep. I can't eat. They really must do something for me.'

The King then astonished Ponsonby by remembering that he was to be relieved, his place taken by Arthur Davidson. He turned to Ponsonby and said, 'In case I don't see you again, good-bye.' But Ponsonby did not think that he meant anything more than what he usually said when he went out of waiting.

A few minutes after Ponsonby left the Prince of Wales came in with the draft of a bulletin he considered should be issued before the day was out. His father did not wish anything to be announced, but Georgie persuaded him on the grounds that there was a certain anxiety because he had not met Alix at the station. Bertie was too weak to put up any sort of a fight. He read it, changed a word here and there, and handed it back to his son.

At 7.30 p.m. the bulletin, which included the words 'bronchitis' and 'his condition causes some anxiety', was issued and was published in the last editions of the evening newspapers. The King's congenital bronchitis was so widely known that it led few people to believe that their sovereign was dying.

By the following morning all members of the royal family had arrived at Buckingham Palace, and when the doctors had examined him again it became clear that Bertie was unlikely to survive much longer. Alix came to his bedside as soon as she was dressed and talked to him as if she were unaware that he was close to death. She managed to hold back her tears until she rejoined Georgie and May, and Toria, in an adjoining room. It was a pleasant late spring morning. The tulips in the Palace gardens were at their best and the birds were in full song amongst the trees and shrubs. Inside, the silence of premature mourning prevailed. The lowliest servants knew that their master was dying.

'I went to B.P. at 10.15,' the Prince of Wales wrote in his

diary, 'where I regret to say I found darling Papa much worse, having had a fainting fit. It was indeed a terrible day for us all. We hardly left him. He knew us and talked to us between his attacks up to 4.30.'

After Georgie, Knollys was the King's first visitor that day. He left after a brief conversation, the tears coursing down his cheeks. Thinking of the comfort it would give Bertie, Alix had a message delivered to Alice Keppel asking her to come to the Palace urgently, which she did, remaining alone with him for several minutes. Another later message was telephoned to Brook House for Sir Ernest Cassel asking him to come at eleven o'clock, but by this time Bertie had lapsed into a coma in his chair and Cassel was regretfully asked not to come after all. Almost immediately Bertie regained consciousness. He lit a cigar, decided it tasted awful, and then said he would dress for his old friend, and formally in a frock-coat.

Cassel was again telephoned, was driven at high speed to the Palace and was at once led into Bertie's room. The King was sitting in a chair and for a moment it might have been any of countless calls Cassel had made during their friendship. Bertie even managed to rise from his chair unaided and welcomed him. 'I knew you would not fail me.' Then he asked after the health of Cassel's daughter who, like her mother, suffered from tuberculosis and had just returned with her father from Egypt, where she had been seeking relief in the dry air.

He looked as if he had suffered great pain [Cassel wrote to his daughter], and spoke indistinctly. His kindly smile came out as he congratulated me on having you brought home so much improved in health. He said, 'I am very seedy, but I wanted to see you. Tell your daughter how glad I am that she has safely got home and that I hope she will be careful and patient so as to recover complete health.'*

Sir James Reid had warned Cassel not to tire the patient and he left after a few minutes. He would have agreed with the decision that was made that morning that the King's

---

* She died eighteen months later, and Cassel was prostrate with grief.

horse, Witch of the Air, should not be scratched from the 4.15 Spring Two-Year-Old Plate at Kempton Park.

A light lunch was prepared for Bertie and brought to his room, but he could not face it. Instead, he walked over to the window unaided and chatted to his two caged canaries. Then he suddenly fell unconscious to the floor. The two nurses present called for help, and he was carried back to his chair. Toria summoned Alix, who came into his room shortly after the doctors had again examined him. Bertie was suffering a series of heart attacks, and he was given morphia to deaden the pain and oxygen to ease his breathing.

During intervals of consciousness he expressed the strong wish to remain where he was and not be put to bed. 'No, I shall not give in,' he repeated in a slurred voice. 'I shall go on. I shall work to the end.'

The Archbishop of Canterbury arrived in the afternoon, followed on a more secular level by a telegram with the news that Witch of the Air had won the 4.15 by half a length from the favourite. This was at once conveyed to Bertie, who had just emerged from a long coma. It was also brought in person by Georgie, and his father replied, 'Yes, I have heard of it. I am very glad.'

They were his last coherent words and could hardly have been more appropriate.

As the evening wore on the periods of unconsciousness became longer, and the doctors ordered the nurses to undress him and put him to bed. He lay there, seemingly without pain, visited from time to time by his immediate family. Darkness fell, and Laking's visits to feel his pulse and check his breathing became more frequent. Soon after 11 p.m. he suggested that the Archbishop should attend at the bedside. Randall Davidson, who had been a personal friend of Bertie and Alix for so many years, entered the room with Alix and prayed at the bedside with her. As the three-quarter-hour chimes of Big Ben rang out, Bertie ceased breathing. At midnight a member of the Household walked out of the Privy Purse entrance of the Palace to the waiting crowd at the gates. He said simply, 'The King is dead,' and returned.

A screen was put round his bed after the family had in turn prayed at his side and said farewell. Later that night Georgie, now King George V, wrote in his journal: 'I have lost my best friend and the best of fathers. I never had a [cross] word with him in my life.'

Through her stunned grief, Alix remembered to tell people close to Bertie who were out of London and would wish to hear the news at once, Redesdale, Carrington and Ponsonby among them. Ponsonby received a telephone message soon after midnight to say that Alix would like to see him. He motored up from his country house at once. He went into the King's room with Alix.

The blinds were down and there was a screen round the bed so that at first I could see nothing, but when we came round it I saw the poor King lying apparently asleep. His face looked natural and peaceful and there was no sign of suffering. I was very much awed and hardly liked to speak except in a whisper, but the Queen spoke quite naturally and said how peaceful he looked and that it was a comfort to think he had suffered no pain. . . . She said she felt as if she had been turned into stone, unable to cry, unable to grasp the meaning of it all, and incapable of doing anything.

Alix did, however, feel one almost desperate need, and that was to leave London and go to Sandringham to bury herself in grief amongst the comforting and familiar surroundings. But there was 'this terrible State Funeral and all the dreadful arrangements that had to be made'.

Redesdale received the news by telegram at his home, Batsford Park, Moreton-in-Marsh, and hastened to London the following morning. Later, he was to write:

When the black news came, a deadly pall fell over the country, and there were many . . . who felt that life could never again be quite the same for them. It seemed impossible. To the last his energy was so vivid, the lamp of life's joy burnt so brightly in him, that men could not believe that the grey mystery had extinguished that sunny nature.

Bertie had survived so many health crises since typhoid fever almost forty years earlier that he almost certainly reckoned that he would survive this bronchial attack. Rider

Haggard, dining at Claridge's a few days later, met his old doctor friend Sir Ian Thompson. The novelist wrote in his notebook:

He told me he did not think the K. knew he was dying. No one told him – thought he would pull through as he had often done. When they told him he had better not see people he sd. it 'amused me' and he did not want any 'fuss'. Sir Ian did not think anything in story that he 'worried himself over political situation'. Not that sort of person. Died because his heart was worn out. Had 'warmed both hands before the fire of life.'* Not spiritually troubled in any way but kept 'all the forms'.

Edward VII had been on the throne for less than a sixth of the time of Queen Victoria's reign, but since young manhood in the early 1860s he had been a figure in the land, strong, positive, amiable, with occasional lapses in behaviour it was true, but the more human for that. The mass of the people could identify with him as they had never been able to do with his mother, and that was not only because he was so often among them, appearing so genial and cheerful, raising his hat (always clear of his head), shaking hands, uttering apt remarks for the occasion. As the nation's 'mother', Queen Victoria had been revered. 'Then came King Edward,' as Redesdale wrote, 'and he, without by one jot weakening the spirit of devoted loyalty which the great Queen had called up, added to her diadem the priceless pearls of personal love and affection. She reigned in the gratitude and reason of her people, he in their hearts.'

Tributes poured in from all over Europe and the British Empire, the grief being most widely expressed in France, Italy, Spain, Denmark and Greece. In France 'the shock was great!' Baroness de Stoeckl recalled. 'Not a rumour of his illness had penetrated. . . . All social events ceased; balls, dinners were postponed – Paris really mourned Edward VII.

---

* I strove with none; for none was worth my strife;
 Nature I loved, and, next to Nature, Art;
I warmed both hands before the fire of life;
 It sinks, and I am ready to depart.
  Walter Savage Landor

"Il était un des nôtres. Il aimait la France et la France l'aimait" was heard on all sides.' At home, privately and publicly, people made their feelings known. Lord Morley, the radical politician and statesman who knew Bertie so well, wrote:

The feeling of grief and sense of personal loss throughout the country . . . is extraordinary, and without a single jarring note. It is in one way deeper and keener than when Queen Victoria died nine years ago, and to use the same word over again – more personal. He had just the character that Englishmen, at any rate, thoroughly understand, thoroughly like, and make any quantity of allowance for. It was odd how he managed to combine regal dignity with bonhomie, and strict regard for form with entire absence of spurious pomp.

Two of the King's closest friends and advisers, Lord Esher and Admiral Jackie Fisher, sang their chorus of praise and love for him, recalling anecdotes to illustrate the points they were making. In his *Memories* Fisher wrote:

King Edward, besides his wonderful likeness to King Henry VIII, had that great King's remarkable attributes of combining autocracy with almost a socialistic tie with the masses. I said to His Majesty once: 'Sir, that was a real low form of cunning on your Majesty's part sending to ask after [the socialist] Keir Hardie's stomach ache!' By Jove, he went for me like a mad bull! 'You don't understand me! I am the King of ALL the People! No one has got me in their pockets, as some of them think they have!'

Fisher sent these memories for Esher to read, who replied:

Tears! that was the result of reading what you have to say about King Edward. . . . I have kept many of his letters. They show him to have been one of the 'cleverest' of men. He had never depended upon book-learning – why should he? He read, not books – but men and women – and jolly good reading too!

But he knew everything that it was requisite a King should know – unless Learning prepares a man for action, it is not of much value in this work-a-day world: and no Sovereign since the Tudors was so brave and wise in action as this King!

Your anecdotes of him are splendid. . . . It was a pleasure to be scolded by the King for the sake of the smile you subsequently got.

Ever your,

My beloved Admiral,

ESHER

Countless writers in their biographies of his contemporaries, in volumes of memories and letters, journals and diaries, make reference to him in anecdotes or in comments on his character. Many people remembered first Bertie's cheerfulness. 'I delighted in the merriment of his kind heart,' Disraeli's wife once wrote. Stamper, who spent so much time with him, commented on the nature of his laughter: 'It was good to hear. I wish I could hear it now. Infectious, merry, and honest. . . . It always rang true. . . . Often I have heard his laugh above all others ring through a theatre. It spoke his genuine amusement, and its heartiness was unforgettable.' Along with his cheerfulness, Lillie Langtry remembered his 'affability to servants. . . . It was well known to all who entertained him, for he seldom passed one without a word or a kind look.'

But, 'Yes he could bark,' recalled the diplomat Henry Bruce:

He had little use for persons who were afraid of him. His Suite were serenely unperturbed by his Royal rumblings. . . . He brought with him to Marienbad one of the Royal footmen, called Hawkins. One day at lunch with Hawkins standing stiffly behind the King's chair, a Royal rumbling began, ending with a thunderclap, 'Hawkins, where's the mustard?' Never a move from Hawkins to get the mustard, only the quietly casual answer, 'Straight in front of Your Majesty.' 'Oh yes, thanks.'

Sir James Rennell Rodd referred to his 'Combining a natural dignity of presence with a cordial kindliness which won every heart. He was such a consummate man of the world that he never missed an opportunity of saying and doing the right thing with unerring tact at the right moment.' Philip James, who became Lord James of Hereford as Bertie's Attorney-General, noted in his diary an evening at the opera with President Loubet: 'Between the acts the King came into an ante-room where several cabinet ministers were speaking to Balfour of Burleigh about a motor regulation bill, and he said,

"You are quite right, tax motors – tax the rich, but never tax the poor."' He was as anti-radical as any Tory, being stoutly in favour of inherited titles, but his feeling for the poor was deeply woven into his kindly nature, and he enjoyed nothing more than mixing with the crowds at race meetings. This was the first reason why everyone called him 'a man of the people'.

Bertie's attachment to protocol, to correct dress for the occasion, to medals and orders correctly worn, and to proper respect for rank, and especially for his own rank, was well known. But he equally enjoyed surprising people with an occasional lapse of protocol, which always amused members of his Household. Almeric Fitzroy, Clerk of the Privy Council, wrote in his diary on 12 July 1904:

Pembroke went to Buckingham Palace the other day to enquire when it would be convenient for the King to receive an address, and found the King having his corns cut. The King asked him whether he had got the address with him, and, on being told he had, said, 'Why not present it now?' Pembroke replied that he had not the Lord Steward's wand, which is supposed to be *de rigueur* on such an occasion. 'Oh never mind,' said the King, 'take an umbrella.'

In late November one year, Jackie Fisher was invited to Sandringham for 'one of Blessed Queen Alexandra's birthdays'.

As I was zero in this grand party [Fisher recounted], I slunk off to my room to write an important letter . . . and began unpacking.

I had a boot in each hand; I heard someone fumbling with the door handle and thinking it was the Footman, I said, 'Come in, don't go humbugging with that door handle!' and in walked King Edward, with a cigar about a yard long in his mouth. He said (I with a boot in each hand!), 'What on earth are you doing?'

'Unpacking, Sir.'

'Where's your servant?'

'Haven't got one, Sir.'

'Where is he?'

'Never had one, Sir, couldn't afford it.'

'Put those boots down; sit in that armchair.'

And he went and sat in the other one on the other side of the fire.

I thought to myself, 'This is a rum state of affairs! Here's the King of England sitting in my bedroom on one side of the fire and I'm in my shirt sleeves sitting in an armchair on the other side!'

'Well,' His Majesty said, 'why didn't you come and say "How do you do" when you arrived?'

I said, 'I had a letter to write and with so many great people you were receiving I thought I had better come to my room.'

Then he went on with a long conversation, until it was only about a quarter of an hour from dinner time, and I hadn't unpacked! So I said to the King, 'Sir, you'll be angry if I'm late for dinner, and no doubt your Majesty has two or three gentlemen to dress you but I have none.' And he gave me a sweet smile and went off.

Bertie's skill at speechmaking was famous throughout Europe. Fluent in French and German, he was especially strong in German slang. Esher claimed that

no one ever excelled him in the power of putting in musical cadence and perfectly chosen words sentiments of courteous welcome or graceful acknowledgement. Those who heard King Edward speak on august occasions can never forget the telling quality of his voice or the emotional dignity of his expression and manner.

In private conversation Bertie was less impressive. His anecdotes were always second-hand and he never acquired the self-confidence of the good storyteller. Alice Keppel once told Princess Alice of Athlone, Bertie's niece:

He likes to join in general conversation, interjecting remarks at intervals, but he prefers to listen to others rather than talk himself. Often he starts a discussion, but as soon as he can get others involved in it he is content to listen and make occasional comments.

The stories about Bertie's memory were legion. Even by royal family standards, it was exceptional. He acquired it and developed it almost to a fine art because he was deeply and unremittingly interested in people. They were his first concern in life and his identification and judgment were unblurred by reading novels. Seymour Fortescue wrote that the King

was endowed either by nature or training, or more probably by a mixture of both, with a memory that really was prodigious.

As an example of this memory, I recollect on my first journey to Cannes, when he had got out at some wayside station to stroll about during the five minutes' wait, some very obvious English gentleman

bowed and evidently rather expected to be recognised. . . . The
Prince at once asked me if I knew who the man was. . . . I could
see that the Prince was trying to place the individual, and suddenly
. . . he triumphantly exclaimed: 'I knew that I should get hold of
his name. He is a Mr —, and he was presented to me just fourteen
years ago at a function at which I was present.' He then proceeded
to state what the function was, and where it had taken place. He
had never set eyes on the man since.

Fortescue did not embellish his anecdotes by mentioning
the dog which would inevitably be at Bertie's side and receiving an occasional reassuring pat. Bertie practised a magis-
terial disregard for dog regulations. At Marienbad in 1907
'Clémençeau was chaffing the King about taking Caesar back
to England without submitting him to six months' quarantine,'
Bruce recalled, 'saying that in doing so *Votre Majesté enfreint
les lois d'Angleterre*,'' to which piece of badinage came the
answer, worthy of Louis XIV, *"Mais puisque c'est moi qui les
fait."* '

Caesar and his predecessors, none of them disciplined or
trained, were ever-present living symbols of Bertie's senti-
mentality.

His Majesty never beat Caesar [Stamper remembered]. The dog
and he were devoted to one another, and it was a picture to see
him standing shaking his stick at the dog, when he had done wrong.
'You naughty dog,' he would say very slowly. 'You naughty,
naughty dog.' And Caesar would wag his tail and 'smile' cheerfully
up into his master's eyes, until His Majesty smiled back in spite of
himself.

Caesar could indeed be a bit of a terror, like his master.
Hardinge recalled how he 'always went for my trousers and
worried them, much to the King's delight. I used not to take
the slightest notice and went on talking all the time to the
King, which I think amused His Majesty still more.'

If George Bernard Shaw had been outraged by the unhealthy
delay in burying Queen Victoria, he learned that there had
been no tendency towards haste in the intervening nine years
to Bertie's death. Alix refused to allow his corpse to be
removed, and as late as 16 May, ten days after he had

expired, she was still taking friends to his bedside for prayers and a last look at him.

Then on 17 May Alix reluctantly authorised the removal of her husband's body to Westminster Hall. It is not recorded who conceived the innovative idea of the body lying in state to permit his people to pay their last respects, but it was probably Knollys or Esher. For three days the body lay there, guarded by members of the King's Company, alternating with the Gentlemen-at-Arms, while the queues of his subjects grew longer over the days and nights, stretching far down the Embankment.

As relations and sovereigns arrived from abroad for the funeral, they were taken to the Hall and the queue was halted while they knelt in prayer and paid their last respects. Never had there been so many Kings in London at one time, including the Emperor of Germany and the Kings of Portugal and Spain, Norway and Bulgaria, Denmark and Belgium.

Alix now fretted at the delay to the funeral and the departure of the guests which would follow it. She was comforted by the presence of Minnie, who was one of the first to arrive and the last to leave weeks later. Not everyone welcomed the Dowager Empress of Russia, however. She was inclined to be bossy and did not treat the staff at Buckingham Palace, or Alix's Household even, with the same easy-going friendliness to which they were accustomed. In Russia servants were servants and 'please' or 'thank you' were not bothered with.

Talking over the arrangements laid down for the funeral, Minnie was shocked to see that the new Queen Mary took precedence over the widowed Queen Consort. This was not at all the case in Russia, and she pressed Alix so hard to have the arrangement reversed that she did so, to the consternation of everyone else. But Queen Mary herself, though surprised, accepted the situation. She judged, correctly, that her mother-in-law was not going to enjoy the loss of privilege and precedence which applied with her reduced rank.

During these tiresome and stressful days between the King's death and his funeral, everyone at Buckingham Palace was saddened and touched by the sight of Caesar restlessly haunting the corridors in puzzled search for his master. He was a favourite with the kitchen staff, whose quarters he visited from time to time for snacks when his master was away, but never much approved of the dog-loving Alix. However, it was to her he turned as friend and companion as the days passed without sight of his beloved master. And it was thanks to Alix that Caesar walked immediately behind the King's coffin, led by a Highland servant, in the funeral procession from Westminster to Paddington.

The pageant was a magnificent one:

The streets . . . were rich in purple; venetian masts wreathed in laurel leaves bordered the funeral route. Houses, hotels, clubs and shops in the vicinity were fringed with purple or white. At Paddington even the girders and pillars of the platform were draped in funeral colours. . . . Immediately behind Caesar rode a cavalcade such as rarely if ever had been seen before or since. . . . Blazing with orders, resplendent in the scarlet and gold and blue and silver of military uniforms, came the kings and a vast number of princes and nobles.

It was more than forty-seven years since Alix, her fresh beauty shining through her veil, had entered St George's Chapel to marry Bertie. Now, with her only surviving son holding her arm, no one could see behind the black veil the tears for her husband, and equally for her first son who was now joined in the vault by his father.

The following day, Alix wrote to Georgie:

How can I thank you for what you were to me yesterday on that truly as you say terrible day! When we laid your blessed Papa to rest. I really do not know *how* I should have borne that fearful ordeal without you by my side. You were indeed my *only* consolation here on earth and your kind and affectionate support helped me through it. God was indeed merciful to me in the midst of such grief, such deep-felt sorrow and pain, to allow me to keep *one* of my darling sons, who now indeed has shown me more than ever his blessed loving and affectionate heart. *Thank* you again and again for all you have ever done and are to your poor old Motherdear.

The element of spoilt selfishness which had always lurked in Alix's nature began to manifest itself more strongly with Bertie's death. She had never suffered from an over-strong imagination and had not given much thought to how her life would be affected by widowhood beyond the grief she would inevitably feel for her loss. Particularly at first, Alix's position was a difficult one, and it was not helped by the continuing presence of her sister. Minnie remained a typical product of the Russian imperial tradition, extremely rank-conscious, full of hauteur and determined to see that Alix stood up for her rights.

There were difficulties over jewellery, over the ownership of Bertie's Garter and the diamond crown worn by Alix at the opening of Parliament. Which of these belonged to the royal family and which to Alix personally was a subject of discreet dispute. Bertie's will was not clear about that. However, it was quite clear about Sandringham, which was to remain Alix's for her lifetime, although she was expected to quit Buckingham Palace and return to Marlborough House, something she was as disinclined to do as earlier she had shown herself unwilling to make the reverse transfer.

In all these and many more petty disputes Minnie was provocative in her support for her sister. The new King and Queen remained tactfully silent, but others in the Household were outraged and were known to express their feelings. The Grand Duchess Augusta, for example, in answer to a letter of complaint from Queen Mary referring to the disruptive Dowager Empress, wrote to her on 24 May 1910: 'I understand every word, expressed or not, and have feared what you so justly allude to. May the pernicious influence soon depart, *then* I hope all will come right.'

The Sandringham dispute, however, could not be described as petty and aroused much resentment. The idea that Alix, Toria and their modest Household should occupy capacious Sandringham, while the new King and Queen, their six children and enormous Household should be confined to the cramped premises of York Cottage seemed ridiculous. On the other hand, George V could easily have bought some other property as his country home. But Georgie hated all change and loved the 'cottage' which had been his since he had married May. And, after all, it was his father who had laid down that his mother should remain in possession of the big house. When it was reported to him that one of his equerries had actually complained to Toria about the discomforts of life at York Cottage, Georgie whipped round on the unfortunate man and demanded to know what the devil it had to do with him.

Lady Cynthia Colville explained Alix's decision to remain at Sandringham in two ways:

The fact that it never occurred to Queen Alexandra to hand over the 'big house' to the King was no doubt partly due to her feeling that Sandringham had been bought and built by King Edward VII as his own private country house, quite distinct from the palaces which belonged to the Crown. It was also partly because she could never quite bring herself to look upon her son and daughter-in-law as the King and Queen.

Alix was certainly thankful that Georgie had determined to remain at York Cottage, which was only a few minutes away from Sandringham's big house and her grandchildren could come unescorted to play. This is what she enjoyed most in her early years of widowhood. Like her own life, Sandringham could never be the same again. It, too, had lost its heart, although Alix did her best to show interest in the gardens which she had always loved. Georgie's shooting parties, on a small scale compared to the golden years of Bertie's domain, were like sad echoes of the past.

By December 1910 Alix had at last been eased out of Buckingham Palace back to Marlborough House.

When the day arrived for her departure [Baroness de Stoeckl remembered], every servant to the last scullery maid stood in the hall as her Majesty slowly descended the great staircase looking so beautiful in her widow's weeds. . . . She said that the only sound was the weeping of the servants – she herself was in tears. She shook hands with each one in turn. She wanted to say a few words of regret at leaving them but her voice was too choked with sobs. When she had shaken the last hand the front doors slowly opened – the car stood ready to take her away. So she turned to the crowd of retainers and bowing her head made the lovely gesture of farewell which was so graceful and in a way her very own.

At Marlborough House it was as if Bertie had been dead for nearly ten years instead of little more than half a year.

She had the house redecorated and there was much new furniture, but the ghost still haunted the rooms and corridors, and when men who smoked cigars or old friends like Esher, Carrington or Jackie Fisher visited her, the memory of Bertie became more poignant still.

'It is all dreadfully sad coming back now in this forever beloved house,' Alix wrote to Princess Louis of Battenberg, 'now so sad and desolate without my beloved Bertie. I miss him more and more. . . .'

Back at Sandringham, where Bertie's quarters were left untouched, just as they had been when he was there on the last week-end of his life, Alix's life revolved around her inner circle. There was, as always, her beloved Toria, loyal and willing and sweet-natured as ever, but borne down with hypochondria and lamentation at her own wasted life. Of equal permanence, reliability and fidelity was Charlotte Knollys, still her Woman of the Bedchamber – 'the inevitable Charlotte'.

Charlotte and Alix were mutually indispensable and of equal influence one on the other. The loyalty was indestructible, and Charlotte gave herself entirely to Alix's service, for as long as sixteen hours a day. She never had, nor wanted, a holiday and days off were extremely rare. If one was ill, the other became nurse. At Abergeldie in 1877 when Charlotte was laid low by typhoid, Alix nursed her through every day, cancelling her return to London and all her engagements. Once at Sandringham when fire broke out, it was Charlotte who ran to Alix's room, woke her up, wrapped a dressing-gown round her and hastened her along smoke-filled corridors. They had not a secret from one another.

The third figure in the trio upon whom Alix utterly depended on the death of Bertie was Sir Dighton Probyn. She had known and loved this gallant seventy-seven-year-old soldier since he had become an essential figure in Bertie's Household. When Bertie died, he was looking forward to a rest from being Comptroller, but at once answered Alix's call to arms and took over those responsibilities again. They were not light, either, for Alix was as extravagant and uncaring about money as ever. He managed to retain some sort of control by a mixture of teasing and cajoling, and affection never cooled between the unremitting crises caused usually by Alix giving large sums of money to one of her favourite charities or some importunate individual.

At first glance Alix appeared to be a rich widow. Her Civil List was £70,000 and she received a life interest in £200,000 she inherited from Bertie. Much of the upkeep of Marlborough House and Sandringham was paid for by Georgie. On the other hand, unlike her son, she was subject to the full rigour of taxation, including death duties, and as the war continued the rate of tax rose alarmingly. Georgie was eventually persuaded to grant her a private allowance of £10,000 a year. A final concession to Alix was the relief of the obligation to pay tax when it was pointed out how anomalous it was for her children, and all other direct descendants of Queen Victoria, to pay no tax while she was treated as an ordinary citizen.

Alix scarcely noted these increases and concessions, but they provided a great relief to old Probyn, who was still struggling away trying to balance the books when he was in his late eighties.

Alix was feeling too seedy, run down and miserable to attend Georgie and May's Coronation. From Sandringham, where she had Minnie staying with her, she wrote to her son:

On the eve of your Coronation, the most sacred day of your life, I must send you a mother's blessing and pray God to guard and protect you in his Holy Keeping till your life's end. May He guide you in the difficult path which you have to tread and make you a blessing to our beloved country as your beloved Father and Grandmother were before you. . . . You will feel and know that *both* our spirits are hovering near you. May God bless you both, and give a little thought to your poor sad and broken-hearted Motherdear.

When Georgie and May left for India to be crowned Emperor and Empress at the great Durbar ceremony, once again Alix envied them their experience but gained consolation from looking after their children. She had a particularly soft spot for their second son, George (another Bertie), who was very vulnerable, sensitive and subject to stuttering. But it was the youngest, John, whom she cosseted most closely because of his need for tender care and the sweetness of his nature. It was long since clear that he would never mature mentally, and his epileptic fits were alarming to deal with. Johnnie was 'the dear and precious little boy' to her. Later, it was thought better that he should be segregated from the rest of the family, and he died peacefully in his sleep at the age of thirteen on 18 January 1919. At his burial, Alix's mind went back inevitably to her own infant son, also buried in the Sandringham churchyard. 'Now our two darling Johnnies lie side by side,' she wrote to May.

On the outbreak of war in August 1914 Alix was at Buckingham Palace and among those members of the royal family who waited for Big Ben to strike eleven o'clock before stepping on to the balcony. The multitude below, silent until that moment, burst into cheers and sang patriotic songs. Her hatred of the Kaiser reached new heights, and there was a note of self-satisfaction in her voice as she exclaimed to everyone, when she could be heard, 'I always told you *he was a bad MAN*. Now perhaps you'll believe me.'

Alix's jingoism was echoed by many British people, but it rebounded against her when Prince Louis of Battenberg, First Sea Lord, was forced to resign in the face of national anti-German hysteria. Like Bertie, she was fond of this able and agreeable member of the royal family and his wife (also German-born) for many years.

She was overjoyed, however, when he was replaced by the ageing Jackie Fisher, who had resigned shortly before Bertie's death. She followed his new and even more turbulent career at the Admiralty with Winston Churchill, whom she loathed. As in peacetime, she continued to follow world events in personal terms.

Alix congratulated Fisher on his appointment at the Ritz Hotel. 'Queen Alexandra and Princess Victoria simply heavenly to me,' he wrote to Lord Ranksborough,* 'and they

---

* Major-General, Extra Equerry to Alix from 1910.

both looked quite lovely! I wish I could have married them both!'

On the night of 20–21 January 1915 Zeppelins attacked British soil for the first time, killing or injuring twenty-two men, women and children in towns close to Sandringham. Alix wrote a letter of appeal to Fisher:

This is too bad, those beasts actually went straight to Sandringham, I suppose in the hopes of exterminating us with their Zeppelin bombs – though, thank God, they failed this time! But they killed as usual* a lot of poor innocent women and children of King's Lynn, I am sorry to say.

Please let me have a lot of *rockets* with spikes or hooks on to defend our Norfolk coast. I am sure you could invent something of the sort which might bring down a few of those rascals. . . .

One of those 'rascals' was shot down in a later raid,† when several Zeppelins ranged along the north coast of Norfolk. It was Alix's last, and alarming, direct experience of war, which she described to Georgie:

We have been living through some gruesome moments here – just a fortnight ago we had those beastly Zepps over us. At 10 o'clock that Saturday evening they began. We were all sitting upstairs in Victoria's room when we were suddenly startled by an awful noise! and lo and behold, there was the awful monster over our heads. Everybody rushed up and wanted us to go downstairs. I must confess I was not a bit afraid – but it was a most uncanny feeling – poor Victoria was quite white in the face and horror-struck – but we all wanted to see it – the house was pitch dark and at last Charlotte [Knollys] and I stumbled down in the darkness and found Colonel Davidson and Hawkins scrambling about outside so I also went out, but saw nothing and for the time the Zepps had flown off somewhere but came back about four o'clock in the night and dropped bombs all over the place!!

Within a few months Alix was appalled at the ever widening rift between Churchill and Fisher over the Dardanelles crisis,

---

* This refers to earlier bombardments of coastal towns by German warships.
† Sixteen Zeppelins were airborne, the biggest raid of the war so far, on the night of 2–3 September 1916. It was an almost total failure. One was shot down spectacularly by Lieutenant W. L. Robinson in a B.E.2c using for the first time new explosive and incendiary ammunition.

and was boiling with wrath over Churchill's stance which was driving Fisher to resignation. 'Stick to your post like *Nelson!*' she appealed to him unsuccessfully. 'The nation and we all have full confidence in you and *I* and they will not suffer you to go, but you are the nation's hope and we trust you! Think of Tirpitz and his Devils how they will rejoice!!! All I say is *stick* to your *post* and God will help us all.'

On 21 July 1918, on learning of the death of Fisher's wife, Alix wrote: 'My beloved Admiral Fisher! No words of mine can possibly describe how deeply I feel for you. I sympathise with you in your terribly sad and irreparable loss. . . .'

Jackie Fisher's death followed two years later, just one more of the contemporaries and friends old ladies mourn. Alix was fortunate not to lose any of her own immediate family during the war. Of her grandsons young Bertie took part in the Battle of Jutland and David was several times in danger on the Western Front. But she saw enough of the depredations the war caused among the thousands she visited in hospitals. This became her war work. From long practice and a natural talent for relating to the sick and wounded, she gave untold comfort. But to the hospital authorities she became a notorious trial, unpunctual in her arrival, unpredictable in her progress (often stopping at every bed when the timetable called for perhaps two or three and smiles for the others), and eccentric in her behaviour.

Shortly before the outbreak of war and on the fortieth anniversary of her arrival from Denmark, Alix had instituted her best-known charity, and the prototype of its kind, Queen Alexandra's Rose Day. At first she was very proud of it, touring the streets and chatting encouragingly to as many as she could of the two thousand or so sellers of the flags in London alone and many thousands more up and down the country. But after a few years she tired of 'that horrible Rose Day drive'.

The Great War brought out the best and worst in Alix. Her profligacy continued unabated throughout, and she turned a deaf ear (literally) to all appeals for economy and completely disregarded rationing rules, including the use of petrol. Her horses and dogs, many of them uncomfortably old, were fed just as before, which put an unreasonable strain on food stocks and on the few staff remaining who had to look after them. Sir Dighton Probyn did succeed in having a few of the most aged horses destroyed, but not a dog was touched. Marlborough House and Sandringham were as richly decorated with flowers as ever, the cost of these running to several thousand pounds a year.

To set against this, not only was Alix tireless in visiting the sick and wounded, in spite of advancing years and poor health, but she kept up a steady flow of letters of encouragement to those running the war. Besides Fisher and other commanders, she wrote letters of congratulation to her old friend Douglas Haig (the C-in-C in France from December 1915) and his wife. It had always been the same: Alix's spoilt selfishness was more than balanced by her charm and kindness and the happiness she brought into so many people's lives.

The setbacks, disappointments and catastrophes of the war at sea and in France, the appalling casualties of the Somme, the ever-growing threat of the U-boat, provided the grey backdrop to the personal blows which Alix suffered. 'Dear, poor Georgie' had a serious fall from his horse while inspecting troops in France and was in great pain for months. Then, after hearing in advance of the proposed visit to Russia of her old friend Lord Kitchener, and warning Georgie of the dangers, his loss at sea was 'fearful news' to her, according to Probyn. (It certainly was to the rest of the country.)

Worse news by far began to trickle out of Russia in March 1917. At first it was hoped that the assassination of the 'holy man', Rasputin, might have helped the cause of the Tsar; but rioting broke out on the streets of the big cities by a people disillusioned with the war, short of food and in search of a scapegoat. Of Rasputin's death, Alix wrote to Georgie: 'The wretched Russian monk caused a tremendous sensation in the world but [is] only regretted by poor dear Alicky [the Tsarina] who might have ruined the whole future of Russia through his influence.' But it was too late. The ruin had already been created. On 15 March 1917 the Tsar abdicated, and after a short interval he and his family were taken away, eventually to Ekaterinburg in the Urals.

On 22 March Minnie escaped with some of her family and her Household to the Crimea, which was not yet under Bolshevik control. For month after month there was no communication and Alix remained in a fever of anxiety about her sister. 'I can hear *nothing* and they are quite cut off from the world and alone in their misery and despair. God help them all,' Alix exclaimed to her son.

On 5 September 1918 she received a letter from Georgie, not about Minnie but about the fate of the Tsar and his family. The rumours had been proved true. They had all been assassinated, including the four beautiful daughters and the little Tsarevitch, on 16 July.

What hope now was there for Minnie? Alix asked herself again and again. The war had been won two months after the news about the mass murder at Ekaterinburg had reached London. Now 'Hang the Kaiser!' was heard in the land, and such an end for Bertie's hated nephew would have given Alix great satisfaction. But wiser counsels prevailed.

Alix's health as well as her mind were beginning to give way. Her daughter-in-law May noted 'a great change in her, she looks so frail, and the deafness is awful'. Even the near-miraculous reappearance of Minnie failed to lift Alix from the half-world to which she seemed to have surrendered herself. The Dowager Empress, with her daughter Grand Duchess Olga and her sons, had been rescued from Yalta by a British cruiser.

The despatch of the cruiser was at George V's insistence. He had earlier argued strongly and at length successfully against receiving the Tsar and his family – a decision about which he and May would feel guilty for the remainder of their lives. The King was fearful of bringing the British monarchy into disrepute if he had encouraged giving sanctuary to his cousin, whose reputation for ruthlessness and tyranny had, if anything, increased with the war and the surrender of the Russian armies. But he reckoned on salvaging something of his conscience, without risking odium, by insisting upon the rescue of this old lady, her daughter and grandsons.

On 9 May 1919 the battleship *Lord Nelson* arrived at Portsmouth with the Russian family as honoured passengers. Alix was piped on-board with Toria to welcome her sister with her daughter. The reunion made an historic and touching scene, but Alix was described as 'very calm' by contrast with Minnie's excitement. The reality was that even the sight of her sister failed to draw her out of her shell of deafness and the confusion of her brain.

Minnie stayed for a while at Sandringham, but found the proximity of a silent and deaf sister increasingly irksome. With tact and generosity (and the further alleviation of his conscience) King George offered her a Windsor residence of her own, Frogmore House, together with a grant of £10,000 a year (£450,000 in today's money).

Later, Minnie returned to Denmark, although life there was as dull and purposeless as at Windsor. In her boredom, she engaged in petty campaigns against her brother the King. Although since leaving Russia she had been living on charitable allowances from the Kings of England and Denmark, like her sister she made no attempt to modify her extravagant ways. She lived in a wing of the royal palace, and King Christian was constantly irritated by her profligacy, especially her excessive use of electricity. One evening he sent a messenger to ask her to turn off some of the lights. She responded by switching on all the lights in every room, ordering them to burn all night. Shortly after this incident, she was asked to remove herself to Hvidöre, where she lived for the remainder of her life.

From time to time Minnie visited Alix at Sandringham, her sister now being unable to travel. These one-time Queen-Empresses made a sorry sight together: now no longer beautiful ('ugly old woman' Alix would say of herself), in their late seventies, and having lived for almost all their lives in pampered luxury, they would grumble about their penury in a loud voice to make the other hear.

Alix expressed her outrage that the royal yacht named after her had been scrapped, that the Ninth Hussars to whom she was Colonel-in-Chief had been disbanded, and that Georgie had refused to intervene on behalf of their nephew, ex-King Constantine of Greece, 'poor, excellent, *honest* Tino', a much-reviled figure in Britain and elsewhere.

Georgie, though noted for his short fuse, was endlessly patient with his 'Motherdear', and her grandchildren visited her more often than they would have chosen to do, especially the two eldest boys, David and Bertie. Of David she once wrote: 'May God grant him a perfect wife!', a wish that was unfulfilled in her own lifetime, or later for that matter. But she was delighted when Bertie told her of his engagement to Lady Elizabeth Bowes-Lyon,* and she recalled for him her own proposal day. Bertie had written to her from Laeken, where her betrothal had taken place: 'We were walking together in the pretty garden following my mother and the late Queen of the Belgians when he suddenly proposed to me! My surprise was great and I accepted him with *greatest* delight!'

In 1925 she was eighty years old, confused, half-blind, totally deaf and no longer with any pleasure left in her life. Aircraftsman J. H. Ross RAF (T. E. Lawrence) was summoned to her presence in the year she died and wrote a few tender-cruel words about the meeting:

. . . I saw the mummied thing, the red-rimmed eyes, the enamelled face, with the famous smile scissored across all angular and heart-rending: then I nearly ran away in pity. The body should not be kept alive after the lamp of sense has gone out. There were the ghosts of all her lovely airs, the little graces, the once-effective sway and movement of the figure which had been her consolation. . . .

Alix died of a heart attack on 20 November. Georgie and May were at her bedside, but there was no time for anyone else to reach her before – painlessly like Bertie – she ceased to breathe.

Tactfully *The Times* obituary the following day gave special

---

* The present Queen Elizabeth the Queen Mother, who inherited from Queen Mary (a purchaser of some of Minnie's jewellery sold after her death) a spectacular diamond necklace and tiara. It is often worn by Queen Elizabeth II today.

emphasis to her reception, and her beauty, when she first arrived in England sixty-two years earlier and Tennyson

gave utterance to the feelings of the whole country that –

> Saxon or Norman or Dane are we,
> But all of us Danes in our welcome of
> thee!

When the Princess was first seen on board the Royal Yacht at Gravesend she was dressed in white, her colour heightened as if by nervous excitement, but with a frank display of wondering pleasure at her reception. . . .

The Times, in this immensely long and moving obituary, later quoted a man of letters who had been present at the wedding ceremony, Charles Dickens:

The Princess's face was very pale and full of a sort of awe and wonder. It was the face of no ordinary bride, not simply a timid, shrinking girl, but one with a distinctive character of her own, pre- pared to act a part greatly.

Dickens had died when Alix was only twenty-five, but that was old enough for him already to have recognised the truth of what he had written, while Bertie's 'sheer joy in the Prin- cess's beauty' was to endure for his lifetime.

Chief Ranks in the Royal Household
IN THE LIFETIMES OF KING EDWARD VII AND
QUEEN ALEXANDRA

LORD CHAMBERLAIN: Responsible for Court ceremonies and also for the running of the Household 'above stairs'. His department included all those such as grooms-in-waiting, gentlemen ushers and pages, who were in attendance at the functions and ceremonies of the Court. His department was also responsible for the furniture and furnishings of the palaces, and included the craftsmen who tended these, the Surveyor of the King's Pictures and works of art, and the Librarian. The Lord Chamberlain did not organise Coronations or state funerals, but did organise other royal funerals (the state funerals being reserved for the sovereign and national figures to whom they are accorded).

GROOM OF THE STOLE: Abolished by the time Bertie became King.

GROOM-IN-WAITING: Gentlemen in attendance on the King on a rota system of 'waits'. He had about seven, with four extra grooms-in-waiting.

GROOM OF THE GREAT CHAMBER: Gentlemen in the Lord Chamberlain's Department, the appointments sometimes in conjunction with others: e.g. the King's Piper was also a Groom of the Great Chamber. As such, they were occasionally called on to attend at the Palace for drawing-rooms and levees, but most of their duties were in the other capacity.

LORD STEWARD: Head of the 'below stairs' part of the King's Household, but the day-to-day supervision was delegated to the Master of the Household.

MASTER OF THE HOUSEHOLD: Supervisor of the entire domestic establishment with the responsibility for the domestic arrangements, the staff, the catering and official entertaining at all the royal palaces and royal yachts.

MASTER OF THE HORSE: Responsible for the general administration of the royal stables, including horses, carriages, and latterly motor-cars of the official residences.

PRIVATE SECRETARY: The most intimate official to the sovereign, who was normally privy to all that occurred, offering guidance and advice when required.

KEEPER OF HIS MAJESTY'S PRIVY PURSE: The controller of royal accounts, who determined the propriety of expenditure.

EQUERRY: The equerries were members of the department of the Master of the Horse and, as such, were in constant attendance on the King in rotation, with particular responsibility for seeing that arrangements were made to get the King to and from his engagements, whether by car or by carriage.

MISTRESS OF THE ROBES: The senior lady of the Queen's Household, who organised the rota of the ladies-in-waiting.

LADIES-IN-WAITING: The general title for the three grades of ladies: Ladies of the Bedchamber, who were wives of peers; Women of the Bedchamber, who were ladies of 'good' family but not peeresses; and Maids of Honour, who were unmarried daughters or grand-daughters of peers. They attended the Queen and usually one of each grade would be on duty, although this was variable.

Select Bibliography

Airlie, Mabell Countess of, *Thatched with Gold* (1962)

Allfrey, A., *Edward VII & His Jewish Court* (1991)

Arthur, Sir George, *Queen Alexandra* (1934)

—— *Concerning Queen Victoria & Her Son* (1943)

Asquith, Margot, *The Autobiography of . . .* (1962)

Bailey, J. (ed.), *The Diary of Lady Frederick Cavendish* (1927)

Balsan, Consuelo Vanderbilt, *The Glitter & the Gold* (1953)

Battiscombe, Georgina, *Queen Alexandra* (1969)

Bennett, Daphne, *Vicky: Princess Royal of England & German Empress* (1971)

Benson, E. F., *As We Were* (1930)

—— *King Edward VII: An Appreciation* (1933)

Bing, E. J. (ed.), *The Letters of Tsar Nicholas II & Empress Marie* (1937)

Blunden, Margaret, *The Countess of Warwick* (1967)

Broadley, A. M., *Boyhood of a Great King* (1906)

Bruce, H. J., *Silken Dalliance* (1946)

Bunsen, C., *Memoirs* (1868)

Churchill, R. S., *Winston Spencer Churchill: Vol I Youth (1874–1900)* (1966)

—— *Vol II Young Statesman (1901–14)* (1967)

—— *Companion* vols I and II (1967–9)

Cornwallis-West, G., *Edwardian Hey-Days* (1930)

Cowles, Virginia, *Edward VII & His Circle* (1956)

Cust, Lionel, *King Edward VIII & His Court* (1930)

Dicey, Sir E., & others, *King Edward VII, Biographical & Personal Sketches with Anecdotes* (1910)

Drew, M., *Catherine Gladstone* (1919)

Duff, David, *Alexandra: Princess & Queen* (1980)

Eckardstein, Baron von, *Ten Years at the Court of St James* (1921)

Ensor, R. C. K., *England 1870–1914* (1936)

Erskine, Mrs Stuart, *Memoirs of Edward, Earl of Sandwich (1839–1916)* (1919)

Esher (Brett), Reginald Viscount, *The Influence of King Edward* (1915)

—— *Cloud Capp'd Towers* (1927)

—— *Journals & Letters*, 4 vols (1934–8)

Fisher, Admiral Lord, *Memories* (1919)

—— *Records* (1919)

Fitzroy, Sir Almeric, *Memoirs*, 2 vols (1925)

Fulford, Roger (ed.), *Dearest Child: The Private Correspondence of Queen Victoria and the Crown Princess of Prussia 1858–61* (1964)

—— *Dearest Mama (1861–4)* (1968)

—— *Your Dear Letter (1865–71)* (1971)

—— *Darling Child (1871–8)* (1976)

—— *Beloved Mama (1878–85)* (1981)

Gibbs, F. W., 'The Education of a Prince (1851–6)', *Cornhill Magazine*, no. 986, pp. 105–19

Gore, John, *King George V: A Personal Memoir* (1941)

Greville, Charles C. F., *Memoirs (1814–60)*, 8 vols (1938)

Grey of Fallodon, Viscount, *Twenty-Five Years 1892–1916*, 2 vols (1925)

Guedalla, P., *The Queen & Mr Gladstone* (1933)

Hardinge of Penshurst, Lord, *Old Diplomacy* (1947)

Hibbert, C., *Edward VII: A Portrait* (1976)

Holmes, Sir Richard (ed.), *Edward VII: His Life & Times*, 2 vols (1910)

Hough, Richard, *First Sea Lord: Admiral Fisher* (1969)

—— *Louis & Victoria: The First Mountbattens* (1974)

Kennedy, A. L. (ed.), *My Dear Duchess* (1956)

Keppel, Sonia, *Edwardian Daughter* (1958)

Langtry, Lillie, *The Days I Knew* (1925)

Lee, Sir Sydney, *King Edward VII: A Biography*, 2 vols (1925–7)

Leslie, Anita, *Edwardians in Love* (1972)

Longford, Elizabeth, *Victoria R. I.* (1964)

—— (ed.), *Darling Loosy: Letters to Princess Louise 1856–1939* (1991)

Lyttelton, *Letters from Sarah, Lady (1797–1870)* (1912)

Madol, H. R., *The Private Life of Queen Alexandra* (1940)

Magnus, Philip, *King Edward VII* (1964)

Marder, Arthur (ed.), *Fear God & Dread Nought: The*

Correspondence of Admiral of the Fleet Lord Fisher of Kilverstone, 3 vols (1952–9)

Marie Louise, Princess, *My Memories of Six Reigns* (1956)

Maurice, F., *Haldane (1856–1915)*, 2 vols (1937)

Maurois, A., *King Edward & His Time* (1933)

Moneypenny, W. F., and Buckle, G. E., *The Life of Benjamin Disraeli, Earl of Beaconsfield*, 5 vols (1910)

Nicolson, Harold, *King George V: His Life & Reign* (1952)

Noel, Gerard, *Princess Alice* (1974)

Pearson, C. Arthur, *The Private Life of Edward VII* (1912)

Pless, Daisy Princess of, *From My Private Diary* (1931)

Ponsonby, Arthur, *Henry Ponsonby: Queen Victoria's Private Secretary: His Life from His Letters* (1942)

Ponsonby, Sir F., *Recollections of Three Reigns* (1957)

Pope-Hennessy, James, *Queen Mary* (1959)

Pound, Dudley, *Albert* (1973)

Private Life of the King by One of His Majesty's Servants (1901)

Redesdale, Lord, *King Edward VII: A Memory* (1915)

—— *Memories*, 2 vols (1915)

Rhodes James, R., *Albert, Prince Consort* (1983)

Robey, Kinley, *The King, the Press and the People* (1975)

Rose, Kenneth, *King George V* (1983)

St Aubyn, Giles, *Edward VII, Prince & King* (1979)

Sermonetta, Duchess of, *Things Past* (1929)

Spender, J. A., *The Life of Sir Henry Campbell-Bannerman* (1923)

Stafford, Earl of, *Memoirs* (1919)

Stamper, C. W., *What I Know* (1913)

Stanley, The Letters of Lady Augusta, 2 vols (1927–9)

Sykes, Christopher, *Four Studies in Loyalty* (1946)

Victoria, Queen, *The Letters of Queen Victoria*, 9 vols (1907–30)

Warwick, Frances Countess of, *Life's Ebb & Flow* (1929)

—— *Afterthoughts* (1931)

Watson, A. E. T., *King Edward as a Sportsman* (1911)

Westminster, Loelia Duchess of, *Grace and Favour* (1961)

Woodham-Smith, Cecil, *Queen Victoria: Her Life & Times* (1972)

Wortham, H. E., *Edward VII: Man & King* (1931)

Source References

('q' = quoted from)
(RA = Royal Archives, Windsor)

1: The Arrival
Page 4 line 10 Sir Frederick
Ponsonby, *Recollections of
Three Reigns* (1957),
pp. 148–9
*Page 4 line 34 Illustrated
London News*, 14 March
1863
Page 5 line 39 Lady Mary
Meynell, *Sunshine &
Shadows* (1933), p. 9

2: A Serene Childhood
*Page 8 line 3 Illustrated
London News*, 7 March 1983
Page 8 line 11 W. Glyn
Jones, *Denmark* (1970), p. 64
Page 8 line 36 Hans Roger
Madol, *Christian IX* (1939),
p. 35
Page 9 line 19 Roger Fulford
(ed.), *Dearest Child: The
Private Correspondence of
Queen Victoria and the
Crown Princess of Prussia
1858–61* (1964), p. 350
Page 10 line 25 Peter
Carew, *Combat & Carnival*
(1954), pp. 147–8

Page 12 line 12 W. F.
Moneypenny and G. E.
Buckle, *The Life of Benjamin
Disraeli, Earl of
Beaconsfield*, 4 vols (1910),
IV, p. 390
Page 12 line 16 Lord Esher,
Cloud Capp'd Towers
(1927), p. 163
Page 12 line 18 Ibid., p. 43
*Page 12 line 20 The Diaries
of Lady Frederick
Cavendish*, 2 vols (1927), II,
p. 145
*Page 12 line 25 The Letters of
Lady Augusta Stanley*, 2 vols
(1927–9), I, p. 72
Page 13 line 7 Georgina
Battiscombe, *Queen
Alexandra* (1969), p. 13
3: A Difficult Upbringing
Page 15 line 1 Esher, *op. cit.*,
p. 158
Page 15 line 17 Queen
Victoria's *Journal*, 20 June
1837
Page 16 line 37 Elizabeth
Longford, *Victoria R. I.*
(1964), p. 125

Page 16 line 38 Queen Victoria's *Journal*, 11–14 October 1839

Page 17 line 30 Prince Albert to his father, 12 October 1839, RA Add. MSS 14/84

Page 19 line 36 E. Stockmar, *Baron Stockmar* (1872), pp. 331–2

Page 20 line 8 Lytton Strachey, *Queen Victoria* (1921), p. 87

Page 20 line 30 *The Letters of Queen Victoria*, three series each of three volumes (1907–30), Series I, vol. I, p. 199

Page 21 line 23 Queen Victoria's *Journal*, 19 September 1838

Page 23 line 32 Queen Victoria's *Letters*, 4 September 1841

Page 25 line 25 A. M. Broadley, *Boyhood of a Great King* (1906), p. 92

Page 27 line 21 Daphne Bennett, *Vicky: Princess Royal of England & German Empress* (1971), p. 25

Page 28 line 17 M. Drew, *Catherine Gladstone* (1919), pp. 66, 51

Page 28 line 21 Sir Sydney Lee, *King Edward VII: A Biography*, 2 vols (1925–7), I, p. 13

Page 28 line 23 Betty Askwith, *The Lytteltons* (1975), p. 83

Page 30 line 30 Lord Esher, *The Influence of King Edward* (1915), p. 23

Page 31 line 7 Giles St Aubyn, *Edward VII: Prince & King* (1979), pp. 24–5

Page 31 line 15 Carrington diary, July 1855, Lincolnshire Papers, MS film 1120, Bodleian Library

Page 32 line 26 q Christopher Hibbert, *Edward VII: A Portrait* (1976), p. 13, Gibbs' diary

Page 32 line 31 q Philip Magnus, *King Edward VII* (1964), paperback edn (1967), p. 26, Gibbs' diary

Page 33 line 27 Broadley, *op. cit.*, p. 312

Page 34 line 19 *The Times*, 29 August 1855

4: A Little Learning

Page 37 line 18 Dearest Child, p. 73

Page 38 line 28 Lee, *op. cit.*, I, pp. 48–9

Page 39 line 29 RA RAZ/443/56

Page 39 line 40 Dearest Child, p. 142

Page 41 line 8 Ibid., p. 174

Page 41 line 31 Broadley, *op. cit.*, pp. 213–14

Page 42 line 12 Hibbert, *op. cit.*, p. 26

Page 43 line 4 Lee, *op. cit.*, I, p. 59

Page 43 line 17 Ibid., pp. 63–4

Page 44 line 18 Magnus, *op. cit.*, p. 50

Page 44 line 35 q Hibbert, *op. cit.*, p. 31

Page 45 line 6 Dearest Child, p. 208

Page 46 line 3 H. E. Wortham, *Edward VII: Man & King* (1931), p. 64

Page 46 line 15 Carrington diary, 3 October 1861, Lincolnshire Papers, MS film 1120, Bodleian Library

Page 47 line 5 Hibbert, *op. cit.*, p. 32

5: *Bertie Breaks Out*

Page 54 line 13 New York Herald, 20 September 1860

Page 55 line 23 New York Times, 9 October 1860

Page 55 line 28 Mrs Stuart Erskine, *Memoirs of Edward, Earl of Sandwich (1839–1916)* (1919), pp. 48–9

Page 57 line 28 The Letters of Lady Augusta Stanley, I, p. 162

6: *Prince Albert's Agony*

Page 61 line 12 q Cecil Woodham-Smith, *Queen Victoria: Her Life & Times* (1972), p. 372

Page 61 line 22 q Dudley Pound, *Albert* (1973), p. 321

Page 61 line 34 Dearest Child, p. 237

Page 61 line 34 Woodham-Smith, *op. cit.*, p. 400

Page 63 line 19 q Pound, *op. cit.*, p. 328

Page 64 line 39 Lee, *op. cit.*, I, p. 118

Page 68 line 21 q

Woodham-Smith, *op. cit.*, p. 417

Page 71 line 36 The Times, 16 December 1861

Page 72 line 11 Lee, *op. cit.*, I, pp. 123–4

Page 72 line 33 Carrington diary, MS film 1120, Lincolnshire Papers, Bodleian Library

Page 73 line 3 G. Villiers, *A Vanished Victoria* (1938), p. 315

Page 73 line 18 E. Fitzmaurice, *The Life of Granville* 2 vols (1905), II, p. 405

Page 74 line 5 Queen Victoria's *Letters*, Series I, vol. III, p. 606

Page 74 line 5 E. C. Corti, *The English Empress: A Study in the Relations between Queen Victoria and Her Eldest Daughter* (1957), p. 72

Page 75 line 3 Hughenden Papers, Lord Derby's memo, February 1862

Page 75 line 34 A. V. Baillie and Hector Bolitho, *A Victorian Dean: A Memoir of Arthur Stanley* (1930), p. 120

Page 76 line 6 Ibid., p. 156

7: *The Search*

Page 80 line 3 Dearest Child, pp. 337–8

Page 82 line 18 Ibid., p. 350

Page 83 line 1 Queen Victoria's diary

Page 83 line 15 Dearest Child, p. 356

Page 86 line 18 q
Battiscombe, *op. cit.*, p. 36,
RA T/3/88
Page 86 line 36 q Magnus,
op. cit., p. 82
Page 89 line 16 q *Ibid.*,
p. 84

8: *True Love*
Page 91 line 1 q
Battiscombe, *op. cit.*, p. 38,
RA Z/4/22
Page 92 line 23 q Hibbert,
op. cit., p. 57; Knollys
Papers, UII86 C1/2
*Page 92 line 27 The Letters of
Lady Augusta Stanley*, 26
September 1862
Page 92 line 33 Roger
Fulford (ed.), *Dearest Mama*
(*1861–4*) (1968), p. 180
Page 93 line 18 Esher, *Cloud
Capp'd Towers*, p. 163
Page 93 line 19 Lord Esher,
Journals & Letters, 4 vols
(1934–8), II, pp. 289, 298
Page 93 line 22 Sydney
Holland, Viscount Knutsford,
In Black & White (1926),
p. 367
Page 93 line 26 Margot
Asquith, *The Autobiography of
. . .* (1962), p. 59
Page 94 line 1 Lord Ronald
Gower, *My Reminiscences*, 2
vols (1883), I, pp. 225–6
Page 94 line 23 A. L.
Kennedy (ed.), *My Dear
Duchess* (1956), p. 215
Page 94 line 33 Daisy
Princess of Pless, *From My
Private Diary* (1931), p. 119
Page 96 line 13 q

Battiscombe, *op. cit.*, p. 41,
RA Z/463/135, 132
*Page 96 line 20 The Letters of
Lady Augusta Stanley*, I,
p. 272
Page 96 line 27 q
Battiscombe, *op. cit.*,
pp. 40–1
*Page 96 line 31 Dearest
Mama*, p. 131
Page 100 line 27 Harold
Nicolson, *King George V:
His Life & Reign* (1952),
p. 51
Page 101 line 15 Drew,
op. cit., p. 105
Page 101 line 17 Esher,
Journals . . . , I, p. 300
Page 101 line 21 Erskine,
op. cit., p. 242
Page 101 line 26 Lee,
op. cit., I, p. 144
Page 101 line 38 q
Battiscombe, *op. cit.*, p. 43
Page 102 line 6 Lee, *op. cit.*,
I, p. 153

9: *The Wedding*
Page 106 line 20 Walburga
Paget, *Scenes & Memories*
(1912), p. 97
Page 106 line 27 q Sir
George Arthur, *Queen
Alexandra* (1934), p. 39
Page 106 line 28
Battiscombe, *op. cit.*, p. 44
*Page 110 line 33 The Letters
of Lady Augusta Stanley*, I,
p. 284
*Page 111 line 36 The Diaries
of Lady Frederick
Cavendish*, I, p. 154
Page 112 line 15 Ibid.

Page 112 line 11 A. G. C. Liddell, *Notes from the Life of an Ordinary Mortal* (1911), p. 46

Page 113 line 9 Lord Redesdale, *Memories*, 2 vols (1915), I, p. 162

Page 113 line 23 The Diaries of Lady Frederick Cavendish, I, pp. 154–7

Page 114 line 3 Ibid.

Page 114 line 29 The Letters of Lady Augusta Stanley, I, p. 286

Page 115 line 20 Winston S. Churchill, *The Life of Lord Randolph Churchill*, 2 vols (1906), I, p. 9

Page 117 line 6 The Letters of Lady Augusta Stanley, I, p. 311

10: The Acclaimed Couple

Page 119 line 4 Dearest Mama, p. 180

Page 119 line 15 Ibid., p. 182

Page 121 line 25 q Magnus, *op. cit.*, p. 101, RA Add. MSS U/32

Page 121 line 28 Dearest Mama, p. 226

Page 122 line 22 q Magnus, *op. cit.*, p. 102, Queen Victoria's diary

Page 123 line 10 Lord Redesdale, *King Edward VII: A Memory* (1915), p. 18

Page 123 line 12 Mrs George Cresswell, *Eighteen Years on the Sandringham Estate* (1888), p. 169

Page 125 line 30 q Battiscombe, *op. cit.*, p. 55, Macclesfield Papers

Page 125 line 20 Holland, *op. cit.*, p. 188

Page 126 line 1 Moneypenny & Buckle, *op. cit.*, V, p. 269

Page 127 line 13 J. E. C. Bodley's review of Lee's biography in the *Manchester Guardian*

Page 127 line 28 q Shane Leslie (ed.), *Memoirs of John Edward Courtenay Bodley* (1930), p. 73

Page 128 line 14 Baroness de Stoeckl, *Not All Vanity* (1950), p. 162

Page 129 line 12 R. G. Martin, *Lady Randolph Churchill*, 2 vols (1971), I, p. 140

Page 129 line 18 Lee, *op. cit.*, I, pp. 178–9

Page 129 line 27 Ibid., p. 179

Page 130 line 9 Ibid.

Page 130 line 22 Personal Papers of Lord Rendel (1931), p. 67

Page 130 line 34 H. R. Madol, *The Private Life of Queen Alexandra* (1940), p. 119

Page 131 line 10 q Battiscombe, *op. cit.*, p. 127, Victor Montagu, Sandwich Papers

Page 132 line 17 Sir E. Dicey, W. T. Stead, Mrs O'Farrell, C. Lowe, *King Edward VII, Biographical & Personal Sketches with Anecdotes* (1910), p. 30

Page 133 line 20 Wortham, *op. cit.*, p. 195

Page 133 line 27 Dicey, *op. cit.*, pp. 31–2

Page 133 line 33 Holland, *op. cit.*, p. 231

Page 134 line 4 q James Pope-Hennessy, *Queen Mary* (1959), p. 375, RA QQM

Page 136 line 12 A. I. Dasent, *John Thadeus Delane* 2 vols (1908), II, p. 197

Page 137 line 8 Constance Battersea, *Reminiscences* (1922), p. 343

Page 137 line 16 Carrington diary, Lincolnshire Papers, MS film 1120, Bodleian Library

Page 138 line 1 Longford, *op. cit.*, p. 392

Page 138 line 23 Carrington diary, Lincolnshire Papers, MS film 1120, Bodleian Library

11: Idle Hands

Page 143 line 14 Roger Fulford (ed.), *Your Dear Letter (1865–71)* (1971), p. 65

Page 143 line 38 q Battiscombe, *op. cit.*, p. 79, RA Y/178/34

Page 144 line 24 Lee, *op. cit.*, I, p. 181

Page 144 line 28 C. Kinloch Cooke (ed.), *A Memoir of Princess Mary Adelaide*, 2 vols (1900), II, p. 44

Page 145 line 6 q Battiscombe, *op. cit.*, p. 80, RA Y/178/34

Page 145 line 13 Ibid.

Page 146 line 3 Ibid.

Page 146 line 33 q Hibbert, *op. cit.*, p. 76

Page 147 line 38 Queen Victoria's *Letters*, Series II, vol. I, pp. 206–7

Page 148 line 3 Dearest Mama, p. 300

Page 149 line 14 q Magnus, *op. cit.*, p. 117, RA 2 448/54

Page 150 line 4 Lee, *op. cit.*, I, p. 256

Page 150 line 23 q Magnus, *op. cit.*, p. 118, RA Add. MSS U/32

Page 150 line 32 Ibid., p. 119

Page 151 line 36 Ibid., p. 106

Page 152 line 7 Ibid., p. 107

Page 152 line 36 Arthur Ponsonby, *Henry Ponsonby: Queen Victoria's Private Secretary: His Life from His Letters* (1942), p. 252

Page 153 line 6 q Magnus, *op. cit.*, p. 154, RA Acc. 372a

Page 153 line 9 Longford, *op. cit.*, p. 365

Page 153 line 16 q *ibid.*

Page 153 line 26 E. F. Benson, *As We Were* (1930), pp. 99–100

Page 154 line 29 Viscount Grey of Fallodon, *Twenty-Five Years* 2 vols (1925), II, pp. 14–15

12: The Accomplice

Page 163 line 5 q Hibbert, *op. cit.*, p. 85

Page 163 line 27 The Times, 10 November 1866

Page 164 line 25 q Hibbert, *op. cit.*, p. 86

Page 164 line 30 q Battiscombe, *op. cit.*, p. 83

Page 164 line 37 Your Dear Letter, p. 126

Page 166 line 3 q Hibbert, *op. cit.*, p. 87

Page 166 line 32 Erskine, *op. cit.*, p. 95

Page 168 line 10 Carrington diary, Lincolnshire Papers, MS film 1120, Bodleian Library

Page 170 line 1 q Magnus, *op. cit.*, pp. 142–3, RA Z 449/80

Page 170 line 13 Ibid.

Page 171 line 26 The Times, 14 November 1870

Page 172 line 17 q Longford, *op. cit.*, p. 380

Page 172 line 19 q Hibbert, *op. cit.*, p. 108

Page 174 line 13 Philip Guedalla, *The Queen & Mr Gladstone* (1933), p. 330

Page 175 line 7 Arthur Ponsonby, *op. cit.*, 5 October 1871

Page 175 line 12 The Times, 18 September 1871

Page 176 line 18 Gerard Noel, *Princess Alice* (1974), p. 171

Page 176 line 23 The Letters of Lady Augusta Stanley, II, p. 148

Page 176 line 36 Noel, *op. cit.*, p. 172

Page 177 line 23 Queen Victoria's *Journal*, 29 November 1871

Page 178 line 8 Longford, *op. cit.*, p. 389

Page 178 line 16 q Battiscombe, *op. cit.*, p. 116, Macclesfield Papers

Page 179 line 6 The Letters of Lady Augusta Stanley, II, pp. 148–9

Page 179 line 14 Longford, *op. cit.*, p. 389

Page 179 line 23 q Battiscombe, *op. cit.*, p. 117, Macclesfield Papers

Page 179 line 36 Queen Victoria's *Journal*

Page 180 line 16 The Letters of Lady Augusta Stanley, II, p. 150

Page 181 line 17 Gower, *op. cit.*, I, pp. 404–5

13: Recovery

Page 184 line 3 Lee, *op. cit.*, I, pp. 327–9

Page 184 line 29 Sir Richard Holmes (ed.), *Edward VII: His Life & Times* (1910), part-work 8

Page 185 line 37 q Battiscombe, *op. cit.*, p. 118, RA A/17/288

Page 187 line 29 Lee, *op. cit.*, I, p. 326

Page 187 line 36 Gower, *op. cit.*, II, p. 318

Page 188 line 37 R. Nevill (ed.), *Leaves from the Notebooks of Lady Dorothy Nevill* (1907), p. 232

Page 189 line 5 Holland, *op. cit.*, p. 184

Page 189 line 37 q Hibbert, *op. cit.*, p. 173

Page 191 line 31 Lee, *op. cit.*, I, p. 372

Page 192 line 30 q Magnus, *op. cit.*, p. 172, Salisbury Papers

Page 193 line 4 Ibid.

Page 193 line 15 Moneypenny & Buckle, op. cit., IV, p. 429

Page 193 line 24 q Battiscombe, *op. cit.*, p. 130

Page 194 line 1 Lee, *op. cit.*, p. 373

Page 196 line 5 R. Hough, *Louis & Victoria: The First Mountbattens* (1974), p. 77

Page 197 line 11 Lee, *op. cit.*, I, p. 381

Page 198 line 18 q Battiscombe, *op. cit.*, p. 130, RA CC/42/66

Page 199 line 16 Ibid., pp. 131–2

Page 199 line 37 Carrington diary, Lincolnshire Papers, MS film 1120, Bodleian Library

Page 200 line 5 G. Bennett, *Charlie B* (1968), p. 57

Page 200 line 24 Carrington diary, Lincolnshire Papers, MS film 1120, Bodleian Library

Page 201 line 15 q Magnus, *op. cit.*, p. 182, RA, Geo V, AA13/13 and 14

Page 201 line 20 Carrington diary, Lincolnshire Papers, MS film 1120, Bodleian Library

Page 202 line 11 Lee, *op. cit.*, I, p. 399

14: Scandals and Tragedy

Page 204 line 25 q Magnus, *op. cit.*, p. 186, RA Add. MSS A/12/302

Page 205 line 18 q Battiscombe, *op. cit.*, p. 134, RA Add. MSS A/2/22

Page 206 line 15 q Magnus, *op. cit.*, p. 188, RA Add. MSS A/12/302

Page 206 line 30 Journals of Lady Knightley (1915), p. 301

Page 209 line 27 Carrington diary, Lincolnshire Papers, MS film 1120, Bodleian Library

Page 210 line 5 Shane Leslie, *op. cit.*, p. 80

Page 210 line 15 Ibid., p. 38

Page 210 line 24 Lee, *op. cit.*, I, p. 551

Page 209 fn. Sir Almeric Fitzroy, *Memoirs*, 2 vols (1925), I, pp. 104–5

Page 211 fn. Loelia, Duchess of Westminster, *Grace and Favour* (1961), p. 70

Page 211 line 10 Esher, *Journals . . .*, I, pp. 324, 326

Page 211 line 18 Eve Adam (ed.), *Mrs J. Comyns Carr's Reminiscences* (1926), p. 57

Page 212 line 23 Lillie Langtry, *The Days I Knew* (1925), p. 45

Page 213 line 16 Ibid., p. 107

Page 214 line 24 Lord Randolph Churchill letters, no. 3392, 1 February 1890, Peregrine Churchill Papers

Page 216 line 5 Ibid., no. 2101, 1 December 1886

Page 216 line 30 q Bennett, *op. cit.*, p. 165, Salisbury Papers

Page 217 line 11 Ibid.

Page 217 line 34 Ibid., p. 166

Page 218 line 37 q Magnus, *op. cit.*, p. 295, Salisbury Papers

Page 219 line 9 q Battiscombe, *op. cit.*, p. 182, RA AA/31/17

Page 219 line 22 Stoeckl, *op. cit.*, pp. 113–14

Page 220 line 30 q Battiscombe, *op. cit.*, p. 187

Page 222 line 3 Magnus, *op. cit.*, p. 285

Page 222 line 11 Ibid.

15: The Reconciliation

Page 228 fn. q Battiscombe, *op. cit.*, p. 198, RA CC/5/57

Page 228 line 19 Ibid., p. 176

Page 229 line 2 Holland, *op. cit.*, p. 198

Page 230 line 5 Lord Randolph Churchill letters, no. 3591, 3 July 1890

Page 232 line 4 Queen Victoria's *Letters*, Series III, I, pp. 418–19

Page 233 line 17 Virginia Cowles, *Edward VII & His Circle* (1956), pp. 278–9

Page 233 line 39 q Hibbert, *op. cit.*, p. 170

Page 234 line 6 Ibid.

Page 234 line 26 q Battiscombe, *op. cit.*, p. 209

Page 234 line 30 P.

Quennell, *Customs & Characters* (1982), p. 26

Page 236 line 10 Robert Rhodes James (ed.), *Chips, The Diaries of Sir Henry Channon* (1967), pp. 43–4

Page 236 line 17 Quennell, *op. cit.*, p. 25

Page 237 line 10 R. Hough, *Edwina: Countess Mountbatten of Burma* (1983), p. 18

Page 240 line 10 Lord Randolph Churchill letters, no. 673, 3 July 1885

Page 240 line 15 Ibid., no. 1607, 31 July 1886

Page 241 line 3 q Magnus, *op. cit.*, p. 249, RA Z/62/10

Page 241 line 10 Lord Randolph Churchill letters, no. 2200, 23 December 1886

Page 241 line 34 Ibid., no. 3601, 9 July 1890

Page 242 line 4 Ibid., no. 3403, 11 February 1890

Page 242 line 20 Ibid., no. 3792, 4 January 1892

Page 243 line 11 Ibid., no. 3045

Page 244 line 37 Carrington diary, Lincolnshire Papers, MS film 1120, Bodleian Library

Page 245 line 7 The Diaries of Lady Frederick Cavendish, II, p. 235

Page 245 line 13 S. Gwynn & G. M. Tuckwell, *The Life of Sir Charles Dilke*, 2 vols (1917), I, p. 414

Page 247 line 21 Paget, *op. cit.*, I, p. 86

Page 248 line 7 B. Oliver, *The British Red Cross in Action* (1966), p. 152

Page 248 line 13 Holland, *op. cit.*, p. 261

Page 248 line 27 Ibid.

Page 250 line 3 q Battiscombe, *op. cit.*, p. 213, Carroll Papers

16: End of an Era

Page 254 line 32 Pope-Hennessy, *op. cit.*, p. 353

Page 255 line 16 Ibid.

Page 256 line 25 Hough, *Louis & Victoria*, p. 204

Page 258 line 9 The Times, 23 January 1901

Page 258 line 36 Letter to *Morning Leader*, 27 January 1901

Page 259 line 18 R. C. K. Ensor, *England 1870–1914* (1936), p. 343

Page 260 line 18 Esher, *Journals . . .* , I, p. 373

Page 260 line 24 Stoeckl, *op. cit.*, p. 109

Page 260 line 33 q Battiscombe, *op. cit.*, p. 219, Macclesfield Papers

Page 261 line 20 Ibid.

Page 261 line 33 Sarah Bernhardt, *My Double Life* (1907), p. 344

Page 262 line 22 Holland, *op. cit.*, p. 187

Page 262 line 27 Lord Hardinge of Penshurst, *Old Diplomacy* (1947), p. 173

Page 262 line 34 Meriel Buchanan, *Queen Victoria's Relations* (1954), p. 175

Page 262 line 39 J. W. Mackail & Guy Wyndham, *Life & Letters of George Wyndham*, 2 vols (1925), II, p. 465

Page 265 line 1 q Battiscombe, *op. cit.*, p. 240

Page 265 line 27 Ibid., p. 242

Page 266 line 5 Redesdale, *Memories*, p. 19

Page 266 line 31 Esher, *Cloud Capp'd Towers*, pp. 180–1

Page 269 line 1 Nina Epton, *Queen Victoria & Her Daughters* (1971), pp. 226–7

Page 270 line 3 q Battiscombe, *op. cit.*, p. 220, Macclesfield Papers

Page 271 line 4 F. Ponsonby, *op. cit.*, p. 151

Page 271 line 37 Admiral Lord Fisher, *Records* (1919), p. 29

Page 272 line 21 Admiral Lord Fisher, *Memories* (1919), pp. 5–6

Page 275 line 5 Earl of Midleton (Brodrick), *Records & Reactions 1856–1939* (1939), pp. 149–50

Page 275 line 21 Carrington diary, Lincolnshire Papers, MS film 1120, Bodleian Library

Page 276 line 10 Mabell, Countess of Airlie, *Thatched with Gold* (1962), p. 109

Page 276 line 29 F. Ponsonby, *op. cit.*, p. 105

17: The Crisis

Page 279 line 12 Erskine, *op. cit.*, p. 242

Page 280 line 17 Esher, *Journals . . .* , I, p. 292

Page 280 line 33 C. W. Stamper, *What I Know* (1913), p. 32

Page 281 line 27 Sonia Keppel, *Edwardian Daughter* (1958), p. 45

Page 282 line 18 R. B. Haldane, *An Autobiography* (1929), p. 208

Page 282 line 36 Stamper, *op. cit.*, p. 111

Page 282 line 9 *Ibid.*, p. 42

Page 284 line 27 George Cornwallis-West, *Edwardian Hey-Days* (1930), pp. 172–3

Page 284 line 30 q Pope-Hennessy, *op. cit.*, p. 361

Page 286 line 15 Frances, Countess of Warwick, *Afterthoughts* (1931), p. 106

Page 286 line 27 Pope-Hennessy, *op. cit.*, p. 370

Page 287 line 10 Holmes (ed.), *op. cit.*, part-work 17, p. 489

Page 288 line 35 Esher, *Journals . . .* , I, p. 335

Page 289 line 13 Battiscombe, *op. cit.*, p. 244

Page 291 line 26 q Pope-Hennessy, *op. cit.*, pp. 371–2

Page 292 line 9 q Battiscombe, *op. cit.*, p. 246, RA Add. MSS U/28

Page 294 line 1 q Nicolson, *op. cit.*, p. 80

Page 295 line 7 Esher, *Journals . . .* , I, pp. 343–4

Page 297 line 4 Holmes (ed.), *op. cit.*, part-work 17, p. 498

Page 299 line 1 Consuelo Vanderbilt Balsan, *The Glitter & the Gold* (1953), p. 167

Page 299 line 11 Lady Mary Meynell, *Sunlight & Shadows* (1933), p. 10

18: Entente Cordiale

Page 301 line 5 q A. Maurois, *King Edward & His Time* (1933), p. 155

Page 302 line 11 Esher, *Journals . . .* , I, p. 346

Page 302 line 15 *Ibid.*

Page 302 line 23 F. Ponsonby, *op. cit.*, p. 21

Page 302 line 34 *Ibid.*, p. 137

Page 303 line 1 Asquith, *op. cit.*, pp. 58–9

Page 303 line 15 Pless, *op. cit.*, p. 201

Page 303 line 32 Holland, *op. cit.*, pp. 357–8

Page 305 line 35 Ensor, *op. cit.*, p. 258

Page 306 line 20 Lee, *op. cit.*, II, p. 119

Page 306 line 21 Baron von Eckardstein, *Ten Years at the Court of St James* (1921), pp. 216–17

Page 310 line 1 F. Ponsonby, *op. cit.*, p. 154

Page 314 line 36 Hardinge, *op. cit.*, p. 95

Page 315 line 12 F. Ponsonby, *op. cit.*, p. 170

Page 316 line 9 Lord Redesdale, *Memories*, 2 vols (1915), I, p. 177

Page 317 line 34 Illustrated London News, 1 August 1903

Page 318 line 8 Wyndham, *op. cit.*, II, p. 462

Page 318 line 35 Ibid.

Page 319 line 22 H. Robinson, *Memories: Wise & Otherwise* (1923), p. 155

Page 321 line 22 Mark Kerr, *Prince Louis of Battenberg* (1934), pp. 170–1

19: A Difficult Nephew

Page 325 line 32 RA W56/120, 16 May 1904

Page 326 line 22 Selborne MSS

Page 330 line 16 E. J. Bing (ed.), *The Letters of Czar Nicholas II & Empress Marie* (1937), p. 84

Page 330 line 30 Conversation with the author, 7 January 1972

Page 331 line 34 q Magnus, *op. cit.*, p. 475, Hardinge Papers

Page 332 line 16 Bing (ed.), *op. cit.*, p. 221

Page 333 line 16 Arthur, *Queen Alexandra*, p. 247

Page 339 line 18 Lee, *op. cit.*, II, pp. 554–5

Page 341 line 15 Ibid. p. 559

20: A Threatening Sky

Page 344 line 2 The Nation, 2 March 1907

Page 344 line 10 Esher Papers

Page 344 line 25 J. Wilson, *Campbell-Bannerman: A Life* (1973), p. 621

Page 345 line 22 Arthur J. Marder (ed.), *Fear God and Dread Nought: The Correspondence of Admiral of the Fleet Lord Fisher of Kilverstone*, 3 vols, II (1956), p. 17

Page 346 line 14 Ibid., p. 126

Page 346 line 35 Ibid., p. 113

Page 347 line 3 Ibid., p. 180

Page 347 line 13 Arthur J. Marder, *From the Dreadnought to Scapa Flow*, 5 vols, I (1961), p. 135, quoting *Fortnightly Review*, October 1907

Page 347 line 26 Marder (ed.), *Fear God . . .* , p. 107

Page 348 line 19 Ibid., II (1958), p. 106

Page 350 line 14 Lee, *op. cit.*, II, p. 580

Page 350 line 22 Asquith, *op. cit.*, p. 248

Page 352 line 24 F. Ponsonby, *op. cit.*, pp. 194–5

Page 352 line 36 Marder (ed.), *Fear God . . .* , II, pp. 180–1

Page 353 line 14 Viscount Grey of Fallodon, *Twenty-Five Years 1892–1916*, 2 vols (1925) II, pp. 19–20

Page 353 line 26 F. Ponsonby, *op. cit.*, p. 195

Page 354 line 18 Illustrated London News, 20 June 1908

Page 354 line 34 F. Ponsonby, *op. cit.*, p. 195

Page 355 line 29 Review of Reviews, February 1910

Page 355 line 36 Marder (ed.), *Fear God . . .* , II, pp. 181–2

Page 356 line 5 Ibid., p. 183

Page 356 line 37 Ibid., p. 181

Page 358 line 25 Illustrated London News, 20 June 1908

Page 358 line 12 Marder (ed.), *Fear God . . .* , II, p. 180

Page 359 line 2 q Battiscombe, *op. cit.*, p. 259, RA CC/42/62

Page 360 line 36 E. T. S. Dugdale, *Maurice de Bunsen* (1934), pp. 203–4

Page 361 line 34 Esher, *Journals . . .* , II, p. 140

Page 362 line 4 q Battiscombe, *op. cit.*, p. 262, RA AA/33/26

Page 362 line 35 Ibid., p. 161

Page 363 line 26 Carrington diary, Lincolnshire Papers, MS film 1120, Bodleian Library

Page 364 line 28 Lee, *op. cit.*, II, p. 396

Page 366 line 18 Ibid., p. 484

21: *A Monarch in Decline*

Page 368 line 1 q Battiscombe, *op. cit.*, p. 264, RA CC/25/19

Page 369 line 23 F. Ponsonby, *op. cit.*, p. 255

Page 370 line 22 Lee, *op. cit.*, II, p. 673

Page 371 line 1 F. Ponsonby, *op. cit.*, p. 256

Page 371 line 18 H. J. Bruce, *Silken Dalliance* (1946), pp. 125–6

Page 372 line 19 F. Ponsonby, *op. cit.*, p. 258

Page 372 line 27 Count Z. Trützschler, *Twelve Years at the German Court* (1924), pp. 258–9

Page 372 line 39 Grenfell, pp. 185–6

Page 374 line 1 F. Ponsonby, *op. cit.*, p. 258

Page 378 line 15 Ibid., p. 262

Page 379 line 12 A. Watson, *King Edward VII as a Sportsman* (1911), p. 211

Page 379 line 15 Lord Esher, *The Influence of King Edward* (1915), p. 45

Page 382 line 28 q Battiscombe, *op. cit.*, p. 266, RA AA/33/41

Page 383 line 9 Esher, *Journals . . .* , II, p. 424

Page 383 line 24 F. Ponsonby, *op. cit.*, p. 263

Page 384 line 34 15 April 1910, Esher Papers

Page 385 line 12 Redesdale, *Memories*, p. 33

22: *'The King Is Dead . . .'*

Page 387 line 14 Redesdale, *Memories*, p. 34

Page 388 line 21 Stoeckl, *op. cit.*, p. 99

Page 389 line 10 R. Cortissoz, *Life of Whitelaw*

Reid, 2 vols (1921), II, p. 144

Page 389 line 37 q
Battiscombe, *op. cit.*, p. 270,
RA AA/37/16

Page 390 line 23 F.
Ponsonby, *op. cit.*, p. 270

Page 391 line 39 Nicolson,
op. cit., p. 105

Page 392 line 38 Cassel

Page 394 line 13 F.
Ponsonby, *op. cit.*, p. 271

Page 395 line 4 Norfolk
Record Office, MS 4694/2/17

Page 395 line 21 Redesdale,
Memories, p. 42

Page 395 line 29 Stoeckl,
op. cit., p. 92

Page 396 line 6 Lord Morley,
Recollections, 2 vols (1917),
II, pp. 331–2

Page 396 line 19 Fisher,
Memories, p. 3

Page 396 line 29 Ibid.

Page 397 line 9 Stamper,
op. cit., p. 47

Page 397 line 11
Moneypenny & Buckle,
op. cit., IV, p. 389

Page 397 line 19 Bruce,
op. cit., pp. 103–4

Page 397 line 21 Bruce,
op. cit., pp. 103–4

Page 397 line 29 L. Rennell
Rodd, *Social & Diplomatic
Memories* (1925), p. 90

Page 397 line 36 Lord James
of Hereford, *Memories*
(1909), pp. 277–8

Page 398 line 26 Fisher,
Records, pp. 26–7

Page 399 line 16 Esher, *The
Influence . . .* , p. 37

Page 399 line 25 Princess

Alice of Athlone, *For My
Grandchildren* (1971),
p. 124

Page 399 line 35 Sir
Seymour Fortescue,
Looking Back (1920),
pp. 210–11

Page 400 line 13 Bruce,
op. cit., pp. 105–6

Page 400 line 30 Lord
Hardinge of Penshurst, *Old
Diplomacy* (1947), p. 97

Page 402 line 11 Lee,
op. cit., II, p. 722

Page 402 line 28 q
Battiscombe, *op. cit.*, p. 276,
RA AA/33/45

Page 403 line 25 Ibid.,
p. 273

Page 404 line 1 F. Ponsonby,
op. cit., p. 279

Page 404 line 8 Crowded
Life: The Autobiography of
Lady Cynthia Colville* (1963),
p. 111

Page 404 line 27 Stoeckl,
op. cit., p. 93

Page 406 line 26 q
Battiscombe, *op. cit.*, p. 279,
RA AA/34/6

Page 407 line 35 Marder
(ed.), *Fear God . . .* , III,
p. 143

Page 408 line 20 RA AA/35/4

Page 409 line 2 q
Battiscombe, *op. cit.*, p. 292

Page 409 line 9 Marder
(ed.), *Fear God . . .* , III,
p. 545

Page 410 line 34 q
Battiscombe, *op. cit.*, p. 290,
RA AA/35/6

Page 411 line 7 Ibid., p. 296

Page 411 line 27 Ibid.,
  p. 299, RA CC/50/1443
Page 413 line 8 Ibid., p. 300,
  RA AA/35/53

Page 413 line 23 352087 A/C
  Ross, *The Mint* (1955),
  p. 185

Index